LIVING THE
BEST DAY EVER

HENDRI COETZEE
EDITED BY KARA BLACKMORE

Copyright © 2013, Hendri Coetzee Trust, Centurion, South Africa.

ISBN 978-0-620-57060-2

Cover Image © Hendri Coetzee Trust
Author Photograph © Peter Meredith
End Papers © Chris Korbulic
Maps © Maddy Leslie

Cover and book design: Matt Swann Creative Ltd

Printed and bound in China by 1010 Printing International Ltd

Portions of this text are reprinted from *African Veins* (ed. Celliers Kruger), House of Orange, 2008.

Back Text: 2010. "Obituary." *The Economist Newspaper Ltd.*, December 29.

For my mother Marie
I am in awe of your strength and integrity.

ACKNOWLEDGMENTS

Hendri's lengthy time writing this book means that there are no doubt dozens of people who influenced him, aided in his authorial development and supported the growth of the text. In his absence, we focus on thanking those who participated in the final publication of this book. The final text you are about to read would not have been possible without many dedicated people:

Emily Hatfield: our unassuming agent/producer who managed and steered the book to publication.

Benjamin Morris: an inspiring friend, editor and word wizard.

Marie Nieman: Hendri's mother and the nucleus of our support team.

Pete Meredith: Hendri's best friend and the guiding voice for decision making.

Celliers Kruger: Hendri's sponsor and friend who was always available for critical input.

Maddy Leslie: A constant voice of reason amongst the chaos and the inspired artist who inked the maps.

Adriaan Nieman: He backed our decisions and hosted the process as we grew from acquaintances to family.

Additional support was provided by Hennie Coetzee, Mary Korbulic, Dominique Le Roux, and Leyla Ahmet.

EDITOR'S NOTE

This posthumous memoir is a patchwork of experiences tied together by years of living. From an early age Hendri Coetzee kept detailed diaries (first in Afrikaans and later in English) to chronicle his life and expeditions. In 2008 his diaries transformed into tools for him to construct this text. On December 7, 2010, when Coetzee was taken from his kayak by a crocodile on the Lukuga River in the Democratic Republic of the Congo, his manuscript was near completion. In fact, he had been amending the text just days prior to the incident.

Two months before his passing, Hendri asked if I would edit his book. When I said yes to my dear friend I had no idea of how this process would unfold. I have nothing but gratitude towards Hendri's friends and family for their faith in my ability, for their understanding that divine happenings exist, and for their belief that I would be able to bring his memoir to public fruition.

The text you are about to read aims both to honour Hendri's voice and maintain the authentic place from which he writes. All editorial decisions were made to enhance that voice. As a result, my additions are mostly contextual and designed to be invisible. I have included additional information about places, political events and individual cultures, all outlined upon his request. My decisions are guided by a wealth of academic resources, mostly a product of Hendri's library.

The most crafted part of the text is found in the end. The blog entries Hendri was writing on his last expedition to explore, by kayak, the Great Lakes of Central Africa, have been turned into their own chapter. In the Epilogue, I threaded a series of expedition reflections and unattached stream-of-consciousness pieces to create the out-of-body voice that you read.

The foreshadowing in this memoir reaches awesome levels of honesty. As the text evolves, so does Hendri; revealing a spiritual path that parallels his rendezvous with nature. Yet in all of these profound adventures Hendri speaks to us, and allows us to see the epic depths that lie within ourselves, and perhaps become awakened to a better way for experiencing our own lives.

KARA BLACKMORE

FOREWORD

It was sometime in May 1997, we were sitting on the cliffs overlooking Rapid 7 on the Zambezi River. We hardly noticed the big glowing amber ball slipping down over the horizon; all our attention was focused on the battlefield between us. It was our second game of chess since we shook hands for the first time. By the end of the evening I had offered Hendri a job as a river guide, despite him never having been on whitewater before. This was to be my first act as the new river manager for one of the premier companies rafting the gorges below Victoria Falls. And so our friendship began.

It was a wild ride, fueled by our passion for rivers, chess, and rum; it would lead to a life of our choice. Among our shared philosophies, was the Best Day Ever. The other was a subheading we called "make it harder". Although our lives weren't particularly hard – perhaps occasionally a little difficult – our tongue-in-cheek phrase served as a coping mechanism. In reciting the byline, "make it harder" we were able to reclaim the humour in each moment.

Twelve years later another sun set, this time over the Nile. A funeral pyre in his honour rushed down the famous Itunda Falls. Hendri had left us but the memories, inspiration and the lessons still influence the way I live. I feel privileged to have shared some of Hendri's short life. Herein lies his story, and his Best Day Ever philosophy. I am sure he will inspire and challenge you as much as he did me!

Pete Meredith

CONTENTS

Introduction 13
Early Days Of Note 16
    Rock Bottom 16
    The Next Level 18
    Tequila Stuntman 19
The Nile 23
    It Was Getting Too Easy Anyway 23
    Nobody Panic 27
    Ready Steady 33
    Crocodile Soup 41
    We Sure Would Be Sorry 46
    A Day Amongst Days 49
    Whitewater Poetry 55
    Harem Girl 62
    Good And Evil 65
    Chess 68
    Hungry Ones With Guns 69
    Nimule 71
    Hole In The Crumbling Wall 74
    Nice And Rustic 77
    Invisible Lines 80
    The Cheap Seats 85
    The Big Bad Wolf 89
    Somali Pirates 93
    Mandari 97
    Soft White Meat 99
    He Has Come 105
    Thank God For Fools 111
    Lost 111

>   Crack..120
>   The King..123
>   This Was The Dream.....................................132
>   A Liar And A Thief...135
>
> Or Die Trying..141
>   Murchison Solo...141
>
> Gangster...154
>   In Over My Head..154
>   Too Old And Fat..157
>   Normality..162
>   Bravado...165
>   Sudan..173
>   Playing The Game...180
>   The Boat Home...183
>
> A Walk..189
>   Day 1...189
>   Day 2...193
>   Day 3...197
>   Day 4...199
>   Day 5...201
>   Day 6...204
>   Day 7...211
>
> Congo Solo..217
>   The Endgame..217
>   Ready Steady Go...218
>   The Forest...223
>   Going In..226
>   Back On The Trail...231
>   Jungle Men..242
>   A Bike Ride...247
>   Getting To The River....................................256

July 11, 2009	264
July 24, 2009	267
Between Light And Dark	277
Kinsuka	281
The Horror, The Horror	287
Diary Quest – H.M. Stanley	292

The Great White Explorer 294
    So Much For Squash 294
    Because It Is There 296
    Stage One 298
    Without the Sex Scenes 298
    Murchison 299
    Out Of This World 300
    The Death Of Logic 302
    Optimistic 304
    Nobody Panic 305
    Another Statistic 307
    Feelings, Do They Make You Soft? 309

Epilogue 314

A Mother's Prayer 318

Life Chronology 320

Library & References 323

Websites & Photograph Credits 327

INTRODUCTION

*I will not live my whole life for a few moments
of bliss, but I am happy to risk it for them.*

On our planet, and particularly in Africa, there are many places that exist like sci-fi movie frontiers on the edge of the known world, all with their own recycled, improvised technology and rules. These are places where the locals live hard lives of poverty by necessity. White people by comparison, live privileged lives in a bubble suspended by their whiteness. Here people live with less and that makes it easier to have more. In the blind spot of civilisation, the rules are not just easier to bend, they are often bought, owned and invented for small sums or lack of better options. Not to say that anarchy reigns. There are basic rules keeping the fabric of society together, often impossible to see, like a continental DNA. For the people who understand these rules, Africa is a land of opportunity, a wild frontier where you can, with guts and determination, do just about anything and, as most governments in the world daily demonstrate in their collective rape of the continent, morals are optional.

I am made from the same odd pieces as this continent. For better or worse, Africa's reality is mine. Life here is X-rated and in your face. It can swing from heartbreak to laughter in an instant, sad and hopeful, cruel and kind. It is not for the weak, yet inhabited by the meek. It is humanity simplified, raw and uncut. Things rarely work out the way you want them to, and nothing can be taken for granted. If you can keep the right mental attitude, every day is a divine adventure into the unknown. Good or bad, the moment you start taking it personally, you are doomed.

The mere fact that a world can function amidst such chaos is encouraging, and in that chaos lies Africa's true beauty. It is not Victoria Falls, nor the luxury lodges and game parks. These are shopfronts, tourist attractions and fantasies paid for in foreign currency. Nice products for sale are always in danger of an environment where decay and creation hold their natural balance. If these are the things you have come for, you will not last long.

Africa's true beauty is intoxicating and paid for in more than money. It is the beauty of extremes. It is not the man without legs begging on the street corner, but the fact that he still dances to the music blasting from a passing car. It is not in the fact that a household has to live on a dollar a day, but that they can be happy while doing it. Africa's beauty is in the enjoyment of simple things, a skill near-extinct in the Western world. There are obvious reasons why we fall in love with this chaos, well-documented things that we read about in books and can see around us. Then there is the part we feel, that grips our unconscious and never allows us to leave.

EARLY DAYS OF NOTE

Rock Bottom

Contrary to popular belief, trouble arrives with the most delicate of sounds. The *pop* of the canister being fired is followed rapidly by the *hiss* of the tear-gas escaping. I grab the rifle at my feet and dive headfirst in the direction of my foxhole somewhere in the dark.

This is a mental war, designed to break us. Most of the other intakes – stronger, fitter and harder than I am – have already collapsed. For me there is nowhere to go, and I have only myself to blame. The spiral of rebellion along with the drugs and drink, through which I expressed my need for danger and excitement, brought me to rock bottom. It was never going to end well and the climax came when my stepfather hit me. Unfortunately it ended badly for my whole family; he with a black eye and a grudge that might never heal. My mother, the least deserving player in the drama, had her heart ripped out. Watching my mother cradle him and asking me to leave was the worst moment of my life. As far as I am concerned, being tear gassed in the rain at midnight is a step up.

My father came to pick me up and made it clear I was not staying with him. He drove to an army recruitment centre and asked the overweight desk jockey for the toughest course they had, starting as soon as possible. I watched myself from far away as I numbly signed up for a unit that trained medics for the South African Special Forces. My idea of endurance was smoking bucket-bongs. I knew what Special Forces meant, and prison sounded only slightly less appealing. A week later he dropped me off at the gates of an army camp with clear instructions not to call if it got too much.

For a month now I have been clinging by my fingernails, and if things go well I will cling for another minute and possibly another minute after that. The gas drifting into the muddy hole brings tears; there is nowhere to go so I cry where I sit, at least it is out of the wind. I have stopped noticing the rain, but am still aware of the cold; which luckily takes my attention away from the hunger. Wrapping myself around my rifle, I stay in the ankle-deep puddle and wait for morning.

The frozen hours just before sunrise are a nightmare during which I am unsure if I am asleep. As the horizon slowly begins to glow I fumble with cold fingers into the inner pocket of my ammo bag. Delicately I straighten the bent cigarette, one of only two. I move carefully. The rain has stopped but everything is wet. On the fifth flick of the lighter a faint blue flame sniffs around. Once the cigarette is safely lit I relax. My back resting against my gear, I stretch out my legs. It takes a minute or two for them to unlock fully. Satisfied they still work, I look up at the sky and whisper, "fuck you" through a smoke ring. I have made it through another night, the sun is going to shine today, at least for a while. I am disobeying the rules by smoking. They have not broken me yet. A strange feeling of well-being comes over me. I am too tired to examine it, so for a whole minute I am not only content but I would be nowhere else.

I am subconsciously aware of the heavy crunch of my metallic reinforced jump boots as they make every step on the runway an act of intent. My hand is resting on the semi-automatic rifle slung across my chest. Friends formed through sweat and hardship create a loose diamond configuration behind me. We walk, in full battle gear, casually toward the helicopter. Humming, its heavy blades lazily chop through the air like a gladiator's axe. Who would have thought things could change so much in a year? The boy is gone; in his place, at least superficially, is this. They tell me I am a warrior and I look the part, even if I don't feel like it. "Warrior..." it is still easier to say than "Man."

Today will be my last exercise. With our training complete and no war to fight, we mostly do nothing. Occasionally we perform exhibitions for generals and civilians. I am not complaining: despite my growing aversion to taking orders from men I don't respect, there is nothing I like more than dangling under helicopters and jumping out of planes. It is the next phase I am not looking forward to.

In a few months we will move to our assigned units, stationed in one-horse towns, where we will talk about how tough we are all day long. We will stage war exercises that we will probably never use, and drink our meagre salaries out in dodgy bars. We will wait our turn to get lucky with the few females who venture near us and settle for a fistfight when they don't. No thanks. I have seen men who have been in this game for too long: tough and fearless but unable to function in a world outside of structure.

I have no idea what I am going to do next, but I am unconcerned. I'm filled with confidence that proves I do not have to back down for anyone;

that I have probably gone through as tough a time physically as I ever will. Despite my own expectations I'm still standing. For months they've told us how worthless we are, until we succeeded in their tests; proving how much better, stronger and braver we are. I know it's propaganda, but there is no denying my body and mind have been to levels over the last year that I never knew existed.

If I could survive what formerly seemed impossible, other impossibilities must also be mere illusions. I now have a powerful weapon: I have fallen in love with discipline and it will open every door with its simple philosophy of 'doing until it gets done.' I believe William James that:

> We may find, beyond the very extremity of fatigue-distress, amounts of ease and power we never dreamed ourselves to own, sources of strength habitually not taxed at all, because habitually we never push through the obstruction. *(Energies of Men)*

I have learned that there is a place where the pain stops, where tiredness ceases, and where limits disappear. Unfortunately this place is guarded by plenty of pain, or at least what I used to think of as pain. The solace is in knowing that you can do just about anything, if you are willing to pay the price.

There is Truth where perceptions become exposed, and even a hint of something greater. A commanding power, unknown in daily life, that rises above the nagging of the body and the mind to rule over both with a quiet will. I don't fully understand this force, and I don't need to. It is there and that is enough.

There are units and men who take this separation from mind and body to far greater lengths, but for me the introductory lesson is adequate. The power and possibility that it emits is undeniable; it is a cold and impersonal power that lives in darkness, not in joy. In the absence of pain and after years of miserable high school and the self-imposed captivity of the military, I am ready for some joy.

The Next Level

Victoria Falls, Zambia, 1997

There was something odd about the way he was looking at me.

"Hi," I said to defuse the silence.

"Hi."

"Hendri."

"Peter."

"Nice to meet you."

"We will see about that."

Unsure if he is making fun of me, I stutter through the tired script for meeting fellow travellers.

"Where are you from?"

"From my mother's vagina."

His point made about small talk, he smiles and asks, "You play chess?" A few hours and beers later, as the sun set over the Zambezi Gorge, the course of my life changed through one man and one simple question, "Is it possible to raft at night?" I ask looking at the rapids fading below us.

"Yes, at full moon." Pete answers. I am quiet for a few seconds, waiting for an invitation. It doesn't come.

"Can I come on the next one?"

"Only guides can come."

"Oh." I feel sheepish for overstepping my bounds. We are silent for a few minutes, focusing on the game in the last light. "Want to be a guide?" He asks as he puts me in checkmate. "OK" I said, I had nothing better to do.

TEQUILA STUNTMAN

Adventure is what all humans need, some humans have just forgotten or never remembered that adventure can be more than the pursuit of adrenaline.

—DEON J. BREYTENBACH

I am a phantom in the boiling pot as the roar and aerated water rise up against the canyon walls of the dark cauldron. I am standing at the base of one of the seven natural wonders of the world, alone and in awe. The river accelerates from the chaos of Victoria Falls a hundred feet overhead and charges the rock wall below my feet that splits the Zambezi's awesome power in two. Right goes to Zimbabwe, left stays in Zambia.

I have already fallen in love with this intimidating basalt gorge. Here, throbbing with adrenaline on one of Africa's main arteries, is some of the greatest whitewater on the planet. We all wish that we will someday find the thing that we were meant to do – I have. I am going to be one of the best kayakers in the world. How hard can it be?

I tighten my life jacket meticulously before leaping from the rock shelf into the silver current, merging completely with its force before surfacing under the old railroad bridge silhouetted mystically above. Without pause I am launched into another rapid. The last of my doubts about this being the best day ever disappears. I have been training as a guide for almost a month; there can't be much more to learn. Everything is going according to plan. Swim the river, climb out of the gorge and get drunk. What can possibly go wrong?

Within minutes the ghost train has me in Zimbabwe. I try to be quiet. I have not seen the small croc in the eddy but apparently it is here somewhere. I drag myself through the water hyacinth, lying thick as mud, fearing an attack at any second. As I reach the bank, the clouds dump a tropical storm fit for the occasion. The darkness is near absolute. I start climbing slowly over the smooth rock. I make it to the metal ladder bolted to the cliff as the first of the storm's downpour washes onto the rock. Progress is slow. I secure each grip on the slippery metal. The rockfalls begin like tracer bullets of sound. *Bugger.* I try to shut out the image of the porter whose head was crushed last week. My confidence wavers as the wind rips at me in the pelting rain. The frequencies of the tiny rock avalanches are increasing. *Think one rung at a time.* A pebble hits me on the shoulder, I look up as a rock crashes into the bar above my head and spins harmlessly away into the dark void. I climb faster.

Once off the ladder and inside the trees I feel more protected. I stumble up the rickety stairs until I walk away from the gorge feeling poised. The rain has passed, but the clouds are still holding back the moon. I walk as quietly as one does when crossing international borders illegally. My mind is already retelling my adventures in the bar when the tale of my bravery is interrupted by the sound of grass being ripped from the ground. I guess it's either buffalo or hippo. Either could destroy my triumph. I stand very still for fifteen minutes as the buffalo graze their way leisurely past me.

Explorers Bar is packed as usual. Livingstone is an adventure town and the nights are as lively as the days, if not more so. Everything goes. I force my way through and throw my lifejacket behind the bar. A glass flies high into the bar wall. Pete and the other rafting legends are drinking tequila suicides in the corner. After snorting the salt and squeezing the lemon into your eyes, it's easy to miss when you throw your glass at the biggest guy in the bar. Claire is the only woman sitting in their group. I hope she will hear how I got here tonight. She is way out of the league of a trainee guide but I am desperate to impress her. Besides, after tomorrow I won't be a trainee anymore.

I get my rum and Coke and move over to a group of skydivers and hunters. We drop our pants: the first one to pull them up has to buy the next round. Five minutes later, the bouncer politely asks us to get dressed. Bored and thirsty we break up into the maelstrom around us. I bump into Hungry, my boss. Without a word we start wrestling. He is a human wrecking ball half my height and twice my size with hair everywhere apart from on his head. After a few minutes we are worn out, and without a word, we go our separate ways, me with my shirt torn off.

I walk past Wayne doing a lone buffalo impression. Around him is the only open space in the bar; he is in a foul mood and ready to fight. Last week he was kicked out and came back with a crocodile stolen from the croc farm, which he released into the bar. It wasn't good for business so now they let him stay. I avoid eye contact. I think we are friends, but I would rather not find out. A few girls are checking me out; they are not yet pretty enough. I join Jim-the-Pig in his booth for a drinking game that involves passing a bottle of cane spirits around and whistling into the bottleneck. I am terrible at it but after a few rounds it ceases to matter.

Hours later they kick us out. I find a girl under my arm. I don't know where she came from but she thinks I'm funny; she must be classy. We stumble down the road to the campsite. The next thing I remember is stealing tent pegs. An hour later I crawl out of the half-erected tent, the sun is coming up and it's time for my big day. I am ready to become a raft guide.

THE NILE

Then he suddenly saw clearly that he was leading a strange life, that he was doing many things that were only a game, that he was cheerful and sometimes experienced pleasure but that real life was flowing past and did not touch him.

—Hermann Hesse

It Was Getting Too Easy Anyway

Everywhere I go people tell me I should have been there five years ago, it was always better, harder or more fun five years ago. In Uganda it is five years ago and I am determined not to leave anything to be outdone by any latecomers. A full existence of adventure, without responsibility, all based around a river where the whitewater limits have not been established and with no one to tell me what I can and cannot do.

As I push on the river for more, bigger, and better, it overflows into my life off the river. The limits with everything are being pushed: a dangerous and intoxicating place. I have met some extraordinary people here and have learned some valuable lessons but mostly I just kayak, party and pose a danger to pretty missionary girls. Life is so outrageous I could not have imagined it, made all the sweeter because it cannot last. It is all about today. Today is *the best day ever* because tomorrow might not happen.

The lack of happy old people in my environment is a good indicator that this is an unsustainable lifestyle. Either I find something better, or I die on the river: either way I have nothing to worry about. The worst possible scenario is that I don't let go when the time comes, that I live out my life by an empty well, depressed and chained to a dead passion.

On the back of my twentieth bout of malaria there is a trigger, a slumbering case of 'Is this it?' I am forced to lie in bed long enough to realise I'm not happy anymore. Reminders of mortality are good like that and are seemingly a reoccurring theme in my life. I have more opportunities in a day than the thousands of black faces around me have in a lifetime. Seeing what one can live without has always made me appreciate my life in Uganda more, but suddenly I feel guilty for doing so little with it. If I can do whatever I want, what is that?

Like a piece of dust behind my eyelid that only hurts when I close my eyes, the thought scratches away, too small to see and impossible to remove. Day after day and month after month the grating drives me crazy until it does not suggest action, it demands it. Since I can't find something to be obsessed with, I will just have to be obsessed about that.

I need something worth living for, or more importantly for my advanced case of superhero dementia, something worth risking my life for. Again I ask *what do I want?* Surely there can be no other question worth asking and nothing else worth doing once you know. With this realisation, in my own start-stop, haphazard, and completely unscientific way, I begin a quest to find out what my desires were before they became afraid of my current reality or got spoiled by expectations. I suspect that if I can cut out the static that distorts my everyday thoughts, I might be able to establish contact with my true self. That true self might even be able to answer my question.

For better reception from the Universe I sit alone in the early hours before humans start to run around in circles. I watch and listen as darkness and light meet in a perfect union of opposites. During this magic hour when a new day is born on the equator, I only need to breathe to feel close to my soul and indeed the soul of the world. Still no answers come, so I exercise. When you are tired, the brain stops circulating the nonsense it believes it needs to pump through your head every second of every day. Ignoring the little voice saying *rest* makes the other nagging voices of the ego weaker. I rediscover the satisfaction and confidence derived from discipline and cut out my recreational crutches. Steadily, with a growing belief in my worth, I start to think more clearly and hear better. Only then does my *want* tune into the answer. It is so simple it has to be correct.

It is hardly a coincidence that I am reading about the exploration and history of the White Nile. I look up from the book, by my feet the Nile's green waters rush past. The answer has been there all along.

Since I was old enough to read, it has always been adventure: Tarzan, Wilbur Smith, Ranulph Fiennes, Henry Morton Stanley, Ernest Shackleton and Wilfred Thesiger. I want to be a true adventurer, an explorer, a really hard cunt. I want to be tested, to live without the safety net and find out what I am made of. I want the freedom of the unknown. I want to be a Great White Explorer. Only a few steps from me lays the vehicle to my dream, a mission epic enough to offer me the challenge I crave. Something so outrageous that it was last tried over fifty years ago and only partially completed.

I would have thought of it sooner, but I had been imprisoned by the belief that the only real explorers left on the planet are men so superior to me that I am only worthy of reading about them. There will be a few details to sort out, but why not? It might be the queen of all rivers, but it's still just a river.

If my new dream is to survive, I will need someone who, unlike me, actually finishes things he starts. The Universe provides this rock of stability in disguise. It has been years since I have seen my brother from another mother. Covered in dirt from driving trucks, up, down, sideways across the dusty, potholed roads of Africa, at first glance and possibly third or fourth, he looks anything but stable. It is the carefully chosen camouflage of someone who considers it more challenging to appear harmless while being potentially lethal.

Forgetting what steps allowed me the clarity in the first place, Pete's arrival sees the last of my good habits disappear. Instead of breakfast, we ordered Red Bull with Tequila, set up the chessboard and proceed to catch up. Twelve hours later, under a full moon, as we stand with rum and Coke in hand, more confident than firm-footed on the narrow deck railing, our backs to the Nile River Explorers bar and our toes leaning over the edge of the drop to the Nile far below, I explain my calling to Peter. He thinks it worthy and most importantly, has nothing better to do.

Not only do I need Peter for this mission, I will not go without him. He is the only one who has ever passed the two-man tent test and he has a way of interpreting life so that it almost makes sense. He radiates stillness behind a frenzy of irresponsible behaviour. To really know how special Pete is, you have to be in trouble, the deeper the better. I love being near him, as one loves being near nature, even if it threatens your life.

It was in Ethiopia where Pete and I first suffered enough to become real friends. What was supposed to be a relatively simple Omo River trip turned into an epic. Every day we were tested a little more, and Pete as expedition leader had most of the pressure on his bony shoulders.

When I lost the repair kit, he smiled as if it was only a matter of time. When rising water levels swallowed our camp at four in the morning, forcing us to pile our gear into a raft tied to a sinking tree, he sang in the rain until the sun came up. When another flash flood washed away our food rations leaving us with three days of food to complete the remaining eight days, he scratched his chin and started working on a plan to fix the situation. When we were crawling through thick undergrowth in the pitch dark of predawn, chasing Merci tribesmen and dodging grazing hippos to retrieve his stolen kitbag, he had some unflattering words to say about the "thieving cunts" but it was an opinion, not anger. When he got up from his malaria bed to stop me from murdering clients after an eighteen-hour rowing marathon, he did so resignedly. When he had to talk a client back into the boat after the freak refused to leave the beach where he figured he could sit and wait for help to arrive, Pete did so without a rash word. Somehow he was holding it together mentally despite being physically ruined.

The defining moment of the trip arrived with a soft plop as Pete accidentally knocked an oar from the raft, his reflexes, for once, too slow to stop it sliding into the muddy river. The soft splash did not do the magnitude of the situation justice. It is the sound that the fabric of space and time would make if you could pass through it. Pete followed the oar overboard. As the water closed over him, all evidence of his existence was erased. The world continued serenely as if what happened underwater was none of its affair. A fly buzzed past in a noisy, erratic arc. Birds were still chirping the same tired chorus. The river still flowed peacefully past, reflecting sunlight and giving no indication of the frantic, dark search happening below.

I glanced up at a few small crocodiles basking on the bank and slapped at a horse fly taking a bite out of my back. As I popped its body between my fingers with satisfaction, I knew the time had arrived, Pete was going to blow his fuse, and he had every right to.

As quickly as it had begun, he landed with a fluid motion back in the raft. Dirty brown water streamed from his red beard and his brown eyes were wide with adrenaline. Oxygen-starved veins pulsed obscenely as they crisscrossed his abnormally lean body. Under normal conditions he had the physique of a holocaust survivor; now fresh from a bout of malaria and an enforced diet, he was almost transparent. There was nothing calm about his appearance, as he looked me straight in the eye and without a moment's hesitation said, "It was getting too easy anyway!"

With those six words, I knew Pete was someone I could learn from. School was far from out; instead of a problem we now had a challenge. After he shook himself like a wet dog, we tied the rafts together and proceeded to tow them until we reached our take-out two days later. Reaching the worn down and unused jetty, I thought we had made it, but the last hurdles are often the toughest. The hunting lodge manager calmly told me in a disinterested tone that you normally get from civil servants, "The kitchen is closed for the night." I proceed to tell him what he could do with his kitchen, but Pete stopped me, "Hendri, you are cracking, leave this to me." "Cracking! The least this guy can do is burn some toast for people who have been dreaming of steak for a week and haven't eaten since yesterday." The look he gave me made it clear that I was dismissed, so I stormed off.

Cracking, me? How dare he even imply it. It took me a while before I got over myself and realised he was right; if you get angry, you have lost. Angry was not something tough guys did. Angry was out of options and helpless. I had heard the theory before but seeing real strength – the strength to choose your response to a situation – in practice was something I wanted to be able to do. Perhaps in twenty or thirty years I will. It was probably the best piece of advice for surviving in Africa because no matter whom you are or what you do, Africa will always present a challenge or a problem.

Nobody Panic

At my first meeting to gather information about the areas we will pass through – northern Uganda, South Sudan, northern Sudan, Egypt – I am told by someone who knows a lot more than I do that it isn't possible. It has been a recurring theme. Personally, I think negativity is the greatest danger to our trip, and for most of the last few months we have been bombarded with it. Pete seems at least immune to rejection and at times to thrive on it. Some nights, particularly after a few drinks, he searches it out, rendering rejection powerless by his rejection of rejection. Taking big sips of it, gurgling it and laughing, he does not bother to spit it back in its face.

I can see where the naysayers are coming from: a complete descent of the world's longest river is a sought-after goal and undoubtedly there are people better qualified to attempt it. Unfortunately, these people are also smart enough to wait a few more years for the political situation to calm down. By which time we freaks will have given it a damn good try.

If it wasn't for the bad language and substance abuse, a Disney movie could be made out of this. The headline would read: "A group of misfits attempt the world's longest river." It is true that we have absolutely no idea what we are doing. Luckily we do know how Africa works.

Everyone seems distracted by the size of the obstacles, comparing our mission to trying to climb a mountain. They have no idea. Problematic structures are merely things we pass over or under. Each has its own solution, how can it not? We put people on the moon; don't tell me we can't raft the world's longest river!

The first challenge is money, and it is a good one. When it comes to money, you could not find two more hopeless souls than Pete and me. Give me a war zone over the corporate world any day. We show up to meetings with ill-fitting 'fancy' clothes and shoes bought from second-hand markets and try to persuade companies to put their logos on our dream instead of billboards. Companies have strong reservations about being tied to a situation that might never get off the ground, evolve into a hostage situation or have a high death toll. We keep telling them not to panic but they remain sceptical. Apart from a few natural obstacles between Lake Victoria and the Mediterranean, there is also the small matter of two war zones.

In the north of Uganda a terrorist group, the Lord's Resistance Army (LRA), has been running amok, killing at random for over twenty years. Beyond the border is Africa's longest-running war in South Sudan. There are talks of imminent peace, and a ceasefire is in effect, but there have been too many false hopes for people not to be wary of a lasting solution. We will be the first since the days of colonialism to pass through this intricate web of government militias, private warlords, freedom fighters, terrorists and government troops, and no one is quite sure what the reception will be like.

While trying to find solutions to these issues, we have been led into the shadowy world of African politics and international aid. Nairobi, Kenya's bustling capital, offers us tireless efforts to suck up to politicians, warlords and generals. We also latch onto aid agencies for information and logistical support as we simultaneously attempt to persuade someone to give us money to play on a river. If we are going to make it through South Sudan, we are going to need to tap the information that is floating around these dusty crime-ridden corrupt streets. All players are in the same game, drinking from the same honey pot of Africa's misery.

Nairobi, for those who have never been here, holds the romance that was the essence of colonialisation, a time when white men shot and rode to fame. With courage, cunning, denial and white skin, the world was yours for the taking. White people pretended to live hard and partied harder. Adventure and excess was the name of the game. Eccentrics became legends, and freaks believed the legends. There is still a residue of the white glory days, but all that excess had to burn out or change its address at some stage. In the 1950s Kenyans challenged the British through the Mau Mau Rebellion. The Empire sent troops to quell the insurgency and maintain their lavish existence. Some families managed to hold on to their money, but they now have enough good sense to keep their fun to themselves and their polo buddies. Drawing attention to white money has not been smart for some time on this continent.

White excess was followed by black. This round took a few connections and a bit of education. The end result is the same: the rich get richer and the poor get nothing. The only difference is, the old-school privileged took care of superficial appearances while the new rulers are too busy helping themselves to bother. The result is a country with few fruits left on the old trees.

Amazingly, despite its best efforts to sabotage itself, Nairobi is still the heart of East Africa and a postcard of the new African city, all-inclusive of corruption, dirt and desperation. The streets are filled with kids sniffing glue and con men waiting to pounce at every corner. Unless you are rich enough to hide behind your estate walls in a plush suburb or the tinted windows of your chauffeur-driven 4x4, you will probably hate it. Naturally, we fit right in and are having the best time ever.

This morning we divide our last coins in order to get to meetings with potential sponsors, knowing that there is not enough money left for lunch. In a strange city, already borrowed into debt, with a few months to go before the trip and sleeping on someone's floor, it is easy to wonder if the dream is worth the sacrifice. Rational people, with things to lose, would have aborted. Luckily, we are far beyond rational. It's possible we never were. The trip has become our reason for existence. Failing would be sad, but if we quit, the emotional fallout would beat anything that an external environment could throw at us.

Coming home defeated and hungry from the failed meeting, I find Pete grinning wildly over a roasted chicken and a fresh loaf of bread. A friend had dropped $1,000 on the table, saying, "You guys go follow your dream and pay me back when you get the chance." We have known him only a few weeks and our friendship is based on a few crazy nights and copious amounts of drugs. Angels come in all sorts of disguises. Turning so close to rock bottom is not a feeling I like, but it's nice to know it's survivable and if nothing else, it enhances empathy.

Wiping the chicken from his lips with his forearm, Pete lights a cigarette and says contently, "It's like fucking desert out here, bru." I open a Tusker lager before he collapses with thirst and get one for myself as a precaution. Knowing the answer, but wanting the pleasure of hearing him say it, I ask, "We going out tonight to spend some of this new money?" It would be rude not to celebrate.

We both believe that since we don't have enough money to fund the trip even if we save, then there is no reason to save. It's only money, and it clearly keeps falling from the sky when absolutely needed. We both chuckle over Pete's same old reply for any irresponsible behaviour. "What good is your cake if you can't eat it, bru."

There is no doubt that tonight is going to get out of hand. The two of us fired up on Red Bull and rum is four hands full of trouble. It is likely there will be scrapes and bruises, confused spectators and more close calls than you can shake a stick at. Pete will end up buying everyone drinks and spending all our money, while using his on-board freak magnet to attract and befriend the weirdest characters in a hundred-kilometre radius. He will no doubt send us into worlds so strange that we will look like the normal ones. Come sunrise, there is no way to tell where or with whom we will be or what we will be doing. Yes please.

We are not just partying it up. This is something else entirely. For us partying is a spiritual system as effective as many more conservative approaches, and we do it with due religious dedication. Drinking is for most people an artificial and hopelessly inadequate attempt to be one with the moment, to forget the past and future, ultimately becoming an observer of yourself. I like to think we merely take it to another level. By living with abandonment we will achieve as much in a final reckoning of life as living rationally, and we will have more fun along the way.

The system makes little theoretical sense, but that is the point, it is based on faith. We are not just a few drunks hoping for the best, I think. There are some rules:

1. Whatever you do, do it hard.
2. Doubt is not tolerated. The ability to surrender completely to life is a must.
3. Never admit to a problem. When one appears, shrug and agree that it isn't hard enough.
4. Hung-over or still drunk, always get up and do whatever has to be done, even if this does not always mean as well as it should be done.
5. Each day's challenge is to outdo yesterday.

It's hard to doubt that we are on the right track when the Universe provides everything we need during a constant stream of outrageous adventures. It seems to me the only prerequisite for a full life is enthusiasm. We are undoubtedly making life harder. Living from hand to mouth while finding the resources to party like rock stars can be an up-and-down ride and a dangerous game to play.

I am over the top, but Pete takes it to new heights. When I see him staggering around on a three-day bender, deliberately trying to shock as many people as possible, I get scared. Take his above-average intelligence, add a religion of detachment, and combine this with a self-destructive side a mile wide, remove all fear, except for dying in your sleep, and you have a potential problem.

As one of his ex-girlfriends said, "Pete comes from a childhood that was dysfunctional in almost every way." In all our years of friendship his history has never been told in more than a few short sentences. Raised in a mental institution run by his parents, the first time he saw normal people was when he was sent to boarding school at the age of six. He is one of the few people I have ever met who is brave and smart enough to be capable of original thought.

My biggest fear is not that he will kill himself on an expedition or during a crazy stunt, but that he won't. The thought that someone with so much life and wisdom might end up as the old village drunk is unimaginable. People who will never understand or see what he is capable of can judge him, but they should never be allowed to pity him. His life is a lesson in so many things; I am still deciphering much of it. For all my belief in him, it is impossible to tell if his story will have a happy ending. It is only the promise of our dream that seems to stop him from stepping off the edge completely. His kryptonite is mediocrity and the Nile project is something even a non-believer can believe in.

Natalie and I were never further than a hug apart. We started the fire and we will watch it die. Together we make fire, usually big ones. To the side of the inferno a bar counter has just caught fire. Complete with its scarecrow customers fully dressed, sacrificed for our pleasure. DJs on the upper balcony play puppet-master with the largest sound system in Uganda, driving the crowd ever deeper into trance.

Travellers, expats, whites, blacks and yellows; the nomads are dancing like it is the last weekend on earth. Blended into a universal frenzy every bit as primitive as the country we find ourselves in. Freaks from all over the world with one thing in common: we left our homes in search of something. For a weekend we have found it.

Scattered across the English-style lawns, surrounding a dance floor, great balls of charcoal, rolled up in mesh wire, glow under the full moon. In the centre, a group of muscular men without shirts and beautiful women in little more are tearing the darkness further apart with streaks of fire chained to their hands. The fire poi hiss around their bodies, while some Scotsman roars flaming clouds into the air.

The fire burns off the last embers of our bitter bickering. She wants to come on the Nile trip and I want none of it. I do trust her, but the only news coming out of Sudan is murder and rape. As bad as things could get for Pete and me, they could get a lot worse for her. I might as well have told an avalanche to go away. A lot of people want to come on the trip until they have to make a sacrifice. This blonde woman from New Zealand is willing to do whatever she has to.

When nagging didn't work, she started researching possible army contacts that could get the team through the trickiest parts of the trip, South Sudan. When she had enough ammo, she invited me to her house where I found some of the other people I had been discussing going to Sudan with. If I wasn't going to listen then she would get them to pay attention. Just entering a bout of malaria, and in no mood for what my fragile ego took as hijacking of 'My' project, I ripped into her. "Who do you think you are? Calling a meeting when you are not even invited." It was nothing personal. I know she is good under pressure. You learn a lot about a person when they have guns pointed at them.

There was one morning at 06:00 after an-all night bender, that we had thought it would be a good idea to watch the sunrise from inside a water treatment plant on Lake Victoria. As it turned out, water treatment plants are considered of military importance. We deduced this from the very twitchy guards who surrounded us after we climbed through the fence. The situation was growing increasingly out of control as the guards whipped each other into a frenzy.

We decided the best option was to walk slowly back to the gate. Few situations in life take as much courage as turning your back on something that you believe might kill you. Trying to project calm, suddenly sober and scared, we ignored the confused and angry shouts ordering us to stop. Fighting the urge to run, we turned our backs on four shotguns.

Later, lying in bed shaking as malaria closed in on my universe, I felt ashamed of how I had acted at the meeting. With what we were about to undertake, we would need determination more than penises. I messaged her an apology, invited her to join the team and settled down for a quinine ride through the malaria madhouse. She is an organiser and provides a good countermeasure for Pete and me, who make it up as we go along. Pete and I have left our 'jobs' as raft guides to work full time on the project, but Nat, having a proper job, will stay on at the guest house until closer to departure. The Nile trip started as my vision but it now belongs to the three of us in equal measure.

Ready Steady

Somewhere along the line we seemed to have confused comfort with happiness.

—Dean Karnazes

After nearly a year, the day has arrived when thought becomes action, the biggest day of my life. The dream has been hanging by its usual thread. Visas for northern Sudan were only granted yesterday, the cease-fire in South Sudan is threatening to dissolve, and to keep things interesting, one of our two financial sponsors had cut their contribution by 75 per cent. We still do not have enough money to finish the trip, but this is no time to let details ruin the mood.

At the Source of the Nile Gardens, beside the memorial to the great explorer John Hanning Speke, we set up the circus that marks our departure. It's a festive affair, decorated with banners, promoting our thirty-six sponsors. Music is playing and important people make speeches about things such as a global community and peace in Africa. Reporters from seven news agencies ask questions and stroke our egos as we run between interviews, changing from one sponsor t-shirt to another, all while doing various product photo shoots. Even if we do not reach the Mediterranean, my wardrobe has quadrupled.

Everyone listens to what I have to say. As the leader I am a superstar. I pose for photos, give speeches, even sign autographs. I never fail to mention how important the journey is to the exposure of the countries we are passing through. Somehow I pretend that it's not really all about me. I am not sure how I feel about fame, but I do like being popular, and I was pretty sure I will never be more so. In all the excitement of my own importance I forget completely about the personal demons that have been plaguing me for the past few weeks.

Throughout my life I have been an underachiever, which is a fancy term for being lazy. The only way to overcome it, I have discovered, is to jump so far in at the deep end, that there is no way out but to swim as hard as I can. The Nile mission is so deep that I can't properly wrap my head around it. I suspect that for the next four months I will have to be at my best just to survive. The thought excites me as much as it scares me.

I will be the leader, the youngest on the team, and even I realise that I am under-qualified. It terrifies me to think a single bad decision could kill the whole team. To succeed we will have to leave our comfort zones. Risks are a given, but how far can one push before one goes too far? There is no rulebook; only people who quit, people who succeed, and people who die trying.

I find making choices between life and death are exciting when I am on my own. The stress factor increases exponentially when I am responsible for others. Being the leader sounded cool at first, but it's starting to feel more like a burden. My idea of leadership is the heroic version and consists of letting the team decide, until I think they are so wrong that the safety or objectives of the expedition are threatened; then I plan to overrule them.

Apart from my leadership reservations, I have also been a bit worried about my people issues. Most of the time I am so deep in my own world that I have no time left for the communal one. I need to think about my interactions, giving them a forced feeling that makes people suspect I am trying to manipulate them. To complicate matters more, at times any contact with people annoys me, even the most well-meaning of interactions. When this happens I usually disappear for a few hours or days. That coping mechanism might be a bit hard when living on a raft.

Right now I'm completely solid and oddly light, as if the world is wrapping itself around me aerodynamically. I am about to embark on something that is completely out of control yet I felt more powerful than ever before. I have manipulated the Universe to make something happen out of nothing. I doubt anything can make one feel as powerful as creating your own life.

We finally set off on our Great African Expedition, all the way to the Nile River Explorers' bar, seven kilometres downstream. If we are launching into the unknown, we are for damn sure going to have a proper bender before we do. Without our community of freaks, eccentrics and misfits from Uganda and Kenya, we never would have made it to the starting line. Most of them have come down for the expedition launch and the party; more likely for the latter.

Some team members I just met the previous week. Marcus, in his late forties, is the team photographer and the oldest member of the expedition. He met Pete on some mission somewhere and asked if he could join us. Since no other photographer asked we said, "Pull in bru." He is English with a Robert Redford look about him; luckily he seems like a good guy. If he has any second thoughts about his choice to put his life in our hands as he watches us dance half-naked on the tables, he keeps it to himself.

We have spent months working out systems and plans to get us through the journey while little thought has gone into the team dynamics. Part of this is out of necessity and lack of options, partly it's because Pete figures the right people are being drawn to us with the blind assumption that natural selection and I together have weeded out his worst picks. As with so many of the decisions we simply believe that they will take care of themselves.

QuiteBright productions will do the filming. Pete met Daniel (Dan), the director, and Amber, the executive producer, in a bar in Nairobi. Once again for lack of a better choice and liking the fact that they were young and hungry, we decided to let them on board only after testing their partying skills properly during a long weekend in Nairobi. Daniel is also a *pom* but raised in Kenya. His girlfriend and business partner, Amber, is from France. How the two of them ever lived without each other is a mystery. Three weeks ago they had their doubts about coming and pulled out of the project. Pete went to Kenya, explained to them that it was OK to be worried, and asked them not to panic.

Somewhere during the festivities Dan asks Amber to marry him. He later explains the decision by saying that since he wasn't sure if he would survive the next few months, long-term didn't seem that long. I suspect it might also have been a case of marking his territory clearly. Not long after he proposes to her at the bar, he passes out. I carry him to bed with Amber following me down the stairs, near tears, not sure if he actually meant it. It is not the most romantic thing I have ever seen and something only Dan can get away with.

I am still playing drunken chess with Pete when the sun finally rises. I ask Pete every ten minutes, "What are we going to do today?" He gives a calm reply of, "Whatever we want, bru." followed by howling at the sky.

I suspect there has never been a more hung-over group of explorers together in a raft as we finally make it down to the river: Pete, me, Nat, Bingo, Marcus, Dan and Amber. Being trained professionals, Pete and I stopped drinking three hours earlier, not counting Red Bull. If you think this is irresponsible, I assure you that if you have ever done an extreme activity on a Sunday morning, your guide had probably done the same.

We are taking two rafts down the forty-eight kilometres of commercial whitewater section that we both can, and at times have, done asleep. Pete's boat will hold the media: Dan, Amber and Marcus. He will take the safer lines to film the second raft, which will go for some more action.

I put Nat into the action raft to try to get her over her fears. She is going to be a liability in whitewater and I have been asking her for months to at least try to become less of one. I am too hung-over to argue when she climbs on the other boat. Leader or no leader, Nat is going to do what Nat wants to do. Also, worryingly, I discovered during a very long day rafting, that in the entire team, only Pete and I are strong enough to pull ourselves back into the raft.

Shortly before sunset we stop at a tourist island called the Hairy Lemon. It is an ideal place to regroup. With so many pieces of the puzzle falling in place in the last week we still have some ends to tie up, and it is easier to hide here than to postpone the launch. We will stay here for two days to organise the new gear and recover from the bender.

During the break, I drive to Entebbe to collect some waterproof boxes still held for ransom at the airport. After collection I stop by our public liaison officer in Jinja. As I am about to leave, he calls me aside and advises me to call off the expedition. The World Food Program has just pulled out of South Sudan because of escalating violence. For him it's a black-and-white issue: don't go. So easily said. "Hendri, call off the expedition, peoples' lives are in your hands, do the right thing." I had not yet heard of the pull-out, but it is a major development. He is wrong if he thinks I can or will call off the expedition that easily.

The Nile has been slowly fattening, letting herself slip into the obesity of Lake Kyoga. The team is hurting after three days of rowing. White skin blushes before the harsh sun with an unprepared innocence. Blisters, buttonholes of pain are in the first phase of transformation into calluses, popping out on hands used to doing little more than open doors. Shoulders, backs and arms, unaccustomed to resistance, rebel against the strain of the oars.

Squinting into the slight headwind, I know with certainty it's about to get harder. High above the heat haze, the sky is twisted in an angry frown of massive cumulonimbus clouds that contain no good news. As if challenged by my thoughts, the flat surface of the lake crumbles. The once light headwind drops its disguise and charges.

Soon the water is spitting at us through frothing white teeth on a two-foot swell. It takes two people side by side on the oars to avoid being blown backwards. We cannot even sustain ten minute shifts. There is no land nearby. We can only continue to fight for our position. Just as it seems we will have to accept our fate and give up, the storm passes. It leaves us in a race to find land before the sun sinks into the vast expanse of water. We make it with minutes to spare. Exhausted to the last one, we crawl into hastily-erected tents and mozzie nets after a simple supper.

A night's sleep is not enough for bodies or brains to forget pain. Over breakfast the team votes to hire a local boat to tow us across the mostly-exposed thirty kilometres of the lake that lies uninvitingly, if momentarily still and calm. Surprised, but sympathetic, I can see no harm in them resting for a day. They dug deep yesterday. Personally, I think being towed across the lake would be nice but I don't feel like calling my parents to tell them I'm a girl.

Slightly worrying is that, apart from Pete and me, no one seems to have bothered to train. I am still too full of optimism to examine the mechanism behind it. Finding a silver lining in the fact that Pete and I will be able to go across the lake without training wheels, I split the team up. Such complete challenges are rare and these opportunities should be taken. If rowing across the lake is too hard that means we are not tough enough.

Natalie is against separating the team, but her opposition is hardly a new phenomenon. Outwardly I am making light of it all, doing my best to ignore her grumblings about the irresponsibility of my leadership. Inwardly I am thinking: it's 08:30, already hot as hell and with a slight headwind, could you shut up so we can get started. The sun is shining, adventure is in the air and everyone is getting what he or she wants, so I find it unnecessary to explain what I see as a basic truth: The fitter and stronger the team is the better our chances of surviving the journey, the weaker the rest of the team is physically, the stronger Pete and I have to be.

They zip the lake open with the bow of the large wooden canoe, trailing their lump of rubber. Suddenly it all seems very quiet. Pete gives me a slightly demented grin from behind his imitation sunglasses. I know it well. It's the grin he uses when we are about to do something completely stupid and utterly unnecessary. Neither of us is under any illusion that we are going for anything but an ultra marathon in forty-degree heat, over a mirror, with the closest shade being nightfall.

Rafts are made for stability, not speed; flat water is uphill. In hour-long shifts, we push and pull, throwing our body weight onto wooden levers which in turn force themselves into and against the weight of the lake. It's slow progress, lubricated by sweat and propelled by continued strain. Trying to rest during Pete's shift is like attempting to sleep in a sauna. Our little blue island becomes a world unto its own. Sweat stings my eyes on the way down to join the salty rivers running across every curve of my body, mixing eventually with the lake below my feet. Watching Pete become an extension of the oars, I want to be nowhere else.

These are the moments that our friendship is based on. Pete is not known for his chitchat. A common view on life – felt, not spoken – has made us close friends for many years. For both of us these are the simple times, in the pure physical challenge of the Now, where nothing else matters but the moment, hour after hour and every single second in between.

Ten hours later, burnt, dehydrated, dissolving into puddles of sweat and mentally elated, we approach the north bank. The wind acknowledges its defeat and finally holds its breath, leaving the lake silent and still. We slow our pace to enjoy the moment we have earned. Sunlight is meant to sleep in the water and around us. The best sunset ever is playing on the big screen. The colours of day linger softly in the mirror before being flushed away by darkness.

Looking for a sign, we radio every fifteen minutes. Finally we establish communication just after 22:00 and are guided into camp by flashlight. We inhale some food before falling into satisfied sleep under the stars.

When I return from my morning walk I find the team deep in discussion over obtaining engines for the next section of the trip. Almost everyone is in favour of the idea. They figure there is no need to go the hard way. I thought if anything they would have learned in the last few days that they are too unfit to handle an emergency. Apart from the physical strength needed to function away from modern conveniences, fitness is a key factor in staying calm. The more fit you are, the less chance you will make mistakes when the going gets tough. No matter how cleverly they try to avoid it becoming tired is inevitable. Why can they not see this?

It will not be hard to organise engines for the next hundred kilometres, but after that we enter a long and dangerous whitewater stretch where engines can't be used. We will have to row and when we do it will be under pressure. Then being tired and having soft hands will become a liability. Overcoming obstacles is a habit and so is backing down from them. We should be embracing the challenges not shying away from them. Discipline is a vehicle we will need over the thousands of hard kilometres ahead.

Bingo is the biggest fan of using engines or any other easy option, as it turns out. He is the mechanic, in his late forties, South African born but living in Uganda. I have known Bingo superficially for a few years but have never really spent much time with him. He has some mechanical and raft skills. Most importantly, Pete thought he would be a good choice for the trip. I am taken by surprise when Bingo states that he does not want to *extend* himself, he just wants to have a nice trip. If he had mentioned his preference a few weeks ago, I would have saved him the trouble of coming. We don't share the same goal on the expedition and I can't see his planet from mine.

I am so disappointed that they are not even willing to get fit, that I overrule the engine proposal without feeling the need for a prolonged discussion.

At first light a few locals start to gather around the campsite. They are the high-water mark of a tide of refugees or internally displaced persons from the war in the north. They are the delta to the sea of misery that we will soon enter. Most of us have been in Uganda long enough to have heard the horror stories about the war, but seeing it is different.

As Natalie and Dan start to do interviews with these people, abandoned, enslaved and persecuted in their own country, it becomes a lot more personal than just newspaper headlines. We listen stunned by stories of rape, murder, sexual slavery, child soldiers and cannibalism. In the soft morning sunlight with the river humming in the background, it is not possible to process this information.

All of them have lost family members. Many are branded and tattooed by torture: proof that the horror is real and living down the road. I marvel at how people can be strong enough to still want to live. In the West, people develop issues when a girlfriend cheats on them, or if their breasts aren't as perky as they used to be. Try having to eat your parents shortly before being gang raped and led into slavery. The unease we feel at their suffering is increased by the knowledge that we will soon enter Pandora's box. If the world can be placed on continuum of good and evil, the compass needle would point to this place as a pole of hell.

The Lord's Resistance Army responsible for this is like a group of unruly punk schoolboys, except they are equipped with a fierce mystical philosophy that drives their deranged actions. Their founder, Joseph Kony, traces his roots to a Holy Spirit Movement that used water from the Nile, at which I am standing, to protect them from bullets and opposition.

Murchison Falls National Park and the isolation offered by northern Uganda is a perfect playground for their antics. Children, as young as they come, are stolen from their homes and enslaved to fight a war that most are unsure of the outcome. The LRA are Acholi fighters who occasionally claim their aim is to overthrow the national government; instead, they are raping, killing and pillaging mostly from their own people. Their aimless fury has engulfed hundreds of villages over two decades and forced the park HQ to move from the north to the south bank of the Nile. This sets an unsettling stage for our next leap into the unknown.

CROCODILE SOUP

Standing below Karuma Falls I am as scared as I have ever been, the roar of the massive rapid dampens everything apart from the dread in my stomach. Waiting for the media crew to get ready does nothing to calm me. Dale, shaking his hair from his eyes, casually chirps, "As soon as we get on the river, we drop from the top of the food chain boys." He looks totally relaxed and straight from the cover of a surfing magazine; I suddenly dislike him a lot.

The raft groans as it is pushed from the smooth black rock, reluctantly leaving our perfectly safe beach for its fluid future. Pete sits in the back. Old Man River has the unenviable position of guiding Thomas, Dave, Dale, Julian, Grant and me through the bridge rapid. I am in front, opposite Dale. We will set the paddling rhythm. Rafting on this section is like being lost without a map while driving in a foreign city at rush hour. Scattered islands mean we have to change intersections a few times to find the right turnoff, taking great care to give the hippopotamus traffic as much space as possible. An annoying voice tells me that I am too close to something that can bite me in half and that statistically, if we have to spend ten days this close to as many as there are, an accident is the most likely outcome.

Still trying to ignore the logic, I freeze in horror. Only a meter from me, I see a dark shape charging straight at me from the depths of the milky green water. Already overloaded, my senses fail to register. There is no time to scream a warning before it breaks the surface a foot away from me. At the instant of my certain death, the all-devouring hippo from hell changes into a harmless clump of vegetation washed up by the current.

The light at the end of the tunnel turns to daylight. I do not even have time to share my near-death water hyacinth charge with anyone.

Commands fly as we paddle at full power, snaking through overhanging jungle-covered islands to avoid real hippo pods and align ourselves for the bridge rapid. Hundreds of spectators have gathered on the bridge. Chanting and cheering, sure of our destruction in the rapids below, they have come to see the crazy *muzungus* get annihilated. They are not disappointed. The first wave hits us hard, submerging me completely; for a second I believe the whole boat has turned over. Dropping off the back of the wave, I am pulled from the water while hanging onto the still-upright raft. By the time we crest the second wave I am back in the boat, just in time for an even bigger, heavier third wave. I have seen plenty of waves and flipped countless rafts to know what is going to happen next. I do the only sensible thing: I close my eyes as the bus crashes at full speed into the cement wall.

Flipping a raft is an experience from another world. There are different categories of flips: there is the recreational one, which you for do giggles with clients, women and children, and then there is this. One moment you belong to the world of oxygen and blue sky, of controlled movement. The next, sound, vision and gravity, smudges into a blur, taking your consciousness with them. The variety of sounds you were obliviously enjoying, are traded for an overpowering muffled roar in which you lose complete control of your body. Up and down is forgotten and you can't breathe. If you are quick, skilled or lucky, you hold onto the raft, it is your lifeline back to all that precious order and air that you were taking for granted only moments ago. If you lost your hold, chances are you are now being rag-dolled like an avalanche victim, with no pretension of control. Your existence is a symbol, painted on a slot machine wheel, spinning for your life. Your only defence is to stay calm while forces far beyond your control are deciding your fate. You have to shut down all nonessential oxygen-consuming functions, which include thinking, until you get the chance to become an active participant in your own destiny once again.

This specific crisis plan sets it apart from other sports, placing it closer to armed robbery or rape, as a way to spend your time. The less you struggle, the slower you think, the less you care, the better you do. Down there you become part of a darkness so complete that you cease to exist as a separate physical being. You remain in this place of nonexistence until you see a splash of light, then once you know which way is up, and once you have restarted enough systems, you may leave your cocoon to swim, really hard. By now your consciousness has shrunk to a pinprick and oxygen is the only thing that will fan your flickering flame.

I have experienced the above enough times to be determined not to try it with the added complication of crocodiles. Fear keeps me hanging on tightly to the raft today. Adrenaline pumping, I climb to the top of the slippery raft in seconds, frantically looking around to assess the situation. Only Pete and Dale have held on and are now squatting next to me. The rest of the 'trained professionals' are scattered across the river. Everyone is swimming for whatever he thinks is the quickest way out of the crocodile soup. Closest to me is someone with his helmet pulled over his eyes by the force of the water, effectively blinding, but not stopping him from swimming as fast as he can in any direction. It would be funny, but only later around the campfire.

First things first: we re-flip the raft. Everyone has to take care of themselves until we have control of the boat again. We get ropes to one or two of the swimmers that are close by. Grateful for the help, they get in. This done, we paddle to shore, a mutilated centipede with the few remaining paddles we still have shared out among us.

Time, according to Albert Einstein, and according to any extreme athlete, is relative. Riveted by the intensity and danger of the moment, your mind becomes totally absorbed by it, something so emotionally powerful that events slow. The speed is completely dependent on how deeply one is in trouble. The second before impact moves in slow motion, and impact itself is so quick it does not even register. The part where you have to deal with the fall-out of your situation happens at a running pace, and is slowed right down again as you wait to find out if your friends have survived.

Hanging onto the thick fraying of jungle vines to stop the boat from floating downstream, the seconds drag by like red traffic lights. We are itching from adrenaline and desperate to act, with nothing to do. Eventually, the safety arrives: Jane Dicey and her safety boat break our stalemate. A quick count shows everyone is present. We had chosen the best raft guides we knew. Between us we must have had thousands of flips, yet this would be memorable for each of us.

As planned for after the first rapid, we spilt the teams up in two boats. One is now guided by me, the other by Pete. Minutes later at a particularly big rapid, we clamber up rocks and overgrown sides to have a look at what awaits us. Not surprisingly with ten different guides, there is disagreement on what is the best route. The two boats decide on different approaches to what looks like the whitewater equivalent of quicksand.

Pete takes the easier option, ironically finding trouble. Sneaking over a rock shelf, he rips a meter-long gash in the bottom of the boat. The ribbed floor deflates in seconds. Rafts are compartmentalised for such an emergency but a flat floor makes for unresponsive rafting. This needs fixing right away. With two guides working and eight directing, we have the boat patched up in roughly one hour.

Big rapids continue for another ten kilometres, testing us properly and introducing me to the most enjoyable rafting I have ever done. The river eventually flattens out into a gentler grade just as the midday light starts to soften. The GPS tells us we are close to our prearranged camp at Chobe Lodge: an abandoned safari lodge reclaimed by forest on the river-right bank. It is only thirteen kilometres from the bridge but has taken us almost six hours to reach it.

I remain behind on my boat while everyone climbs up the slopes and crawls through the undergrowth. The first day is supposed to be the easiest. I am not really sure how much harder it can get without killing someone. Fortunately, my fears from the morning are gone. We are in deep, but we are swimming. With the human chatter gone, I lie, eyes half closed, to catch the sunlight in my eyebrows. Surrounded by the bush, I listen to the sounds of insects, birds, river and animals, weaving a hammock in which I lie suspended in ecstasy. I see clearer, think purer and feel more at peace here, under this tree, surrounded by my great adventure, than perhaps ever before. For long blissful minutes I fit perfectly in the world.

The once-luxurious lodge is a one of the remains from Idi Amin's rule, Uganda's most infamous and flamboyant psychopath. The carcass of lavish living has been greatly enhanced, in my opinion, by nature's landscaping. What once strived so hard to blend African wilderness and western comfort now looks like a film set where Rambo would choose to hide from the Vietcong. Natalie and Bingo have driven Land Rovers here, accompanied by AK-carrying game rangers as protection against the LRA. Looking at the map, it should have been a one-hour drive; instead it took them seven.

Considering the condition of the road, if it still exists, we decide to abandon the backup vehicle idea. The boats will be heavier, but secretly I am glad to be rid of the ground crew. With them comes clutter we don't need. At the moment our tally is eighteen, turning the simple procedure of camping into an organisational nightmare with rules and regulations. I want quiet campfires, the sounds of the jungle and close camaraderie, not queues waiting for food.

After dinner, the campfire continues a puppet play of orange shadows on the derelict walls. Dale, Pete and I leave the team and the nicely framed Milky Way inside the skeleton lodge. Our after-hours mission is to collect more water. In the patchy light of my headlamp I swear I see that crazed grin from Pete again. Not far from the river's edge, this task seems like an acceptable undertaking for such big tough explorers.

We travel using hippo trails that make tunnels through the thick vegetation. It is the only way to travel faster than a crawl. The problem is, hippos also use them. These burrows make forwards and backwards movement joyous but leaving the path in a hurry is problematic.

As our ears adjust farther away from camp, the more restless the jungle sounds. Flashlights are a nuisance. They blind anything not in the small artificial light circle. They make you soft, and should not be used by real explorers for anything other than emergencies, or perhaps reading. Since we are all South Africans it goes without saying that we have the lights off. Once entombed in our jungle cave, I start to get that too-familiar feeling that I might be doing something I shouldn't. The voice in my head is doing calculations again. If hippos leave the water to graze at night, and this is the densest concentration of hippos in the world, then this must be the best chance ever to walk into a hippo. Damn it! I wish I was this clever when the lights are on.

Sneaking along as quietly as we can, my paranoia is interrupted by a twelve-year-old girl screaming. I am doubly surprised to find out the cry came from my lips. Almost instantaneously Dale joins in with an undignified yelp of his own.

Ants are the real kings of the forest. Unlimited numbers of fearless, unemotional, determined and well organised biting-things. They can make life unpleasant, as we are now experiencing. It is a mistake to think of an ant as small, because there is no such thing as a single ant. It is merely a part of a larger organism. If a scout ant ends up on a human and realises that it is being led away from its mates, it will not try to escape. Instead, it will bite down in honourable suicide. If a whole colony has climbed on board, the trouble rises exponentially.

Along the path, ants have been dropping onto us and spreading over our bodies. They are ferocious and sneaky. Once the entire colony is in position, the order is silently transmitted to the hungry masses. As one, they try to swallow us. We beat ourselves in the hope of killing some ants – all thoughts of hippos are forgotten. Eventually after a few minutes, our frantic strip-dance routine slows. The battle is still far from over, but it seems that we have gotten rid of the worst of them. As the rough, tough explorers stand semi-naked under the faint glow of a head torch we know full well that there is no other way to describe our actions than pure panic. We burst into prolonged, slightly hysterical laughter, interrupted by the occasional shout as another ant, who has escaped detection because of a particularly strategic position, bites into its host.

Finally we make it down to the water. Dale does a quick sweep with the flashlight, revealing two pairs of blood-red crocodile eyes in the water. Paper-scissors-rock for who fills the containers. We fill them about halfway before retreating with some pride still intact. Somewhat reluctantly, we leave the nice open beach and the devil we know to enter the caves leading us back to camp.

We Sure Would Be Sorry

In contrast to the strong flow we experienced yesterday, the river is now almost a kilometre wide. There are still plenty of rapids, but they are smaller and swirling between islands of various sizes, turning the river into a maze of channels. From a whitewater perspective, it's easy. That said, the risk of colliding with a hippo in the reduced depth and width of the many small channels keeps an edge to our wild paradise. From my extensive knowledge of flora, I identify the tall trees and thick vines as Tarzan vegetation. With every second I am falling more deeply in love with this place.

The sky looks different here. Why? Maybe, when seen together with wildlife, an African sky stretches back to the beginning of our kind, to an ancient genetic memory of home. In all directions birds and antelope decorate the scene. Hippos are so abundant that the priority is not to run them over. Pods of twenty or more appear in every eddy; dripped like candle wax over one another, they cuddle in great pyramids of blubber. Every so often we surprise a pod on the bank; they speed across the land and plunge into the river, stirring even more discomfort beneath us.

The sky is dotted with hundreds of birds. My personal favourite are the fish eagles that look snobbishly down at all the lesser life forms. Goliath herons, with a distinctive deep flap from their massive wingspan, somehow keep themselves in the air whilst, like Christmas decorations, sociable little yellow weaverbirds chat excitedly from their intricate golden nests drooping along river. Large flocks of silver terns twist and dive at incredible speeds, flying like good music past our rafts.

Shortly before lunch we come within twenty meters from elephants hosing themselves down, blissfully unaware of our presence. We hear other members of the herd trumpeting their position from deep in the jungle. It's impossible not to be awed by their size and odd appearance. The sight of them in their natural environment, is as wild as can be, close enough to observe the hairs on their wrinkled skin and to smell their body odour.

A sandy beach seems like an ideal spot for lunch. The island is straight from a Peter Pan movie set. High palm trees throw permanent shade over hippo paths that are so old that they have worn the white ground two feet below the palm roots. Large boulders are scattered to form different rooms. In some, bones of prehistoric size lie half-buried. It appears we have stumbled onto a hippo burial ground. Perhaps poachers made this a base years ago, or perhaps this is where hippos come to die. Aware that I am dependent on good karma in this environment, I wonder guiltily if I am committing sacrilege as I slip a foot long tusk into my bag.

The relative calm of the river is soon flushed away unto a single channel. Over a series of ledges it creates the kind of rugged beauty that can only be found in things of incomprehensible power. Seeing one of the world's largest rivers drop over this kind of gradient is the reason most of us are taking the risk to be here. We have arrived at our promised-land, but will have to be content to be spectators. Without a doubt, it is too big for the rafts to attempt. We carry, drag, and slide the boats along the left bank, past the meat of the rapid. Even though the distance is short, it is hard and hot work, and takes hours.

Past the danger zone, we wrestle the boats to make a re-entry; watching the sun hanging by a thread. Caught up in the excitement and anticipation, we continue downstream hoping to find a camp around the next corner. The jungle has started to thin but is still pretty overgrown along the banks, leaving few good places to camp. Large pods of hippo guard the banks and further reduce our options.

Another big rapid turns the horizon into a threat. If anything goes wrong now we will have to deal with it in the dark. There is simply no option but to camp immediately. We look at the left bank for a long time but still can't see a camp. On the right there is a slight opening in the bush, which could just hold the two tents. I promised the park authorities that I would not camp on the LRA-controlled right bank. They have used the isolation and size of the park to hide from the military for two decades, but sometimes you just run out of options.

The risk seems small compared to the other more immediate threat. Alone I would not give it more than a few seconds' thought. When I see the team jokingly setting up camp, I start playing the 'what if' game. Soon I progress to paranoid level. The chances are slim that the LRA will stumble across us, but if they did, we sure would be sorry. Unnecessary risk with high mortal consequences is stupid. To ease my mind, I slip into the jungle and walk a wide perimeter around the camp, searching for any sign of recent human activity. After thirty minutes of sneaking around like Rambo, machete in hand, I return to find the group relaxing.

As a team, they are already working well. Everyone is chipping in to get everything done as quickly as possible. Firewood is collected, water bottles are filled and filtered, veggies are diced and tinned meat is opened. All this happens in complete harmony despite the continual harmless teasing, or perhaps because of it. These are the explorers of our era: board-short, sandal-wearing misfits; at the core still the same type of restless souls who will forsake safety and comfort to venture into the unknown. We have more possibilities than our forefathers had to express our travel-lust in productive and safe ways, yet here we are, risking life with no prospect of money or fame.

A Day Amongst Days

We try to make an early start. Our enthusiasm is blocked by a fine mist of uncertainty hovering above the water. The lack of visibility adds mystery to an already magical atmosphere. As part of the jungle soundtrack, hundreds of birdcalls drift over the rumble of the river. We eat a modest breakfast of oats, made digestible with copious amounts of sugar. We contemplate where we are and prepare mentally for what will be a day amongst days.

I am nervous about what lies ahead yet confident with the system we have established. My sixteen-foot raft serves as scout, being more mobile and carrying less gear than Pete's stable eighteen-footer, the latter having more stability and therefore carrying the more important supplies. A metal frame is mounted in the middle of the raft, which holds two heavy wooden oars that provide the main driving force. In addition, each boat has four people with smaller plastic paddles. A moderately loaded oar boat is an effective machine in big whitewater; adding four paddlers makes it turbo charged with power steering.

Without a warm-up, we get into the big rapid that forced us to camp last night. Like a mathematical virus gone mad, it grows. We find ourselves in a complex formula, dividing, adding and multiplying around islands so quickly we don't even know where the true riverbank is. The environment and speed of the occasion forces us to push past the boundaries of safe rafting.

Scouting is good and necessary, but when you have to weave between pods of hippos in order to get into position, it is demoted to being overrated. Even if you stop on an island there is still no guarantee of any view into what lies ahead. The rocky outcrops are layered with barbwire vegetation to impair such sightseeing. Rafting here has to be approached differently. In other words, we make it up as we go along. The goal is to go as far as we can into a rapid while maintaining an exit route to the safety of land.

Dale is my front-right paddler. The longer the trip goes on, the more I rely on his input. This is the first time we are on a mission together but he came highly recommended, and I can see why. We both started at the same time as young punks on the Zambezi River. The standard joke is that we share a life. We had worked the same jobs for the same companies, lived in the same house and dated the same girls. We just never did any of these things at the same time (as far as we know). Born in Bethlehem, deep behind the boerewors curtain in the Free State of South Africa, he comes from a place as Afrikaans as it is conservative. How an English-speaking pretty boy like him survived out there is uncertain, but if anyone could, and make it seem cool, it would be Dale.

In our future I will have the pleasure of walking through rain forests, getting lost in swamps and kayaking some crazy water with him. I have yet to hear him complain or see him tired. He is the one, at the end of a hard day, who brews the cup of tea that everyone needs but no one has the energy to make. He is too laid back to ever organise an expedition himself. In spite of that, his positive and useful attitude makes sure he gets invited on any trip he is near. He has a way of doing what needs to be done, without making a fuss and without shouting me, me, me; an attitude I have always respected and secretly envied.

In the front-left position sits Thomas. Professionally he is a telecommunications executive, genetically he is all Viking. Tall, strong and scared enough to paddle his heart out, he is a close friend and one of the original brains behind the source-to-sea concept. He had to pull out of the complete trip due to a severe case of adulthood. Thomas has doubts about coming on even this section and whether he belongs here amongst us professionals. What he lacks in experience he makes up for in willpower and guts. Inside he is fighting his own demons, but he has not let that interfere with his performance as a team member.

The rest of my crew are non-rafters. Marcus, with his delicate English skin, is painted with white sun-block under a large safari hat; his freckles constantly threaten to coalesce. He is never without a camera, and is a perfect foot soldier. When he is told to paddle, he does so without hesitation, and as hard as he can. Before the week is out he will show me a thing or two about courage and calmness under fire.

Dan occupies the remaining position on the raft, making our boat the media centre. Filming is Dan's only priority. He seems blissfully ignorant of how deep down the rabbit hole he really is, while frantically trying to film as much of the process as possible. I am not making life easy for him. We are moving fast and most of my focus is survival, not making films. Since he knows nothing of whitewater, it is impossible for him to anticipate good shots. Too often he has finally set up for the shot just as the action finishes. He does the best he can but is too far out of his comfort zone. He is the butt of the jokes from both rafts, as much for his girly paddling style as for his witty responses to the friendly banter.

We have far less experience than Pete's all-professional raft, but better off for it. On my boat the decisions are made by Dale or me, and then followed blindly by all. The pros on Pete's boat all have their own opinions of the best way to proceed. Indecision is a decision, normally a bad one. Standing in the middle of the raft I have all the control and most of the power. In the really big stuff, when I am throwing my body in behind the oars, it is easier to leave strategic decisions to Dale. I am becoming dependent on him as navigator. While everyone else rows, he has time to stand up in the boat to look ahead and make educated guesses about future risks. Pete and his boat follow at a distance close enough to see us but far enough back to change their course if we did run into trouble.

We are driving the oar boat like a kayak, swinging into small patches of calm water only meters before steep drops, and zigzagging across the river, making last-second decisions and pulling them off with pinpoint precision. The environment, the complexity of the water, the unknown, and the great group, makes this the most fun I have ever had in a raft, and probably ever will.

We blast down giant tongues of water and crash through waves big enough to worry lesser men. When it gets so exciting that I am not sure if I am enjoying it anymore, I figure it might be a good idea to stop. At this speed our safety margin is starting to resemble a 747 water-landing procedure. Worst-case scenario, we go blindly over a horizon line. Searching frantically for the brakes, we find some water moving in the opposite direction of the main flow. We gladly accept the offer and force our way into this little respite to wait for Pete. Meanwhile we try and figure out what to do next.

Spinning slowly, round and round the eddy, the rest of the Nile is heading past us like a freight train. The only thing we know for certain is that we don't want to be in the middle of the river; unfortunately it's where we are. Ahead is an island over which we can carry the boats, albeit with some difficulty. This would still leave us in the middle of the river and a few meters closer to whatever has all this water so excited. On either side of the island are horizon lines with just enough visibility to get us interested. Using the outer edge of the eddy's gravitational pull, we sneak as close to the horizon as possible before scurrying back to safety.

Our brief inspection suggests that we can make it through upright. Scouting horizon lines from your boat is, however, not an exact science. Instead of looking for dangers that you can see, you look for dangers that you cannot see, then make an educated guess about what to expect in the blind spot where you will land. I have a lengthy discussion with Dale while the rest of the boat tries not to look worried. We decide to go for it. Pete waits to see how it turns out. He will not be able to see us once we drop over the horizon and we will need to radio him as soon as we make it down. If we don't make it, radio contact will be postponed for a while.

I splash some water on my face, take a deep breath, and try to think happy thoughts as we confront the cliff of water. A big wave is expecting us at the bottom; fortunately our speed takes us through the guts still upright. It's by no means the end. Things are moving at high-speeds and we still have a few more moves to make before we can manage to stop in some calmer water. I get on the radio to tell Pete we have made it through and so can he. I am unable to reach him. For lack of better ideas, I scratch my chin; this is going to complicate things. Have I lost the team? I am annoyed with myself. I should have a better backup plan.

If it was anyone other than Pete guiding that raft I would have been more worried. When groups get separated in action it is vital to know that no one will do anything rash – the last thing you want is multiple incidents. I know Pete will go into super safety mode and look for an alternative route. We carefully find our way to the right bank. From here we walk back upstream to find them. Eventually we re-establish radio contact. They are out of options, having taken a route left and ended up above what they describe as certain death.

With great difficulty they carry the boat back up a few hundred meters and make their way across to us. Both boats are safely tied to the right bank. Dale, Dan and I walk downstream to find a way past what we now know is a massive rapid, climaxing somewhere near. We leave the hippo trail to stay by the river. This will provide the necessary view of what is ahead. It's called a jungle gym for a reason. After thirty minutes, Dale and I feel the ants again. This time there are no girlish screams, only immediate action accompanied by a lot of 'F' and 'C' words. Hearing the commotion, Dan comes crawling along the same route hoping to film our misery. Unfortunately, he is unaware he is collecting little devils of his own. He reaches us just as we shake off the worst of our ant problem, leaving us free to laugh at him getting a full dose of what he wanted to film. Watching my friends being terrorised just never gets old.

Eventually, clinging to a rickety cluster of vegetation that overhangs a waterfall, we get a glimpse of the rapid ahead. We don't need to look for long. It's obviously out of our league. Time to portage. Inland we split up to find a path for the rafts. Dale returns with good news. The mainland turned out to be an island. If we carried the raft over the relatively open ground through the middle of the island, using the well-worn hippo trials, we can raft down a dodgy little side channel and rejoin the main stream below the rapid.

Two people with machetes go ahead, carving the trails wider and higher. Their excitement at being given such manly jobs is soon tempered by blisters. The rest of us strip the rafts down to carry across the island. To complicate matters a bit we keep the rafts inflated. Due to some pre-trip problems, we only have one very limp raft pump. If our fifty-dollar priceless pump breaks, we will be up the river with plenty of paddles but no boats.

Reloaded, we launch into a tight channel, the raft bumping from side to side at an increasing pace before it squirts us from the shadows we have been in for the past two hours into brilliant sunlight. My eyes blink rapidly to adjust to a world with colours other than variations of green, and for the effort they are rewarded with one of the most spectacular sights ever. Four magnificent waterfalls plunge between island cliffs high above us. Reuniting at the bottom of the turmoil, the converging currents ferociously oppose a ninety-degree turn, creating a ripple of power in the air. If this place was accessible, it would have tourists from all over the world flocking to hotels built on its edge with postcards for sale at quaint cafes located in the spray of the falls. Instead, it stands unmolested, sheltered by inaccessibility, as unspoilt as the day it was created.

The days of the great explorers who walked and sailed into blank continents and oceans are gone. People like me are cheap copies and wannabes. I don't care. To be here, to see this piece of art, to be allowed into nature's VIP lounge reserved for the viewing pleasure of those willing and able to pay the entrance fee, still beats anything else I know.

These falls lie halfway on our journey and mark another change in our environment. The dense forest along the banks gives way to savannah. The increased visibility reveals a greater variety of antelope grazing on the hills. Rapids break long flat pools. The first of this new type drops a bit more gradually, resembling a slide more than a waterfall, with ninety per cent of the water flowing into an incomprehensible hydraulic machine. We stand silently on the brown rocks under the blanket of its thunderous sound. Staring at it transfixed, it's all-crushing, swallowing vortex sucks away our thoughts. Eventually we use the inviting ten per cent of water to sneak past, aided only by ropes that align the rafts to the shore and us.

Safely back in the boats below the monster, we still have an hour before sunset. The huge pool vista suggests a campsite in our near future. We see many good camps, but none are accessible. Hippo pods, trapping us on the river, cut off every approach to the bank. The sun is setting fast, the fearless leader has made the same mistake on consecutive days. With only minutes of light left, we dissect a pod to force our way ashore. They don't like it; neither do we.

Exhausted from a day of high tension and hard physical graft, everyone goes straight to bed after a quick meal. The team fits perfectly into the two tents. Pete and I return to our beds – the rafts. The wooden plank that doubles as an emergency stretcher, tabletop, and raft seat is my favourite place in the world to sleep as the boat breaths lightly on the swell beneath me. Not tonight. I lie on the raft listening to a hippo blowing and splashing meters away. I don't need to speak hippo to know that we separated it from the pod and are exactly where it wants to get out.

Feeling vulnerable, I try to think of alternative sleeping options. None seem much better. I glance over at Pete, sure that he must also have assessed this situation as exposed. He is rolled up in the sleeping bag cover he has been using as a sleeping bag since I met him, already asleep, wedged in the foetal position under the raft seat, using it as a roof instead of a bed. This new position offers only a slight psychological advantage. It will have to do. For ten minutes I listen to the hippos becoming increasingly frantic before eventually abandoning myself for a sense of peace that only the truly tired can get in a situation outside their control. I roll over one more time, into a deep sleep where a whole new world of adventure and aggressive hippos await.

WHITEWATER POETRY

There is no better time to see a sunrise than on a mission next to a big river. It's hard not to feel hope and awe as this new day starts. The tell-tale signs of a massive rapid roaring and rising ahead gives this day a shot at the best day ever only five minutes after breakfast. When approaching an unknown rapid, the trick is to get as close to the point of no return before stopping to have a look at it. I have been practicing for days but as with everything, eventually I go too far. I assume that behind the caravan-size boulder, lying half submerged on the left bank, there will be a calm pool.

Assumption is the mother of all fuck-ups crosses my mind and quietly slips though my lips as the boat is sucked down a small side channel. We have lost our brakes; I hope we will like the ride. A blind corner under a canopy of trees is approaching fast. This level of commitment to the unknown is what we have tried to avoid. The team, sharp from days in the deep end, reacts well. We force our way to the inside of the turn. Next we manoeuvre around a giant tree standing on a rock island in our path; its thick branches narrow into twisted fingers, clawing at us as we pass. Another slick move towards the middle of the river we avoid a crashing wave, and we are in the clear. Success comes with high fives and rebel yells.

Somewhere in the blur of the last twenty-seconds I saw Pete trustingly following me down my mistake. I look upstream in concern. They don't quite avoid the overhanging branches but still slip by. As they enter the calm water, instead of high fives, everyone apart from Pete jumps out of the raft. "Celebrations are going a bit too far." I mutter self-righteously to Thomas. His reply puts the mystery into context. "It would take more than that to get me into this water." Perplexed, I wait for them to catch up before I can get an explanation. A monitor lizard dropped into the boat from the overhanging tree. Any reptile longer than a foot triggers the fight-or-flight reflex. The two-foot lizard was tolerated as it did panic laps around the raft while they dealt with the bigger threat of the rapid, but as soon as they were in the flat water everyone, including the lizard, found a way out while an amused Pete watched the antics of the "kids".

The river soon tightens into a fast flowing valley. If crocodiles could send postcards, this would be the photo with "wish you were here" printed on the back. We are used to seeing 'flat dogs' regularly, but this is a new level. Uneasily we float past the cold-blooded killers baking in the sun. More than a few slither ungracefully into the river to have a closer look. Slapping our paddles on the water and shouting at them with hardly any fear in our voices, we make enough noise for them to doubt a free lunch.

After a handful of these close-ups I see one coming in from my right that looks different, more determined. He is coming for more than a look. Pointing it out for the benefit of those who haven't yet seen it, I turn the boat to face our problem. We beat the water and scream with the vigour of a heavy metal band. It is either too hungry or too brave to care. There is no chance of out running him and absolutely nothing we can do as he swims up to us.

The eerie thing about a croc charge is the utter silence with which it happens. Dale and Marcus positioned in front are in the greatest danger. Calmly and without any instruction, they sit on the inflatable raft tube staring into the approaching row of teeth. The croc launches itself out of the water as it lunges for the raft. It is met mid-air by our last line of defence, Marcus and Dale's paddle blades. An explosion of sound shatters the complete silence that has given the situation the suspended disbelief of a movie scene. The plastic yellow blades make contact with leather, flesh and bone. Dale slightly misses to score a deflecting blow, but Marcus is on the money. A 900-kilogram Nile crocodile takes some stopping, especially in its killing lunge. Perhaps it is the surprise of being treated so disrespectfully, but the blows do the trick. I see flashes of its white belly as it twists in the air like a sporting marlin before splashing back into the water never to be seen again. Stunned, we sink back into silence for a second. Once we have processed what just happened we explode into, "HOW FUCKING COOL WAS THAT!!!!!!"

A minute after the crocodile-hunter episode, mist rises over the horizon to tell us another mighty rapid is coming up. Dodging the usual hippo or two, we pull in above it. By now we have all become so accustomed to seeing the beasts everywhere that they have to be closer than ten meters to be considered worrisome. Once on the bank, my eyes stretch, my jaw drops and an unspecific feeling that can be described as either excitement or fear rises from my bowels. A standing wave emerges like a giant cobra about to strike, bigger than anything I have ever heard of and certainly bigger than any I have ever seen.

It is a sheer green cliff standing as fierce and fragile as a gas flame nearly eight meters tall. Defiantly the freak wave holds its form while tons upon tons of water pass through it. Just when it looks as if gravity will drag the mountain down, it jerks back up like a punch-drunk giant teetering on the edge of collapse. It is too big for the raft, but in a kayak, oh my goodness, it might just be possible. As if looking for confirmation that what I am seeing is real, I make eye contact with Dale. He reads my mind. "I reckon it might," he says quietly before turning his gaze lovingly back at it. Without a word we both decide to come back with our kayaks another day. We manage to get the rafts past using a chicken route that clips the edge of the titan, close enough to have a peek and get the heart racing. It is turning out to be a day with more action than most people experience in a lifetime, and we have not even had lunch.

The epic flows into another piece of whitewater poetry. The Nile is revved up to top RPM, the noise makes it clear we have stumbled onto something enormous well before we can see it. The GPS says we are close to the end. This could well be the final rapid, and it looks like the Nile has saved the best for last. Stretching out ahead of us until the bend in the low canyon blocks our view, we can see virtually continuous, intimidating, dangerous – but possibly navigable – water. The only way to handle it will be to break it down into digestible parts, turning each into a destination in itself. The unsurvivable Murchison Falls is lurking somewhere close, if we are going to attempt this we have to get it right.

Breaking the rapid down is harder than we hoped. Part one is OK but we can't get a good look at what lies below part two. The canyon walls rise steeply on the right bank with trees obstructing our view. The Albertine Rift shelf refuses the plan of unassuming river explorers. Finally, after two hours of back and forth, I think I have seen enough to make the call to go down.

The first part is negotiated perfectly. It's more difficult than it looked but eventually we are on the relatively calm water that leads to the mysterious water cliff. Sniffing like nervous rodents we slowly sneak up to its edge; it is only once we are committed to go over that concentration displaces nerves. A feeling of great joy and relief lights up my insides as I get the first clear glimpse of the previous blind spot. My instincts were right: this is going to be fine.

To search for a route through the whitewater stretching indefinitely ahead, we scamper up the canyon walls. From above it is clear that we have to make it to the river's left side. If only it was that easy. Before us is almost a kilometre of fast-flowing water, booby trapped with all sorts of nasty looking river features. No easy options are on offer, but on closer inspection we notice a weak spot in the river-wide wave that should allow access. The downside is it will force us to wait until we are half way down the rapid before we can start pushing to river-left, presenting fatal consequences if we miss.

I notice that Pete has not climbed the gorge to scout the section ahead. I am annoyed. Even if he will be following me through the rapid, I want him here. He has a good eye for whitewater and always has valuable input. I decide he is being slack when the end is in sight and I grumble to myself about his shortcomings. Even though we have shared thousands of hours together on expeditions, under the heat and the pressures of a hard day, we still become irritated with one another. The unspoken rule is only that it is dealt with internally. I know that the voice in my head criticising him has nothing to do with him. Being angry with someone else, focusing on their faults, makes me smarter, makes me harder, at least by comparison. Their weaknesses make me believe in my own strength and righteousness. I am thinking of clever ways to tell Pete off while he has gone down to the first and smallest obstacle of the upcoming challenge. I am not sure why he didn't come up with us, perhaps he just needed to be alone – perhaps he had a feeling.

Whatever it was, it possibly saved our lives. He sat alone on a rock staring at the river. A hippo surfaced and started playing in a small waterfall. Time and again, we have seen them doing this, playing in seemingly impossibly strong rapids, walking over rocks with tons of water pressure smashing into their stubby legs. This one was bobbing up and down, having a great time, climbing up on the rocks that form the waterfall and diving back into the water. Treating the mighty Nile as its personal splash pool, it seemed in complete control. All that power and elegance slipped as it lost its footing, going headfirst and on its back over the waterfall, its four short fat legs pointing to the sky. After a few seconds it popped up to give Pete a guilty look and an embarrassed grunt, Pete reckoned it was the funniest thing he had seen since George Bush promised to eradicate evil.

The problem for us was, after its little accident the hippo stayed in the calmer water that was created by the backwash of the waterfall, in the exact place we would have passed through with the rafts. If Pete had not seen it, we would have gone right over, or into, its head. Together we sit contemplating, mostly silently, baking in the afternoon sun, watching and waiting for Harry the clumsy hippo to move.

The S-Bend is undoubtedly the biggest rapid yet. A fitting final challenge. Held up by one hippo when we have already passed so many thousands. It appears this one is obstacle. The guardian of the final gate. The finish line is in sight but we will be spending another night in the bush. A golden rule in expeditions is not to relax towards the finish. In mountaineering, more people die coming down the mountain than going up. Rushing is a natural tendency of mine, and a dangerous one. A good night's sleep before attempting the last obstacle does not distress me at all. In fact, it will give me one more night to take it all in. I have been able to live a complete fantasy for a few days. If we can finish without killing someone this trip will be the greatest thing I have ever done.

By nightfall the hippo has still not moved. It's time for a new plan. Around midnight we throw rocks into the pool to establish as best we can that it has left the water to graze. Then, using ropes, we swing the rafts past the spot in question. A complicated process in the dark using many hands and quick movements with the risk of being pulled into the water from the steep bank. I warn everyone to be especially careful, and proceed to fall myself. Luckily I grab onto some protruding tree trunks and stop just short of what would have been a terrifying swim at best. The close call leaves only my ego bruised at the little puppy yelp I let out as I felt myself slipping.

In the thick undergrowth there is no space for tents. Sleeping bags are laid out in hippo trail trenches, tunnelling through large tree vines, protruding from the yellow dirt walls of the underworld. Every day the group reminds me more of soldiers than raft guides. In their eyes glints the same steely resolve of people playing for keeps. There is little talk around the small campfire. I am guessing we have all had moments where we felt in over our heads. Every time a challenge arose, the entire team has jumped in to defeat it. I am proud to have been part of it.

With a cup of tea, I climb onto a rock facing upstream. Pete and Dan join in watching a forest fire in the distance paint the dark canvas of night with a red brush. Words are used sparingly, just three guys in the Now. I am having an immense feeling of well-being. In most of my life I feel out of place, but not here. During the last four days I have felt one-hundred per cent involved, focused and alive. Everyone, somewhere deep down, wants to know how they will perform when their life is threatened. This exercise has answered that question for me. I was scared before leaving, the real-deal scared. A large part of fear is the belief that we can't deal with the consequences of certain actions. Inevitably once we are forced to deal with those consequences we find ways to cope, or even thrive.

Shortly after first light, the boat is rigged and ready to go. It's a cold morning with a clear sky. Superficial jokes are tossed round, but there is an edge to us all. Things are going to start happening fast once we commit to the flow. Dale unties us from the split tree trunk and jumps nimbly in as I start to pull on the oars with everything I have. Going backwards enables me to pull on the oars instead of pushing, giving us twice the power; unfortunately it becomes harder to judge angles and position. Long hard strokes make each one count as we move sideways across the river. Dale notices it first, and yells out the bad news that we have overshot the soft spot in the river-wide crashing wave. With a sickening feeling I know he's right.

It's not good! We are moving too quickly to reverse our momentum and are going to have to deal with it. Time is up. In the last seconds before hitting the crashing wave I take a reflex chance. When facing up to a big wave it is essential to keep the boat straight, for impact. Now, without thinking, I changed our angle from ninety degrees to seventy-five degrees, pointing right. If the angle is perfect, it should surf the boat back to the soft spot and through. Too little or too much angle, and we will go over.

It works. The boat takes a big hit, but the speed of the water ushers it through the window before it can flip over. A few more strokes, dodging another hippo pod, and we are safely in the slower-moving water along the right bank. Pete notices my mistake and avoids it, managing to come through easy and right on line.

We have another small waterfall ahead of us that we rope the boats over and suddenly we are at the take-out. Just like that, it's all over. We have made it. There are some big hugs and a few high fives; the overall mood is strangely quiet. Normally after such an ordeal there is a lot of back slapping, hooting and hollering.

Personally, I know how close that last call was on changing the angle. I am annoyed with myself for getting the lines right all week, only to come that close to killing at the end. Why the rest of the team is so quiet, I can only speculate. Perhaps we are all a bit shell-shocked. We know enough about risk to realise that we have been playing the odds for five days. We are all alive with no injuries, but with more close calls than can be considered healthy. Possibly we all feel that in the end we are just lucky to have survived, more relieved than excited to finish.

I suspect I am missing an opportunity to learn something that might make me a better leader in similar circumstances. It is my first trip as leader in a combat situation. I eagerly want to be good at it, but receive no feedback. Not one of the guides thanks me or criticises me afterwards, and it's not like you can ask them to fill in a form.

The whitewater is done. We still have twelve kilometres to go before the Red Chilli Rest Camp. We deflated the raft so that we could carry it past Murchison Falls and down the gorge, but as we inflate it, our pump finally breaks. We knew it was bound to happen and to be fair, it could not have happened at a better time. A few plans are in the pipeline to get a new one, but for the moment we are stuck with a deflated raft. Dale suggests we blow the raft up by mouth, figuring it is nothing but a big balloon anyway. Three hours later, hyperventilating, we have enough air to float it, barely. The floor is all but flat, the sides no more than half-inflated and the cross sections completely limp.

Pete, Nat, Dale, Marcus, Dan and I pack into the raft while the rest of the crew gets in a Land Cruiser and sets out in search of rum and Cokes. The river is well-behaved and flowing regally through beautiful wilderness. Big animal herds graze all around and the width of the river leaves us plenty of space to avoid hippos. It's all rather touristy and relaxing; a big herd of elephants on the right bank lifts the mood even higher. Staring contently at the scenery I notice a log that looks like a crocodile, a lot like a crocodile. The only reason I know it is not one is because crocs don't get that big. As I point out the interesting similarity to the rest of the crew, the log proceeds to charge through the water straight at us.

Gone is the bravado of slapping it in the teeth; this croc looks big enough to swallow the raft. I say, "Forward paddle," unnecessarily and as calmly as I can. There is at least two hundred meters between the monster and us. Normally this would be more than enough. Suddenly the half-inflated raft feels like a plastic child's swimming pool. Even with six of us paddling as hard as we can, it keeps gaining on us. Magically, as it comes closer we manage to go faster. Eventually after a good ten minutes of this ridiculous situation, the crocodile-god gives up, or at least dives underwater. Another five minutes of sprinting, just to be sure, before we slow down, exhausted. The novelty of dodging crocodiles and hippos now well and truly over, all we want is safety, rum and Coke.

Harem Girl

I cherish the freedom of access provided by our rafts. The world outside is nothing but a vague notion, our main concern is day-to-day survival. Life is close to perfect. Free from whitewater concerns, we appreciate the other gifts of Murchison Falls National Park. Barely through the delta, the river tentatively joins Lake Albert then decides it would rather not visit the Congo. Making a right turn, without a stir in the little lake it shakes off the stagnant, slightly malevolent personality of the area, and regains its individuality and purpose by heading north. We are not far from the LRA stronghold in northern Uganda, and once we pass into the red zone, we will be moving 24/7.

Before we leave the Victoria Nile and join the Albert Nile, we find a suitable campsite under a tree. Its century-old branches frame the lake and the mountains of the Congo in a graph of decline. In the distance an ominous afternoon thundercloud gives it an appropriate tint of doom.

I am desperately trying to endure constantly being in the company of people. Even though I have loved the mission so far, moments alone are the deep breaths that keep me from drowning. While everyone lazes around reading, writing, doing whatever they feel like, I take the empty raft out on to the lake and strip down for a wash. I bask naked in the afternoon sun, submerged in a lake I have only read about. For a long time I sit sucking up the precious solitude.

My gaze scans over Lake Albert onto the shores of the Congo and gives me that magical feeling that I am living my dream, finding what I came for. Here the Nile's ancient secrets and allure have not been trampled under millions of tourist feet; the owners of each pair robbing a little of its mystery with a carelessly aimed camera and cheapening it with their visitor's fee. Here, even one hundred and fifty years later, relatively few Westerners have followed on the great African explorers' trail.

This lake and the falls was named by my favourite two, Samuel and Florence Baker. An unlikely couple in the dramatic years when man's greatest ambition was to find the source of the Nile; something he had been unable to do since the beginning of recorded history. Explorers of the nineteenth century were celebrities who wrote books about how brave they were and how tough they had to be to survive in the African continent. The Bakers did not fit into that mould.

Sir Samuel Baker had no reason to risk such a dangerous journey. Unlike Stanley, he had money and social standing; unlike Livingstone he was not exploring for the glory of God; and unlike Speke, he was not a loner out to prove himself. Most importantly, unlike them all, Samuel brought his woman along to share in the marvellous adventure. Samuel was larger than life, but Florence was possibly without equal before or since.

The men strove for glory and immortality, while Florence Baker was just there to keep her man out of trouble and neatly dressed. Young and beautiful from eastern European descent, she stood by her man during two extraordinary expeditions. The first to discover the sources of the Nile and the second to put down the slave trade. Their life together is perhaps one of the greatest love stories of all time.

They stood isolated, in a world as foreign, inhospitable and dangerous as ever existed: A middle-aged English lord and a stolen teenage Hungarian slave girl. Europeans, Africans and Arabs died all around them by the thousands. They risked their lives for one another more times than most couples have romantic weekends and barely uttered a complaint. They pose a stark contrast to today's explorer who has to make it sound harder than it was in order to sell a book or movie. The masses want drama and they are spoilt for choice. Provide it or they will change the channel.

Being entertained by my own thoughts drifting light as clouds on a blue sky, I witness a scene that will remain with me forever. Two bull hippos emerge in a battle for dominance. They force their giant jaws open, trying to swallow the other. It's all happening slowly, as if the mechanism is run by hydraulics. Gradually, the oval breach that can be seen through their gigantic orifices grows, until it allows a perfectly clear view of the opposite bank. The foot-long teeth protrude through corners to mar the tranquil view. Eventually one bull backs down, diving under. The other follows in pursuit. On the surface a wave mirrors the chase. A ridge of water, displaced by torpedoes burrows under the surface. The speed with which these reaction waves move and turn is frightening. I knew the statistics before, but I am glad I did not see this until we were safely through the Murchison section.

The unassuming bridge and elephants mark Pakwach town at the edge of the national park boundary. As a feat of engineering it doesn't say much, and looks like a pretty basic affair, its steel garters covered in thick spider webs. Symbolically it says goodbye to peace, and welcome to war. Before we reach Sudan we have a tricky two hundred kilometres of LRA-infested territory. Since there is nothing of interest here, apart from people being killed and people killing, we decide to skip the sightseeing and head directly for the Sudanese border. The only thing we need from the misery industry is a few interviews to show the world what is going on and to make them realise how brave we are for passing through. We can get these film interviews in safer surroundings.

We decide to travel through the night to make us less visible and shorten our exposure time in this volatile zone. It is a good reason for rowing through the night, not that I need one, especially during a full moon.

Loaded on our rafts is enough gear and supplies to get us to Juba, the capital of South Sudan. We hope the shops will be open when we get there, whenever that is. Somewhere on the route is a gorge, but we have no idea how deep or how steep. The few accounts by people who have seen it are localised and mostly from the fifties. A worst-case scenario is that the walls become so shear that we cannot portage around the dangerous rapids, forcing us to portage overland through a place with notoriously unfriendly people with a littering of land mines.

We have to keep the rafts manoeuvrable enough to handle big, unknown whitewater and they have to carry seven people with food and personal gear for twelve days, three video cameras, a sound recording system, blank tapes for six months, solar power system including car battery and panel, comprehensive medical kit, five still cameras, satellite phone, kitchen (including Dutch oven and two washing bowls), two laptops, ropes and climbing gear (in case the canyon did wall out on us), rafting equipment, air-band radio, fishing equipment, and miscellaneous personal items. In Sudan we will add two soldiers with guns and sleeping mats.

Overloading is my pet hate. My idea of an expedition is to leave home, not bring it along. When I go on a mission alone, I take as little gear as possible. If you don't use it every day, you don't really need it. This is obviously not a minimalist trip. I know it, yet I feel like screaming every time I see something that I think is unnecessary. Pete loves his gear and follows the "it's better to have it and not need it than to need it and not have it" approach. Fine. It annoys me as much as his reckless driving but we usually find a balanced middle ground.

As a non-camper, Doctor Ian's personal gear exceeds everyone else's. Experience tells you what you absolutely must have. Unfortunately for Ian, he asks me to help him repack. I halve his gear but it is only when I put his thick pillow on the Land Cruiser to Kampala that his face drops. It's not the pillow. I like pillows. I will sleep on a jagged rock shelf if I have a good pillow. But its far more efficient to stuff the case with clothes come sleep time. He doesn't seem convinced, neither does Bingo. I wonder if he expected this when I asked him to leave the comforts of his desk and busy life in Kampala? It occurs to me that I am being a space bully. Making a fuss over a pillow seems small, but I am desperate. I try to explain myself. Unfortunately I have a way of expressing myself when convinced that I am right that comes over a bit too forcefully, altogether defeating the purpose of an explanation.

Good And Evil

The river is almost four hundred meters wide by now and the banks are completely covered by papyrus. These smooth green pipes with their scrub-brush heads keep us fortified. Just the thought of the LRA is enough to charge the rafts with a strange energy. For all the talk, the threat is probably minimal. In the unlikely event that we do come across one of their small patrols at the exact moment that we pass one of the few openings in the papyrus walls, they will have to be ready to shoot or see us pass by in seconds – I think.

The day takes the last sip of colour, fading pink to night. Adventure is ready to punch around the corner. Our senses are amplified to compensate for our loss of vision. What had minutes ago been wide open becomes a hyacinth and papyrus labyrinth. Islands of plants, not planted at all, silently creep down. Green clots suffocate the river. If one of these narrow channels closes up, we will have to row kilometres upstream to try another.

We are sucked abruptly down diverging channels, trap doors in the darkness, leading silently and suddenly on different courses within a lost horizon. In the disorienting surroundings and dead of night, the rafts occasionally lose each other. Through radio contact we manage to find one another again in the occasional open pools of water. Blinded, I make choices based on little more than gut instinct, always seemingly heading for a dead end, never actually coming up against one.

I row for hours unwilling to give up my position on the oars, absorbed by the meditative routine of pushing on the sticks in the unfamiliar and eerie surroundings. The silence is alive and the full moon turns the world silver. The most level-headed of humans cannot deny the mystique that encloses a river at night. It is a night passed in examination of the things we so rarely talk about, things our cluttered lives seldom give us an opportunity to question. Sure, there may be no answers, but if abstract thought is man's greatest achievement then it must be exercised.

Our talk is punctuated by deep silences about the only debate that could do such a mystical night justice: God. Ian came to Africa as a missionary, and if you are going to talk God, with whom better than a card-carrying member? I admire the alternative road he has taken, the success he has made of it and I think his opinion carries far more weight than my own.

His conclusion, as I understand it, is that he has seen too much random suffering in his years in Uganda to be able to still believe in the 'greater good' that he came to Africa for. Too many bad things happen to good people, and even more unforgivably, too many good things happen to bad people. Idi Amin, the man responsible for the carnage that Ian saw while working in Luwero, or the killing fields, spent the final years of his natural life in a penthouse in Saudi Arabia. A man responsible for the killing of an estimated 300,000 people, and a symbol of evil in our time, lived to die of old age. A tough fact to swallow in our framework of good and evil.

I admire Ian's uncertainty on the matter. Most members of organised religions are world leaders in selective information processing. Personally, I am just sceptical about any ideology and too busy living. With so many things I do not understand in my own life it would be arrogance or desperation to pretend to understand a sphere so much larger than myself.

Ian is not the only one who finds the Bible of little use in explaining all the amazing and terrible things that we are surrounded with. I have read some of it, and have heard it spoken since I was born. It has never really made any sense to me, but I pursued that path for all the wonderful hope it promised. On at least three different occasions I sat crying on my knees offering my life to Jesus, asking God to accept me, to make me feel whole. Ironically the times I have felt whole, certainly did not happen in church and most definitely not as I was on my knees. Besides, I find no enjoyment in reading instruction manuals. I agree with the Buddhist saying, "There are as many paths as there are monks. When we choose our path in life we choose that as a path to God." The answers are all around us or nowhere at all.

Trying to sound smart, I favour the 'no energy can be destroyed' theory. That it merely disbands and comes back as part of something else. The idea that nature is just a continually dissolving puzzle trying out new forms sounds like heaven to me, an immortal VIP pass to experience everything in the multiverse. When the earth does eventually hit the sun and gets blown to bits, it is only to propel us further into the unknown. It would be a worthy ride to evolving through billions of years for. Apart from the scientific proof for this, of which I understand little, it fits into my personal experience of God. If I had to describe my most satisfying moments in life they would be when and where I felt part of the world around me. Unfortunately this clever little theory does not explain the nature of evil, and its obvious presence in the north of Uganda.

Imagine your worst day, multiply it by a hundred, and pray to your God that you never experience what some of the people in this war zone go through, every day, without any hope of it getting better. Ever. Compared to these people, every day, no matter how bad, is *the best day ever*. I know nothing about pain, nothing about suffering and hopefully never will. I have no tools to deal with these people's suffering, and luckily I don't have to. I am merely passing through. I can pretend to understand, to be compassionate, and I do, within limits and preferably during short film interviews. Other people's suffering doesn't make us wiser, only our own can do that. The best we can hope for is that it will make us realise how good we have it, which might be a step toward wisdom after all.

Chess

The first rays of sun find us wrapped up, already warm in sleeping bags, waking from a few hours' sleep or unwinding from a rowing session. After staring into the night for ten hours, the colours around us are staggering in their diversity and clarity. The mood is high as we share the drug called sleep deprivation.

The most consequential event of the morning is Pete creating the breakfast of champions. Somewhere along the line a friend gave us support in the form of muscle-builder protein shakes. When sprinkled over breakfast (and most other meals) it transforms whatever you have on your plate into a strawberry milkshake. Genius, but for some reason not an instant hit with everyone.

Too soon the cosy-morning feeling burns away under a sun that does not tolerate such foolish sentiments. Not wanting to risk stopping to cook, the corned-meat-mayonnaise special comes out for lunch. Luckily we have some stale bread left to top it off.

Affected by the midday heat that sticks to everything like Velcro, Pete and I have a bite at each other over some trivial matter. Since neither of us is right or wrong, we do not apologise. When we finally stop, lured in by the implied safety of seeing women and children at a small cluster of scarecrow huts, Pete brings the chess set over as a peace pipe. Our latest in a long line of sets broke days ago, so we stretch out a sponsor's t-shirt, mark some squares on it and proceed to do battle, peacefully.

The chessboard is our private place. We enter it as a ritual, a celebration, a board meeting, a treat, or a cleansing exercise. The fact that there is no luck in chess anchors us both. We have absolute control over that board if nothing else. We have played many epic games through the years, but the only one I can remember the result of is the first time I beat him. It wasn't that I had beaten Pete, it was that I had arrived at his level. A good game has never been judged by the outcome. The aim is simply to make the challenge harder, ultimately to become better. Between us, bad moves are retracted and strategies discussed to expose weaknesses. When I get cocky after a few wins, Pete patiently reminds me, "The race is only against yourself, bru."

Hungry Ones With Guns

He doesn't look like he is about to die, but he is. A tall Austrian man in his sixties, he has walked life uphill both ways. Living in this magnificent place, his dream has become a nightmare. The tourism he counted on for income died because of the war. The wife he came to settle with left shortly after, apparently with the architect of his dream lodge. Emphysema has made it impossible to even walk down to the water for fishing, which is the reason he built the lodge in the first place.

Throughout our time at Ara Lodge, he seems to have a quiet humour and dignity about him as he waits out here, alone, for his lungs to slowly suffocate him. He has given us the keys to his castle while we make a final re-supply before South Sudan. It waits menacingly, unknown, now only a few kilometres away.

There is perhaps no place that knows more about violence than Sudan. The earliest explorers write of fierce tribes that love a fight regardless of reason. It was the commercialisation of the slave trade that decimated most of Africa from the fourteenth century onwards, setting a new standard for brutality. The Arab world and Africa don't play well together. Slavery had been the main industry in Sudan since way back when the Meroe and Cush civilisations were the middlemen.

When the massive swamp known as the Sudd, that separates north from south, was opened up in the 1800s, the floodgates for the slavery industry opened with it. Born and raised with a sense of superiority that can only be justified in the name of religion, the Arabs of Sudan still believe their God has given them the right to do whatever they like to the heathens that live in the south. The overall effect of the slave trade was the estimated death of thirty-million people in Africa, and in Sudan, the moulding of a country where no one was safe and no one could be trusted.

The preferred method of harvesting slaves in the South was through fortified camps deep in tribal lands, called Zaribu camps, and from here they would do excursions into the surrounding areas or bribe local tribes, hostile to one another, to do their dirty work for them. Turning primitive people against each other was a fruitful tactic. In the South it is only the Shilluk tribe that is united under one King. The Nilotic tribes of the Nuer and Dinka only have loyalty towards their clan. The Madi are known as the chosen ones, the ones who stood up to the British Empire and delivered Charles Gordon's head to their leader. They would pay in the thousands once Lord Kitchener arrived with unmatched heavy artillery.

The current war in Sudan is the longest-running war in Africa and like almost every other war on the continent, child soldiers are doing most of the shooting. The clever rhetoric about religion and freedom is only partially true. At its core it is little more than a fight for who gets to eat. All the fighting happens in South Sudan, between the Government of Sudan (GOS) and the Sudan People's Liberation Army (SPLA) while the Lord's Resistance Army (LRA), armed by the GOS, plays a significant role. Thrown into the mix are a few warlords loyal to either or controlling their own areas. Even if the cease-fire is holding, we still expect the country to be full of some of the most dangerous kinds of people in the world: hungry ones with guns.

So do we fly our flags? Some of the team believes it will be safer to show that we are not part of the war; others feel that as foreigners we will be an even more prized commodity for terrorists. Unable to resist a good debate I get stuck into what is really a trivial matter: flags or no flags. If the bad guys get sight of a group of pasty skinned foreigners we are in for some attention.

Nervous about the severity of the consequences of any wrong decision, tempers rise. A smart leader should stay out of emotional debates, or mediate a compromise. Instead, I heroically decide for the group: we will fly the flags. At our leaving ceremony the South African ambassador presented me with a huge flag, making a beautiful speech about us all being ambassadors. It made me feel important, and at the very least they give some shade. My aim should have been to calm feelings before Sudan, not inflame them; when I finally realise this, I take the flags down, but emotions can take a long time to heal in a war zone.

NIMULE

Long before we reach Sudan, Nimule town winks at us from a dusty hilltop, sunlight reflecting from its corrugated iron roofs simmering above the papyrus-covered banks. Eventually, scattered and worn buildings appear along with a few small gaps in the papyrus, but nothing large enough to suggest it might lead to one of the biggest towns in South Sudan.

The river accelerates after turning away from the hill and we start to suspect we have missed the most important border post of our lives. The GPS agrees but refuses to take any responsibility. Skipping international borders anywhere can irritate the army. I imagine it's worse when they're actually at war. With no break in the papyrus and at an increasingly fast pace we are being swept into an unknown section of rapids in an area inhabited by notoriously hostile people. The papyrus finally opens up for a glimpse at the riverbank, unveiling two men with guns. They gesture frantically for us to stop. Since they are not wearing uniforms I decide not to. I figure it's better to ask for forgiveness from the good guys later than to beg for mercy from the bad guys now. Following us at a little run along the bank, they become increasingly aggressive, as people with guns often do when ignored. We wave back in self-defence.

Out of sight, we tie the boats to a tree spreading its twisted limbs out over the river. The runaway train has to be stopped now. Asking the team to stay behind, I commandeer Dale's kayak and proceeded to paddle back upstream, on a mission to find the town. Walking would have been easier but here, in the river, I have a slightly lesser chance of being spotted, never mind the nesting land mines.

The current gets too strong to continue. I force my way into the papyrus barrier, falling shoulder-deep into the stagnant water trapped below. I grab straws to pull the kayak and myself forward. It is slow, muddy progress until I finally crawl onto hard ground. I rest for a few minutes, camouflage the kayak as best I can and sneak into the tree line. Using all his skills the Great White Explorer becomes almost invisible to the naked eye while his keen jungle senses miss nothing. Moments away from actually believing this, I almost walk into a man before I see him.

His black skin is perfectly camouflaged in the shade of a tree; the first sign of this new danger, is his brilliant white teeth, like a scene from a children's program. I guess if you have to surprise someone with a gun, it's not all that bad if they have their pants around their ankles. Mid-process, still squatting and quite relaxed at seeing a white man appear from the river, he proceeds to start up a conversation of which I understand not a single word. It is hard to feel threatened by someone on the toilet and his tone sounds friendly enough. Through hand signs I manage to get directions to town. Leaving him still squatting and chatting away, I resume my stealth mission with a smile.

Ten minutes later I come across burnt buildings. The story of their demise is written in braille by heavy gunfire on their walls. Cowardly roofs have completely surrendered to gravity, while the foundations stubbornly fight a losing battle to keep the rest of the constructions from deserting. Snotty kids, half dressed, covered in dirt, start to appear, following me at a cautious distance, not sure what to make of me. I use my camera to show them their faces on the little screen. It's a huge success and soon I am quite popular.

Eventually I come to a military setup. Tattered pieces of uniform hang lifeless and faded over a wire. Spent ammunition shells, stuck upside down in the dirt, appear to be the Sudanese equivalent of white picket fences. Men sitting on the shady side of the building in rickety wooden chairs watch me with interest. Their AKs are within easy reach. It appears a half-naked white man covered in mud is not a threat.

From here I am led to another house, where an old-timer dressed in an Arab robe perches on a throne watching the world through memories. I am surprised at the Arab getup. This is supposed to be a war between Christians and pagans in the south and Muslims in the north.

Grey hair and a neat white beard give distinction and wisdom to a sunken face that seems impossible to age, rare in a continent where the life expectancy is around forty-six. He squints at me, as if he has already seen too much in life. Even shrunken with age he is almost a head taller than my six feet, towering even amongst the physically impressive Dinka tribe that makes up the bulk of the SPLA. We sit in silence watching kids play with toy guns on the cracked steps of the crumbling barracks. Through the gaping holes with frayed edges serving as doors, the buildings seem empty inside. Skinny, bald chickens scratch around on a dull courtyard, hardly bothered by vegetation.

This is one of the biggest bases of the SPLA. Nothing more than a shantytown is The Stronghold. Somehow these barefoot soldiers, with weapons stolen from the enemy and filtered in from Ethiopia, have managed to resist and finally force the Government of Sudan with its army and air force built with oil money, to at least consider letting them have their own land and religion. The issue is still far from settled but I feel obliged to marvel in their relative success.

In 1972 the Addis Ababa Peace Agreement ended the first war in Sudan after seventeen years. It was a time of great hope for the continent and in particular for Sudan, its largest country. Investment flooded into the country that is roughly the size of Western Europe with a population of fewer than forty-million. For a brief time Sudan looked like it was going to break from its violent past, and Africa looked hopeful. Over thirty years later perhaps there is a glimmer of hope again.

Bingo shows up to tell me the team has moved downstream. After our local contact arrives, we are driven to their campsite. We pick up two expedition members on the road. They were bored in camp and decided to go for a walk. I stare at them unbelievingly. Social walks on the front line of a combat zone without a guide is utterly stupid. No one seems to be concerned that we have the team split into three groups with no way to communicate. I am angry at how little control I have over the team, but decided to work on the *angry* part instead of the control part. At the camp my mood does not improve.

Nimule National Park has been decimated by the war and is only a park in name, or so we thought. The officer in charge of the park is upset about us not stopping in town. Ian and Natalie try their best to calm him down. He is taking our invasion as a personal insult and a direct threat to national security and the safety of the three animals still alive in the park. To be fair, he is also concerned about our safety. Long after we have admitted to our mistake, he continues his rant.

I would like to get involved with the discussion but suspect I will only make it worse. These lectures from people in authority are often a process that has to run its course. Any new person addressing the official can easily repeat the process from the beginning. Say yes, say you're sorry, nod your head, ask for forgiveness from the officer, or even God, if you think it will help. Allow him to show his men that he is in charge and then he'll run out of steam. Our SPLA contact, Commander James Akol, eventually manages to calm the situation down, only slightly ahead of its natural conclusion.

The team is eager to have a look at Nimule: the mysterious border town holding back Sudan from Uganda. Pete, Dale and I stay behind with the gear. As the team squeezes into a Land Cruiser I start the tea as Pete sets up the chessboard.

Hole In The Crumbling Wall

Under the tree canopy swatting at flies, patience seeps out of me with every drop of sweat. It is 10:30 and the team was supposed pick us up at 08:00. Something is wrong. It's the only explanation. As the imaginary crisis escalates in my head, I set off on foot through the remains of the Nimule National Park.

It's a long, sweaty mission until I finally find them sitting in a large blue room, paint not so much peeling from the plastered brick walls as melting away. Stick men and women drawn on ancient anti-malaria posters relay messages unconvincingly from the wall. A huge wooden desk sits with a sole purpose: command centre for the colossal man clothed in a solemn green ceremonial uniform. A large Sudanese flag covers the wall behind the local army general.

The team is listening from the unevenly sized chairs while Dan films the General explaining the local security situation. Too late to join in the meeting without disrupting the flow, I stand by listening to the last few lines of the hour-long safety briefing. Pete needed to be at this meeting. I desperately hope that there is a reason the team has not come to pick us up; my temper starts to flare at the possibility there might not be one.

Everyone has a role to play on the team. Pete has many, but above all, security. He spent months researching and planning our progress through Sudan, finding and getting to know the people who knew what was actually happening on the ground. He tracked them down over East Africa and infiltrated their tight circles. Most, if not all of them were in some way involved with the aid organisations, which have found a centre in South Sudan and more particularly with Operation Lifeline Sudan.

In April 1989, in response to a devastating famine and the aftermath of the long war, as a result of negotiations between the UN, the Government of Sudan and the Sudan People's Liberation Movement/Army (SPLM/A), Operation Lifeline Sudan was established to deliver humanitarian assistance to all civilians in need, regardless of their location or political affiliation. The GOS did not want their enemies or anyone who might potentially be an enemy to receive food but they were smart enough to know that the Bush administration might do it any way. They figured it would be smarter to have some control over the process and have UNICEF be the ones who distributed it.

Their kind of operation and our partially dependent security relies on real-time information, lots of it. For them it is to make sure that at least some of the assistance they send drips down past the military to the local population and, just as importantly, to keep their own staff and operations as safe. For us, it is to know who is in command of the territory we will pass through. Gaining information about these places is a secretive, lucrative and often a shady industry. The people who run it are not people you find in the yellow pages, nor can you walk into an office asking, "Excuse me sir, but would you mind spending some of your precious free time telling me what people pay you big money to know?"

In the shadowy outer limits where most of this story plays out, the actors are freaks. People who can't exist within the confines of normal society are drawn to places like Locichockio, South Sudan, DRC and Uganda (to a lesser degree). Once there, natural idiosyncrasies are allowed to grow unchecked. A lot of these hard men and women in the security side of the misery industry are from army backgrounds, prone to antisocial behaviour and weary of outsiders. They are overworked and stressed with matters far more serious than a few joy riders wanting to go down the Nile.

Pete won them over. He drank beer, swapped stories, slept on floors, did house calls and loitered at offices, but most importantly, he listened. It's an accomplishment that cannot be overstated. By the time we left for the trip, he had the personal phone numbers of the who's who in security information about South Sudan. He could pick up the satellite phone at any given time to get up-to-date information about specific areas we were passing through. He had effectively established a wiretap into the system through personal contacts, vital when passing through a place as volatile as a forty-five year old war zone. Bringing all these threads together, Pete is equipped to orchestrate our progress through Sudan like a traffic warden. He tells us when to go, stop, speed up or slow down.

These sources are immensely valuable, but even their information comes from the local commanders. On the ground people live and die by the quality of their information. If there is a movement of troops or conflict in their backyard, they will be the first to know. It was important for Pete to hear what this Big Man had to say. My resolution not to get angry lasts only seconds after I hear the team did not think it necessary to pick us up, believing they could just pass on any important information. In their naivete, they don't realise it's not only the answer given but the question asked that makes information a science. This is fine when we sit around and discuss trivial points, but the margin for error shrank when we crossed the border. We need to think about every move. Instead we are a team of individual tourists, playing at exploring. The only person to blame is the team leader, but it's much easier blaming everyone else. I need to get everyone on the same program. Tomorrow we leave Nimule, and the margin for error shrinks again. We are running out of crutches.

Outside, the town tour continues. While Dan does interviews with SPLA soldiers, I find myself alone with Natalie for the first time in weeks. We disagree on almost everything, but we each like the core of the other person, and this has been enough for it not to matter. Somewhere in the last few months, something cold has crept in-between us.

A few weeks before departure, one of our major sponsors threatened to pull out. Natalie was the one dealing with them and I emailed her from South Africa, where I was finishing some exams, to tell her to tell them to make up their minds. One way or another, we needed to know, for sure, how much we could count on. There is no doubt I could have been more subtle and supportive, but I hardly know how to define either of those two words. She misread the email as me criticising her, and sent me a harsh reply. The thought had never crossed my mind that it was her fault. I did the only sensible thing: I ignored her.

There is a direct negative correlation between my friendship with Pete and mine with Nat. Pete and I have our language. A line or a single word sums up a situation. Everything has an inside story, a history attached to a certain philosophy or a past adventure. It is difficult for anyone to be around us and feel included, especially when we get into our physical world. Anyone would feel pain at being excluded from an inner circle they once enjoyed, and perhaps she reacted in the only way she knew how – anger. It became a downward spiral; the more we avoided her, the more she sought confrontation. Everything became a competition and a power struggle. If I said this, she said the opposite. If I wanted this, she wanted that. Soon Natalie's imaginary rejection by Pete and me had become real.

Standing under the shade of an Acacia tree, inside the shell of an old house, I talk to her about not coming to pick us up. She should have known better. I am not angry anymore, just tired of the drama and desperate for a solution. Unfortunately, I have not yet learnt that it is more important how we say things than what we actually say. My words can come out like punches, when all I mean to do is to point a finger. Natalie starts to cry.

Girls cry, some men cry, I cry, but Natalie does not. Before today I can't even remember seeing her sad; she prefers pissed-off. Seeing her break makes me forget the last few months. This is my friend and I want to protect her. She is having trouble with Bingo and my clumsy words were the final psychological straw. I had noticed the snappy conflict between them, but because I thought she could handle herself, I didn't think twice; one more tick on the growing list of slip-ups by the fearless expedition leader.

According to her, Bingo disrespects her contribution to the mission, undermining her authority. I should find it ironic, but her tears bring things down to an emotional level. Bingo lives in the same town we do, but has hardly lifted a finger to help with the project. This puts him a long way from having the right to disrespect Natalie.

For the briefest of moments the reality of how bad the group is fractured surfaces above my own needs. As she wipes the tears from her eyes and walks away to compose herself, I am left looking at the river far below, albeit through a hole in the crumbling walls.

NICE AND RUSTIC

Friendly soldiers with rippled black muscles and shining sweat, their AKs swung casually over their shoulders, help hoist our gear over the rocks and through the high yellow grass into a small pool. By the time the black rocks start burning in the midday heat we have dressed our bodyguards in lifejackets, accessorised with automatic weapons, and are ready to go. They have obviously never rafted before and it's doubtful if they can swim. Poking out of a new red life jacket is Charles' bald head. His boyish grin makes him look younger than his forty-three years. Far from intimidated by the strange assignment his superiors gave him, it appears he might have volunteered. Already telling his mates how he is going to conquer the Nile, he demonstrates how to paddle.

Moses, our second guard, is his opposite. Tall and shy he seems to understand English, yet is reluctant to speak it. Charles, on the other hand seems unable to shut up. Moses looks doubtfully at the rapids downstream. Meticulously, as if the success of the mission depends on it, he rolls up his army pants to just below his skinny knees. I don't have the heart to tell him he is going to get completely soaked. His disempowerment is complete when I replace his AK with an aluminium paddle.

I don't like that "it might go" gleam in Dale's eyes. We might make it through the falls alive, but he sure will be sorry if we didn't. The rafts will be carried around Fola Falls, but he has his kayak with him and is itching to use it. I have enough to worry about without Dale playing stuntman and am relieved when, with a faint twinkle of longing in his irrepressible smile, he breaks eye contact with the rapid and says, "Next time."

Under loud applause from our armed escort, we force our way into the unruly current below Fola. The single channel is only fifty meters wide and can barely contain the force of the water. The transition between the calm pool and the water rushing past is a tricky traverse, and for several minutes we struggle. Then suddenly, the heavily loaded boat is lifted effortlessly onto the massive waves. Tossed around like a toy in a bathtub, it never threatens to capsize. For as far as we can see, the river runs straight and true, exhilarating and refreshing after weeks of flat water. Twice we stop to have a look at blind horizon lines. The canyon soon opens out.

At lunch I give the long-overdue team talk. The meeting is a disaster; that I realise straight away. Only later will I discover the extent of the damage. I raise my voice hoping to achieve unity; I take us further from it. My intention to address the issues may have been right, but my execution could not have been worse. When being a bad leader, good intentions count for nothing. I offended everyone by adopting a broad tone and not identifying specific people and their mistakes. They are justifiably nervous and here is their leader sprouting on about some vague issues and telling them to take it more seriously. I should have said why I was worried, why I was angry, what I was afraid of. I should not have treated them like children.

If I had been a better leader, I would not have needed to give a speech at all. Mediocre leaders have to raise their voices and bad ones get angry. With an effective leader the team should not even know he or she has spoken. The truth will carry itself to the conclusion if introduced correctly. Once a team is on the right track it is preferable to let people arrive at the answer by themselves. With such a splintered group, a few smaller meetings would have been better than one large confrontation. There would have been less risk of me going off in the wrong direction. I might have understood better what each person was feeling and thinking.

There is peace in seeing beautiful and familiar landscapes, but there is awe and wonder in unfamiliar surroundings. My cup is overflowing with the latter. Months of anticipation have sweetened the fresh tracks, and the view is even more striking for being devoid of human life. The river flows at a lively pace and rowing is necessary only for steering. Large trees crowd the banks, sheltering the river from the harsh semi-desert that starts above their tree line. Are we in an oasis? With so much adventure around, I forget about the meeting.

A gunshot kills my serenity; the echo is filled by Charles' laughter. He let off a round to scare Dan. It worked; he managed to scare all of us. He has been telling stories of his life and showing off his collection of bullet holes smudged across the skin of his scrawny body. He is a cowboy, and cowboys are dangerous on expeditions. However, I admire him for maintaining his sense of humour during a life of fighting.

Eventually a beach sprinkled with driftwood promises soft beds and a large fire. We accept the invitation. Pete and Charles, who have been bonding over hunting stories all afternoon, head off into the bush. The AK hanging from Pete's shoulder is not for protection. In his life before rivers, Pete was both a poacher and an anti-poacher, sometimes simultaneously. He lived in the bush for months at a time with nothing but his gun. Between the two of them I will not be surprised if they return with a dead animal. This return to his past will become a ritual as we pull into shaded campsites along these stretches of river. He will pick a direction and slip away like a fish released into water.

Inevitably he reappears just as quietly, after stalking something wild, eyes glowing with pleasure and excitement.

In the morning the gorge begins to flatten and we start to see glimpses of people. Women drop their bundles and collect their kids in practiced sweeps. They run up the riverbank in panic. Charles screams loudly after them not to worry, that we are the good guys. No one waits to find out. Eventually we 'capture' a man in a dugout canoe, too slow to escape the invading *muzungus* with the flat-sided branch he is using as a paddle. Once reassured that we are not going to harm him, he sells us the large fish lying in a puddle by his stubby toes.

Apart from the fish, the inside of the *pirogue* is almost bare. A tattered fishing net, a single broken and faded sandal used to float his net, and a bowl cracked along its entire length used for the continuous bailing needed to keep the *pirogue* floating. Its edges are now barely above water and resemble the last whispers of a dying man's heart-rate monitor. Anywhere else the boat would be a museum piece, retired a thousand years ago. The marks left by the rough incisions of the chisels at its metamorphosis from tree to boat have been erased by time. Yellow plastic patches have been nailed crudely over large cracks to stem the haemorrhaging.

The *pirogue* is the symbol of Africa. It looks nice and rustic from afar, pretty even. It's only when you are close to it that you get the whole picture. Years ago, it was hastily and crudely cut from a mature tree, for a purpose it would never understand. Splitting, it is forever sinking, with plastic aid nailed over the biggest holes. No matter how many layers are applied, the water finds a way past the inflexible Western solution. For the African in the puddle, patiently scooping out water with a bowl, it is still just a boat.

INVISIBLE LINES

I squint as Charles points toward another old tree. This tree separates the good from the bad guys, depending entirely on which side of the tree you are standing. As far as invisible lines go, this one is as important as any other. This is the front line, the entrance to a whole new rabbit hole. I am not sure what I expected, but this doesn't come close. This is where we leave our new friends Charles and Moses behind. Surrounded by the unknown and helpless, they have become synonymous with safety. It is a moment I knew would come but just not so soon. I get that feeling in my stomach normally associated with kayaking and waterfalls. It is with resignation that I turn for the bank.

Ian looks at me and I see the fear in his eyes that we all feel. For a moment I register the extent of his doubts, and completely forget my own. In my years of raft guiding I have seen it many times. Bad fear, the emotional kind, not the fear that freezes your actions, instead the warm one that muddles and melts clear thinking without even realising it is making the decision for you.

He starts rambling about it not being safe, that we shouldn't go ashore yet. It makes little sense. Where else are we supposed to go? I struggle to fit this reaction with Ian. I suspect it is not death but the lack of control that he fears. Still he is asked to be a bystander in potentially the most dangerous moment of his life. I don't know how to deal with it, so I keep focus on the banks for a sign of that which surely lurks in these woods. Women washing clothes under drooping branches, who had frozen like deer in the headlights, bolt in a panic. By yelling Charles manages to persuade a few to remain at the edge. Their apprehensive body language indicates the matter has not yet been decided.

The next step is to find the local area commander. If there are LRA or GOS hostilities, we need to know ASAP and get out. According to Charles, the SPLA base is at least four hours away. In African-speak this could easily be as much as eight hours. With six hours of light left, two soldiers and no real idea of what is going on in the area, I decide to make a run for the base. If we get there and the area is unsafe, we can come back with reinforcements before midnight. If the area is safe, we have lost nothing.

I inform the team of what I plan to do. Daylight is running out and there is little time for discussion. I don't want to separate the team, but with only three of us remotely capable of running that distance before dark, I have no choice. The team is scared and still angry over my outburst a few days ago, I know I should stay with the group and send Dale with Pete, but with a dangerous physical mission ahead, the last place I want to be is in camp listening to people complain that it is cold on the top of Everest.

Ian wants the group to stay together for the night. I try to reason with him, but we have stopped listening to each other. Precious sunlight is being wasted so I leave saying, "Sorry if you don't like it, but that's the way it's going to be." Like so many decisions a leader makes, there is no guarantee my plan is right. To see the commander of the area is standard operational procedure. If Ian had been at any pre-trip meetings he would know this. In my eyes he is reacting out of fear, not reason, and fear doesn't reason. Throughout my life I have trusted my instinct when it came to high-pressure situations. I have no intention of changing a strategy that has worked well, especially when there is so much at stake.

Charles agrees it's the right option, but he agrees to everything, and given the option of running for hours or flirting with the women in the nearby village, he graciously offers to stay behind. Moses gets the short straw and leads us from the river at a running pace familiar to Pete and I from our army days. With this slow, low shuffling of the feet that can be sustained for hours, we set off under the midday sun. The Zulus in South Africa call this "eating the earth," not walking, not running. Our feet tap a soft rhythm on the dusty path swinging lazily between scattered trees, occasionally passing through tight little clusters of huts. Adults stop mid-conversation to stare stunned as an unknown black man and two dirty *muzungus* run through their backyard, unable to grasp the situation before we slip from sight again. As the hours drag on, I stop noticing the surroundings. Hypnotically I follow the blinking ivory soles of Moses' feet. Twice we hear gunshots in the distance. We don't stop to discuss it. We run.

Around another lazy bend, a soldier lays motionless on his back in the dirt, shirt unbuttoned. I assume the worst. With a burst of adrenaline, I regain focus, all senses heightened. Without stopping Moses bends down mid-run and grabs the lifeless soldier's AK. Once out of sight, he hands the rifle to Pete and makes a quick gesture that indicates the soldier drank too much.

I allow myself to detach and look at this strange scenario from above. I like the view, a lot. We are three tiny dots in motion as remote as one could ever hope for and as far from the everyday as humanly possible. Covered in sweat and dust, we run on the calming effects of endorphins. Moses floats effortlessly in front of me like a phantom. Dark sweat streaks underline the anatomy of his muscles. The way he simultaneously runs and holds his rifle leaves no doubt that he is a soldier.

Behind me is Pete. His body, built solely for purpose, is without a single luxury for appearance sake. Every sinew flexes. His wild beard and unkempt hair, which daily reveals more red, blends perfectly with his dusty camouflage. He looks like a mix between a holy man and a lunatic, which he might just be. He runs in the easy, alert shuffle of a paratrooper, his AK held across his chest, hand lovingly on the wooden grip, ready to lift it to his chin and double tap the trigger with a second's notice.

I am between two hard men from different tribes and of different colours, their essence the same. They would be elite warriors in any culture. If we do find any trouble, I can't think of better people to confront it with.

Moses finally eases the rhythm of his feet and slows to a walk. I doubt he is tired; we must be close. As far as he is concerned, the job is done for the day. Unfortunately we have to get back to camp tonight, regardless of the security situation. Ian's reaction has set off all sorts of warning bells. I need to get back before the well is poisoned beyond repair. Using hand signs, I tell Moses I want to keep running. He shrugs and steps on the gas once more.

Just after 18:00 we arrive at a clump of huts surrounding a rusty anti-aircraft gun pointing to the sky. A few soldiers sit talking, playing checkers and listening to a radio that is hooked up to a car battery. Moses is warmly greeted. After a few minutes of catching up on each other's lives, he flashes his big grin our way and proceeds to tell our story. Immediately we are invited to dinner as guests of honour.

Some of them speak English and after light banter, I slip it in that we need to get back tonight, feeling like a typical demanding white man. The commander, a tough-looking bear of a man, dressed like the other soldiers in dribs and drabs of uniform, grants us a few minutes of shop talk. The news is all good. It has been weeks since the LRA has been anywhere near. Just to be sure, he will give us three men to escort us back. Moses, who must have been looking forward to a proper meal and a quiet night around the campfire with his mates, turns back without a frown.

Thirty minutes after arriving, we are back on the trail. Our fears about security calmed, some of the urgency leaves us and we join our escort in a strong walking pace in a moonless night with no flashlights – Great White Explorers don't need them, and freedom fighters can't afford them. Anything more than a few feet away remains solid black. After two hours we are lost. The soldiers argue amongst themselves. They ask for directions from the small clumps of nervous huts we weave through like insects scavenging for food.

We have been going for almost eleven hours, and even if the area is *safe*, being lost on a frontline of a war zone is not ideal. We keep stumbling along; as good as blind, tired and hungry, thinking this is *the best day ever*. This is why we endured begging for sponsorship and permission in our ill-fitting suits and uncomfortable feet in not-so-shiny shoes. Now barefoot, dirty and drained, it seems like a good trade.

It is not the first or the last time Pete and I would be lost together. My favourite is the time in Rwanda, while tracing the most distant source of the Nile, the Akagera River. We followed a damp smudge in Nyungwe Forest for three days, cutting our way through thick rainforest until it resembled a stream. On reaching the edge of the forest, our guides and the rest of the team took vehicles back to base camp. Pete and I wanted to follow the whole course of the river and arranged to meet the team at a bridge about twelve kilometres farther down. At that point the river was wide enough to float a kayak in, even though you could still easily jump from bank to bank.

Since I am notoriously hard on equipment, eventually losing or breaking everything given to me, Pete always carries The Tricky Box. Inside it sleeps the sat-phone, some extra money and other valuable pieces of kit. As I got into my kayak I realised the bag did not fit, and since it was only 11:00 and we had all day, I left it behind. My bag had the warm clothes, bits of food, cigarettes, etc. By 17:00, according to the GPS, we still had ten kilometres to go in a straight line and there was not a straight line in sight.

The river had swung back into the national park and become completely strangled with vegetation, making kayaking impossible. It was a gradual realisation that we would have to spend the night; no big deal for two Great White Explorers like ourselves, apart from the fact that the lighter had stayed behind with the dry clothes. Schoolboy error. We found ourselves in one of the highest rain forests in the world, where it gets a bit chilly at night, especially when all you have for warmth is the wet shorts you are wearing.

When darkness had dumped over us like an ice bath, we had reached a buffer zone of pine forest, which protects the park from the surrounding villagers. Already passed through several buffer zones, which bent right back into jungle, we were a bit undecided on what to do next. Sitting still was painful, and walking barefoot in the dark was dangerous. Teeth clattering, I watched Pete rub sticks together, knowing that even MacGyver couldn't get a spark out of those wet sticks. I mentioned this fact, perhaps unnecessarily to him. His answer came evenly as ever, "I know bru, but I have nothing better to do."

Eventually we built a pyramid with pine needles and buried ourselves under it. Spooning for warmth is an art we refined during that long night. It was too cold to sleep, at best we tranced out for a few minutes at a time. When one of us wanted to turn, he had to warn the other. Normally the response was, "OK, just give me another five minutes on this side." Then oh-so-slowly we would turn together, trying to keep any warm air from escaping. I could see the stars faintly through a small opening in the leaves. I knew even at that moment, that it was better than sitting at home watching TV, at least I felt alive. Cold, very. Hungry, yes. But there was also humour and camaraderie, and a certain honesty and intimacy with the moment that made it a day to remember, not file under 'average', and moved to the recycle bin of life's memories. I wouldn't have swapped that night, holding my skinny, hairy friend, for any woman's warm bed. 'Make it harder' was designed to get through nights like this.

The Cheap Seats

You can only allow yourself to become a victim.

–Peter Meredith

At 01:30 we finally reach camp, exhausted, famished and elated. Natalie and Dale saved food for us. The soldiers take a look at the *kawajha* food, shake their heads and make their fire at the edge of the camp. Charles is already telling tall tales, no doubt about how brave he was and how lost we would be without him. Laughing and content, they close their circle. For us the reception is less friendly.

"Nobody panic." Is Pete's standard response to any argument that approaches excessive emotional levels. It goes down like a cup of cold vomit with Ian. This is exactly what is eating him, the fact that we don't seem worried enough and even worse, telling him not to be. He says we are not valuing his contribution. Worry is not a contribution, I think, but don't say.

Ian does most of the talking. He feels he is not being included in the decision-making process and that his experience is not being respected. Bingo feels the same. Marcus says little but agrees that we (Pete and I) have not been open enough. These may all be valid points, but after having been on the move for twelve hours, I am not in the mood for complaints from the cheap seats.

Bingo has, during the entire expedition, not washed one dish, not cooked one meal and contributed nothing but criticism. My belief is, if you want to be a tourist on a trip, then you should shut up and do what the tour guide says. As for Ian, he is right; I don't trust him to make any non-medical decisions. He has been out of his depth since the day we started. I follow Pete's lead and try not to say anything I might regret, but I am angry and hurt by the fact that they think I am being a bad leader. The fact that I am a bad leader doesn't matter.

I cannot see what the fuss is about. We are in a high-tension area and yes, everyone is not happy; but we are alive and the right decisions have been made. They have been sitting in the shade, next to a beautiful river, with fishing rods, more food than they can eat and a guard for protection. If anyone should be complaining, it should be Pete and me. We have to volunteer for every hard, dirty or dangerous job because they can't physically do it. It was our efforts pre-trip that made this possible. I have made some mistakes with interpersonal relationships, but I have made the right choices tactically. Stroking their egos is not part of my job description.

The last of my warm feelings for Natalie die around a small pre-dawn campfire under that tree in Sudan. Only a day after asking me to defend her against Bingo, she backs him against me. Dan remains impartial, or at least stays out of the discussion. Weeks ago with the engine issue, he had become so involved that he forgot to film entirely. He must have realised a documentary filmmaker's task is to observe and record. Dale can understand their point but adds that he is, personally, just happy to be here. Amen. Surely *happy to be here* must be the starting point.

I know I have to stay calm, listen and compromise. When Pete asked me to control my temper before the trip, this was the night he knew would come. I swallow my true feelings, apologise to the group and promise to try to keep everyone better informed. Later, lying under my mozzie net, too tired to sleep, the argument grows out of proportion in my hot little head.

I begin a conversation with myself. "Fuck them! I have nothing to apologise for! All of them are here on my invite, a present given free and undeserved." That's it Hendri, you tell them. Go boy. I say to myself all the things I packed into my held tongue. "You have done little more than show up for a trip of a lifetime, and a chance to make history, but instead of thankful you are telling me how to run it!" I roll over now, very excited. "You may be part of the team, but in no way do you have equal shares in the adventure. Time, money, even some good old fashioned hard work will buy you shares but they don't come free." The Great White Explorer rages and rants but knows he is beat and that makes him even angrier.

There is truth in the criticism that makes it more uncomfortable. I do not stop to wonder how else they could have put across their grievances. My insecurities as a leader turn it into a personal attack and I retaliate in equal terms. How well one takes criticism is a sign of maturity, and I am not about to let maturity stand in the way of the best trip ever. The problem is that my life *is* this trip and there is only so much I am willing to share with them. I am also scared. I can't lose this trip. For the first time I doubt that I can pull it off. The life I lived before will never be good enough again. Who are these people, and what are they doing in my dream?

My choices as are: A) tell them to leave the expedition, B) concede and shut it all up inside, or C) admit I am wrong and try to do better. Realistically C is not an option, the Great White Explorer just doesn't have it in him. The correct choice would have been to say, "Here is where we are, I am not prepared to change and have invested too much to feel I have to, if you don't like it you can fuck off right now."

I see my biggest mistake was inviting them. Some people should just never be on an expedition. This is becoming a reality TV show – unacceptable. I have no desire to bicker my way down the Nile. Neither Bingo nor Ian is crucial to the success of the trip; they could stay and get on with the project or go home and whine about it there. Either way, group conflict solved.

I suck it up and try to do the right thing so as not to hurt the sponsors by sending the two most prominent members of the team home. I decide it is entirely their fault but choose to act superficially from the moral high ground. I concede in public, while hating them in private.

To overcome this, it is essential that the leader chairs regular internal meetings, even if they are, as I prefer them to be, informal. Plans on my trips are continuously being formed in conversations. This makes them fluid and ideal for African conditions where reaction time is more important than structure.

The problem is that anyone who is not involved in the conversation is unaware that plans have changed, and not everyone is good with rapid change. I have not yet learned that the more input everyone has in the forming of plans, the more they enjoy and the more responsibility they are forced to take. Sharing decisions makes for better team dynamics, but it has its limits, and everyone on the team should know that. Our disintegration as a group when entering Sudan proved that. It is an impossible situation and a dangerous one. If you are taking strong-minded people on an expedition (and that's really the only type you should take) you have to be sure they respect your experience. As I am learning, I have neither experience nor respect.

Expeditions are too rare to dilute with people who don't share your appreciation. There will always be conflicts on trips in the heat of battle. The problem occurs when conflicts overflow into other moments. It was ridiculous to have chosen people so randomly. Making up the mix of personalities in the group is crucial. With the right group you can swim through a swamp for a week and have a good time. With the wrong ones an outing to the beach is agonising. What ever happens from here on my new rule for anyone who wants to come on an expedition with me is, "There will be no complaining."

Ernest Shackleton is possibly my favourite explorer of all time. I thought he was the greatest leader ever, for bringing back all of his crew alive. Now I think differently. He was a great motivator and leader, but for a lot of the time he was away from his crew, his strength was in the attitude he established before the team departed. He placed the advertisement for the *Endurance* expedition of 1914: *Men Wanted: for hazardous journey, small wages, bitter cold, long months of complete darkness, constant danger, safe return doubtful, honour and recognition in case of success.*

The result: everything bad that happened on the trip, they accepted and signed for on the dotted line even before they left. He knew all about making it harder.

THE BIG BAD WOLF

Resentment is like drinking poison and hoping that it will kill your enemies.

—NELSON MANDELA

My morning walk greets a freshly risen sun. The crisp air is not concerned with the unpleasant thoughts lingering in my head. I would rather be sulking alone, but we still have a movie to make and we need to film the SPLA camp. To get back before dark, we must leave shortly before dawn. The painfully slow progress is not helping my mood. We are loaded with gear and constantly having to stop and wait. Inside me, something has formed that I have never experienced – hate. Hate for these people who have taken my most beautiful moments and reduced them to meaningless petty squabbles.

In my clouded, troubled mind Ian and Bingo, who I respected so much before the trip, have become nothing but scared, complaining old men, so used to being the boss that they are unable to follow. They were never going to accept my leadership when snap decisions were needed under pressure. Why should they? For them I am just a man half their age, from a different world. Their weakness has become my weakness. I know it and it makes me even angrier. For Natalie I feel pure hate. I even wonder if she set me up so she could play Bingo and me against each other.

The trip, as I imagined, is over. From now on it will be compromise after compromise and I hate them for that. I hate them for being soft. I hate them for being scared and I hate them for dulling the colours of the only bright thing in my life. I know their attitude is another challenge, I know their behaviour is only making it harder, so that the mission becomes more worthy. Knowing the path does not give you the strength to walk it.

Faintly in the background I hear a voice saying this is an opportunity to learn one of the greatest lessons. Everywhere you go, you will find negativity and pettiness. What could be more valuable than learning not to be influenced by it? As true challenges often are, it is on a front that I do not want to fight. I was prepared for danger and physical hardship. I imagined myself emerging the conquering hero. It is all slipping away, my image of myself as the great leader, my image of myself being able to handle everything.

At the SPLA camp I manage to handle introductions and then excuse myself. Even when I am in a good mood I can look like someone stole my last chocolate. When I'm unhappy it is impossible for me to hide the fact. I need to be alone until I can get a grip on myself. I must not let my thoughts spill out.

I lie on my daypack in the shade of a mango tree and fall asleep almost instantly, exhausted physically, but more so emotionally. In the last twenty-four hours I have had some of best and the worst moments of my life. The power nap stabilises cabin pressure enough to enable me to rejoin the group. I walk up to the group of men Dan is pointing his camera at; the soldiers explain various methods of torture they have endured. Hearing about being tied upside down from a tree and having melting plastic dripped on you while someone beats the soles of your feet, thankfully puts my little internal struggle into perspective, at least temporarily.

Having been captured and recaptured, it took heavy fighting to control this hundred square meters of arid bush. Again, it amazes me what they have achieved. Barefoot men and boys with nothing but AK-47s, fight against tanks and helicopter gunships. Another example of how someone defending his home is worth ten paid soldiers and all the expensive hardware they bring with them; a lesson America never seems to learn.

More surprising than their courage is their humanity. I expected cold men with dead eyes. Instead they are full of humour and seem to have taken well to their brief introduction to peace, able to enjoy what they have right now instead of what tomorrow might bring, and without resentment for the positions they were born into. They are philosophical about it. Peace would be great, but they have their guns and will keep fighting if needed. It is the only life they know.

They don't trust the Government of Sudan who has a bad reputation for keeping their word or valuing peace. Even if lasting peace does come, there will be other challenges. It will take many, many years to untangle a world that has seen nothing but war for its entire recorded history.

As the only visitors they have received from the outside world and looking important with our cameras, we are treated like royalty and invited for an exceptional lunch of fresh meat. It is wise to be cautious when invited for a meal in such a poor community; their delicacies can be disgusting to a white boy raised on leg of lamb. Still I salivate at the prospect of bush pig. I am hungry and a bit of wild animal will go down well. "Yes I love pig, and I am very hungry, thank you so much."

My enthusiasm drops as they carry the carcass into the room. It looks like it stepped on a land mine. Lying in a pool of blood, it is half cooked with bits of hair and skin, spiced with pieces of rock and shrapnel for extra crunch. Bon Appetite! Unable to play the 'I am not hungry' card, there is nothing to do but get stuck-in.

After lunch there is no time to let the nausea settle, or allow fatigue to penetrate my bones. We have to get back. Leaving the cool shadow of the mango tree, we step onto the hot windy path, for our second lap. Halfway, Ian is suffering. Pete stays with him for the last two hours of the walk, continually reassuring him that the end is just around the next corner. While Pete coaches him into camp with the patience of a parent, I enjoy his weakness, as it feeds the dark cloud that is again building over my world.

"Make us proud," was the first serious thing I heard Charles say. He has not seen many people return from where we are going. We scan the banks nervously, trying to hear past the gossip of yellow weaverbirds that are frantically building and destroying their hobby homes. It's early, the air is still fresh, the sun merely playful. It is a morning like a thousand others, but in the moment it seems large enough to be the only one. The SPLA told us to expect a dead zone. This is no man's land. Being here makes you everyone's enemy.

Crossing into SPLA country, we had come in through the back door via the relatively friendly border of northern Uganda. Now, progressing into GOS territory, we are entering via the business end, the side trouble arrives from. Lack of good GOS contacts is perhaps the weakest part of our plans regarding known evils. We can only hope that news of our arrival has filtered down. Contact with the GOS has been minimal and always through Khartoum, more than a thousand kilometres from our current position.

While holding our collective breath so as not to startle the universe, we put away all cameras and get ready to roll onto our backs and expose our stomachs. Any second now a hundred things could go wrong. The first sign of the big bad wolf is a well-groomed man in new army pants and an LA Lakers vest, collecting water in a yellow jerry can, his AK relaxing nearby against a tree.

Giving him our best 'lost tourist' look, we try to appear as harmless as possible. He accepts the scene without too much fuss. We shake hands, he slips his plastic sandals on and indicates for us to follow. Dan and I take the few steps up the bank and into the bush while the rest of the team waits. Led through the army base, it's clear our fears were exaggerated. It's so easy it's almost anti-climactic, the fear is gone and the unknown once again turns out to be a nice-enough place. These guys are hardly sitting with their fingers on the trigger.

The atmosphere might be Sunday morning but the setting ain't church. In contrast to the SPLA base where they can pick up everything and disappear if a helicopter gunship arrives, this is an organised military establishment. Simply put, they have bigger guns and more of them. It is a well-kept garden of war with all the African favourites – semi-automatic rifles standing side by side, neatly, row upon row. Rocket-propelled grenade launchers rest on sandbagged hedges, their deadly pollen budding at the end of simple looking pipes. Mortar shells stand around ready to be dropped down short stubby stems.

These heavily fortified camps have been the Arab way from as far back as the slaving days, oases in enemy territory from which to wreak havoc on the local population by raiding local tribes, or ideally arm them to raid each other. Perhaps fifty men, all in new uniforms, are in the business of everyday life but not one is further than a few steps from a weapon. A small group sits playing cards with a Titanic movie memorial deck and listens to what passes for music in Arabic.

The base commander is a short man with a potbelly and commando moustache. Sporting a red t-shirt with crispy uniform pants and new flip-flops, his smile reassures me more than his broken English. He seems to take great joy in sitting down and asks us to do the same, calling over his shoulder for sweet tea and dates. It is obvious he doesn't get much opportunity to entertain.

The team is called and settles in comfortably under another giant mango tree. Ten minutes ago I feared for my life, now relaxed on a chair with my second cup of sweet tea, sucking on a soft date, I study the men around me, trying to see the devil I have heard so much about. All I see is young men. Some are chasing a chicken around the camp, laughing and bantering. Their Arabic descent is drawn with finer features and in a lighter tone. These northern born fighters dig themselves in for long periods behind sandbags, doing duty for Islam or merely serving a term for a paycheque.

I sit back contently watching the chicken as the circle of soldiers closes in; it makes a beautiful swerve, side-stepping between camouflaged legs, and into a green canvas tent. I still have open wounds in my mouth from the SPLA's Frankenstein pig yesterday, and for once am not rooting for the underdog. I like and admire the SPLA and these are the very guys who committed the atrocities we heard of just yesterday. Over a good chicken dinner I am prepared to listen to their side of the story.

Somali Pirates

With a look that could melt butter, Dan starts to shoot from the hip. Bingo doesn't like it. He and Ian are at their twitchy best. They have every right to be. We are in a country where people fight to the death over camps under mango trees. They are bound to take the security of its only bridge seriously.

I assume we can get away with Dan stealing a few seconds on film, military secret or not. We are mid-river, and as long as he is cool and hides the tapes immediately it should be fine. It's time to throw him a bone. He deserves it. At every transition between rival factions or sign of political tension, I have asked him to shut off his cameras. Cameras make people with guns nervous and that tends to make everyone else nervous. Even if the straight lines of this Lego structure don't look like much, it is an important shot for the film. We are passing under the most fiercely contested piece of rusty metal any of us has ever seen.

We cause a bit of a stir as we pull into the shade of mango trees that have dropped fruit on Juba since the war was over slaves and not oil or religion. Pete and I are whisked away by military intelligence on the back of two 125cc motorbikes, over the bridge to the nearest army camp. Outside a small guardroom we are asked to sit down at a plastic table next to the river. We make small talk and sip sweetened tea in shot glasses.

A colossal man from the Nubian Mountains, skin black and shiny as a sergeant major's boots, inspects our paperwork. He bears a striking, but hopefully insignificant, resemblance to Idi Amin. Leopard-print bedroom slippers and dark aviator glasses suggest he has ambition. When he is satisfied with our piles of paperwork, we are driven back to the team. Another lieutenant stomps into the scene. Obviously more impressed with the size of Pete's beard than with the fluff debuting on my chin, he seems disappointed when he hears I am the team leader. We are ordered to move our boats upstream to the guard post.

To make this manoeuvre possible, we tie our rafts to a navy boat. I have a thing for boats and this one appeals to me on many levels. Shark teeth are painted across the back of the sleek eighteen-foot hull that gives the boat a 'fuck with me and I will enjoy it' look. Two 300-horsepower engines bulge excessively with a FNG machine-gun (the type Rambo prefers) mounted on the front deck. With their black bandanas, the crew looks more like Somali pirates than navy boys. Their AK-47s are draped over ripped and shirtless torsos and each sports a machete-sized knife in his belt. Knowing it's the kind of photo chicks would dig, but afraid to appear like a dork before the real men, I resist the urge to take out my camera. There are few things as cool as an action photo of yourself and few things as uncool as stopping the action to take one.

As the boat starts to pick up speed, Pete's raft digs into the water and floods, causing the satellite phone charging on the solar panel to fall into the water. Our most prized piece of electrical equipment is soggy. It threatens our communication with the outside world. This piece of kit is essential for monitoring the fluctuating safety situation and for keeping the various balls of our juggling act from bouncing and breaking. The only good news is that for once it wasn't me who caused the catastrophe.

The boats are tied up and we join the team in a worn out minibus. Ignored, we are driven around for a few hours by a stone-faced driver and a security officer. Without reason for the route, and unable to get a word from our escort, we complete a tour of every government building in Juba. Presumably they need to figure out what to do with us.

Eventually we stop outside a blue and light-green supermarket, the same colours as every other newly-painted object in town. The doors are unlocked and we are told to help ourselves. Not sure if we understand the instructions correctly, we stand reluctantly in the doorway. Someone reaches for a chocolate in slow motion, followed by a guilty look at our handlers. Sensing no reaction, a can of soda is next, and all still seems fine. Soon we are buzzing from one sugar rush to the next; high on chocolates, soda pop and the pure relief that the ice between our handlers and us has been broken.

For the last few hours we have been treated not rudely but very indifferently. Like dogs waiting for attention, our tails stopped wagging as we emotionally shut down. An unexpected pat on the head from our masters and a snack, and we are jumping with excitement. All we need now is a ball to play with. Dan sums it up nicely with a mouth full of chocolate "Juba, South Sudan? What on earth was the fuss about?" I hand him another cold Coke.

After the feeding frenzy we briefly enjoy the only tar road in the southern capital, before being escorted through the courtyard of a flat house, past a kitchen and into two large dormitories where beds await occupancy. After more food we are invited to witness Juba's nightlife, as it tries to find its feet after two decades when no fun was allowed under the stern eye of Sharia law.

On a basketball court, I witness something so bizarre it takes a while to comprehend. Under a few Christmas lights dangling from a barbed-wire fence is a dance party for sober grown men. From our rich cultural heritage we dazzle them with renditions of the moonwalk, the sprinkler, the truck-driver and various other tribal dances. Soon we have a square-dance going. Because it is an alcohol-free zone, I am unable to break out my best moves; they pretend to be impressed nonetheless.

At 22:28 Big Brother decides we have had enough fun and escorts us home. I have become so used to sleeping without walls that I carry my bed into the courtyard and slip into sleep, filled with wonder at where I am.

Sleeping outside ensures an early start. It's the first time in weeks that I have been in an area where I can run. The first rays have barely climbed over the glass splinters that are stuck on the concrete wall before I sneak past the armed guard, and down the street.

Running is one of my favourite ways to explore any new place. Importantly, it's also a solo activity. I am dodging potholes, while trying to take in the shantytown, built on the ruins of better bad times. Some anaemic dogs run sideways and panic between the war-machinery that lies rusted and blown up everywhere.

I am thankful for the quiet streets. *Kawajhas* (foreigners) are rare but most of the early risers seem too sleepy to care, too polite to make a fuss, or just not that impressed. I am left to my own randomness, but it couldn't last. At some point a man joins me on my run. The size of his belly bulging over his red tracksuit is taunting me. To hurt the Great White Explorer's ego even more, fatty is brushing his teeth, chatting away and easily keeping pace.

Later in the day we are visited by National Security, a department not normally associated with courtesy calls. They can't seem to do enough for us. I go shopping for lunch. On the way back, the captain in whose house we are placed picks me up in a battered Land Rover. He is visibly insulted that I brought food.

Doc Clarke and the rest of the crew spend time in the hospital doing interviews and filming. I decide to walk around the market, followed by military guards. I admire an aluminium cup, made from one of the hundreds of Land Rover carcasses that litter town. The shopkeeper gives it to me with a big smile. I cringe with guilt knowing how much these people's hospitality exposes my own selfishness and my culture's obsession with possessions.

If this guy makes a dollar a day, it would be a good day. It becomes apparent he is giving me a sizeable part of his assets for no other reason than I liked it. If the gift was from the government it could be a public relations exercise, but from a street merchant? I start to believe something special might be happening here.

We hardly have time to get stuck into the fridge that is overflowing with cheese, sodas, chocolates, yogurts and fresh fruit before we are driven to dinner with the district commissioner. In a public park without vegetation and a tatty-looking bandstand, we are packed around three tables. A constant procession of meat and vegetables is brought to our table, with a variety of sauces for the *injera* bread that is eaten by hand. As soon as a dish approaches its last quarter, another replaces it. We do the best we can but there is just too much. We are rolled into the car and driven home.

In our wildest imagination none of us would have expected to be treated this well. Our remaining days in Juba continue in this trend: over-eat, go to sleep, wake up and do it again. On our last day, in a final gesture, the military officers who have already done so much for us give us wooden carvings; little elephants and rhinos of the standard tourist variety and no chance of surviving the journey. It must have seemed to them exactly what Westerners would want. The gesture does not go unappreciated. If we had ever doubted the sincerity, the warmth of our departure ceremony puts it to bed. It is with a touch of sadness that we leave the large crowd of officers and soldiers waving us off. All of us will soon be no more than a footnote in each other's lives.

With their goodbyes fading behind us, I hear a strong voice drifting from the bank in English. Silhouetted against a field of countless yellow and brown rusting tanks that will never kill again, left to die from lack of maintenance, an old man stands tall and straight, wrapped in a brilliant white Muslim *jallabiya* robe. "We see you, *Kawajha*," he yells. "We see you, and we see peace is coming."

I desperately want to believe him. In the vein of modern sponsored expeditions, we try to put across that we are in some way making the world a better place by embarking on this journey. We hope that through our exposure of the situation, somehow, our presence will help to make a positive difference. The pretext all sounded so good, we even started to believe it. In reality, though, we take more from these people than we can possibly repay. I have stopped believing that we can have an impact on a mess of this magnitude. But perhaps, the old man is right that by doing what these people have not seen done, by traveling where no foreigner has travelled for so long, we provide a spark of hope, and just maybe we are participating in something bigger than ourselves.

Mandari

The sun has started its free-fall, and shadows are spilling lazily on the ground. A cloud of smoke lies thick as morning fog across the horizon. As we enter Mandari territory, the present moment fades to a faraway place. What my eyes are seeing is so surreal that I suspect my imagination has conjured them. Tall stick figures, covered in ash, as if born inside the fire, stare back at us. Frozen in ancient salutes, their arms are pointing to the sky in awkward angles. The smudging of daylight colours through the smoke and the unnatural greyness of the naked statues transfixes everyone into silence.

The fragile freeze-frame is shattered by children erupting. Their curiosity cannot be contained by their tribal salute. A single shriek ripples through them before splintering into a dozen individual voices; it sends them running along the bank screaming and laughing. Rationalisation invades the dream and we blink again. The adult figures on the banks are caught in the children's excitement. They drop their strange poses and start to move their long limbs. The whole tribe seems to be running along the yellow twisting bank. They think us every bit as strange as we do them. A man with orange hair bangs excitedly on a suitcase-sized brass bell. A little grey boy, head cleanly shaven apart from a tiny black comma on the back, is blowing on a cow horn as tall as himself. White cattle stand contently around smouldering dung fires, their long horns contort into the same shape the cattle-loving Mandari were imitating only moments ago.

Giant young men, naked and painted grey, yell and jump to the rhythm floating from the banks. Curvy girls are dressed in red skirts decorated with beads; their bodies shining with scarifications. Every tiny spot of colour draws attention against the canvas of dry grass, white dirt, smoke and ash. We are no more than strangers inside the hazy world they have created to shelter themselves and their beloved cattle.

The sight of the Mandari for the first time, under these circumstances, is one of the purest moments I have ever known. If the trip ends here and now, I will consider it worth every effort and more. For an instant I feel perfectly woven into the fabric of Africa I believed was long gone. It does not even occur to me to stop. There is nothing more the cattle camp can offer me at this moment; lingering might only diminish our breath-taking introduction. There will be time to learn and understand, but for today they will stay a glorious mystery.

I watch them laughing and living their simple lives, unashamed by their nakedness, exotic in their plainness and confident in the belief that their cows are the only fortune they will ever need. My mood turns sad, sad for knowing that we are the first ripples of the turning tide for their lifestyle. I feel guilty for playing paparazzi. Intoxicated by the powerful effect of the Mandari, I think of bringing tourists here to see an endangered and prehistoric way of life, a way to make a few dollars and have a good time doing it. This way of life will end. It is too innocent to withstand the introduction of *want* that will come with comparison to my culture. Once they start to mix, this proud culture will die in beer halls and be buried in plastic. Beautiful naked bodies will be covered in the T-shirts of pop culture idol idiots. It is an end that is inevitable. But I would rather not be the one to bring vultures to snap pretty pictures, without an ounce of understanding. Experiencing their lifestyle, however brief, is misconstrued into some sort of proof of the Great White Explorer's accomplishments.

These are the type of people we came to find, and we are not even giving them the honour of a stopover. If we were genuine we would have stayed to get to know them and granted them the courtesy of understanding what we are taking photos of. Instead we are rushing off to our goal thousands of kilometres away. Our biggest concern is not their culture but our own petty problems. I make a vow to come back. Will that time be too late?

Soft White Meat

The gunshot is close enough to make everyone instinctively duck. By the way the man on the bank is waving his AK, we suspect it came from him. It was either a warning shot or a bad shot. I decide not to wait around to find out. Throwing my weight on the oars, I speed up the river's magic to make us disappear around the corner. The man along with all consequences of our potential meeting, dissolves into an unwanted universe of possibility.

We are again without a guide or translator, in one of those uncertain zones where they cannot follow. We were getting overconfident before the shooting started. This is a reminder we still have a long way to go, and many gun-toting strangers and permutations to negotiate. This is old-fashioned warlord country, literally for the last two decades. Around here it is common for people to have never gone more than thirty kilometres from home. Territory is shared out between the SPLA, GOS and other smaller armed groups, loyal only to themselves. It resembles gang warfare more than civil war. People fight hard for their pieces of land and the enemy often is within a few hours' walk.

We are hoping to get to the biggest town since Juba, Bor. We are also hopeful there will be a free goat dinner on offer. At the very least we will know who is in control of the guns around us. By the time the sun sinks, we are still in no man's land. Not only is there no man but there is also hardly any land. We are forced to camp on a spongy reed clearing in what is fast becoming the Sudd, one of the largest swamps in the world. Like many place in the Sudan, little current information is known. For centuries this swamp formed a natural barrier stopping penetration into the heart of Africa from Egypt.

In this swamp, like many, the view is boring, it's humid and the nightlife consists of mosquitoes. I am a bit of a malaria collector with strains from Namibia: three normal and one cerebral, Ethiopia; only one, but particularly feisty, Zambia; six, Zimbabwe; one, Botswana; one, and Uganda; ten, give or take a few bad hangovers. Millions die from malaria yearly but here it seems mozzies are capable of inflicting immediate death by sucking you dry. In size, ferocity and numbers, I have never come across anything like it. A prehistoric ancestry with dark clouds of vampire demons and evil spirits is constantly in motion. Their howling grows increasingly angry and demented, as millions of tiny needles are frustrated in bloodlust. The noise alone would make you run if there were places to run to.

When mozzies are biting through jeans, repellant is futile. Dropping my pants for a squat is a test of endurance. They zone in on my fat white ass, for an all-you-can-eat buffet. What I don't understand is what they eat when there are no people about; there is nothing here but water and papyrus. In their lifetime, we must be the first people ever to be foolish enough to stop.

Slapping at the noise, more to make myself feel better than for effect, I cook a meal of corned meat and rice. It is gulped into the interactive food chain before we run to the shelter of our tents or nets. Once there, it's like being inside a beehive with a bee suit on – safe but far from relaxing.

It's the end of an era. Umbrellas and flags are flying like a colonial tea party as the Care International boat speeds toward us. They have come to tow the brave explorers to Padak, where our new engines await. The mood on the rafts is euphoric. For the others it is the end of punishment. I say nothing about my own feeling of loss. I would have loved to row the whole way, to pay our respects to the river and the men who went before us. The moment we tie onto that boat the physical challenge is over. It never became as hard as I thought it might.

The Care crew is almost as excited as the team. Cold bottles of drinking water are handed out and photos are taken. Their excitement wanes a bit as they realise towing our rafts means a severe reduction in speed. This ensures we will not make it to the base before nightfall. They decide to move the rafts by road instead. The group splits. Bingo, Nat and Ian climb into the standard aid-white Land Cruisers waiting at a little fishing village. Marcus, Dan, Pete and I don't want to risk a full descent just to arrive at base a few hours earlier. Unsurprisingly, Dale also chooses to stay on the river. As the Care boat cruises through kilometres that would have taken us days to row, I sit happily in the front watching the bow scribbling our by-line on the blackboard of Nile history.

I find myself at a loss with the sheer magnitude of our surroundings, trying to place myself in this trajectory of history. Under a clear sky the stars are so bright, their reflections seem to shine from below, as if we are floating through space. Papyrus openings reveal lakes beyond, and beyond them lie many more, a vastness blossoming out of itself and seemingly into infinity. Eventually we leave the wide channel to force our way through a tight reed alley. The sensation of space is lost.

We are in contact with the world again and dragging the boat through channels barely larger than footpaths. It's terribly exciting, midnight in the legendary Sudd. Our boat and the vegetation rustle with sounds like holiday tinsel; it would rather not let us through. Our flashlights shine blunted light against the encroaching papyrus walls. Eventually we squirt out from a cluster of papyrus onto dry land. Under the headlights of the Land Cruisers we drag the boat up. Driven for thirty minutes over a bumpy track that we can only see from what little the headlights allow though the dirty windscreen.

Finally after midnight, the big yellow metal gates of the Care campsite shut behind us. The high wooden walls are the most impressive part of the camp. Some tents with beds and a few grass-roofed huts are scattered in a circle around a communal kitchen and dining room. It is the most civilised place we have seen for some time, but far from fancy.

In the morning, eager to walk, we are escorted around the few buildings that comprise the town of Padak. For the first time since entering Sudan we are met with cupped hands instead of waving ones. It's tempting to believe this is because Padak is one of the few aid stations in the South accessible by road, even if only in the dry season, and only sometimes.

On the drive back, we see through the dirty back windows, and the No Guns Onboard sticker, a group of Dinkas, ashen from dust and simmering in the midday heat, carrying a crude stretcher. Our car, with a doctor inside, is contributing to the dusty spray. We are already well past before Dan suggests we stop. The thought had not occurred to me.

I am not sure why I can drive past a man too sick to walk, and not offer him help. Perhaps a lifetime in Africa has made me thick-skinned when it comes to human suffering. Every day one is passed by someone in trouble, and if you help them they might follow you home like a puppy to be taken care of indefinitely. Or it could be that I am cold hearted? I prefer the first explanation.

Numb rejection is a decision made thousands of times and yet only rarely do I even question it. One instance that stays in my mind happened in Addis Ababa, Ethiopia, the begging capital of Africa. There, begging is a socially accepted way of making a living; step out the door and you find masses of deformed, even dying, people. On one particular day, I had been sitting at a workshop, waiting for welders to make a part for an oar frame, sipping tea and taking pictures. As a seasoned African traveller I pretended it was 'no big thing' when two feet of twisted man crawled towards me with no legs and barely any arms. It became more difficult to ignore him when the malformed claw reached out with his pleading eyes.

Usually this is when I would wind up the window or increase my walking pace. If I was feeling really guilty I might even have crossed the road. He had me cornered and he knew it. Being a man of principle, I refused to break my 'no money for beggars' policy. I tried my best to explain to him, with a shrug, that I can see he is in need but that I am not a tourist and therefore above his tricks.

Something must have gotten lost in translation, because he kept staring and waving his stump at me, not aggressively, just persistently. Stalemate. He was just doing his job and I was refusing to pay guilt tax. The welder slipped a hand into his torn overalls and produced a few crinkled notes that he handed over with a smile. If I thought about it longer I would have been disgusted with myself, spending more on a river trip than any of them would ever see, along with a body that has never let me down. Instead I only felt mildly embarrassed, spent a few dollars on beer and nearly forgot all about it.

I have never found an answer to the begging scenario. My mother in her middle-class innocence and inborn wisdom has a good system: she gives with her heart only when she feels moved. There are several possibilities daily for this to happen in any given African country. My current plan is to carry small amounts of money (when I remember) then give them out when I'm moved. It's a great system. In exchange for a minimal total cost in a weak currency, I get to feel good about myself and they get a few cents to do with as they please. Everyone is a winner at a bargain price.

When I think they are demanding, I refuse out of principle. Usually this leaves me feeling slightly worse, but we can't have the poor being demanding; it smells of anarchy. The anti-begging campaign's justification is that payment promotes more begging. This might be true, but in all the years that I never gave, I don't think I stopped one person from begging.

Haves-and-have-not's guilt is worldwide, but in Africa it is colour-coded. I do not feel the guilt. Being White in Africa means you are assigned a role. My travels in Africa are based on this undeniable and fortunate fact. Stinking, and in dirty torn clothes, I can show up at any doorstep, empty-handed, in most rural society in Africa, and expect to be treated like royalty. My whiteness is proof that I am connected, if not rich. Whites are rare and therefore valuable. For that reason alone, a white man would never be left sick in a blanket by the side of the road.

I get away with what I do in Africa because I am white, simple as that. For me the colour line is reinforced by an upbringing under apartheid in South Africa. No amount of exposure, experience or psychoanalysis will ever completely erase the effect of those formative years. Power, given to us for no other reason than our skin colour, is neither deserved nor earned, and it is often a heavy burden for the black people dependent on us. It takes a very strong and rare person not to start believing in his own ranking when he is constantly being treated as if he is inferior.

When the first explorer arrived in Africa his technological advantages made him seem like a god to the tribes he encountered. Today the white man has lost his god status but in most rural communities, he is still seen as being from a high social order. We have even sold them a picture of a white God. Can you imagine white people worshipping a black Jesus?

I know how to operate in Africa, but my skin creates a barrier of tinted glass. This keeps me on the outside looking in. I can glimpse at what lies beyond, but it's murky and I will never understand what it is like to be truly African. So instead I try to focus on what I am: a white African. I try to find my place in a continent that does not allow me camouflage. Here I am judged as quickly and as stereotypically as I project judgment onto these people. In desperately poor places like the Congo and South Sudan, the people do not want you to be their equal. You are a white person and attributed with certain characteristics, mainly qualities which promote hope or at least an excess of money. Whether you can deliver or not, you have already been positioned in your symbolic role.

You can try to fit in, but it's no use trying to be black when you're not, people will notice. Besides, white people just are not tough enough to be black. If you want to experience Africa on the ground level, and I recommend that you do, the best you can do is to use your whiteness cleverly, with consideration, and not be scared of getting dirty. Because whiteness corrupts and absolute whiteness corrupts absolutely, it is essential to at least try to know where black people are coming from, to try and see it from the vantage point of the less privileged, to remind yourself of your good fortune, to cure yourself of any notion of superiority. Unfortunately this knowledge will not make your life any easier, which seems fair in some twisted way.

We pay for our Whiteness in every transaction. In places like South Africa, being white makes you a target. The sins of our fathers have poisoned the water and justifiably given us a lot to answer for. I suspect though, that the problem is even simpler than that: hunger and hopelessness. Going without food for a few days is bearable, but over a sustained period the gnawing can erode even the strongest principles. The constant primitive drive is demanding, unceasing and desperate. The intensity of true hunger can only be understood by people who have experienced it. It is the force revolutions are built upon.

For the most part, being white is a 'get out of jail free card' and an all-access pass rolled into one. In Uganda especially it is like being a rock star; people stop and stare and children run after you, screaming with joy, "*Muzungu, Muzungu.*" Whiteness is a wonder so beyond belief, that it has to be said out loud. The world is at your feet. The white man is a goose that lays golden eggs, and a person with no opportunities will be stupid not to ask for, or try to take it, when they have nothing to lose. This is a fact. If you don't like it, move to Norway.

Being a white African can be compared to winning the lottery. I didn't ask for it. I only play the cards I am dealt. To their credit, most black people don't hold my luck against me, they just think that I should share more. We pay them for their ability to suffer and endure, for most of them it's the only skill they have. They do the most mundane tasks if they are lucky, the most tiresome if they are not, either way they get to do what we don't want to do for ourselves. In Africa there are so many people doing things for you that it is easy to forget that they are people. I am not suggesting you remember every name, but something as simple as a greeting and a minute spent on idle chat, will go a long way. It gives respect and recognition. More often than not it brings greater humour and enjoyment in the small things, and at the very least a larger portion at lunchtime.

The inequality is unfair and I don't deserve it, but the position of white people in African societies is not going to change in my lifetime and neither is my skin colour. All I can do is to try to be the best white man I can, to accept my limitations of the help I can give and to use my guilt for some good.

Africa is a harsh continent where unpleasant realities exist every second, on scales larger than we want to imagine. Good intentions aren't enough. Change does not happen overnight and if you want to survive out here you do the best you can with what you have. That is the African way.

HE HAS COME

The square contains warriors throbbing with colour, passion and raw emotion. The crowd is driven into a frenzy it can barely contain. Hundreds of voices scream for violence as their bodies re-enact it. Bare feet are stomping hysteria onto the soil, rhythmic like a drum.

At first glance it seems to have a carnival atmosphere: sports day, a fashion show, a chance to sing, a chance to dance. All over Africa are dusty football pitches like this, where young men kick half-deflated balls or knots of plastic bags past termite mounds and potholes. This however, is much more to my liking: wrestling, the Dinkas' national sport, where the judges carry AK-47s.

The crowd walls in the battlefield. The energy is thick and threatening. Most of them are naked apart from token pieces of cloth. Clothes were made a legal requirement here only a few years ago. As long as you have something on, it will do. Threads of bright yellow, red, green and purple, are faded, their seams are splitting, and their messages are without meaning. Reduced to their most basic function, only colour matters.

Particular men, removed from the crowd by the seriousness of their responsibility, are the only ones permitted to carry guns to the carnival. With the amount of testosterone flying around, it makes sense to have gun control, enforced by superior firepower. Sudanese, for all their lovely characteristics and incredible hospitality, are quick to anger and no strangers to violence. Sparks turn to flames quickly out here. Last week a chief was shot at a similar festival over a disputed result.

Inside the frenzied human square, sit two groups of men, motionless. Stone-faced, focusing for battle, they feed on the crowd's energy. Once a warrior reaches fighting point, he rises slowly. The small physical gesture creates a ripple, exponentially amplified by a rolling wave of expectation that flows freely from the tribe onto their warrior, turning the young man into its weapon. Locked, loaded and ready to fire, the muscled, yelling, jumping, flexing, chest-beating warrior carries his tribe toward the advancing and opposing train.

In their loincloths, they move closer. Their movements grow larger and wilder. Once face-to-face, showmanship makes way for focus once again. Under instruction they embrace tentatively and suspiciously. Their eyes lock first, then their thick arms as they keep their bodies as far away from the point of contact as possible. At a signal from the tribal elder, flanked by armed guards, the contest begins.

Tense muscle erupts inside the violent embrace: turning, twisting, kicking, pulling, and eventually falling. It's as if I am looking at the

Coliseum or standing on a timeless battlefield. Here, on this square, one can feel the tension of an ancient bloodlust that contact sports were created to replace. The match is brief compared to the long-lasting celebrations that follow.

Inevitably there is commotion over who touched the ground first. It is a dispute taken up by the whole tribe; it is as serious as their own collective warrior pride and it is defended as vigorously. This is clan warfare, thinly camouflaged as sport and begging to explode into an age-old rivalry. A clan's reputation is built on how well they fight, and a man's honour is married to his results.

The emotion for every fight is built on the last. After an hour I can stand it no more. I want – no, need – to be released into the intoxicating, simple honesty of the savagery. My fingers are clenched into fists. The hair on the back of my neck is erected in a growl. A western upbringing allows me to smile and joke about the clarity of a genetic drive to battle, but my unconscious is following the command to obey.

Drifting toward a group of warriors, the frantic crowd sweeps me up. They don't need language to know why I am here. It doesn't matter who fights as long as someone does. Within a few steps I have my own entourage, dancing, jumping and willing me on. Face to face now with the enemy, I look down to see I am beating my chest. I am laughing but this is not funny, far from it.

No one rises to meet my challenge. I'd like to imagine that I am an unappetising prospect. In fighting me there is little to gain and a lot to lose. Two months of pushing oars for hours a day has made me strong. I feel, and possibly look, like I can do some damage. If they beat me, so what? They beat a *kawajha*. If they are lose, they must accept defeat from a *kawajha*. More likely, they are confused by my unexpected appearance. Before the stalemate is resolved, I am surrounded by another group of men who break into the inner circle, flashing clubs and automatic weapons and yelling aggressively at me. I don't remember this as part of the program. It takes me a few seconds to get a grip on myself and accept that this situation is out of my control. Everyone and everything is charged with emotion out here in the middle. They want me to get out, NOW! It is all said in Dinka but the tone is clear.

I am reluctant to leave, but rapidly turn from sun-blushed to pale at the sight of spit flying. Wild gestures demand that I should get the fuck out of the square. One of our translators manages to drag me out without igniting the crowd. Only later do I get the official explanation – apparently, the middle is not a safe place to be.

An old man approaches slowly and politely. "He has come." My eyes follow the direction of his bony finger, towards the swampy bank. I see a man rising from a canoe. It takes him an awfully long time, and he grows ever taller while doing it. "He is The One," the old man says knowingly, and with a touch of pity, as he turns and walks away.

A circle is formed. 'The One' is wearing a loincloth. I, on the other hand, have my rainbow nation South African flag wrapped around my waist. It has none of the edge of yesterday; a small crowd, eager but not hysteric. This is just a little sideshow compared to the battles we witnessed. Yesterday I had given myself a good chance of beating some of the warriors. With this guy, I am merely amused. He is close to seven feet tall with arms that dangle to his knees and a bounce in his step that sends ripples of muscles playfully running up and down his frame. It is clear, he is 'The One'.

Yesterday the warriors had started from bent-over positions. It seems however, that is not how real men do it. "Be careful bru, he looks like he can be harmful to your health." Pete comments unnecessarily, not even trying to hide his smile.

I step inside the ring. We circle each other like boxers. He lets loose a few slaps to my head. They say a great white shark hunts like that, a few bumps before they bite you in half. I take the first blow on my arms, covering my head, and realise this is only going to end one way. He threw that slap with careless ease, yet I felt the vibrations from the point of contact all the way down to my feet.

I am still marvelling at how strong he is when he decides that I have no surprises in store and rugby tackles me to the ground, ending the sideshow painlessly. Thanks for coming. School is out. Now go play with the other kids. He seems terribly happy to have won and so do the masses. We hug, he dances a bit, he squashes me against his chest some more, and I go back to packing the boats.

One of the best things about this lifestyle is that most mornings my environment is a mystery. Comfortable in my sleeping bag, I watch the swamp form around me, the papyrus walls fill with green, the water slowly shedding its dull coat as the sun creeps across the surface. Like a puzzle, the growing light keeps filling in parts of the world, colouring them into shapes as they first absorb, and then reflect it.

Last night's camp was erected just before sunset on one of the precious few pieces of dry land in this water-verse. We were thankful to camp at the Monothany fishing hut. They are closely related to the Dinka, but somewhere down the line they were cast out to be fishermen. In a society that values cattle above all else, they are at the bottom of the social ladder. The good news is they have mostly escaped the war. None of the bad guys were desperate enough to enter this part of the swamp. The bad news is that life here is miserable, even without a war.

Fish, I can smell it everywhere. Slowly, I locate the main source; dried fish, hanging like baby clothes from a washing line. Just below the raft a few old canoes are materialising from the mud. Cracked, damp and slightly misshaped, they represent a fortune considering how far away the trees must have been that gave birth to them. Even in Padak, trees are endangered. Here there are simply none. Canoes are essential to life in a swamp, without them you will go hungry and lonely, quickly.

I roll over slowly, careful not to disturb the fragility of the moment with a sudden movement. Behind me two small huts with reed walls lean toward one another, their roofs almost touching, like an elderly couple whispering secrets. In the small courtyard, a patched-cloth mosquito net is erected over a few sticks to create another bedroom.

From inside the rectangular tent, children's voices drift excitedly across the hard-caked mud. A distinguished man, tall in the Dinka mould, but slighter in build than the powerful Mandari, stares back at me. Scarred, straight-shouldered and muscular, he looks dignified even in the tatty green boxer-shorts that are his only clothing. Sucking nothing but air from a beautiful long-stemmed wooden pipe, he watches me as closely as I do him. It's time. Let the day begin.

I climb out from under my net while brushing my teeth, spit the toothpaste overboard, jump from my bedroom to the edge of the raft, using the bounce of the soft tube to launch me over the meter or so of mud onto dry land, take another five steps and shake hands with him at his front door.

On hearing the greeting, kids peek curiously from under the mozzie net. Once their curiosity has overcome the fear of being eaten by the *kawajha*, they spill from a space too small to hold them all. Grandmother staggers out from around the back and babbles something at me through a toothless mouth. She seems impossibly old. From the form of her body only skin remains. Mother is already busy with chores, helped by the older kids, who shoot glances up at me from eyes still filled with sleep. The youngest are carried and cared for by any one big enough to lift them.

This easy interaction between members of the family is striking. Once the rest of the team is awake, I stand back to observe it better. There is only one person to watch. Something is different about her. A distinct aura surrounds her, so much so that she imposes it on everyone else, making us react to her rather than the other way round.

It takes me a few minutes to recognise that sounds die in her vicinity. She carries silence around. Far from handicapped, there is a peacefulness about her, uncorrupted by needless noise or by the shortcomings of speech. She has the confidence of nature, loud enough for everyone to experience it, if only prepared to listen.

She fascinates me. I take as many photos of her as possible, hoping to capture her aura on camera but failing spectacularly. I try to be discreet, but she, like all women, can tell when a man is watching her. With confidence she should not possess, she looks at me with eyes full of life and smiles. What a smile it is, as powerful as any human expression I have ever seen. She smiles because she cannot speak. A brief moment passes before she shyly looks away. She can be no older than fourteen, just becoming a woman, and for her I would imagine life is as good as it is ever going to be. Soon she will get married and leave the comforts of her father's house, and be worked until any curiosity and lust for life disappears with the smoke of the cooking fire she will be chained to. Not much future for a deaf girl out here; not much future for any one out here.

Perhaps her uniqueness will save her from that. I would like to think so. There is no need to interrogate her, no need to question her. Her smile speaks to stories I will never know. I marvel at how, on this fifteen square meter patch of black mud, in what most would consider hell, I have never seen a happier family – close, loving and completely integrated.

As we leave them surrounded by the water and isolated by the full force of the swamp, I pause to wonder how they managed to tame hell. We leave a few bits of our food and take with us some of their love and happiness. Best transaction ever!

Thank God For Fools

Thank God for fools! – for men who dare to dream
Beyond the lean horizon of their days;
Men not too timid to pursue the gleam
To unguessed lands of wonder and amaze.

Thank God for fools! The trails that ring the world
Are dark with blood and sweat where they have passes.
There are the flags of every crag unfurled;
Theirs – ashes and oblivion at last.

Thank God for fools! – abused, of low estate.
We rear our temples on the stones they laid;
Ours is the prize their tired soils might not wait;
Theirs – the requiem of the unafraid.

–Anonymous

Lost

I reluctantly come to the conclusion that our guide has no idea where he is going. I stop listening to him completely and start making it up with help from the GPS, instinct, blind guesswork and hopefully, good luck. Mostly we are in a channel wide enough to seem correct, but when it occasionally splits into equal parts, I worry. People are so rare that when we do find one we question them intently.

We are all in a trance induced by the monotonous scenery. It's only when the first mosquitoes descend on us that urgency is introduced. Even drifting mid-stream, no amount of repellent keeps them off. The most effective defence is movement; we dare not stop.

Through the night people drift off and wake up at will. Everyone gets a driving shift. The journey takes on a dreamlike perspective, a papyrus and water mantra, underscoring the extent of our isolation. The sound of the engine has woven itself into my subconscious. At first I thought it rude and obtrusive after the quiet of the oars. Now it is barely the whisper of a soundtrack to my life.

The GPS has become the golden calf we worship; proof of the world outside. Continuously we to turn to it for some sign that our ark will find dry land. It measures in straight lines between here, there and heaven, leaving us to figure out the meandering maze of the world. Still when in the Sudd, for which there are no maps and the swamp is ever-changing, this is information you treasure. The great gods of Global, Positioning and Satellites imply that we should expect the town of Shambe quite soon, a single dot on a screen filled only with obscure swamp drawings. This is the sum-total of our information on the only town we will see for days.

The guide swears he knows where it is. I choose to ignore his increasingly heated instructions. It is already deep into the night, past the witching hour, and I have been questioning myself for some time. If there was someone to whom I could delegate navigation, I would, but I am out of options. To relinquish it now, even if anyone wanted the responsibility, would only lead to more confusion. I am halfway through the calculation. Mathematics is not supposed to be improvisation, but there you go. Only my autopilot overrules the doubt, which threatens to derail the last bit of confidence I have.

We escape from the papyrus tunnels for the moment, and around us a large lake spreads out. It is swallowed by the dark horizon on all sides. The long hours on the boat and the growing belief that we are lost have dampened the mood. The guide sits smugly, arms folded, waiting for me to admit I am wrong. Our relationship is past repair and I am feeling tension between the team and me. Going against local advice and getting lost is a great way to become unpopular in a critical crowd.

They are beyond the need for assurances from either the guide or me. Rationally, we have enough food and fuel to last days, and as long as the GPS doesn't die, we will eventually, probably, force a way through to somewhere. The problem is this hostile environment invites emotions to get involved. If I am wrong there will be "I told you so's," perhaps even a rebellion. No doubt it will produce more proof of my shortcomings as leader. As the guide frantically points left, I go right. This is it. If we don't find Shambe on this side of this lake, we are lost.

My eyes strain toward the all-encompassing horizon. I start to think of a way to admit my error. Suddenly, dark forms rise above the symmetry of the black horizon. Can it be trees? Trees mean dry land, and on dry land there will be people and a town. I never doubted it for a second. We slowly motor toward the trees, so as not to trigger any fingers of slumbering soldiers. A long flat jetty develops out of the darkness, a fossil from times when this was a port where boats stopped.

And the GPS says, "Let there be Shambe." No one congratulates me so I do it myself. I glance over at the guide to make sure he knows, that I know, that he knows, before voices from the bank bark nervously, inquiring what our intentions are. The guide finally proves useful, and eases their fears, which are disguised as aggression.

Even at 03:00, the banks are full of people. Marcus, the official tea maker, struggles with the chronically-ill stoves, eventually managing to produce a few cups while the team sets up camp. We are all tired and I can hear Dan and Bingo biting at each other. I am glad that for once I am not involved. As I rig my net under the stars, I contemplate the team dynamics. Still a long way to go, and I wonder if Bingo will make it. Pete is as short-tempered as I have ever seen him while Nat is looking unfazed.

My father once told me about his selections for the South African Special Forces, a challenging period that lasts for months. At any time, during any given day, one person could come up short. According to him, sooner or later everyone did. I was a child at the time and was surprised to hear this admission of inherent weakness from a man who symbolised ultimate strength. He went on to say that when your day came, when it is just too much, your friends picked you up and carried you until you recovered, physically or mentally. There is no shame in it because tomorrow you will do the same for them.

As a team we are far from there. Dan and Amber have each other and the film. Pete and I will reach the Mediterranean together. Marcus seems to be getting older every day, but I don't doubt he will make it; he has his cameras, he has purpose. Natalie has invested too much in the project and still holds many strings for its completion. Even if she did not, she would persist out of pure stubbornness. Ian is leaving in a few days anyway, and I know for him it is not soon enough. Has he even enjoyed it for a single moment? Bingo has no close friends, no purpose and nothing invested, not even a goal. He came for a holiday and it is turning out to be anything but that.

We get rid of our guide, a process that becomes quite heated. He wants more money, $100 more. It's ridiculous, that's more than he would make in six months, even if he had a job. I refuse. All the while a crowd stares and creeps closer. With our backs against the river I allow myself to be extorted for $50 just so I can escape this place which is making me feel increasingly uncomfortable. With a dash of speed and a new guide we leave Shambe.

The days stutter along; only the temperature varies between hot, uncomfortable, and very uncomfortable. The few people we come across live in sad-looking settlements on flattened papyrus, half-floating, forever sinking. The stink of fish hangs over tattered reed shelters along with dark clouds of flies. People sit with bowed heads, disease-ridden and covered in festering sores, numbed by heat and lifelong bouts of malaria. They are too needy to know where to start asking for assistance; they simply watch us as we take a few photos and leave them to continue.

Large chunks cut from the papyrus walls indicate we might be close to Adok. In some of the openings temporary shelters stand with small fires smoking weakly, while men hack a living from the endless supply. A few canoes piled high with papyrus and reed matting float downstream.

Our party reaches a crumbling dock beside a metal boat with plants sprouting from holes in the rusty hull. Downstream lies a goods container, shot full of holes, askew and burnt, its doors crucified on broken hinges. In Sudan, towns are synonymous with military bases. Even here, deep in the swamp, there is a reason to fight. As it turns out Adok is in the oil-rich region. Since the 1980s, when the black gold was discovered, companies, governments and rebel factions have all vied for a square to plant their bases. It is a perfect place to transport materials and has plans to be part of a pipeline project. This is of course, if the fighting stops. With that resource, here, now, comes a large bull's-eye and a lot of blood and gunfire for whoever is unfortunate enough to land on this square.

Dan and I, cautious after our experience in Shambe, hop on the carry racks of some old bicycles and are driven by eager soldiers. The muddy, potholed footpath leads to the base commander's compound. Once inside the reed fence, we are greeted with sweet tea. We exchange pleasantries for three minutes before begging for cigarettes. While the commander is in a giving mood I ask about fuel. He offers us sixty litres from his limited stash.

Soldiers are dispatched to collect the team, so we move outside in the hope of a breeze. Cigarette in one hand, a cup of tea in the other, I talk to the commander. I ask the major, jokingly, what he did wrong to be placed here. He laughs, saying it's 'only' a two-year deal; after that he will be living in Khartoum, his road to promotion paved by this tough assignment. I'm surprised at how nice a man he seems to be; yet I wonder how many men he might have killed and tortured. He would have to be ruthless to be given such an important command. Hopefully, it's a side we will not see.

We get to talking about Shambe, the eerie town we passed a few days ago. Apparently rumours of cannibalism are abundant in that region. As he says *cannibal*, it clicks. That look I found so uncomfortable and yet familiar was exactly the one I have given many a last piece of chicken, trying to figure out if I could get away with eating it and not seem rude. I doubt they would have tried, but I bet they were thinking about it.

I sit and smoke late into the night. Even the last few days of maddening boredom have been an enjoyable challenge. A part of me wants to keep going past the Mediterranean and never stop. I have no lack of ideas on where I would go and what I would try. The fact that we have come this far makes anything seem possible. I have wanted this for so long. Now that it is a reality, I am afraid that a return to my old world might turn this into a dream again.

I can't find any reason to return. All the parties and the crutches that have given me pleasure for so long, the women I love for a week, the superficial friendships and the social politics. Once upon a time I thought them challenging and fun but they're not the substance I want to fill my days with. Here, far from it all, it seems easy to turn my back on the only life I have known, to choose uncertainty over certainty. What would I really be giving up?

The major at my side, dapper in his new uniform, underlines his sentences with an elegant wooden cane as we walk down the badly-drawn path. A chain gang wrestles a papyrus snake fifteen meters long and as thick as a Boeing engine. It will form part of the base of a 'raft' used to transport reeds, mats, and papyrus to the market, five days away in Malakal.

Feeling inspired, we redesign the shade frames for our rafts. It turns into a competition as different philosophies on aerodynamics meet needs for comfort. Reeds, sponsors' banners, and 'rekking' (the rubber strips cut from inner tubes that seem to hold Africa together) are woven and tied together to repel the sun. In the end both boats resemble floating shanties, each as rickety as the other. We then settle back into 24/7 travel. Conversation has long since dried up. With no new input there is nothing but my own stagnant thoughts going round in slow, broken circles.

When your head starts to throb from inhaling engine fumes, it means your driving shift is over. Apart from that there is only day and nighttime. Luckily for me, being a cricket fanatic, it easy to sit and watch nothing happen for days at a time.

Somewhere in the night I wake up. Light from head torches and voices spill into my consciousness. The banging of fuel drums being refilled is barely enough reason to raise my head, and I am about to slip back into sleep when my mind hooks on something: the swamp walls are not behaving as they should.

The thought tries to force its way through a mind clogged with sleep and lack of use. The walls are moving backward, faintly but unmistakable. We are moving upstream. We can't be moving upstream. I point it out to Bingo and Pete. Bingo shrugs it off as impossible, as if ignoring the fact is going to make it go away. Pete takes out the GPS. It confirms we have been driving upstream for a long time, burning precious fuel. During the last refuel the boats had spun round and in the disorientation of the swamp and darkness we kept going the wrong way. At least something exciting has happened.

The firefly on my right does not change position. My mind, dulled from days without input and struggling to stay awake, sets off no alarm. When I connect the dots, I am jerked awake by an unsettling reality. Light means people, and people mean military. Military at 04:00 means trouble. My brain stalls before it can shift into second gear. Pete was told yesterday by sat phone that we are entering a particularly volatile area. The government has been clamping down on rebels. It is something to do with a problem in Nylwak. We were told to stand by until Pete got further information. On our next communication we got the all-clear. Apparently some United Nations aid workers were shot by a rocket-propelled grenade in a village.

I judge our distance by the light. They are still some kilometres away. I cut my engine and yell over to Bingo to do the same. Luckily, for once the boats are close, and I don't have to raise my voice. I need time to think. This time of night, scared soldiers shoot first and ask questions later. I am still trying to figure out what the right thing to do is when we float around the corner to find the light much closer than I anticipated.

I would like to think that if I do have a skill in life, it is risk analysis. I do get it wrong, but as a rule I am good with summing up a situation quickly and accurately, and reacting accordingly. One look ahead of me and the terrible knowledge that I have committed a serious error slides down my spine. Instead of a military settlement with a sleepy guard we find a war ship at anchor. *Bugger*. The green light I noticed is set on the fourth-story control tower. Its deck, five meters above the water line, looks like a Somali gun market. Guns big enough that even a blind man couldn't miss from this close. The boat's bulk fills a quarter of the river's width.

I am close to sinking in fear. I try to adjust to the fact that I am the bull's-eye for a modern and deadly weapon. I have had guns pointed at me once before, even a knife against my throat in the middle of a bar fight. All unpleasant, but none made me feel as helpless as this. No amount of talk, clever reflexes, or begging for my life, will get me out of this one.

I can't see the eyes of the person holding my life in his hands, and he can't see mine. If Pete's information from yesterday is correct, its crew will be twitchy. Killing us will be standard procedure, as easy as a two-second burst from the deck's guns currently pointing just over our heads and designed to shoot planes from the sky. My worst fear has come to fruition. I have led the team into a dead end. If they do open fire there will be no survivors.

Helpless, all I can do is watch and use my Jedi powers to wish the situation right. Seconds drip by like Chinese water torture as we float silently towards the ship, towering like the Gates of Mordor over us. Almost level with it now and still no rustle from the monstrosity, except for the low hum of its generators.

Up close it looks even more threatening, unnatural in the green light. As we draw level, I start to relax a bit, it is 04:00 after all. African law of averages says the guards will be asleep inside, hiding from mosquitoes. With that thought, someone yells from the deck aggressively. We have surprised them.

I yell back "friend" in every language I know. We are halfway past, dreading the moment when those deck guns will swivel from their resting position to focus on us. The shouts on the deck grow more urgent. Activity continues to increase, presumably as the gun crews move to battle stations.

A part of me desperately wants to start the engines and make a run for it, but I don't want to escalate the situation by adding any more components to the equation. My hairline has receded two centimetres by the time we are past the stern. Clear of the deck guns I start the engine and open up the throttle.

Eventually everyone drifts back to sleep. For me there will be no sleep for hours. One of the most petrifying moments of my life, I allow the adrenaline to evaporate slowly. I replay the situation, over and over, trying to reassure myself that I overreacted, that it really wasn't that close. The rest of the team was nervous, some might have been scared, but for me it seemed like the end.

Pete has things on his mind. He is attempting to make food fall from the sky. Even for the best logistics man on the continent this is a neat trick. He pulled the trigger yesterday by remote control as he leant against the rickety shade structure of the raft in the middle of the swamp.

Months ago in Nairobi, he packed two barrels with 'emergency supplies' then somehow got them on a plane to the UN base in Lokichokio. Next he conned a local contact to collect and keep them until further instructions. He found out who flew which routes over the swamp, befriended the particular department head and organised for the barrels to be left at a designated destination.

Once he knew the flight plans, dates and routes for the UN, the barrels made it onto the plane, and he made sure we were on converging times and coordinates. Now the pilot just has to fly low over the water as the loadmaster dropped the barrels, hopefully, from a height that will not destroy them.

The plane makes a low sweeping turn as Pete talks him in position with the air band radio he brought for such an occasion. The pilot levels the silver wings out at what would have been treetop level, had there been any, aiming straight at us.

The first blue barrel tumbles slowly out the door, increases its rotation until it hits the water like an oversized rubber bullet, skipping and somersaulting on the surface before settling down lopsided and dented, followed by the second treasure chest in the same swirling, blue trajectory.

The boats are spaced along the green corridor to increase recovery speed and to decrease the chances of getting hit by a flying barrel. Engines are revving and ready to go. The barrels were designed to float but when it comes to chocolate we don't take chances. This is as serious as we get.

The first figure I see walking through the soggy green mattress is a black man, naked apart from a pair of pink Joe Guest boxers and a heavy machine gun. The second man is equally scantily-dressed and slightly-heavier armed. Dangerous men walking light-footed and determined; at home in this place where land and water meet halfway. It makes me realise the desolation and danger of our position.

Immediately that thought is challenged by a bundle of blonde dreadlocks. She is armed with an old-school film camera, no doubt finding it all terribly exciting and completely unaware that she should not be here. It makes quite a sight, the little Scottish girl between the partially naked warriors, so at ease she could be a woman strolling about her garden. As harmless as she looks, so potentially lethal do they.

The first time I met her, I wondered if she knew her head was on fire, but was too polite to ask. Some days I still can't tell. At first glance she appears every bit the oblivious little Scottish girl that she might just be, far from home and too naive to realise what she gets herself into. I have seen her walk into the fire and come out the other side with ash in flower patterns enough times to think that *oblivious* might be a weapon she wields with intent. I used to worry; now I know better. She is protected by angels, they look after their own.

When she proposed to follow us down the Nile, alone, I was not convinced. I wanted to know her plan. "I think I am going to catch a ride up to South Sudan with a transport company. Hang out there for a bit, and then take it from there." Not what I wanted to hear. At that point, we were already six months into planning our own trip, and by comparison it seemed a bit simplified, even to me. I sighed, shrugged my shoulders, and walked away, muttering. I figured she might get up to South Sudan, realise the country is at war, find some child soldiers and spend a few months teaching them how to make sculptures out of cow manure, before drifting back to Uganda. I should have known better. The problem is that even though most people think they know better, Maddy usually – for some reason that is beyond me – does. It's an annoying trait.

She is a mental picture that will make me smile every time I hear a girl say it's not possible to travel alone. How exactly a single white female got to this muddy patch in the Sudd, a thousand kilometres deep in a war zone with nothing more than a smile, enthusiasm and a few hundred dollars is still not clear to me.

The warriors leave her with us and escort Ian back to the small airfield ten kilometres away. Ian is leaving us today, to considerable relief amongst all parties concerned. Aware that the security in the area is deteriorating quickly, we don't waste time on long goodbyes. We motor hard to get out of the danger zone and spend the night in Atari, where our initial cool reception turns into the unavoidable warm Sudanese welcome.

At dinner we hear that the government has unleashed an air strike on the area we just passed through. The thought of Maddy's escort, the three fighters and their families, subdue our own joy at making it out. If they are still alive they will be out there tonight, plotting revenge and mourning for loved ones, while we sip tea with their killers.

Crack

I am not covetous for gold,
Nor care I who doth feed upon my cost;
it yearns me not if men my garments wear;
such outward things dwell not in my desires.
But if it be a sin to covet honour,
I am the most offending soul alive.

—William Shakespeare

It's the end, even if we are not yet halfway to the Med. The end of the swamp, the end of war zones, the end of the South. For almost a year Malakal seemed to be at the other side of the world. We were told that reaching it was a fool's dream we would pay for with our lives.

Natalie has been on the sat phone organising a reception, and as we approach our hopes grow. Our wildest dreams are outdone. The governor of the state, a well-set man in a khaki suit, comes down to welcome us personally. Along the dock are at least fifty people applauding us. We are walked down a short road dripping precious shade and purple flowers from jacaranda trees. After ten days of reeds, trees have never looked so beautiful or solid.

The procession of cheering admirers follows us into a government compound that looks like an old colonial recreation club: a sprawling area covered in large trees with the Nile flowing peacefully past. Once inside a large white house with high ceilings in a 1950s style, we are fed, properly.

I am wedged between the Governor and an unidentified but truly massive man. The three of us comprise the heavyweight eating division on a table seating twenty people. No time is wasted on table manners and not nearly enough cutlery is used, both would slow us down. Bumping elbows we tear flesh from animal bones clenched in our fists. It is every bit as savage as a Dinka wrestling match, except that this time, I keep the pace effortlessly.

Malakal is important so we decide to stay on for a while. We fill the days with filming, organising logistics, making courtesy calls or simply roaming and resting. In a game of volleyball, the locals, not surprisingly, beat us. Dinka and Nuer are the kind of tribes a Disney movie would send a down-and-out coach to search for. He would inevitably discover a superstar who then goes on to change the game of volleyball, unite his team and fall in love, while learning some valuable life lessons about being a team player.

Dan starts a rumour that there are two sexy girls working at the War Child charity. Pete and I, thankful for the lead, follow up on it. It's a cruel joke; the bastard is rubbing it in. Amber has arrived and it is nice to have her with us, for Dan especially. He is in top form, refusing to make any plans; adopting the standard Arabic reply for any statement, *Inshallah*, meaning "God willing." It has grown on all of us, very appropriately non-committing for any occasion.

We sit in the backyard of our compound, eating with our right hands, dipping in the sauce which is licked off our fingers. Afterwards I lie back in my chair as a bowl of water is brought for me to wash my hands. I offer cigarettes around. It's early evening, the heat of the day is forgotten in the Arabic social hour. We are sitting or lying on beds in the courtyard, under the stars, listening to our security officer Steven explain the complicated web of politics and tribalism that is Sudan. Steven is a young intellectual and hails from one of the smaller southern Sudanese tribes that seems to be everyone's victim.

It's great to be able to talk to someone who speaks good English and is so intimately knowledgeable about the tiny sparks that keep Africa's longest war burning. He has become our first real Sudanese friend. Listening to him, Sudanese culture comes alive in context: they do this, and it makes him feel like this; or that happens and it affects his family, who we met yesterday, in this way or that way.

Leaning forward secretively, he motions for us to draw the circle closer under the light of a dying bulb. He confides that he is a SPLA spy and asks for our help in gathering information. We let him talk, but refuse to get drawn into comment. This is no place to be taking sides. Even if I am sympathetic to the SPLA, there is no way we are going to get involved. It is more likely he is testing us. To be arrested for espionage by the militant Sudanese government would mean no more VIP dinners – at best. Politely, I tell him that we are non-political and only wish to see peace in Sudan, for all its people. He nods, we lean back and smoke our cigarettes in silence.

Our day trip to an SOS Children's village is a ray of hope for international aid after seeing so many failed attempts. Despite having met so many genuinely good people, the severity of the situation makes it seem hopeless; too many people with too many differences who are too far behind with too many obstacles to overcome. It wears down even the most optimistic. Hope is truly a candle in a dark room. Just one flicker and we are all willing to believe again that the story of Sudan might have a happy ending.

Over tea we are told the sad stories of the kids who end up here. For all the criticism aid organisations get, their worth cannot be overstated. If it is measured in laughing children, then here at least, it is a success. The staff are competent and serious about their calling.

On a tour of the facilities, we are thrown to the kids as entertainment. They seem to have no attachment issues. Soon we have them hanging off us, jumping up and down for attention, trying to out-do each other for cuteness. I see Pete swinging a few kids around and even his big beard can't hide the smile underneath. He has always said that he never wanted children and it's an unfortunate fact that many of the people most qualified to have children have this opinion.

Later in the afternoon we watch a soccer/football match. In my opinion, football is boring no matter in which country you watch it. More interesting is the squad of riot police deployed on the sideline with shields, helmets, clubs and tear-gas, all ready. The Sudanese have perfected the art of finding things to fight over; nevertheless, it seems excessive over a ball. Steven is non-committal on the subject, blowing it off as standard procedure. The crowd does not seem threatening, so I mark it down as more over-regulation by a military regime.

Later, reading a book in the courtyard, the faint but unmistakable traces of faraway teargas forces a sneeze. I will never know what caused them to use it. All I can do is scratch my head at the world presented so convincingly to us by our hosts, GOS and SPLA alike. How safe we feel in both territories, how friendly the people are, and how a thin line drawn in grotesque violence separates this country from prosperity.

The King

I am sceptical. The beast stares ahead blindly with empty eye sockets, having lost its windscreen decades ago. The engine cover is its only part with hinges still attached and currently the only hopeful sign. The rusty shell has shed its skin. Even the pieces added in later decades, from long-dead relatives, have succumbed completely to the infection. Above the radiator a translucent sun-bleached plastic jerrycan functions as the fuel tank. There is still enough shape left to suggest the truck might have once been of eastern-bloc origin, but the last fifty years have been filled with body transplants. It is too old to pretend to be anything other than an African bastard.

To get the dinosaur moving all male passengers have to push, and then get back on as it sputters and jerks past. Stopping is even more fun. On command from the driver, someone jumps from the moving truck while the rest throw him logs from the back. These are inserted under the wheels, causing the truck to hobble to a halt, over one log too many. It might sound dangerous to jump from a moving truck, but considering that even at top speed we are over-taken by goats grazing, it is an acceptable risk.

I watch the routine play out with a few planned and unplanned stops. From the back we wave like royalty at the few scattered villages we pass. Eventually, as if it had known all along where we were going, the beast gives a final cough and comes to an undignified halt in the closest shade near the palace. It is the home of the King of the Shuluk. Perhaps 'palace' is a stretch, but it is certainly the prettiest African village I have ever seen, distinguished from a million other huts across Africa by their artistic grass roofs; works of art from a people rich in culture. There is nothing new in the materials used; the only difference is in effort and skill. Approximately twenty mud huts with their fabulous hairdos stand neatly under acacia trees.

It's mid-afternoon and not even the breeze can be bothered to move across the silent scene. A group of large and tough looking men appear from the shadows to greet us. They are all dressed in pink togas. It's not easy to look tough in a pink toga but the look is completed with traditional tattoos, cut until the knife scraped against the skull, and the mixture of weaponry.

The King shows up in his Royal Pink Toga. He is a charismatic man with a good sense of humour, even if he is little more than a figurehead and a player for the GOS. His thoughts on Sudan's peace and related matters offer a bleak outlook.

He excuses himself for his evening ritual. As he sits on a folding chair outside the royal hut, which differs from his twenty wives' huts only in size, a soldier in a brand-new camouflaged uniform marches up to his side, pulls out a bugle and proceeds to blow a reveille for an evening parade. The King's guard then marches up for inspection. The King is amused and waits with a glass of Scotch whisky, listening to BBC World Service on his wind up radio.

Behind him, his tribal warriors stand idly leaning on their walking sticks, watching the parade of men they would probably rather be fighting. Their pink togas are starting to grow on me. We present the King with some mosquito nets and bid him farewell. We resuscitate the truck, and roll, rattle and cough into the sunset. Our expedition is a few nets lighter, but richer by a royal goat and bottle of Scotch whisky.

Nasser, an officer in the GOS, has been assigned as our minder, a handsome, intelligent man with fine Arabic features. Once his national service is done, he will study to be a lawyer, *Inshallah*. Turns out he plays chess. Two minutes later the board is set up outside the run-down mess hall, coincidentally painted in the same green blue as every other government building since Juba.

Spectators watch over our shoulders as we start to scrap. A good game finishes in a draw. Pete takes his place and we play till late in the night, drinking whisky, telling stories; some we already know and some we don't. There is nowhere I would rather be and nothing else I would rather be doing. Before we go to sleep we put the royal goat in Dan and Amber's tent. It turns out that I am hilarious when I am drunk, not to mention a good dancer, incredibly handsome and immensely brave.

Even before opening my eyes, the taste in my mouth and the throbbing in my head tell me that the day is going to hurt. I would prefer to go back to sleep, but someone is babbling at me in Arabic. Now feeling very unfunny indeed, I open my eyes to find a soldier trying to tell me something. With the utmost respect I tell him to, "Shut the fuck up." By the hurt look on his face I am guessing he understands English. Yes, it's going to be a long day. The desert is no place for a whisky hangover.

Muslims, pagans and Christians, black skins and flowing white robes, people and livestock block the narrow alleyways where shops sell and mothers cook while kids play. It's too much, too close to each other, but somehow it all fits on this floating town. I have always wanted to be on a real African ferry. I hate crowds, but it is a boat class on its own, and something about the utter chaos seems worth experiencing. This large blue, dirty bathtub stuffed with people, animals and smells will do nicely.

We are assigned to the top deck, where there is enough space to lie down, walk around and look at the peasants below. Pete notices a faded 'No Smoking' sign, from a time when the boat's owners still cared about such little things. As a joke, he reaches over and takes Nat's cigarette from her hand and flicks it overboard. The wind blows the burning butt into a group of Muslim men, kneeling solemnly for sunset prayers to Mecca. We watch, horrified, waiting for one of the robes to catch fire, while preparing to sacrifice Pete to an angry mob demanding infidel blood.

Squeezed between the outside rail and the bridge, seated on a rusting metal plate, with our feet hanging into space, Nat and I find a place to be alone. We have both become experts at avoiding each other, but with another few thousand kilometres to go, we will have to sort it out. I tried to speak to her a few days ago, but she had still been too raw from the fight in Malakal.

On that day Nat had changed the date of our arrival in Khartoum. Apart from it being the wrong date, she had done so without consulting me. I went to confront her. She claimed it was my fault. I'd had enough and I lost my temper. Screaming back, I finally lost it completely. The whole team was not listening. I stormed off with enough rage to punch holes in walls. I was in such a state that no one dared to even make eye contact. I disappeared down the street kicking rocks and cans. It was all shame when I realised that I'd cracked. Self-loathing crept in. I then understood I was the problem.

Rather than talking she gave me a letter, the kindest words I had received from her in almost three months. The letter explained the small details that have led her to become angry with me. She further explained how her spiteful behaviour arose because I made her feel unwelcome and unsuited to be on the expedition. The letter finished with some beautiful words about our past together and the good times we shared. I knew it had taken a lot from for her to write it.

The letter leaves me in two minds. I am weary of her. She has shown me in the last few months a level of viciousness that I don't want to be near. I have few friends and do not use the term lightly. Pretending to be friends is not an option; faking my feelings is a game my face can't play. The solution is simple, but I am afraid she handles rejection at least as badly as I do, and slightly more aggressively.

We sit close and we talk, honestly and openly, as if discussing other people. We track the deterioration of our friendship. We have both had plenty of time to think about it. Ironically, her greatest grievance, the belief that I don't want her on the trip, is without base. I realised long ago how valuable she is to the expedition; the only reason I don't want her here, is because she drains me. I hate conflict in my own aggressive way.

Neither of us are prepared to admit we have been wrong; we can only agree that we want to finish the expedition and that we can't continue this way. We decide to drop the friend pretence and just be good expedition members. Ours is not the first friendship to end from this expedition, and it will not be the last.

It is likely you will see the worst in any person on a trip and hopefully the best. The nakedness of the experience is what forms camaraderie and close friendships – or if the mix is wrong, mortal enemies. On a long trip like the Nile, with a group our size, we were always going to have some issues. If you apply the two-man tent test, of how many people in your life you could stay in a tent with for four months, you would be fortunate to be able to name six people, and even then the chances of them feeling the same toward the other five people on the trip is minimal. It is an unavoidable hazard and a great motivator to do solo expeditions. In the future I will make sure everyone is crucial to the trip or really funny (which is mandatory). Just because someone wants to come is not a good enough reason.

The days go by peacefully on the ferry. We have more personal space and lots of visual stimulus. Bingo has decided he will be leaving. He thinks the trip should have a different leader, and I think he is lazy and negative. Other than that I think we like each other just fine. Maddy, who had become everyone's release valve, tells me that Bingo and I are actually a lot alike: we both prefer to be left alone to do our own thing, and neither of us are in any danger of working ourselves to death. As with so many things that come from that lovely soul's lips, there is some truth in it.

With Ian already gone, and the improved working relationship between Nat and me, there seems a chance that the team dynamics might be sorted out.

Pete and Maddy and I sit until late in the night, talking. It is a cold windy night and ours are the only voices on the upper deck. Maddy entertains us with how she missed the ferry in Malakal and had to chase it down with another boat. What is even more hilarious is that it is not the first time this has happened to her. Artists!

We should be at Kosti tomorrow morning by eleven, but then that is what they said yesterday. None of us are too worried, we use the time to reassess the last few months and start to look forward to the next phase. I search for a phone to find our local contact, Mohammed. I reach him, but he doesn't speak a word of English.

While I am trying to project my thoughts over the phone with hand signs, a man approaches and asks if I am with the Nile expedition. He has heard of our mission. Fame has its benefits. I get him to call Mohammed and translate some directions. Two bridges down, take a left.

Marcus wants to do a coffee-table book on bridges and I think it a great idea, starting with this one. It's the first bridge we have seen for an undetermined amount of kilometres, and although I would have painted it rainbow colours, it's still a beauty. The modern arch spans hundreds of meters taking all the glory that once must have belonged to the now-rather bland, blue railroad bridge behind it. Its low clearance explains why the ferry could not go all the way to Kosti.

Hunkering down below fishing lines and spider webs, we pass it to end up in a boat graveyard. Lines and lines of ferries, barges and various other boats are tied along the bank to rust in peace, reminiscent of a scene from a world after a nuclear holocaust. When the war broke out they stopped and died without another day's work.

Eventually we find our man, Mohammed. He leads us to a hotel in town and leaves. No more security officers, no more free accommodation, not even lunch. We must be getting close to civilisation.

Preferring to sleep on the river, Pete and I find a campsite on one of the hundreds of rusting islands in what must have once been a busy harbour. The flat deck of the old barge is slightly slanted but wonderfully smooth. The surrealism of the scenery puts it in contention for best campsite ever. Flocks of storks and pelicans are our only neighbours, nesting around us in the carcasses of luxury cruise liners.

Inhaling the wonderfully blessed space, we play chess, smoke cigarettes and occasionally grin at the each other. The ferry was interesting, but we both badly need a break after being surrounded for four days.

We make slow progress into a heavy headwind and by sundown we have moved only thirty kilometres. Unless you can find humour in discomfort, you will detest motoring a raft into a head-wind. Waves break without rhythm, blowing heavy drops into your face. You can only crawl over the irregularly-spaced mounds. The engine growls hysterically between water and air, as it is lifted clear from the water by the slow, shaking motion.

Because I am cheap and stubborn, I probably would have kept going. Knowing the team's aversion to discomfort and fearing a rebellion, I decide to go back to Kosti to arrange a boat to take us north. Marcus is upset. Rightly so. I had the option before we left, but had thought we could save some money by doing it ourselves. After all, how hard can it be?

Marcus accompanies me on a hitchhiking mission, back the way we came. He seems to have accepted my apology and we have a lovely trip in what is now Arabia. Skinny kids with long hair herd goats between square mud huts with flat roofs, and camels dot the horizon.

A few trucks roll by on the bumpy road, covered with slogans written in cryptic, flowing script. Colourful tassels swing to keep rhythm with the music blasting from distorted speakers. We find space on wooden benches laid out for paying customers. We rattle along passing donkey carts loaded heavily with water containers, leaking their precious cargo slowly onto the long, dusty plain.

There is a boat in Kosti big enough to take all our gear and it's affordable. Its narrow shape makes it easier work through the waves, but it is still sunset by the time we find the team. In the morning all six of us jump into the ten-meter, banana-shaped boat, comfortably perched on our rolled-up rafts.

The river is the width of a lake, with small dunes and sandy beaches drawn in white on the banks. Every so often we pass tiny wooden boats with tatty sails made from rough overlapping stitched cloth and decks worn to the texture of polished glass by time, water and wind. We are the only representatives of the twenty-first century as far as the eye can see.

Ahmed, our driver, sees the fishing nets that fence off little patches of brown water as nothing but a hindrance, instead of people's livelihood. At first we show disproval of such random acts of 'don't give a shit', but we can't be bothered to nag. Soon we embrace the local custom, yelling "Fuck it uuppp" each time we rip through another.

I am not sure what the elderly lady did to be here, but she looks calm in the back of the armoured car. Ahmed looks less so. We were minding our own business, trying to get past the dam wall, when the military pulled up and ordered us in without explanation.

The light from outside our metal box draws a cartoon picture of a jail cell on the iron floor. Ahmed, not as accustomed as we are to being in police custody, is uneasy. As for the old woman, she is cool as a cucumber. She stays behind as we are escorted into the commander's office.

The Best Day Ever

They say to survive in Sudan you need three things: patience, patience and some patience. The bureaucracy is obese and had its legs torn off. It still crawls, but oh-so-slowly. On the positive side, in our case at least, the snacks are great. During dinner we are gently interrogated while they wait for official clearance to let us go. It is well past 23:00 when we are driven back through the quiet streets to our boats.

By 02:00 we have completed the portage around the dam and have our rafts reassembled for another early departure. Khartoum is so close that no one needs any motivation. The few hours till sunrise pass in a blink. The morning wind has died down and allows good progress. No more need to save petrol. We go full throttle until we hit the sandbanks. The river here is so wide that at places during the dry season, it is knee-deep or less.

My ninja sense for locating the deepest water is not working this side of the equator. The end result is that we keep getting blocked by wave after wave of mud banks, centimetres below the surface. Nothing left to do but push the boats. It's easy work, even enjoyable after sitting for so many weeks. It's only the delay we are resenting. We are in Khartoum mode, having built up our personalised city fantasies for weeks.

An hour of tedious pushing later and we resume our speed. Another hour and we can see her. The peaceful moments unveil a stage set with ancient *dhows*, magnificent mosques, and dignified men in white robes followed by herds of camels. The morning sun holds the landscape in the still, quiet tones that desert life reflects so well. It speaks to the heart about space beyond and times before Khartoum was marked and scarred by the immediateness of modern-day life. The first official sign is a majestic bridge spanning the Nile.

We pull over to give the rafts their first wash in months, albeit, a superficial one, and get our banners out. These get a quick scrub on the stencilled letters hiding under slime. Our main sponsor's banner, Worldwide Movers, is missing. What are the chances of losing the most important one? Some caveman carpentry follows. We twist and tie sticks into a frame, a few marker pens, cloth, and a new banner is born. Truth is, I nap. I am a danger to art.

The mood is high. I have no idea what to expect in Khartoum. I am hoping they have a decent steak, maybe even a cheeky rum and Coke. By coincidence it's my 28th birthday.

It is a fitting place for the two sources of the Nile to finally meet. Without fuss, the Blue Nile and the White Nile, intertwine to form the Queen of Rivers. Minute after minute, century after century, it is here that the Nile is born again and again. The Blue Nile is clear and confidant, its annual flood is forgotten and no doubt happy to have left Ethiopia. The White Nile, tired, worn out and just about beaten from its long journey through the great swamp lands of the South, is a mere shadow of its former self.

We have followed it from the source, thousands of kilometres away in the heart of the continent and the lush banks of Lake Victoria. Still, we are only half way on our journey. Behind us is strewn a catalogue of challenges that at times seemed like lifetimes. Forests, swamp, whitewater and war zones had been the easy parts. We had earned the right to be here. We had every right to be happy.

A hovercraft comes flying down the Blue Nile, takes a left and heads back up the White Nile without so much as a wave. Soon more boats do the same. This must be our reception! They are blind to us only a few hundred meters from the rivers' confluence. We pull over onto a small sandy beach on the left bank and giggle as we watch our welcoming party drive away from us. It's a beautiful African mix up.

Realising their mistake, the flotilla turns around. Suddenly we are drinking champagne, eating strawberries, smiling at TV cameras, posing for photos and shaking hands.

People line the riverbanks waving at us like celebrities. Our river convoy has now grown to almost fifteen boats, including ones that hover, speed, sail and row. There is even a geeky marching band, complete with brass instruments, funny caps and drum sets. "Happy Birthday to me. Happy Birthday to me." At the Blue Nile sailing club hundreds of people rush to shake our hands and take our photos. We are superstars in a country under Sharia Law where no alcohol is allowed and women are covered in black curtains. So much for the perks.

Eventually we are left with only a few friendly faces. Mohammed, a new acquaintance, is quizzed on the chances of finding a bottle of rum in an Islamic city. He returns in minutes with a water bottle containing *Aragi*, the bootlegger's drink of choice. He just happened to have this in the back of his car. We must attract a certain type.

We proceed to get pleasantly drunk. After dark I stumble back to the

Blue Nile, motor out into the middle and fall asleep under the stars. It has been a birthday I would never have imagined. A drunken Pete and his raft float away during the night. He wakes up by himself somewhere downstream, but he makes it back by sunrise.

THIS WAS THE DREAM

There is only one thing I dread: not to be worthy of my sufferings.

–FYODOR DOSTOEVSKY

Two hundred thousand of the neediest people I have ever seen fill a barren hole on the outskirts of Khartoum. I keep to myself, which is hard when visiting an Internally Displaced Person's (IDP) camp. I try to engage but my hangover seriously restricts my functioning. Pete picks up the slack, playing both TV presenter and public relations manager. He is making the press and the sponsors happy while the fearless leader sulks behind sunglasses.

Scattered in the desert around the city, millions of people are living in boxes isolated by seemingly endless kilometres of sand. Not even the surroundings want them here. This windswept open wound is made of cardboard, devoid of a single green thing. The usually majestic desert looks pathetic, covered in plastic bags that are trapped in the few dead shrubs and wire fences surrounding the homeless, country-less and hopeless. This slum is one of four official IDP camps; altogether there are between 1.8 and 2 million people stranded out here in the desert. Massive graveyards stretch across the horizon with human bones sticking out of shallow graves being dug up by the hot wind.

Some say that Sudan has the largest IDP population in the world. Currently forty per cent of Khartoum's population is displaced persons. Whole families fragment and move to these dusty enclaves; generations are born out of their forced nomadic existence.

Away from the suffering, I sit on the narrow mosque wall, legs dangling into space, squeezed between two boys. With wicked colours and holy robes, the swirling dreadlocked Sufi priests dance themselves ever closer to their God. They are twirling dervishes, spinning religiously into trances. In the midst of this spectacle, a Syrian VIP shows up in a black Mercedes with tinted windows. His armed guards manage to carve a hole in the packed crowd for the dark suited man in his aviator sunglasses to pay his respect to the dancers.

Between the solemn postures and the steady hum of the worshippers, beggars sit or crawl, while the spiritually possessed pace and jerk. One, depressed with slumped shoulders, cries and shouts, another yells happily from the top of his lungs in joy; he greets everyone by hand, trying to share his joy before he explodes with it. These two opposites never see each other, occupying different worlds or working different angles. Another looks like he is on serious drugs slipping back and forth between worlds we dare not imagine. It's a freak show and I am loving it.

Before we leave, the mayor of Khartoum honours us at a function. Chris, one of the owners of Worldwide Movers, shows up for this historic night. Six months ago I was a raft guide, yesterday I had the powerful listening to my opinions, even though I still don't own a pair of shoes. To see so many people making such a big deal out of it makes me wonder if this is something to be proud of after all.

I swell with pride, but it is temporary. Inside, I feel fake. I see all the fuss as just more paint on a rusty frame. These people don't know us, they are praising us for their perception of who we are. If they had seen our petty squabbles as we looked past real suffering and its heroes, they would not be so quick to clap and cheer. All this glory for what? What have we really accomplished for this country or these people? We are in this for ourselves, we have done nothing super human. We conduct interviews and talk to people who feed us more propaganda, then pretend to ourselves that we understand as we profit from others' suffering.

Wednesday morning we are frantically trying to construct a transom for the engines to hang off our new boat. Departure date is today, and with all our hangers-on and VIP government groupies ready for the departure, we have to leave, ready or not.

Normally we would be prepared to go in ten minutes, but last night some of our Khartoum friends gave us a boat. While Pete and Nat were having a smoke with them on a ten-meter raft, Pete remarked that it would make a great boat to do the rest of the trip in. "Oh this boat? It belongs to my family. Please take it." Seriously? You have to love the Sudanese.

While we find a way to attach the engines, the rest of the crew make the boat more comfortable: pillows, blankets, *shisha* pipe, table, fruit basket. For the rest of our journey north we will be driving a raft big enough for all of us to be together in one boat, with room to spare. It's big enough to walk around and cook on, we can even save petrol by only using one engine, which is handy since we don't have enough fuel. The boat is in essence still a raft, which means we can still do the cataracts that lie ahead of us – we hope.

We are being given a new beginning, if not a clean slate. Beyond this point is one of the most isolated and historically rich stretches of river anywhere, through the world's largest desert, and we will be doing it in the lap of luxury.

"This is how I imagined the trip would be. Me and you sitting together, laughing and surrounded by all this beauty." Nat says, turning her head to look at me. We are both quiet for a while, contemplating what has not been said.

"This was the dream," Nat says again, this time with a sigh. We are sitting shoulder to shoulder without touching, a light wind blowing in our faces. It is possibly as close as we will ever be again. Behind us sit two men cleaning their cameras. One I will never really know, the other, I will one day wish I never had. Farther back, driving the boat, Pete in his own world, and if I know him half as well as I do, he is likely to stay there for a long time yet.

I watch Nat closely for the first time in a while. She has a way of looking at the world around her as if it belongs to her. An arrogance that would be threatening in a man, but mistaken in a pretty little blonde for mischief. When she smiles it is even possible to miss the steel in her blue eyes. As friends we had opened our souls to one another. We had taken on the world. This *had* been the dream. I know what she means. Perhaps the two of us had loved it more and therefore felt its slow mutilation more painfully than the others.

Something has changed, even if we haven't yet. We are asked questions by this journey and have nowhere to hide from the honesty of our answers. Found wanting, we fall back on our defence mechanisms, mine withdrawal, hers attack. Yes, we have made it this far, but dreams lose their sterility when they are lived and this one has seen far too much pettiness.

We eventually finish the Nile in Rosetta, Egypt, 128 days after we started. Pete and I fly to Switzerland to start work the day after the trip. It was the worst possible thing we could have done. Direct from the freedom of the Nile, we sold our souls again to commercial rafting as if it was no big deal, as if it had truly been for nothing. Switzerland, as beautiful as it is, had too many rules and too many people to tell me what to do. It was not the ending to the trip I had imagined, just as the trip had not been what I imagined.

Because Pete and I never felt that the trip itself was that hard, we never got much satisfaction from achieving it. Pete shrugged it off like it was of no concern, but I was intensely aware of my inability to rise above the group conflicts and my failings as a leader. Frankly, I thought I was better than that. I felt sorry for myself, thinking that I deserved more for all my hard work or perhaps that I did not work hard enough and failed myself. I tried to escape the failings of my personal identity and ideology in an ocean of frivolity, and nearly drowned in it.

A Liar And A Thief

"Hendri Coetzee is a liar and a thief." It can't be! I am the Great White Explorer. I have fan mail to prove it. Steward Goddard disagrees, and is accusing me of claiming what is not mine and stealing what belongs to his father, a man I respect immensely.

While other kids were juggling a few half-formed dreams in their peer-pressured pimpled heads, John Goddard plotted a course for a life unlike any other. At age fifteen, without giving up quality for quantity, he sat down and wrote a list of 127 goals he wanted to achieve. They included exploring the world's longest rivers, climbing the world's most impressive mountains, and visiting the natural wonders of our globe. He has made over one hundred ticks on the list, and last I hear he was heading off to the Tsangpo Gorge, China, deep in his eighties. It's a little structured for my liking, but he has achieved more than any man can hope for and is not to be compared with a restless, fickle misfit like myself. I knew before starting that John and two Frenchmen descended the Nile in 1951. Most importantly for me, they did none of the whitewater sections. I know because when one of the Frenchmen returned to try, he was eaten by crocodiles in the very first rapid.

The email could not have come at a worse time. I am already disillusioned with what we did. This threatens to destroy the integrity of the trip, for me at least, completely. Had I claimed something that was not mine to claim? Was I just another big-mouth or worse, a liar and a thief?

I had not given it much thought pre-trip, but I am starting to realise the complexity of the claim *First*. Where does one draw the line? How much of a river do you have to do before you have 'done' the river? I believed that the fact that he walked around the eighty kilometres of whitewater in the Murchison Falls stretch, the hardest and most dangerous section of the river, was enough to disqualify a full descent. Add to this all the other whitewater sections, and the total kilometres missed by their expedition were no more than two hundred, barely one per cent of the total distance covered. The most dangerous one per cent to be fair, but I walked around three rapids myself. By the end of our trip I missed eleven kilometres of the Nile, one kilometre of whitewater and ten kilometres of a security area after Lake Nasser. The first, because I could see no way through, the last because I couldn't be bothered with Egyptian red tape. If someone comes along one day and does more rapids than I did on the Nile, will he or she have done the 'Complete Nile'?

It is hard for me to let go of the 'Complete Nile First Descent' but the fact that the answer is so blurred is answer enough. If you have to add little by-lines like first 'full' descent then you are splitting hairs. Delusions of grandeur and the thought that I am making history are gone.

I would have done the trip even if it wasn't a first full descent of the world's longest river. The mission itself is legitimate enough in its complexity and challenge to not need any of these qualifications. As a political web it has more pitfalls and dangers than when Goddard did it. Back then Sudan was under Anglo-Egyptian rule. Nowadays this is balanced by things such as satellite phones and engines.

We were doing separate trips with different challenges, fifty years apart, but he was first. Claiming a full descent was an easy sound bite for the sponsors that we never got. The ones we did get would have cared less. Technically true or not, 'full descent' is a moot point. We discovered no new areas, we only became the first people to do all of it in one go. Does that make us harder or smarter than Goddard's expedition? I seriously doubt it.

I started the journey to do something I could be proud of, and it turns out my assumptions were based on personal interpretation and not broader consensus. It also seems that Jinja is considered by many not the true source of the Nile. The fact that we could get something as fundamental as that wrong, I guess, says a lot. To be the longest river, the Nile must be traced from its farthest source, a muddy hole in a swamp deep in Rwanda. In our amateurism, we did not even consider that we had to go and do another river far from the actual Nile for it to be an attempt on the longest river in the world. John Goddard had also not completed this 1600 kilometre Akagera River. He and his companions had started their journey in Rwanda but almost drowned on the first day and decided to drive to Jinja. This of course meant that if we did do the Rwanda section, we would have done 1800 kilometres more than Mr. Goddard. Significant, but still on a sliding scale.

The following year we figured we might as well do the most remote source so that we could claim a first descent with a slightly clearer conscience and get on with our lives. We went to Rwanda and the Akagera River. Then we found the source of the Akagera, high up in Nungwi Forest. A muddy damp path like a hundred other muddy damp patches in the same forest. We then walked, paddled, rowed and motored all the way back to Jinja. We had done the first full descent of the White Nile, doing 1800 kilometres more than Goddard's team, and become the only people to have completed the world's longest river beyond doubt.

The true ridiculousness of the modern expeditioning world was illustrated two years later when another group of freaks claimed to find a 'new' source. In other words, another muddy patch somewhere in the same rainforest. Just so they could claim that they had done a First – neglecting in their press statement to mention that they too tried and failed to complete the Murchison section. During their rescue in a tragic chain of events, one of the rescue team was shot and killed by the LRA.

Robert Collins, author of *The Nile*, the book that inspired this journey, said: "They're talking about a difference of a few miles. ... These chaps are really just out for adventure, and I'm all for that." Well said. None of us should take ourselves too seriously. There are biologists out there like Mike Fay who are making the world a better place through their expeditions, but the rest of us, no matter what we will have you believe, we are just out for a bit of adventure. The state of the expeditioning world and my own behaviour left a bitter taste in my mouth.

I hyped my own achievements for the marketing machine. All adventurers do it to make us sound more impressive and get that elusive 'First' that the media and public crave. Marketing organisations get paid millions to do it every day. It is nothing but the art of making something sound like more than it is; a crucial part of the age of extra super sun block and double deluxe burgers. Reality's limits have changed little, so to promise more, we find fancier ways to say the same things. It's a lie that is told so often that we find it acceptable.

In an era of information overload the most important thing is to grab someone's attention for a few minutes, and that's just not long enough to tell the truth. Reality TV is such a fine blend of fiction and truth that it might kill the truth completely in our lifetime. Watch a documentary and what you see is an embellishment, another false layer to make it better than the old version, another coat of paint. We all know it, but because the lie is so easy to pass on again, it suits everyone in the short term, and time is money.

Adventurers are in competition. Like everyone else we try to outdo one another. No one is interested in a mission with no danger or discomfort. The more the Earth is explored the more those two elements become the explorers' only way of selling their product.

I sold my integrity so I would sound impressive to people I would never know. I twisted a fact so it suited me, but a half-truth is a misleading truth. I made something seem a little bit more than it was to make myself seem a little bit more than I am. Good intentions or not, I became part of the problem. In that simple act I destroyed any pride I might still have had in the Nile expedition.

For me the Nile mission was about much more than the expedition, it always had been. I tied myself and everything I thought I was to It. I hoped to cure any existential angst I might have had. Ironically I only made it worse.

This is the part of the brochure they don't give you to read when you decide to pursue your dreams. The small print of life states that if you work hard at something you will get what you desire. In reality it is not the way you desire it.

The trouble with turning dreams into goals is that dreams give hope whilst goals create expectations. A dream can be a cruel mistress. Only someone you love can break your heart, and only losing the things you care about can hurt. When we extend ourselves, we expose ourselves; we experience the highs and lows that come with putting it all on the line. I knew that all along, but I also believed in happy endings, and this wasn't it.

The Dream. It is hard to remember it now. It had all started so full of excitement, hope and joy. I was so sure it was what I wanted. Perhaps I wanted it too much. For me it was never just a journey, it was a reason for existence. Something changes in you once you really try something. Failing yourself while winning is worse than not achieving your goal, because at least then you can try again. I risked it all for something and found nothing. The best day ever is over. It's night-time.

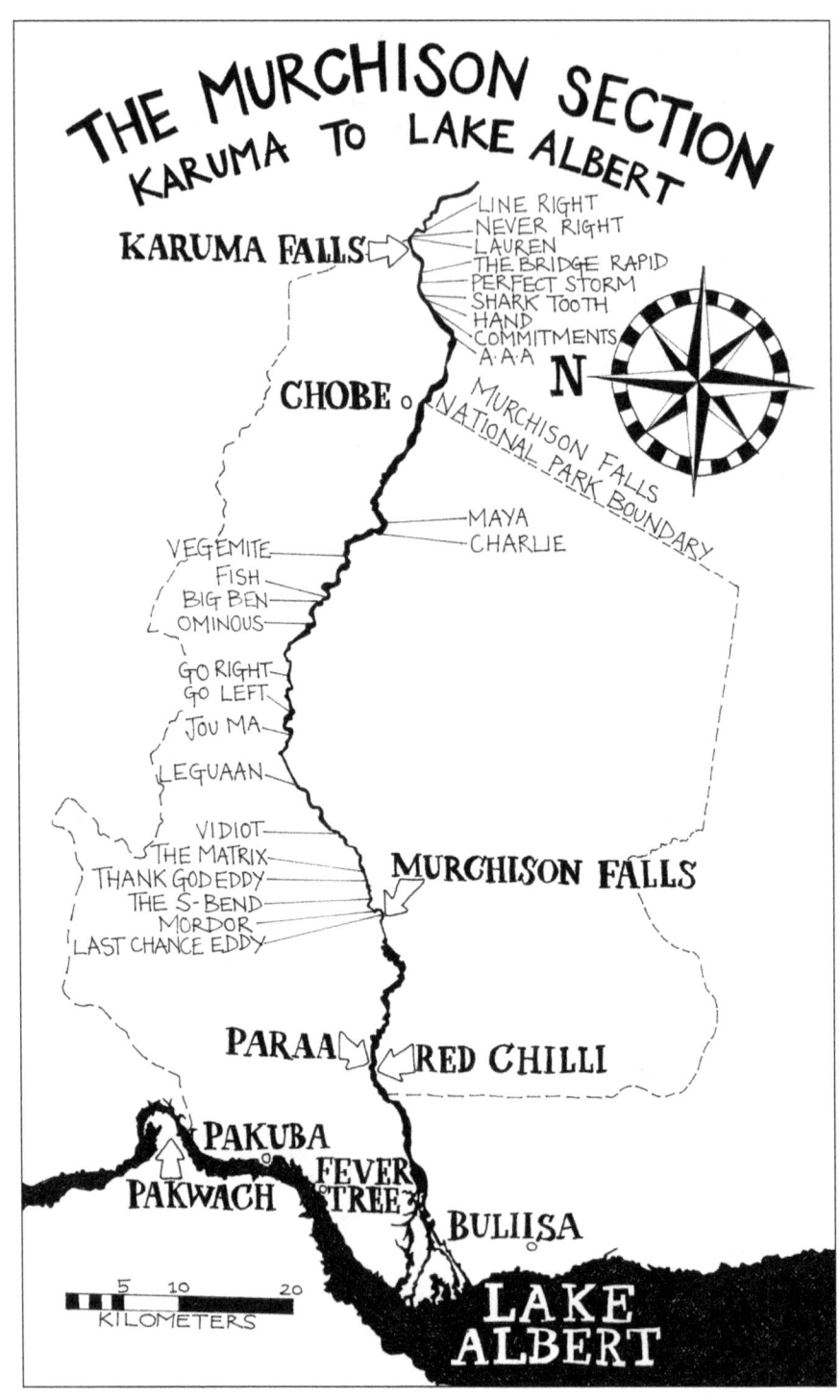

OR DIE TRYING

He talks almost as if going into battle against overwhelming odds as a holy ritual – a way of offering his death to God, to see if he would accept it.

—Pat Shipman

Murchison Solo

I am back to doing what I do best, unsure if I am still good enough, unsure if I ever was, and gambling my sanity on an insane journey. While doing a silent meditation retreat I had an idea. I would return to Murchison Falls National Park. This time alone. It was not the first time a mission of mine had been called suicide, the only difference was that this time I wasn't so sure they were wrong.

Psychologically the hardest part of an expedition for me is the penultimate week before departure. Last minute preparations and excitement can distract me. As I struggle to justify the risks, the all-important 'why' and 'what if' questions loom the largest. Theoretically, there is still time to pull out, and that tiny crack can threaten the wall that is holding back a tide of fear and doubt.

In its own way, preparation is one of the most challenging and exceptional times of the mission. If you wish to overcome any monster, you need to love it. Beating fear and overcoming doubt serve a valuable function. Through this effort you establish commitment and grow strong enough mentally to overcome obstacles on the journey.

Fear and doubt should not be all-consuming. If they are then you are probably doing something you should not, and the chances are you will mess it up. It is, however, allowed to be pretty intense. If you know you are going to be playing in a place where mistakes carry a heavy stick, your emotions will swing between terror and calm more frequently than you might feel comfortable with. There is nothing glamorous about your own fear and doubt. By definition they are uncomfortable feelings, and just because you deal with them once, does not mean you will not have to do so again. The best part about this ongoing battle is the long-lasting benefits. Doubt forces you to evaluate your motivation as best you can. This helps to stop it from becoming a weakness later. Looking closely at motivation for your trip, you can't help but get to know yourself better. Questioning motivation is a wonderful tool to force you to assess your life. So much of our lives are spent doing arbitrary tasks and fearing things that will never happen.

Confronting fear has even more potential benefits for self-growth. At the very least, we will have something real to be worried about instead of the imaginary dangers that stalk our existence. During expeditions we live the extraordinary. The result is you stop taking your thoughts, actions and possibly even your life for granted; then start to question what you stand to lose, how good your skills really are, and if this is really what you want to be doing with your time. Only then do you begin to balance the books of your life.

I am ready, can I do this? I really hope I don't get eaten. To get my affairs in order I send my mother a text message, casually mentioning that I will be on a river trip for a few days, trying to slip in an, "I love you" without ringing alarm bells. The reply makes me smile. "It sounds lovely son, wish I was coming with you." I doubt it.

It is as intimidating a put-in as I have ever seen. The river is angry because it can't flow fast enough down the thirty-meter wide funnel. Overhanging rainforest covers both banks; raggedy green curtains allow only superficial glimpses into the mysteries hidden behind them.

Battle-hardened soldiers guard the bridge I am standing on. One look into their hollow eyes reminds me that life is cheap in these parts. Wildlife wait under a bridge where Idi Amin's troops dumped bodies and the LRA burnt out vehicles. A single white man failing to return from the jungle will receive little sympathy. A few hundred meters down, the river takes a right turn and disappears ominously into the jungle. Unfortunately I know what happens after that.

I can't remember the last time I was so scared. I need to get on with it. Within fifteen minutes I'm ready to go. A friend takes a photo. In case this is the last photo that will ever be taken of me, I try to look happy and content. I am neither. I break into the current without looking back at the figures waving me off from the bridge. I paddle into the jungle aware of being very alone.

Around the first corner, and I have not seen any hippos. As that thought passes through my mind I see a crocodile. With that I turn from tourist to participant. Zimbabweans call them flat dogs because when they swim their tails wag and they have that stupid expression of singular purpose on their faces.

Charges from the front are a nuisance. They leave few options. On past expeditions we would charge back when they could not be outrun. Now, alone, as I see it coming straight at me, that option seems like a bad one. Mouth too full of teeth in a retarded smile, there is no doubt that it wants to eat me. Playing chicken seems silly.

I have to make it past the reptile on the outside. It all happened fast but somehow I do. After the initial two-hundred meter full-blown charge he follows me for a kilometre or so, but is eventually forgotten as I focus on the whitewater. Only seventy-nine kilometres to go.

Take a deep breath. No time to doubt, no time to panic, it is just forward now, some big rapids coming up. Running on memory, I do not stop to scout. I settle into the rhythm of my surroundings. Thoughts float in my mind: random subjects, ex-girlfriends, and experiences with friends, things far removed from this place – but I am here, completely. My senses feel superhuman. I can smell and hear the jungle; my eyes continually scan the water and banks. Picking up small details I file them away under harmful or harmless. Every hundred meters, I make a complete turn to check for crocs approaching in my blind spots. They are silent hunters; the only detection is visual.

I reach a rapid I don't remember. Slowly I approach the horizon's edge, trying to keep an open line to the nearest bank in case it turns out I cannot make it down. The river is split into channels. I commit to the middle; surely if I can't remember the rapid it can't be that big.

The relative safety of the eddy just before the horizon line is cut off by surfacing hippos. I go for the only other eddy still available. It has to be a portage now. No hippo trails here, so I drag myself and the boat through the thick undergrowth on the island. Some minutes later I find a small stream. It doesn't look great, but it could be a possible way out.

The jungle is thick, making the portage almost impossible without a machete. I know the stream will be overgrown and that being washed into a strainer is a real possibility. I can see calmer water through the branches and decide to paddle there, gambling that I will be able to get out of my boat before the next horizon line. It would save me at least thirty minutes of serious jungle bashing. Again I feel the fact that I am alone, no mistakes now, this would be a bad place to be stranded. It works out, two minutes of paddling, a short portage past a strainer and I am back in the main channel.

Still, I don't rest. Adrenalin is pumping strong so I continue into the next set of rapids. Soon I am in the 'hippo maze' section. The river widens and flows into a labyrinth of smaller channels, rapids become easier, but the risk of running into hippo or crocs in the reduced width and depth rises. Continuously I judge, calculate and guess which is the biggest channel. I don't want to end up where I cannot outmanoeuvre a pod of hippos or a croc.

Hippos seem to be in every eddy, worryingly even in the main flow. I try my best to stay in the deepest water, but inevitably I have to cross shallow places in order to join up with larger currents. These are the intense moments, while I cross within meters of hippos. The ones I can't see are the ones that really scare me. My main defence is muttering, "Please don't eat me, please don't eat me."

During past trips I have made as much noise as possible to warn hippos lurking below the surface that I am approaching, hoping they will pop their heads up and give me a chance to avoid them. Now that feels wrong; every sound I make is a lunch bell for every croc in the valley.

In these small channels I will not be able to avoid a charge from the front, so I decide to go silently. Somehow it just feels right to make as little noise as possible, to be as unobtrusive as I can in this place; to let sleeping wildlife lie.

I see a hippo and a calf on an island; such weird animals; an obese, four-ton pink river horse and its exact miniature copy. You look at nature differently when it confronts your mortality. You see more because it matters more. Being alone strengthens this bond with nature. Momentarily I flow with the current. For the first time since I have been on the river, I relax, I am filled with a sense of wonder, of peace and for a few minutes I allow myself to just enjoy what I am doing.

The peace doesn't last long.

Even though the recognition of channels is hard in this maze, the next configuration of islands looks similar to a tricky rapid that has caught me by surprise in the past. Before I can confirm my location, I see another croc. He sees me at the same time. It's very simple from there on. Neither of us hesitates. He charges. I run. This time, the rapid saves me. I slip into the faster water and leave him behind.

Darkness comes quickly on the equator and time is running out for today. I pull into the first river-left beach I see. The right bank belongs to the LRA terrorists and I have enough to worry about already. It is good to get out of my gear. I collect some firewood and send my GPS location out to my 'rescue squad' in the park. These coordinates will give them a place to start looking if I don't make it out and serves as current proof that I am still alive. I make some coffee and sit down to watch the sunset. It is awe inspiring.

By the tranquil aura of the fire I am able to think for the first time since starting. I do not even begin to congratulate myself; tomorrow will be harder with more crocs and bigger rapids. There were a few close calls today but nothing I did not expect and I still believe with everything in myself that I will make it. I do not question myself for being here, that would be bad for survival. An itch best not to start scratching.

It is no accident that I am here alone. This section has been paddled only four times successfully, with a fair number of failed attempts. The first descent was done in 1998 by Adrift. Since then the only successful attempts have been by me and my usual partner-in-crime, Pete Meredith. Every descent with a different crew, every time by the skin of our teeth. It is no coincidence that I fear and love this place like no other. I knew I would return after our first descent in 2004. I was deeply touched. A year later I was back again. It would be my last. *That's it, no need to go back, been there, done that.* A year later, I put on for the third time.

Committing to the third descent was the hardest. I couldn't stop thinking that I was pushing it too far, that twice was enough, that my 'luck' was going to run out. Even worse, we were being paid to do it. I was close to pulling out when Pete reminded me of the simple fact that there was nowhere else I would rather be. He was right, thinking logically the risk is almost unacceptable, but there is something so unique about this place that despite the risk, any opportunity to experience it is a privilege.

Our third descent was four days of non-stop action, with more close calls and adventure than you could explain to anyone who wasn't there. I can think of no other time when I felt so alive. I made peace with the fact that I would be coming back, and already in the back of my mind I knew how.

I have always liked paddling alone. For me, paddling is an individual sport. It has never been between the river and me. I believe the river does not care, does not even know you are there; it just flows timelessly, obliviously onwards. Nature provides the stadium, but the race is only against myself and life is the only prize.

I have dreamt of a solo mission from the first time I saw the section, but then it was more like a fantasy. Like scouting a massive rapid without your boat, you imagine it, you go away, you dream of it, and every time you see it, you believe a little more that you can do it until, if you're lucky, one day you know you are going in.

I eventually drift to the question: Am I ready to die? In the context of where I am, I give it serious thought. In our society we avoid the thought of death as if recognition alone could trigger the event. Thinking about your own death is seen as a sign that mentally, all is not well. Some people live their entire lives with the sole purpose of minimising the chances of it occurring to them, instead of preparing for the inevitable.

After spending so much time avoiding the issue, it is almost soothing to invite death on my terms. This is death's natural environment, and even if it is threatening, it is not malicious. It is just the two of us out here; the illusion of death belonging to someone else is gone. The interaction is positive. I am very aware I could have a faultless run and still come up short. The wildlife brings a factor of unpredictability that cannot be ignored.

Fear has been ever-present since making the decision to go. At times it felt so right. Other times, fear gripped and suffocated me as I thought of the dangers outside my control, of how good my life was and of what I stood to lose. In those moments all I wanted to do was quit.

I knew I would not quit. I knew that I would do this despite the risk; I would do this because of the risk. It is something I am drawn to. I have tried to analyse this part of myself, without success. It is my kind of trip, my perfect challenge in my most beloved environment. I have never tested myself to this level.

I don't expect most people to understand; I would like them to understand, but I do not need them to understand. I hardly understand it and I have given it months of thought. For me it is a chance to do something which can feed my soul for the rest of my life.

Death is coming for all of us, and if that doesn't fill you with fear then you are ignoring the fact. We know how we will begin and end: I would just like to give the middle bits a chance to surprise me. The day when we will have to face the crossing will come sooner than we think. I hope my day is many, many years away, but I am not sure if I subscribe to dying in my sleep. I was at my grandfather's deathbed as he did that, grasping big gulps of stale life through his tired lungs, unwilling to let his physical form go.

I do not want to take the greatest leap in life in a vague dream. I want to have the chance to look it in the eye, to say, "You have had me in your sights all your life, but it's on my terms that I come to you." Tibetans believe that one can find enlightenment at the moment of your death, as long as you prepared yourself for it during your life.

I back myself to do the right thing at the right time, but I know that I don't control all of this, and that I will need something extra to make it through. That is the really scary part, because it means surrendering to something I don't even understand: spirituality. I suppose there is a spiritual aspect to this journey that is as much a justification as anything else. I will call it the 'fifth element', some call it luck, chance, providence, divine intervention, God.

Every 'extreme' athlete knows that it is a numbers game, the more times you play, the better your chance of a fatal mistake or an accident. My number will come up, but there is a belief in me that it will not be on this trip.

In preparation I have been spending hours solo paddling, night and day, but more than that I feel my whole life has been preparation for this. Surviving this is about so much more than being able to paddle well. The last few weeks have been filled with calm and peace despite the underlying fear. I have simplified my life to kayaking, meditating and good people. I have tried to make the most of every day; I have taken time to see the sun rise and set.

Someone once said, "In order to make the most of your life you need to know that you are going to die one day." From my own experience I can tell you nothing makes you experience life more to the fullest than if that day has a potential date.

I have had *the best day ever* more times that I can remember. So yes, I believe I am ready to die if that is what is needed to live as I want to.

I look back on my life and I see that it is only in these moments that I have truly lived. My memories seem bigger, more real in these circumstances: the good times, the friends, the hard times, the lows, the awe and wonder I have felt. I know I am here by choice, and am glad I am here. I can be nowhere else.

In between these deep issues, I visualise my next mission. It involves me, a big gun and some croc hunting. The hippos below my camp are huffing and puffing. That and an unrecognisable sound from the bush behind keeps me on edge. I try to sleep but am still high from the day and feeling too vulnerable to close my eyes. I start fantasising about that gun again.

One of the biggest challenges in this place is the continual intensity. Never can you say *I am safe*. Nowhere in this jungle are you at the top of the food chain. I knew it would be like this, but knowing and experiencing are worlds apart.

Across the river a storm is approaching; it is still far off so I watch the lightning display until it fills the sky above me. What started off as a spark in the distance is soon a short circuit of the whole world.

Zipping up my bivy bag I cut myself off from my surroundings, at least symbolically. I fall instantly asleep from sheer exhaustion. During the night I am aware of the rain, of cold water inside the bivy determined to destroy the warmth in my body. A small puddle sneaks around, eventually invading every position. It is a restless night fighting demons in my sleep, but I never fully wake, reality would be scarier. When I feel the approach of dawn, it takes me some minutes to extract myself from my bag, I can't find the zipper and it is with relief that I finally emerge from my cocoon.

I am excited about what lies ahead glad to have made it through the night. It was an exposed time, a sitting snack for anything that likes meat. I made a big fire as some sort of protection, but the rain put an end to that illusion.

Within ten minutes I am back in my boat. I am cold, but feeling good, feeling ready. There is relief from tension in action. It is not long before I am back in the big rapids. The Nile is flowing in one channel again, gathering all its power and rushing at everything in its path.

Scouting only when absolutely needed, I try to build up momentum. Soon I am at the crux of the whitewater, a massive rapid Pete understatedly called "go right" leaving out the "or have a very bad day." The Nile drops over a series of four waterfalls, breath-taking in view, humbling in power, almost certainly un-runnable.

On my last mission we had a croc charge as we tried to make the last eddy before the falls. Then we were five kayakers, drawing courage from each other, we shouted and screamed, meeting its charge head-on. I doubted I would have the same intimidation factor. The eddies seem too small to share with wildlife, but the main flow is not an option. I negotiate the whitewater while scanning 360 degrees for the crocs. Nervous times.

All goes well, I make the last eddy and use the network of hippo trails to re-join the river after the waterfalls. I put in next to a pod, trying hard not to disturb them. I tell them not to worry; that I am only passing through and of my great love and respect for hippos. They seem disturbed nonetheless.

At nine, I stop for chocolate and biltong; I have been going for two hours and have made better time than expected. I am in the biggest rapids of the section. Crashing waves and holes of dismembering power feed inescapable currents. It is essential that I stay out of the main flow.

Since the calm pools and riverbanks are almost as dangerous as the rapids, I try to avoid them also. Running blindly over horizon lines, trusting my memory, I race between mountains of water and the few rocks still defying its power. There is no need to look back. I lose myself totally in the powerful, ever-shifting, roaring world in motion. It is the kind of kayaking you can only do alone. I am moving as fast as my environment, with fear biting at my heels. It is only when I slow down that it catches up properly.

The end is not far now, but the worst is about to come. I enter the crocodile gallery and know that this is make-or-break. This is where we have encountered most of the crocodile charges in the past. The river is at its narrowest and without sufficient whitewater to provide speed, I have to worry about flat dogs on both sides of the river. I feel like a postman on an uphill road knowing the angry dogs are out.

And so it is. The last hours turn into the most intense hours of my life: charge after charge. If I see the armoured green shapes sliding threateningly from the rocky banks I can get away, so I look really hard. I get away from the first two easily, but my unease is growing. I will only have to not see one.

I increase my routine 360 degree turns to check for any incoming, but there is just too much water around to be sure. Stagnant and without speed after a turn, I see it only as an afterthought. Some deep instinct drags my eyes back to where seconds ago they noticed only placid green water. In its place is a crocodile, only fifteen meters away from me, at full charge, closing the almost-irrelevant distance between us. Estimated safety distance for outrunning a croc is thirty meters. It is time for Plan B.

I throw a decoy, in the hope that it would confuse the beast enough to slow it down. I had kept my helmet on my kayak deck for just such an emergency. Every second now is crucial. I lob the helmet at the croc and without looking back to see if it works, I start sprinting. A few seconds later I steal a look, the croc is still coming hard, but it seems I have at least maintained the distance between us. The race is still very much on, but at least it's a race.

From my experience it seems that crocs have a short sprint speed and it must have used most of that to get close to me. It finally gives up the chase. Once safely away, I look back to see it swimming toward my helmet in the distance. Now the concern has become being chased by one croc into another's territory, having to deal with two charges at once.

Therefore during the next few chases, I keep focusing on the bank and river ahead, trying only to glance back every twenty paddle strokes, to see how I was doing with the present issue. I am not sure how much I have to go to take out, but it hardly matters. I bolt through every flat pool. If another croc is going to get close, I want it tired by the time I see it. I finish the last bit of the section in nothing short of an Olympic sprint record.

The last rapid, a one-and-a-half kilometre S-bend work of art which has often in the past troubled us, passes without any problems. Within sight of the takeout, I run into a hippo pod. Less than five hundred meters to go I find myself surrounded by the blubbery anthills. Unable to move forward I sneak out on the bank before they can decide what to do with the stranger in their midst. I carry my kayak past the irritated family, before paddling to take out.

A friend is sitting on the hill overlooking the stretch of water above

Murchison Falls and comes down to greet me with the inevitable, "How was it?" "Fine" is all I can manage.

I feel no relief at being done. I am in shock from the last few hours. For a few minutes I sit alone by the river, trying to decompress, to find some feelings. Nothing comes. There is no joy, there is no sense of accomplishment, not even relief. My brain is unable to make sense of what it has done to itself.

Murchison was a turning point in my life, even if I did not know why at the time. For all the uncertainty about why I did it, I realised that if I could risk my life for something as vague as my hope of *the best day ever*, then there are no excuses real enough to not pursue all things I know I want.

I am still high from the experience that is never far from my thoughts. I have finally impressed myself. After the disappointments of the Nile and the following years of mediocrity, I believe again in the outrageous.

The more I realise what I have done, the more I am looking for a reason. Reasons are important when you keep risking your life for something; not merely as a justification for the risk but as an important answer to life. Normally the joy from an expedition lies in the camaraderie, in the sharing of the experience with friends. Apart from the helmet trick, a nice short story with a happy ending, I find it hard to tell people about the journey. It is as if the telling cheapens the doing. Every time I tell it, it becomes more of a myth.

Above all, this was an expedition of the mind. Everything happened in my world, and only I can make sense of this. I know that I did not enjoy the experience in any conventional way, by any stretch of the imagination. I know that I tempted fate and that I have tested myself to an extreme that I will probably never again willingly approach. I know I am alive when I could have been as easily dead.

I have been in the adventure game long enough to know that someone will always do something harder; that people you know and many you don't know will criticise what is pure and true to you. It matters, but only little. This was my private World Cup. There is no applause, no photos, no medals. Once in my life I went as big as I could imagine, and made it. The thought leaves me feeling powerful.

Does this fact I made it prove that there is a fifth element? If only it did, but there are always so many other more rational explanations that the doubting mind grabs hold of. I doubt myself because I do not want to invent a God just because I need to believe that there is more to this than I can see. I need to believe there is magic out there and will pursue any sign of it, but I am weary of self-deception.

Belief is mental but for me it also needs to be physical. It has to be lived, to have any chance of soothing the soul, of proving that we can do things that are bigger than ourselves, that we are part of something bigger than ourselves. I needed to walk through a minefield to feel protected.

Perhaps reason has no place out there, or that reason is what I hoped to leave behind. Perhaps I was right when I said before the Nile trip that, going on a journey that will put your life at risk is not a decision made by the mind. Reason does not support it. Besides what could be more ironic than dying when you feel most alive?

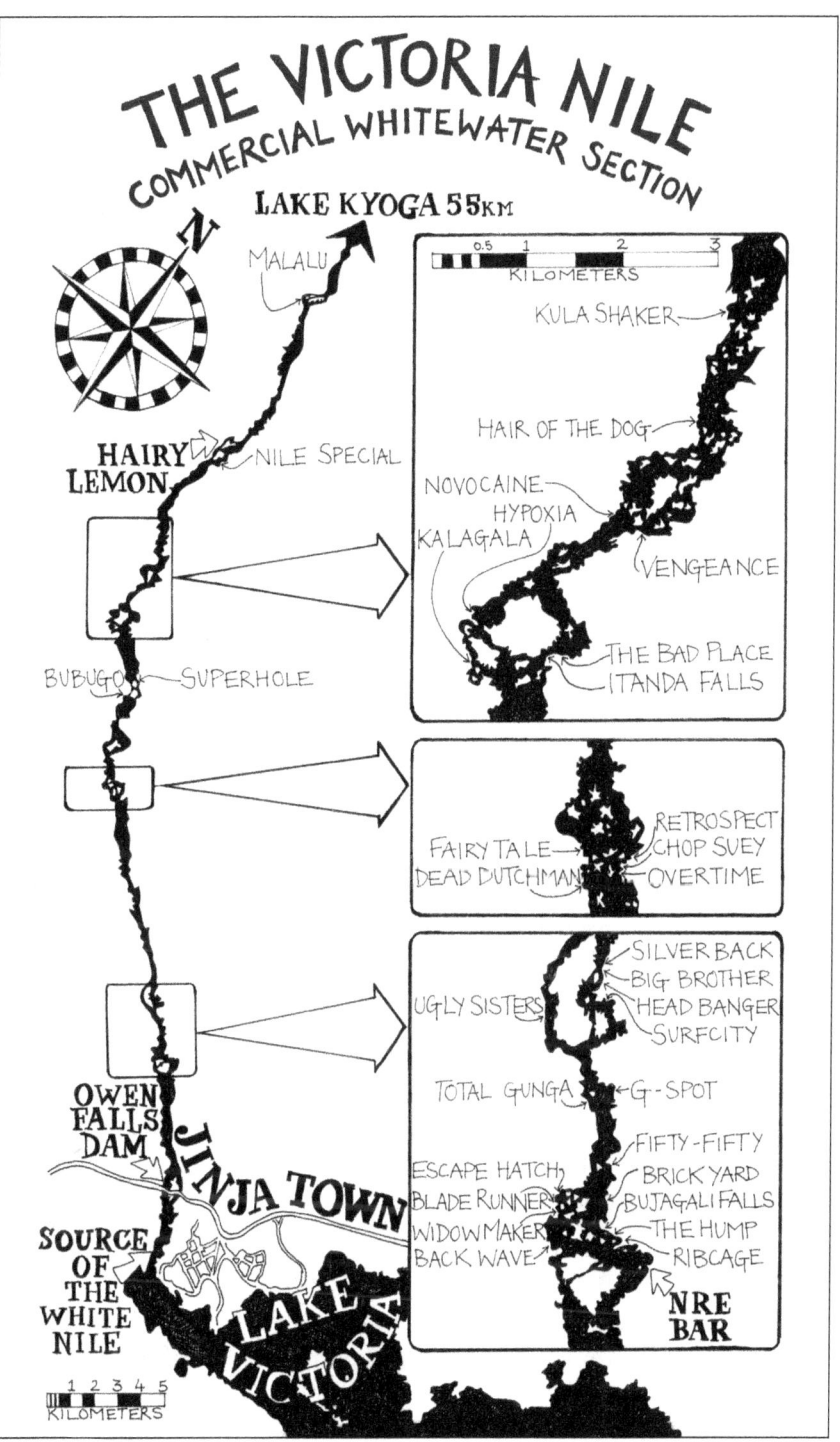

GANGSTER

Soul Growth

Rebellious heart, in the grip of fate,
Have patience, wait!
Calm you and attend to the great wind's blowing,
Bearing winged seed to your hands for the sowing.
Drive deep the plow of sorrow and pain,
Turn up rich soil for the golden grain,
Spare not the tears: they are needed as rain;
Too long, too long has the field lain fallow,
Now well prepared and no longer shallow.
Please God, a soul is growing!

—Annerika Fries

In Over My Head

Uganda, 2008

For nearly two years my little life in Norway was fine. My job as a social worker turned out to be not as fulfilling as I had hoped, but it left me with lots of time to run in the mountains. I was making a decent salary, lived in a house, and had a car for the first time as an adult. It was all going rather well until – I had another idea.

The project I worked for was funded with the purpose of giving the hopeless youngsters as much quality of life as possible, a best day ever for the spiritually handicapped. The only way I knew how to live *the best day ever* was on an expedition, so I worked out a budget for a trip to South Sudan and got the Norwegian Government to fund it. I love the Norwegian social system.

It's not home, but as close as it gets. I would know where I was even with my eyes closed. After the mountains of Norway, the African sky seems even bigger than I remember. The smell of the air is comforting as I step from the airplane. Like a favourite old pair of jeans, the humidity fits perfectly around my skin. Like a river, a chain of linked events, has again washed me up on the lush shores of Lake Victoria. My life has taken one of those sudden, yet gentle and beautiful turns, that allow me to believe in destiny. Ahead lies a mission I could not have imagined a year ago.

Squeezed between some of Africa's baddest boys, Sudan, Democratic Republic of the Congo and Rwanda, Uganda does not have the same fearsome reputation as its neighbours. It is here that I have had my greatest moments and some of my worst, experienced the extremes of dreams broken and dreams achieved, evaded catastrophe by a second and been that second too slow. Here I walked hard miles toward becoming a man. If you can't find adventure here, you don't deserve it. It's a place where anything can and often does happen. Never have I landed here and not felt this tingle of anticipation in my stomach.

It's a challenge that brought me back, this one so unforeseen that I grin at the irony. The gods are having a laugh, and again it's at my expense. Uganda has always represented freedom to me, a place where I needed no one, where I could do whatever I wanted. This time it will be all about responsibility: the world's most reluctant babysitter becomes a parent. Somehow in the last six months I had acquired a rebellious teenager. As his social worker I thought it would do him good to see what problems really look like.

I think of it as, 'I am not OK, you are not OK, but some people are really fucked' therapy; a legitimate mission to the experience-frontier. The only person in deeper over his head than me is the skinny, pale rebel behind me, trying his best to look like he steps off planes in Africa every day. It brings another little smile to my wannabe bearded lips.

Just remember this is what you asked for. I mutter to myself as I walk towards the new and improved airport building. Inside, the continent's standard issue yellow paint falsely labelled 'khaki' instead of 'African airport,' has been replaced by a much more high-maintenance cream colour. The tacky safari wildlife paintings have made way for working TV screens. Old health warnings that remind me to "wash my hands after going to the toilet" and "abstain from sex" have been substituted for cell-phone ads showing attractive young people fulfilling their dreams over the phone. The visa office even has change for my British pounds. The West is getting a foothold in Uganda. I am not worried. The wheels will come off soon enough.

Thomas is there to pick us up. Danish, he came to Africa for a short contract eight years ago. Like the rest of us, he still wonders why he is here sometimes, but has made peace with the fact that it is too late to go back to the safety of the womb. In his new life he has a wonderful wife, a healthy son and it would seem everything else a man might desire.

The official 'voice of reason' for the expedition, Thomas is a man who has been in the picture for most of my decade-long love affair with Uganda. From the early days when I lived on his couch for months at a time, we have seen each other grow through different life stages. Our friendship is based on a mutual respect for each other's stubbornness.

The van is covered with his company's logo, advertising safe and comfortable sightseeing tours in Kampala. Tours that allow plump white flesh to sit safely behind the tinted one-way glass and stare without being stared at. I briefly wonder why you would bother leaving home if you wanted safe and comfortable. To each his own. Personally, I am all for risky and uncomfortable over the next month. One look at the twinkle in Thomas's clear blue eyes tells me the bus is heading in that direction

For our first exercise in unsafe, we have to make it home to fight another day. The freak show called traffic plays out on a stage and we are also actors. The oncoming traffic in our lane is as natural as the piles of green bananas, oversized grey bags of charcoal and beer crates that huddle around the rickety wooden shacks and brown freckled brick structures that funnel the chaos. We weave through traffic abiding by the only traffic rule there is: *Don't assume anything.* It is a system that can only be understood once you stop looking for a deeper order. This abandonment of logic is useful since most of the people who do have driving licenses, bought them. I know, it's how I got mine.

For my driving test, I drove past a fence post resembling Roman lettering and up to a square building fading away peacefully under the shade of a large tree. Inside an obese man was reclining behind a desk littered with receipt books, swollen with moisture and cracked open like overripe fruit. We greeted one another, and I explained I needed a license.

He leaned back in his chair; raised it on its hind legs and pointed at a grubby pamphlet of road signs half pasted to the wall. He tapped at different signs with a short stick. An identification game, I see. After I got the first three right he grinned and nodded. I failed the next two. From his sad smile I suspected he was using me to try and find out what they meant. Since Uganda has few road signs apart from road blocks marked with tree branches lain across the road and real men with guns, he decided three out of five would do.

Changing the angle of his chair without moving his body, he closed back in on the desk and proceeded to write me a license. Unable to help it, I grinned and asked him if I would not be required to drive as part of the exam. He looked up at me perplexed at why he had to explain himself, "Ahh, but you drove here."

On these roads the actors are all stuntmen. Cars overtake on blind rises, overloaded trucks stop where they die, and motorbikes carry whole families. Bicycles are loaded with anything from pigs to double beds and driven by kids too short to reach the pedals. Right-of-way is awarded according to size. Pedestrians have only slightly more rights than cats and dogs, and decidedly fewer than cattle.

Women bent under bundles of wood, scamper alongside chickens, goats, and cows, all partaking in the death-defying trick of crossing the road. Indicators are used in a secret code, best to be ignored completely. God help the vehicle attempting this course without a horn.

My little gangster rebel from Norway tightens his grip on the upholstery. He is thinking what everyone thinks the first time they see this: the whole scene should implode on itself in a huge crashing heap. To be fair, often it does.

Too Old And Fat

> *An expedition... is a reflection of life, reduced to its simplest form. Staying alive, having something to eat, a place to sleep. Trying to keep dry, trying to keep warm. Excitement, extreme happiness, challenge, danger, camaraderie, sometimes sadness, loss. It's a basic, yet complete way of life.*
>
> —Celliers Kruger

I bend over the raft to wet my hands. A little habit I have developed through the years before dropping into the big stuff. The bigger the rapid the bigger the splash; later in the day I would be taking a small shower. For now a splash will do.

It's *Silverback*, one of my all-time favourite rapids. What makes it so distinct is the view. As you glide through the event horizon there is plenty of time to be impressed by the sheer magnitude of what you are about to crash into many meters below. You will soon pick up speed on the smooth green slope. To play it safe you have to move aggressively left or take your chances with the crashing wave that owns the centre; it swings vicious punches at anything in its vicinity. As it happens, centre is exactly where I plan on taking Gangster.

It's a gamble, this is his first time on a real river. If he falls out here, probability is high, it's going to be hard to get him back on the river. We are not here for haircuts, so I decide it's time to test his mettle.

"Get down, hold on." The wave connects, sending Gangster flying. Skinny jean-clad pins spread-eagle over his curly head. He is a tough little bugger, and to his credit he still has a hand on the raft.

Unfortunately for him, things are about to deteriorate further. Making it upright through the first wave is only a rite of passage to face the Silverback: the bad-tempered, baby-eating, cocaine-sniffing, alpha male of commercially-rafted crashing waves.

Experience has given me the gift of detachment while my body does what is necessary. I notice Gangster's facial expression as we crest the last wave before impact. It says, "I don't know what's happening but I think its bad." I feel a little pity as I square the raft into the inevitable ass-kicking he is about to receive.

As the raft is swallowed, he is unceremoniously ripped off the side. It's basic maths from there on. Fifty meters down, he pops up and is washed into a safety kayaker like a bug on a windscreen. It's a man-sized swim, and dragging him back into the boat I am ready to play a Jedi mind trick I learned back in the USA. A rebel yell and a high-five before they get their focus back and you can convince a terrified client that they actually enjoyed the experience. It is not necessary. He gets back in with precisely the smile I was hoping for, the corners of his mouth inches from terror but still pointing in the right direction. He is shaken but not destroyed.

Midday, on the flat pool after lunch, the world is moving like it's stuck in quicksand and too hot to care about it. With soft Scandinavian skin sizzling in the heat, smarter people would be hiding in the shade. It's all just about perfect. As I reach into my dry bag for one of the cheap cigarettes I have been terrorising my lungs with, my phone rings. Imagine! Okay, *nobody panic*, so what if there is reception on the Nile? I calmly press green on the little buzzing box.

"Hi, Thomas." From there the conversation progresses to "Mmmhhhh, that's not so good. Okay, get back to me when you know more. There has to be a way around this."

Thomas has been attending 'Sudanese Bureaucracy 101' at the embassy. It is a fast lesson for a slow course. Seeing their shock and lack of comprehension at someone wanting to go to Sudan as a tourist, he changed his angle of attack to business visa: a safer path with more established guidelines. It gets the wheels moving again, only to lead him to the next little bombshell they forgot to mention a month ago on the phone: the Government of Sudan has no sense of humour. Apparently the Sudanese are still upset about the cartoon of Muhammad printed in a Danish newspaper in 2005 and have banned all Danish people from coming to Sudan. Thomas must be the first Danish national to actually care.

It's been a great day. Any responsible adult would be calling it quits right now, but I am not really listening. Instead of following the other rafts I am rowing my empty raft in the opposite direction. The voice doesn't seem to mind being ignored. *What are you trying to prove?* Still no answer. Unperturbed it continues to state its case, "You are overweight, unfit and rusty...oh and did I mention you haven't seen Itanda Falls for eighteen months?" *Blah blah blah.* "Too many cigarettes, you won't last ten seconds without air." *Blah blah blah.* I let him ramble on. Perhaps he has a point? *No, he doesn't, shut up and row!*

It is no use getting into an argument with yourself, especially when you know you're right. The voice and I have played this game a hundred times and paddled across the flat pool to Itanda. I know the price for failure. A few years ago it cost me a hairline crack in the base of my skull, allowing brain fluid to leak out of my ears. It's not the most difficult rapid on the Nile, but it is a distinct symbol of power on the world's longest river. Today I will be dangerously close to overstepping its boundaries. I feel a gut-wrenching fear that almost makes me vomit. It threatens to shut my brain down.

Why take the risk? I might know the answer but can't remember it, so I just keep leaning on the oars for no good reason. At some point, while crossing the pool, I find a sense of peace. I convince myself that it is fitting I try this, even if it is a little outrageous.

I speak to the rapid asking for an indulgence for old time's sake, I even imagine it can hear me. If only I could see my fish eagle. I look hopefully at the trees but there is no sign of my powerful *totem*. It would have been a bit too much to ask for. I speak out loud, like I do when alone and pretend not to be scared.

I slip into the narrow jungle channel that will eventually bring me to the top of Itanda, my eyes are drawn to the left. Sitting in the water barely twenty meters from me, close enough to see the black tip on its crooked yellow beak, is the largest fish eagle I have ever seen. Its white crown marks it as royalty, as surely as the arrogance with which its gazes down on the world. I stop moving; flowing past, we look silently at each other.

It could be a coincidence that I see my totem before this test, but I have lost count of the times it has worked this way. Besides, when you're scared, you take what you can get. All doubt is gone now, I smile and nod my thanks. Not thanks to the Nile for allowing me to get away with all my foolish games, but for allowing me to believe in magic. Gratitude for supplying a canvas on which I can paint life and watch with surprise as it unfolds – for helping me to look at life with wonder – a point of view for things I don't understand instead of bitterness at the things I do.

I drag my eyes from the thin misty veil that hangs over the roaring finality of the horizon and dunk the helmet filled with water over my head, with it thought and doubt are washed away. It is unfortunate that the best part of me is unconscious, and that to be truly at peace I have to stop thinking and just be. It is fortunate there are places like this to facilitate the process.

In the thick of it, it's just like old times. The roar of the water becomes the soundtrack to a movie I watch of myself. Things happen fast, move in slow motion and are over too quickly. You either make this rapid look easy or painful; today it is easy. With a last pull I bend the oars to slip out of harm's way. A moment's realisation of what I have done, I let go of the thick wooden oars and float out the run.

The sun has softened, letting light and shade achieve symbiosis in colour. The roar of the water is still keeping out the other world, and the river reflects enough beauty to stun me into time and space. I would not trade my life for anyone's. If perfection is unattainable, then this is a glimpse not worth a bit of risk. Maybe that was the answer I couldn't remember earlier?

Older, fatter, it's all true, but you can kiss my ass, I haven't even peaked yet. I grin broadly at no one as I glide into calmer water. It's good to be back.

If anywhere can wake Gangster up to the fact that life is what you make of it, it will be here. His problem is not the alcohol, the violence or the drugs. They are merely symptoms; ways with which he is trying to start a fire inside himself. All it does is starts fires around him, leaving him colder and more isolated from a life he just can't seem to get going. If he refuses to move because it might not save him, he will die from old age where he stands, scared, bitter, shrivelled and scarred by things that never happened.

He has character and intelligence to spare, what he lacks is motivation. He is rebelling against a world he does not think is fair. I can't change his mind; I think he happens to be right. We all pretend to have it figured out, trying to convince others and ourselves that we know the answers when most of us are equally clueless. I arrived here a confident young man who had been traveling for years, with no idea that I still had no idea. Sometimes it seems I might grow old enough to realise everything I once believed was wrong.

I was born in apartheid South Africa and never questioned the fact. I grew up in a middle-class family and had the same middle-class worries as most other kids: parents, girls, looking cool. When I was twenty-two I read a book called *My Traitors Heart* by Rian Malan. I realised for the first time what my father had been part of, what I had been part of. The realisation that everyone could be wrong has never left me. Even if life is fair to us, it's terrifying to think you could do everything right and still lose. For many in Africa, reality resembles a vendetta from the Old Testament.

It takes a force stronger than fear to overcome paralysis. Meaning can come in many forms – passion, love, work or plain stubbornness – take your pick. This is life, and the only real choice we have is to live it, even if we don't understand or like the rules. The good news is that interpretation is entirely up to us, which at least theoretically makes us God.

Never before has a generation been granted so much choice. We are *free* to pursue any goal, but success is portrayed as physical beauty, money and fame; these, in turn, are supposed to lead to happiness. Any other outcome is seen as a failure. Society's script might destroy a few funny-looking and sensitive teenagers like Gangster, but it will keep the rest of us in line. Gangster would be the first to say this out loud. But, having the confidence to totally believe the world is wrong, rather than yourself, is normally reserved for the mentally insane.

Gangster needs a personal reason to generate the enthusiasm necessary to fight the demons he has inside. For me it came in the form of passion for one of the greatest rivers on the planet: the Nile. Surrounded by a good group of like-minded people, we lived in the moment, good or bad, and greedily drank it all up. I lived a life I could never have imagined when I was kicking and screaming at Gangster's age. Some good role models showed me that life did not have to be a path defined by others. The only requirement is that you go after it with everything you have. We are about to go on a trip to South Sudan at the expense of the Norwegian Government to prove it.

I can't show him the exact way because I have not found it yet. I can't tell him not to be too serious. I can't tell him it will be okay because there is no way of knowing. All I can show him is that he is free to search for an answer, whether he finds it or not. Like trial and error, we can test our answers, discard the wrong ones and keep searching for right ones. Often we return to the same lessons. Possession of this power at the very least brings us *hope*. I brought Gangster here in the hope that I could show him that life can be lived on your own terms if you stop being so scared of it. No one gets out alive anyway.

Normality

Walking past our campsite, you can pick them by their fresh faces. They treat life like everything can be cured with enthusiasm and prayer. Crisp clean crusaders for God. Everything is a simple matter of good versus evil, and they know the difference. I am jealous, it's the kind of certainty I would love but can't ever imagine having.

In their own way they are no less freaks than my own group, their intentions are just more noble. I have known too many men and women better than me who play instruments in that band to dismiss them as simply idealistic. Still, as a group they make me itch. Give me an obviously-flawed person any day.

I look back at my own group of misfits. The missionaries' neat lines provide the perfect contrast to our rough edges. We walk around shirtless, tattoos showing, calling each other cunts to our unshaven tanned faces. Exhibit A, Reuben walks past. Maori tattoos ink-dark lines cover his body and even the fisherman's beard can't hide the fact that he is rock-and-roll. I have known him for years, and there is no dodgy dive in the world where he would not blend in. Yet under that lies a heart pure enough to get him into anyone's heaven. You would have to search a long time to find a funnier, kinder soul with more zest for life than Reuben.

And then there is Joe. Our friendship has an unlikely history which started with me saying: "I don't mean to be rude, but you're too fat, go ask the other guide." He seemed to take the news well. Luckily, he really is a big boy and isn't fat. I was told that if I showed up for work I would be taking a five-foot brunette down the river in my tandem kayak.

An hour later as I am standing by the river, he walks back to me still smiling. I relent. This should be a good challenge. "Hop in, big boy."

My safety talk is brief and to the point. "You are too heavy for this activity and chances are we are going to spend a lot of time underwater. Do what I tell you and don't panic. This is going to be a big day, ready?" His smile grows a few inches, "What can possibly go wrong?" He replies with a slow-burning excitement that never seems to leave.

The next time we met was in Ethiopia; I sent him an email:

> Hi Joe,
> I am not sure if this is the right email, but if it is, I am going on an expedition in two months, it might be something you would be interested in.
> Best,
> H

His reply was as short:

> Hi H,
> Sounds good, I am in, when should I be where?
> Best,
> Joe

Normally I don't like nice guys, we have nothing in common. Joe is as nice as they come. The thing that saves him is that he believes, secretly, that he is a wild man. This might be true, but he is still the nicest 'wildman' I know.

On our first day in the Blue Nile gorge in Ethiopia, I flipped the raft. It was as good a wipeout as you can walk away from, the raft frame was stripped beyond repair and the camera man had to go home with a hole in his leg. It was not an excellent start to the best trip ever. Our relationship up to then was built on one day of tandem kayaking followed by a big night in the bar. I was not sure what he would make of this.

Joe found it all exhilarating. For the next two weeks we paddled a loaded gear boat with the only two paddles left through unseasonably high water in Africa's deepest gorge. It was a proper experience that would have tested any skilled raft guide. Joe's job as mechanical engineer in the UK turns out to be only a front; he is actually a heavy weight Tin Tin.

The last email I sent him, read: *Interested in going to Sudan?*

I am happy with my team. I chose this them with care. Thomas says it's because I can control them all. It's not the whole picture. As a leader it's my job to be able to guide the team, especially with Gangster here I can't afford for things to slip. It's not because they are weak; far from it. Other people's weaknesses annoy me only slightly less than my own.

The first thing I looked for when I chose this team was mutual trust and respect. Trust can be formed on a trip, but it needs a base built on respect. A production line engineer who designs water-cooling systems, a rock-and-roll raft guide joker and a telecommunications project manager. Their day jobs don't define them, but these are good skills to bring to our undertaking. That, and they have enthusiasm, possibly the greatest asset to any expedition. It's contagious and powerful.

They might not be the obvious role models for Gangster but all of us, apart from seemingly Joe, have our own demons and have fought them. None of us have been victorious. We know that cosmetics don't make the man. My father used to say, "Be careful of the man who looks the part; he is normally trying to look the part." Some people might be born squeaky clean, but for the rest of us we can only try to be as good as our deviant selves will allow. I figured Gangster might be more inclined to listen to these guys, who for all their faults, are golden where it matters.

EARLY DAYS OF NOTE

HENDRI WITH HIS FATHER AND SISTER

A YOUNG EXPLORER (LEFT) HENDRI WITH HIS MOTHER (RIGHT)

TARZAN

SELECTION FOR 7 MEDICAL CYCLE BATTALION GROUP.
BLOEMFONTIEN, SA

EARLY DAYS ON THE ZAMBEZI WITH THE FAMILY

ZAMBEZI RAPID #9 LEFT LINE

THE NILE

MADDY AND HENDRI SPINNING FIRE

HENDRI WITH HIS BEST FRIEND PETE

LIFE AND ACTION ON THE NILE - MURCHISON SECTION

THE KARUMA BRIDGE RAPID (LEFT) A FLIP ON THE PERFECT STORM (RIGHT)

EXPEDITION MORNING COMMUNICATIONS. LAKE KYOGA, UGANDA

THE LAST STOP IN THE SOUTH ON THE FRONT LINES OF SUDAN

LIFE IN THE LIMELIGHT

NEGOTIATING SAFE PASSAGE THROUGH CONFLICT ZONES. NIMULE, SOUTH SUDAN

THE NILE SOURCE TO SEA EXPEDITION TEAM

THE MEDITERRANEAN SEA. ROSETTA, EGYPT - 4620 MILES LATER

MURCHISON SOLO

MURCHISON SOLO. BEFORE - AFTER

THE MATRIX WAVE (LEFT) HENDRI WRITING IN HIS JOURNAL (RIGHT)

GANGSTER

RELAXING ON THE FLAT WATER

HAND PADDLING ON THE NILE

WATCHING THE BEGINNING OF THE BEST DAY EVER

TACKLING THE FIRST RAPID IN SOUTH SUDAN: FOLA FALLS

A WALK

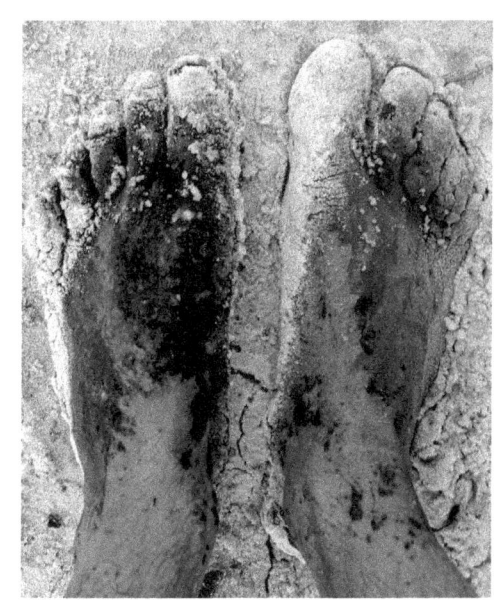

SELF PORTRAITS FROM THE SWAHILI COAST

CONGO SOLO

TREKKING IN TL2 FOR BONOBO CONSERVATION

LIFE ON THE CONGO RIVER BARGE.
KISANGANI - KINSHASA

HENDRI ASSISTS RESEARCH BY FITTING HIS KAYAK WITH A DEPTH SONAR DEVICE

HAND PADDLING THE KINSUKA RAPIDS, KINSHASA

THE GREAT WHITE EXPLORER

MURCHISON FALLS NATIONAL PARK, UGANDA (LEFT) LUKUGA RIVER, DRC (RIGHT)

THE GREAT LAKES EXPEDITION IN THE RWENZORI MOUNTAINS, UGANDA

MEDITATING ON A BARGE CROSSING LAKE TANGANYIKA

HENDRI'S COMMEMORATIVE PYRE BURNS IN THE SUNSET BEFORE DISAPPEARING DOWN ITANDA FALLS, UGANDA

Carl Jung had a hunch that what passed for normality often was the very force which shattered the personality of the patient. That trying to be 'normal', when it violates our inner nature, is itself a form of pathology. He believed that everyone has a shadow side: the side of our personality that we do not consciously display in public. The shadow may have positive or negative qualities. If it remains unconscious, the shadow is often projected onto other individuals or groups.

He goes on to say: "Filling the conscious mind with ideal conceptions is a characteristic of Western theosophy, but not the confrontation with the Shadow and the world of darkness. One does not become enlightened by imagining figures of light, but by making the darkness conscious. The latter procedure, however, is disagreeable and therefore not popular."

BRAVADO

"*Ogambaki nyabo?*" are my first words to the police officer.

I am not sure if I have the local greeting correct, but with languages, as with most things in life, I figure you get bonus points for trying.

"Ehh, *njebale-ko*." She replies. There is no smile. I know I am on the right track when she continues, "Do you have citizenship?"

The longer we can stay away from the topic of the overloaded roof racks, the better the chances are of avoiding the issue.

"No, *nyabo*, I am looking to marry, would you like a *muzungu?*"

"Ah, but I am taken."

"Ah, this is a problem. You have a sister?"

"I have, she is there."

"Is she beautiful?"

"Like me."

"Awww." We slap hands as the deal is agreed.

"You bring."

No bribe, instead a fair trade, paid in conversation and humour, two things Ugandans appreciate more than any other nation I have come across. No matter where you are, you can spark up a conversation and expect to have a laugh. A gas-station attendant will ask for your car or possibly your girlfriend, rather than die wondering.

As a people they stand for the best in what Africa can teach the world: the gift of having little, striving for more, but never too busy for a laugh and a chat with a stranger or friend. This place is merely amused by our Western obsession to master time, like watching a dog chasing its tail. Ugandans own time by doing the opposite. Time is priceless and Ugandans know how to make time; still, they think we are the rich ones.

On our way to the next section of the Nile, we are stopped twice more for no other apparent reason than to chat nonsense. Obama has been elected, Bush is out, and the world is a better place. The fact that he is replaced with a black man, half Kenyan, seems too good to be true. It's as if his election has validated the whole continent. Kenya has declared a national holiday, and Ugandans are stopping white people in the street to tell them the news.

We can't sweet-talk the roof racks, though; eventually gravity gets the better of them, tearing the roof open so that no amount of black rubber or duct tape is going to stop our gear from ending up on the road.

Not by coincidence, this happens on the only forty-kilometre section of new road. It is wide enough for all road users, without a pothole to blemish its crisp-lain surface. You would expect this to be a nice change from the narrow crumbling lanes that lead up to it. You would be mistaken. To keep it new, it is protected by speed bumps every thirty meters. They are built up so high that forty-five degree angle approaches are the only way to clear them without scraping the bottom of your vehicle. Traffic moves in and around each other from opposite directions in a helix formation more common to an ant colony.

It would be ludicrous anywhere else in the world, but here it is merely a lot of speed bumps creating a uniquely African traffic pattern. We spend the time playing that favourite Western gazing game called, 'what on earth could they have been thinking?' We eventually crawl into the next brightly-coloured cell-phone branded town. The roof racks are still attached, if only barely.

The gas station attendant has the answer to our problem and three minutes later a pick-up truck appears. It's seen better days but the wheels are still generally pointing in the right direction. Negotiations begin. We baffle the driver with our clever calculations and undeniable logic; he strikes back using emotion and pity. We meet half way. The price is more than a local would pay, but white-man tax is as certain as a Catholic Pope.

The team will follow behind, while I go in front with the gear and the new driver Godfrey, or "God" as he likes to be called. Who wouldn't?

Tarmac turns to dirt and eventually to mud. I can't see the boys anymore, suspecting they fell back to avoid dust, but noting their absence I enquire from God if this is indeed the way to Murchison Falls. "It is the one," he replies. "You're the expert," I think as I switch my concentration back to bracing myself in the seat, attempting to minimise airtime. The tyres are bald, the suspension shot and we have yet to try the brakes. God isn't risking getting stuck in the mud by slowing down.

Still no sign of the boys, and it's just not feeling right. God has no doubts through, I'm just being paranoid. Besides it has been years since I have been on this road and never in this direction; who I am to question God?

An hour later we stop at the lodge that marks the end of the park, one hour in the opposite direction of where we should be. I start the verbal abuse that God deserves, but halfway I realise it is ineffectual. I go for a beer at the lodge instead.

We have been at Murchison Falls for two days already and it's time for us to get on the river for a proper expedition. Gangster has started to become more involved, but as can be expected he still keeps to himself. Transported from a small industrial town in Norway to being surrounded by ruffians in Uganda would be a big step for anyone.

He is unbelievably inconsistent. From night to night his views change. His mental constructs are built on so much faulty logic that trying to fix one piece endangers the whole rickety structure. To do repairs you have to work on the whole system, an impossible undertaking without his surrender.

The task for the morning is to carry all our gear to the bottom of the falls. Charged up by the energy of the whitewater and the coming adventures below them, I throw the first load on my shoulders as light sneaks over the hill. I make just enough noise to make the others, still lying in their sleeping bags, aware I have started. I chuckle at the thought that they are probably swearing at me from under their mozzie nets. Hard manual labour before breakfast, out of choice, is an action as rewarding as any other. It is however not an opinion shared by all.

I am still playing strong man when a few eager hands arrive looking for porter work; they find it. I am immediately put to shame with the heavy loads they carry, shattering any illusions that I was being tough.

By midday the boats and gear are ready to be loaded. Dehydration is a whirlpool draining my energy and stirring my temper. It is impossible to drink enough while doing physical work at this hour; every move is washed in sweat, and every thought sticky with fatigue.

I need a scapegoat for my irrational, simmering anger and Gangster supplies it. He is not working hard enough. He is not behaving like I want him to. His actions are a ladder for my temper. I know I am probably making a big deal out of nothing, so I bite my lip to stay quiet, straining to see the situation from outside my hot head.

Eventually we are all on board and push onto the confused, foaming water below the falls. The current tries to establish some structure again after its traumatic experience in the Murchison gap. Like my own temper, the water has no reason to be angry; like me, all it needs is to be on the move again. Time will be sufficient for both of us.

We travel less than five minutes when we pass two crocodiles on a small island. At the sight of these creatures, motionless as statues, mouths open to reveal triangular teeth, suddenly I can't remember why I was angry. Ahead stretches wilderness and adventure, places and times so real that they will strip away the complications of excess, at least for a few weeks.

Already I feel lighter. We see all the usual suspects: buffalo, elephant, giraffe, and warthogs. Gangster's 'too cool for school' attitude is temporarily forgotten. Unable to hide his delight, he yells out the name of every new animal he sees for the first time in the flesh. If the boy had ever dreamed of Africa, his dreams have just come true.

Bordered by Congo and Sudan, this whole area has that 'monster under the bed' feeling. Everything looks peaceful, but with a premonition that things could go wrong when the lights go out. We are deep in the delta; soon we will be in Lake Albert. The Blue Mountains of the Congo are on the horizon. They look sufficiently hazy and mysterious as to mark the most troubled region known as 'the deepest and darkest' of Africa. Unfortunately we don't have time to dwell on imaginary dangers, something more pressing is staring us in the face from tiny pink nostrils located high on their square jaws.

The channels are becoming uncomfortably narrow, forcing us closer to the hippos, a situation neither species enjoys. I have passed within a stone's throw of thousands of hippos in my life and they have never given me any trouble; I really would like to keep it that way. I sneak left, then right, as each new obstacle appears. Eventually there is nowhere to go, a pod is spread across the river like a fishing net.

I continue to go forward not out of bravado but because we are fenced in by papyrus banks. My cunning plan to get us out of this traffic jam hasn't come to me yet but if I slow down a bit, maybe it will.

As I lightly push towards the left bank, sweat trickles down my back. The hairs on my arms react to the electricity in the air, my grip tightens on the sweat-polished wooden handles of the oars. I reflect briefly on how fear affects my memory. Right now I can't seem to recall why I do what I do, and if I had remembered earlier how much I dislike being this close to hippos, I would never have come.

The next move is up to the hippos. A few bulls on my right grunt in protest. To avoid them I take us towards a mother and her baby. I am hoping they will want to join up with the main pod at river right; we are all reasonable adults after all.

Eyes are expressionlessly set on me, she seems a bit indecisive herself. It's an uncomfortable situation as neither of us can conjure the appropriate response. Almost on top of them now, the mother is still standing her ground. The baby looks very un-cute popping its head up; this does nothing to ease my worries.

I glance hopefully at the game ranger and his AK-47. He seems calm as a Hindu cow.

"Sir, please keep your gun ready, if this is going to go wrong it will do so quickly."

"Joe, Gangster, get down, if he has to shoot then you want to be out of the way."

Ranger: "Do not fear, they will run, just go."

"My friend, we are not on the big park boat, they can eat us."

Ranger: "Just go."

The truth is I am afraid, and I am not above firing a warning shot to prove it. I would prefer not to run over a mother and baby. The burden of choice is taken away. Pushed by the fast-flowing current, we run out of options. I hold my breath to focus all Jedi powers on a happy outcome as we head straight for where mom submerged just a few seconds ago.

I wish I could say that as I entrusted our boat's destiny to the universe I felt complete calm, but that would be a lie. Long seconds later we leave behind the line of hippos still stretched out across the river. The mother pops up for a disgusted snort at the rudeness of it all before returning to her midday nap. Feeling brave all of a sudden, I tell her where to stick it.

It is the last obstacle before the river opens up into Lake Albert. Fear turns to elation so quickly I am reminded that they are the same chemical cocktail. Low hills cup the lake, its shimmering surface dotted with floating papyrus. Some fishermen paddle up to sell us overpriced fish, but one look at them and I don't feel like arguing. The sun has burnt their black skins to ash; their bodies are as rundown as the grass huts that line the shore. There is no joy in their eyes, for them life is one long struggle to put food on the table with too many mouths to feed.

We drop off our rangers with a few shillings and some fresh fish as a tip. We think about camping near the ranger station but decide against it in the face of some stellar logic from Joe. "The rangers might come back, they might have rules. We don't like rules. Those are the rules."

A gap between two hippo pods allows us access to a sandy beach. We prepare camp in the happy, haphazard way that marks the first few nights of a mission. It's a process where you need everything and no one knows where anything is. We are caught off guard by the storm that we have seen approaching for hours. The fillet steaks burn as we huddle under the smoky tarp that covers the fire.

After the storm, Gangster and I sit on the rafts. The stars defying earth's gravity leave plenty of space for contemplating big issues while the river flowing past our feet smooths and softens ideas. Something he said a few nights ago has been sticking in my mind. He felt he wasn't free. As if it was his right to be free. There are many kinds of freedom, none are free. I have spent my life chasing that dream. Not even God is free: He can do what He wants but he has to run the world. At best it is a process, hard-won through sacrifice, in pieces that can just as easily be lost. In the end, the only real freedom is from your own needs and expectations.

Freedom requires the sacrifice and surrender of everything at least at a symbolic level. Understandably it can be a heavy burden and a lonely road. Many search for freedom, but once they come close enough to grasp the depths and scope of the loneliness they have to cross to achieve it, few have the will or desire to take the last committing steps across a barrier of no return.

This is not what Gangster wants to hear. He sees freedom as waking up and doing what he wants instead of what he has to. He doesn't realise that he is already a master at this, and that is the very reason he is so unhappy.

I talk, but does he listen? Would I have, if our roles were reversed? Probably not, I don't even listen to myself. Even when I know what the path looks like, I still struggle to follow it. I have walked the path, but inevitably I have gotten lost or side-tracked. What is this human drive to sabotage ourselves? Are we simply not yet ready to be free?

The closer I come to the end of a two-hour rowing stint the less I want to stop. Somewhere in the shift I become an extension of those oars, and by definition the water over which I am gliding. My entire body moves the boat, its rhythm and power, a non-violent martial art. The cool night air combines perfectly with warm sweat. What began as a strenuous exercise evolves into meditation, only more manly.

In the silence the voices of the night are expressed with increasing clarity. First the soft lick of the wooden blades break the surface tension, then the gentle rush of current against the hull of the raft, later the faint drip from the oars as they swing forward over the mirrored, moonlight surface. Their hushed tones of simplicity calms endless thoughts until one stroke becomes all strokes and all strokes become one. It sets your mind free to wander where it may please, often finding no reason to wander at all.

Ahead of us lies two hundred kilometres of some of the flattest water in the world through one of the hottest areas on earth. Throw in some pesky LRA terrorists and it's no coincidence we are doing night shifts. I would have kept the oars for another hour, but there is no denying Joe his time on the sticks. It's dangerous to scratch your nose with him around. Like an alarm clock, he wakes exactly at the start of his shift.

Any break in the rhythm of the oars and he will offer to take over, pretending to do you a favour. I give up my position and sit back to enjoy the peace that comes along with full-body tiredness, leaning against a dry bag, staring into the darkness. As a welcome to Joe, thunder crashes in the distance, the full moon suddenly looks fragile, threatened by clouds so colossal they seem to contain entire worlds.

The heavy hand of heaven unfolds aggressively over us. Its rage and violent intentions are made clear as the roaring lightning spits thunder. We are inside a giant dark box, alone, trapped with its fury. Gangster, has never seen so much raw power in his life. He looks worried. I pass out rain jackets, assuring him that I have been in this situation many times; I make a mental note to avoid any further ones.

I would get off the river if there were somewhere to go. I have researched the issue and scientists agree that during electric storms is not a good time to be on open water surrounded by nothing higher than your head. Not to mention the metal frame on which the oars are mounted. I have always thought a lightning strike would be a perfectly reasonable way to die. There can be no clearer sign that your time is up than the Lord striking you down personally. The other guys knew there would be situations beyond our control. Losing Gangster would be devastating; everyone is expecting me to bring him home.

Heading for the jagged papyrus shore we find a hollow big enough for the rafts to be blown into. Hope encourages the act of camouflage. Rain comes in sideways and makes it painful to look up. Joe, still smiling, takes out soap and washes while we are pressure hosed, battered and blinded by the water.

The lightning strikes are so close now you can feel the electrical charge in the air. The sky breaks in giant waves over us. This is no place for fear, only awe. Well, okay, maybe a little fear. The only sensible option is to surrender to the brilliant white pulses, so profound they leave the darkness quivering.

The storm does not end, it only leaves us behind, cold, wet, and speechless. The tempest continues to vent its anger at the world beyond as the moon peeks out of the shredded clouds like a scared child. Our universe has turned the blue grey of a contusion, bruised by the violence. Overwhelmed by the immensity of what we had been part of, we sit and watch the spectacle of light and water in the distance, occasionally muted by lightning flashes.

The serenity of night eventually makes way for the harshness of day. Even in the heat of the hottest day ever, there is humour, just a lot less of it. We row slowly, we talk slowly, and slowly we live through the day. We awake from heat-induced zombie states just as the sun begins to sink.

Apart from relief from the heat, the night also intensifies the sense of adventure that helps to digest the hardship.

This night doesn't disappoint us. In pairs we keep moving. Gangster finally manages to push himself through the thirty-minute pain barrier. His arms have been buckling under the strain, unused to any exercise more than rolling a joint. Watching him row is equally painful. For some reason tonight he persists: an hour turns to two before he accepts an offer of help from Joe. I am not sure who is more proud, Joe, Gangster or me.

While I am asleep, Reuben almost runs over a three-meter python; later he hits a crocodile. I try unsuccessfully to make the timing of my second shift seem like coincidence. Joe is not fooled. Every shift has its ups and downs but 03:00 till sunrise is a gem. The dead of night almost guarantees that everyone will be asleep and that you get to push into the sunrise.

By the time sunrise comes we are ten kilometres from the Sudanese border. It's a slow, beautiful blossoming of daylight. Pink light flirts shyly over the horizon, stopping just out of our reach. Delicate clouds are so fragile and soft they might have been cut from the fabric of heaven. Egrets, strung out like a pearl necklace, fly low over the water, dragging their reflections effortlessly half a meter below. Wings are inches from each other, never touching: birds white as the clouds above them.

A hippo charges into the water from the papyrus bank. It's nowhere nearby, but I force my tired arms to row a few more minutes. Finally we tie the boats together and watch the sun creep closer still. Each is left to his own thoughts or lack thereof. This is a time for feeling, not thinking. Our bodies tell us we have gone hard for thirty-six hours. Amongst us we have done our best, something we so rarely take the chance to do. This assurance makes the departure from the night into day even more remarkable.

SUDAN

Blood in the water attracts fewer sharks than a white man at an African border crossing. The first day in a new country, you are always at your most exposed. Everywhere are trained professionals waiting to relieve you of your money and annoy you while doing it. They attack in packs and the only question is how badly you will be done in.

I was hoping to avoid it crossing into Sudan by having a branch to catch hold of as soon as we swung over the border. Our local contact is nowhere in sight. Instead of a man with friends in high places, I am now just a clueless white-faced dollar, waiting to be ripped off by anyone with a good strategy.

The first and most demanding man who forces himself into my face claims to be from the Wildlife Authority. I remember them being a stubborn lot from my last visit. Their aggressive approach comes as a surprise after Norway and Uganda; it briefly hurts my feelings. I am forcefully told to get on the back of a motorbike and driven into town. I sense the price rising.

Behind me, the boys are hiding in a papyrus clump. This cover might ease their roles as circus freaks in the busy little river port. A little market has sprung up where passengers move between piles of dried fish, bananas and various assortments of vegetables piled neatly in little pyramids. The dock itself is a muddy patch located under a steel construct that either never became a building or never will be again.

The motorbike swings from left to right across the road, avoiding goats, people and other vehicles; it only slows for potholes filled with water. Everything else is done at speed. When puddles resemble rivers, my driver descends alone, revving, dragging and pulling the little 125cc out the other side in puffs of two-stroke smoke.

Nimule has grown since my last visit here in 2004. The shot-up army barracks bordered by dusty roads have sprouted into a shantytown. Corrugated iron shacks have grown with the same planning and aesthetics as weeds. It's a clever balancing act that might connect a few despondent trees into footpaths and roads.

The runaway bike ride stops at a derelict building with Sudan Wildlife Authority painted in freehand by a five-year-old. Round the back by a green army tent, I am introduced to Charles. In his fifties, he seems important enough to be able to make decisions. His round face is dominated by a beaming smile consisting of irregular buckteeth.

The topic of a fee comes up pretty quick; the problem is they don't know how much the fee is. This could be good or bad. It appears we are the first people to officially camp in the park. Charles makes a suggestion; I look shocked, and make a counter-suggestion. Negotiations begin.

After a few bouts of back-and-forth it turns out Charles is not 'The One'. This means I have him beat and he has run out of ideas. Back on the bike and off to go see 'The One' at a bombed-out army barracks.

New tents linked with camouflage nets form some kind of command headquarters. Soldiers in brand-new uniforms look smart and efficient; it seems this is a place where decisions are made.

Distinguished-looking grey-haired men, shoulders filled with stars and stripes, emerge from under a tent made of artificial leaf cover. Their faces have been chiselled by decades of war. They carry the confidence of men who sentence others to death. These grizzly old warriors must have fought many battles to become trusted leaders. These men should not be mistaken for petty chiefs, for this is a gathering of some of the best warriors on the continent, possibly the world. When our time comes before one of the hardened-old combatants, he looks us over before asking our business. On hearing my team and I wish to stay in the park for a night he replies, "I don't think it is a problem young men, just go sort out your visas at immigration." Refreshing. Yes please. A quick handshake and we are off.

At immigration we are greeted with a different story. They charge us $5 each for the privilege to pay $40 per visa. Foolishly, I fall back on logic to explain the system has no logic. I know we are being taken for cash-boxes, but when a system is based on something so absurd, it takes a while to establish an even more-absurd response.

I settle for the small victory of getting them to write me a receipt on the back of a scrap of paper retrieved from a pile of trash. I would love to play the game for an hour or so just for the practice, but I am in a hurry to get back to the boys who must be roasting on the rafts by now. We pay our white tax, jump the next line and are off.

Dodging sharks left and right as they try to 'help', I make it back on board the rafts only slightly poorer. Not far from town, above Fola Falls, under a thick tree canopy, with enough firewood we set up camp. We will portage around the falls in the morning.

One of my favourite parts of a mission is making a fire. I pride myself on being able to do it quickly and effectively; it makes me feel savage, useful and manly. You can flirt with my girlfriend, give me your opinion on how I live my life, or insult cricket, but don't you dare tell me how to make *my* fire.

What this means in practice is that the longer I struggle to get my fire going, the larger the bruise on my ego becomes. Working with damp wood, this is turning into a large lesion. Gangster wants in on the action, it's only natural; no man can watch another struggle with fire and not make suggestions.

I am the Great White Explorer. What does this kid know about fire? I have nothing to fear here, so I stand back to let him realise the folly of his arrogance by his own hand. Within minutes he has a fire going by means I would not have given a chance. Turns out one of Gangster's hobbies is pyromania. Well-done, sir. It must be hard for him being new and clumsy at everything in this world and being told what to do all day. He is handling it better than I would have.

We have gone almost three hours without a seeing a single local. Surely it doesn't have anything to do with that gunshot a few hours ago. In an area with so many guns it's much more likely to be game hunters than a destabilisation of the area's security. I try to convince myself that the two occurrences have nothing to do with each other, that any second now we will run into someone.

Outside of national parks, it is almost impossible to be alone in tropical Africa; stand still and a few figures will pop up from the bushes eventually. Of all the days I wanted to be alone in the world, today is not the one. We have time and money and I want fresh meat. Somewhere around here there is a little goat that will look good on a spit.

The wild scrub of the last few days is disappearing. The banks open into large cattle-grazing areas. Everything indicates people close by. Eventually we spot a herd of long-horned cattle walking through the thin bush. We go on shore, confident that our spit-roast is now only a formality.

It is a massive herd, lazily grazing their way over an area one-kilometre wide. Uniformly ash-white beasts with crooked horns thicker than a man's arm and many meters long. Still no humans. It is getting a bit creepy; in the way you tell ghost stories with your friends until you start to believe them yourself. Dinka love their cattle, the men even share a name with their prized ox. For a herd of this size to be unguarded does not seem right.

Down by the river would make a great campsite: ample shade, loads of dry wood, even a grassy field we can play touch rugby on. It is tempting, but a gunshot and the unguarded cattle have triggered a gag reflex in my psyche. I want to get away as quickly as I can without starting a panic.

I get everyone back in the boat while trying not to look over my shoulder too often. We continue for another hour or so until I have convinced myself that we are far enough from the gunshot and that it was probably nothing. We are all rapidly turning red in the merciless sun. It's time to get off the river.

We stop below a sand cliff, and use tree roots to climb from the water level to the flat ground above. There is wood, shade, and as added bonus, a jumping platform for shenanigans. All day we have practiced flips from the rafts for just such an opportunity. After some extensive, if not scientific, depth-checking with Reuben's fishing rod, he and Gangster launch themselves off the dirt cliff, head first.

We get stuck into an early supper of Soya-mince pasta special. I have hardly scraped the last of the yellow gunk from my orange plastic plate when another gunshot rips. I look at Thomas. "Did you hear that bro?" He enquires unnecessarily. My reply is instinctively understated to avoid worry, "Definitely a gunshot, didn't sound that close."

Nothing is said as everyone deals with the issue privately. I go through a few permutations before saying, "Okay boys, it's probably just hunting but since we don't want to get it wrong, I propose we pack up and push on till we get closer to Juba." Thomas, "Fine by me bro, lets get out of here."

Joe is already packing, "Yeah man I have been feeling like someone has been watching us the whole time, let's get going." I wake Reuben who is asleep, book on his stomach, with the news of our imminent exodus. He also needs no persuasion.

The exodus threatens to turn into a panicked retreat as we toss gear into any open space. Twitchy glances pierce the suddenly hostile-looking bush around us. Expecting hell to break loose, we have the boats packed in seven minutes. Reuben is the unlucky last one still on the cliff, earning him the final sweep of the campsite for any gear left behind. He does it remarkably fast, then slides down the tree trunk into the raft.

Darkness is only minutes away. Radios are passed out and a quick safety talk given. It's full action. "Okay Gentlemen, we keep in sight of each other, radios on. Try not to make noise and keep head torches off unless absolutely needed."

Thomas asks, "How long are we going for?"

"Let's keep going for four or five hours, nice and slow. If there is trouble in this area, it's bound to be LRA. Their normal mode of attack is small groups, hit-and-run. We should be safe near Juba, it's too big a military force for them to contend with. But we don't want to get into Juba at night, especially if there is shooting in the area. I want Reuben on the sticks for the first hours, I don't remember there being any more big rapids but rocks might be problematic in the dark, he is best qualified to avoid them."

"You happy with that bro?"

Reuben: "Copy that, Colonel Coetzee."

"Lekker, stay in the middle of the river. Let's make like an elephant's cock and hit the road."

Already a week past full moon, we will have no moonlight until 23:00. I have never see Gangster so alert. He is the first to spot the orange flicker ahead of us barely ten minutes later. He points it out solemnly and I nod in acknowledgment.

Looking at Reuben's boat, he is chatting away, oblivious to his surroundings. "Psst...Reuben" nothing, "Reuben," nothing, "REUBEN! Shut up, fire on the right."

They see it immediately and drop down in the raft. We are mid-river and will flow past the fire in a few minutes. All sound from us is silenced, even the sloshing of the oars in the water. We drift toward the threatening flicker of orange blowing kisses into the darkness. As we pass the fire it disappears as if hastily covered. Another perfectly reasonable explanation could simply be that a solid object blocked it from our view as we passed. Another serving of paranoia is handed out and swallowed.

We settle into night-rafting mode. Beds are made in dry hollows between gear and rowing shifts decided. Nothing much happens for a long time. Occasionally we pass through small rapids that can be heard long before their contours, sketched in silver, can be seen.

Fortunately, I know that there is nothing to fear from the rapids apart from getting the sleeping bodies wet. Without that nugget of past experience, it would have been impossible to proceed. Hours slip into each other on the winding black path in near-complete darkness. The silence of the night amplifies any sound, the oars dipping into the water sound as loud as footsteps in mud. The quiet becomes its own enforcer. Even talking above a whisper is somehow offensive to the environment.

By midnight we have covered thirty kilometres. The thin slice of moon has made little improvement to visibility. Our weak flashlights do more harm than good as we strain to find a crack in the one-dimensional darkness. The overgrown banks repel all attempts to find a place to stop for the night. Eventually, for lack of a better option, we tie onto a rocky island for a meeting. Now that we are presumably past any fighting that may or may not have occurred, we need a new plan.

While water is boiled for tea I put forward two options. We can either stay here tied to the island and leave early, or we keep going slowly, aiming to reach Juba by sunrise. There are points to support both. After some discussion swinging both ways the team decides to keep going.

I watch Gangster's reaction closely. It's one thing to do a twenty-four hour stint if you are mentally prepared for it, but another entirely when it is forced upon you. What I see makes the whole experience worthwhile: he is making tea, looking for biscuits to hand out, offering to give up his bed space, all without a negative remark. He is serious but I am not fooled – he is loving it.

During my shift, floating close to Thomas, our radios blurt out rough military commands. The harsh, angry ghost voices violate the silence. A newly-established feeling of well-being is replaced by a paranoia induced by not knowing the location of the bodies who house these voice-boxes. The owners could be ten kilometres away or only one. The temperature suddenly drops and the hair on the back of my neck stands erect. I search for clues in the ominous blackness.

I check personal databanks for established procedure in such a pickle but can't find any. By switching the radios off, we find a bucket and stick our heads in it. We drink the sweetness of ignorance, if only briefly. At least this way no one else needs to be disturbed by the news that there are upset soldiers awake at 04:00 somewhere in the vicinity. Fear grows quietly in the dark. It's a preferable alternative to hearing angry voices without bodies in a language you can't understand.

We expect anything at any moment but move along unchallenged until we can make out the first lights of Juba on a hill in the distance. Our timing is off by an hour. The last thing we want is to approach the all-important bridge before daybreak and get shot over the mistake. We pull over on the bank and tie the boats to the roots of a mango tree dipping its toes in the water. Then we fall into graves of sleep dug by physical exertion and tension.

Playing The Game

The annoying man with the missing front teeth whistles at me: "Your friends, they are being arrested."

I have been trying to secure transport back to Juba all morning and have achieved nothing but sunburn. We have been camped outside Terekeka for a few days hoping to organise a wrestling match between the boys and some Mandari warriors. Even this seemingly simple task has proven to be a problem.

The proud pastoral warrior I was so in awe of when I passed through here four years ago has apparently disappeared to the highlands for the rainy season. Instead we find ourselves surrounded by people calling themselves Mandari. This morning we did get invited to a cattle camp for a wrestling match, but taking one look at Reuben's tattoos, and the sum total of Joe and Thomas, they suddenly found ample excuses not to wrestle.

Diluted as these leftover herders are, it is still an interesting experience for Gangster and the rest of the crew. Personally, the heavy disappointment is at not finding the people who supplied me with some of my best African memories: purity of a world inside the smoke. I knew the real thing and I am worried that my fears about the preservation of their traditional lifestyle might already have come true. Deflated, I take the opportunity to get some space and to organise our trip back to Juba.

Approximately one-hundred and fifty kilometres upstream there is a road that research indicates is in good enough working order to sustain regular traffic. It turns out 'regular' means there is one decrepit Land Rover that drives there once a day. Even if we did pay the extortionate white-man fee charged for a private hire (more than the cost of the vehicle) we would not be able to fit our gear on it, and I am doubtful it would make it to Juba anyway.

Which brings me back to talking to this irritating man. Instead of answering my questions about transport he has been grilling me on the why, where, and what a group of five white men were doing this far from Juba. Curiosity is understandable, but demanding answers is not the way to my heart. After establishing that he is only a taxi driver, I have been ignoring him, enjoying the little game and watching him become increasingly aggressive.

The game has changed. He now has something I need, information. A change of angle is required. Two minutes later I am walking toward a plain brick building, placed in the middle of a large square courtyard watched over by a man with an AK and a faded Sudanese flag.

I have an idea of what is coming: the only question is severity. Taking out a packet of biscuits, I have a quick lunch. I fold the packet into a V shape, sliding the last few sugary crumbs into my mouth before crumpling it up and sticking it into my board-shorts.

I bend over to cross through the narrow doorway, and with that the game begins. It is impossible to see much in this dark room, even though the door is open and the sun is bright. It is important to come out of the blocks well. I need to know what I am dealing with ASAP. Glancing around the basic room, I see my crew dejected, listening to five men trying equally to be more serious and important than one another. All heads turn to me.

There are many cards to play with your first hand. I choose a standard 'I am important but so are you' approach. To look important, it helps if you have a pair of shoes, but since I never do, I try to at least look hard. I introduce myself as the leader of the expedition, increasing my status and power. I am offered a seat to join the contest officially.

Next, I have to establish who the real players are before I play any more cards. I sit back and let them talk for a few minutes while stroking my beard as if I am slowly digesting each word. Instead I am reading the room to find out who am I playing against and what the stakes are.

It's important to know the *who*, because every time you play a card, it is spent. Play your weak cards against lesser opponents and save your face cards for the later rounds.

Right, now we are just throwing paperwork at them. It is impossible to have all the paperwork, but the more you have, even if it's unrelated, the better. This ensures that you can show them that whatever the problem is, it's only a misunderstanding. The guy doing the talking has the best English. After every monologue he glances over to an older man sitting in the corner.

Time to find out what we are playing for. Different stakes require different approaches. This is where your homework comes in. You should know most of the answers before sitting at the table. What is the usual outcome of similar situations by the authority holding you? How good are the structures outside of your situation? Is there a higher authority (embassy, law, etc.) that will eventually come to your rescue? Being detained in certain areas is significantly more serious than others.

There is also a difference between being arrested and merely held for questioning. Are you in a holding pattern with a chance of going somewhere less pleasant, or merely being played with? If they are interested in showing muscle, how much do they need to show before being satisfied?

Armed soldiers without any explanation picked up the boys from the cattle camp. From there they were driven here, where they have been lectured for thirty minutes before I showed up. My guess is that we are not being arrested, only slapped across the wrist for not reporting to the local authority when we arrived. This would bring the stakes down to merely wasting our time, a cheap commodity. I can now enjoy the match instead of fearing the outcome.

Because they have the guns does not mean they have all the face cards. As a white-man there is a distinct possibility that you are important or have 'connections'. It's a standard bluff to play, but a fool's trap that they will be suspecting. It is too easily proven or disproven with a cell phone.

Instead I go for a loose combination of plays. The key to playing the mix bag is fluidity. Keep an eye on how the process is developing, ever ready to change strategy and emphasis. Try never to play a card until its conclusion, only use it to lead you to the next play. This approach works in a number of combinations. Let's look at the standard options:

First, *reward*. Why I am here? "To look for possible opportunities for tourism ventures." This leaves an undertone of future reward for whoever helps me. Next, I use *apologetic ignorance*. "I am terribly sorry sir, I just didn't know the procedure. If we had known, we would have surely gone about it another way." This is the sugar to get them to start swallowing. Also known as the *foot in the door* approach. I am telling them something they want to hear. I have their attention, so I turn my focus to the real decision-maker addressing him directly.

I move on to *flattery*. "Sir I am a huge fan of Sudan, in fact, it is my second visit. What I liked so much the first time was the amazing hospitality I received from everyone." He nods. I know I have him. All that is needed now is to yank the hook so it catches. It's time for *guilt*. "But this sir, this is unacceptable. You take my colleagues in like criminals and bring them here while they are visiting with your neighbours." *Guilt* is effective and tempting to overplay, but don't. If used well the first time there is no need.

I give him with a nice out. "I am happy to sit with you and discuss this matter, you seem like a wise man, but please let my friends leave. They have yet to have lunch and as you know, we white people are not used to missing meals." At this point everything should be played with *humour*. The game is won; just make sure everyone departs thinking they won it. Then get out of there before they can regroup. Lastly, leave nothing that can be used as leverage later.

There are cards I have not used but that need special mention. *Anger*. It has its time and place, but is to be used sparingly and with awareness to cultural context. Getting angry at a Sudanese man will get you nowhere near where you want to be. Conversely, getting angry with a Congolese is merely part of the game. If it doesn't work, you will probably end up with the default option of *begging*. Another favourite is *pity*. It can make for a good endgame, especially if you had been outplayed mid-game. *Confusion*, used by a master, is an art and can be used as often as possible.

This was only a back-room game but if you are ever in real trouble without a doubt the best option to complete a royal flush is *religion*. Played by a pro, I have seen it pull the rug from underneath even the most skilled and cunning authorities.

Warning: be very aware of your circumstances, they dictate the cards. Try to enjoy it for what it is; at the very least you provide entertainment for the people of the land you are passing through.

The Boat Home

From my perch on a broken cement block, I draw mental shapes between the bullet holes in the rusty, corrugated iron building. My analysis confirms that at least as many were fired from the inside as from the outside. Must have been a bad day.

I was told to be here at 08:00 to secure our places on the boat back to Juba. I figured it was excessive but I don't mind. I would rather not spend another week in Terekeka, and three weeks of expedition life has slowed my internal clock. I am happy smoking Supermatch cigarettes while people-watching. Teaching the annoying kid with the buck ears some new English words did my good deed for the day. Focusing on the pronunciation of the "F" and "Off" sounds.

A few Mandari women sit in the sun around large bags of beans, presumably keeping their position in line. I decide not to follow in line. Instead, I sit in the shade, respecting tradition. The women seem happy, joking, doing each other's hair, gossiping. It appears to be a big day out to town.

Around 12:00 a man appears. He identifies himself as the boat driver and disappears. At 14:00 a different man arrives and proclaims to be the boat driver. Loading begins, women haggle over taxes and the size of their baggage. There is no system, everything happens according to opinion. Yawning, I wonder why logic never got a foothold on the continent. It would be so easy to make rules that could simplify the situation, but then I remember how much I love this place for all its chaos. I suppose I can identify with the disorder. I sip some warm water and try to guess the unwritten rules.

I have already booked the front of the boat for the expedition, forcing everyone else into the back half. Crates of sodas are piled between sacks of food, while kids are tied to mothers and guns slung over soldiers. The driver, who has changed identity again, is part of a gang of three young men ordering everyone around. He seems to be the only one who is not drunk.

One drunk young man stands out as particularly annoying. He briefly harasses me but he is not yet drunk enough to ignore the look I give him. I suspect that might change in the fourteen-hour ride ahead of us.

The boat is the supply line for everything between here and Juba. It is a constant stream of stops in every village to collect and leave people and goods. We have made ourselves comfortable in the front; it is all rather peaceful. Thomas writes in his diary, Gangster listens to his MP3 player and I try to suppress the pain of watching Joe teach Reuben to play chess. After every stop we play a variation on musical chairs and switch activities.

By sunset we are halfway, pulling into the largest town along the route. It takes me five seconds to dislike this place. Stopped next to a local bar, every drunk in town is yelling out demands and comments at the white guys. When they see Thomas take some photos the aggressive atmosphere goes up a notch.

The transfer of goods and people on the boat happens on an uneven, moving path, consisting of people's heads, sacks, oar frames, jerry cans, fish traps, crates of Coke. It leads in and over our legs, a tricky act in which we are intricately involved. We move essential gear out of the way and try to point to the most stable footholds. Mothers balance loads on their heads with babies on their backs. So far everyone has made it without any serious falls.

The more we ignore the crowd on the bank the more demanding they become. A few men leaning over a reed fence are now positively threatening us. I have no desire to go ashore and find out what they are so upset about, but an incident forces the situation to boil.

The driver's mates have been getting increasingly drunk on local spirits and even though they have been mostly ignoring us, it is hard to do the same with them. The arrogant drunkard from this morning stumbled his way to the middle of the boat yelling orders in his red tracksuit. Standing unsteadily on one of our gearboxes, stinking of alcohol, he bumps his knee into Reuben's head one time too many.

As a reflex Reuben pushes him away. It's too much for the drunk; he falls head-first onto an oar frame, bounces once like a lazy tennis ball, lands on a waterproof camera box and then rolls slowly into a crack between some personal gear. The magnitude of the wipe-out stuns the crowd into silence. Everyone is watching the drunk. I am relieved to see him move as he tries frantically to get to his feet amidst the piles of gear. With the grace of a donkey on ice, he finally wobbles to a position from which he can wag his finger and yell abuse at Reuben through a mouth full of spit.

The crowd is increasingly hostile. I have seen crowd hysteria boil over into violence, and it's unpleasant. I help the drunk up and make a show of friendliness to set the tone for Reuben's apology. Leaving Reuben to it, I jump ashore to try and calm the masses.

Focusing on the oldest and most sober-looking ringleader in his dirty white singlet, leaning over the reed fence of the bar, I try to make him feel as important as I can in the shortest possible time. A few minutes of shameless flattery and I am in an office signing a first-grade exercise book called The Register. It seems all they wanted was recognition.

During the night I slip in and out of sleep to smoke cigarettes or chew on dry bread. At some stage the whine of the engine dies. I have been waiting for the engine to die because no trip would be complete without it. I light a cigarette as we float backwards down the dark current. I know there are no spare engines or paddles because I checked.

Since just about everything I own is on this boat, I am interested to see what the plan is. Before the burning coal between my fingers gets halfway to my hand, the engines start up again. It seems we are looking for something. The banks are covered in thick reeds and solid darkness. I am impressed the driver can even pick this spot from a hundred others in the dark. Then I hear a man yelling from behind the reeds.

The driver, unable to find the landing site, is edging the front of the boat like a knife into the layers of reeds. Inside a man is hanging in the middle of nowhere. Once we are close enough, he is dragged on board. He looks more dead than alive, and crumbles to the floor in a wet heap. I am at a loss; how did the driver know how to find a man in the middle of all that at night? Our translator looks as stunned by the events as we are. "He is the one who was making the troubles," he whispers.

By now he has recovered enough to start shouting. His passionate abuse and fury is flung into the darkness. The whole boat is forced to listen as it swings between bouts of wailing and self-pity. Under the dim light of our head torches we piece the story together.

The demented wet figure in front of us waves one arm around at invisible foes, with the other holding his red tracksuit pants up. It is the same idiot that Reuben pushed earlier. It seems someone had enough of him and helped him overboard; the next thing he knew he was crawling along the bottom of the river. Lucky for him, he crawled to the correct side and up into the reed walls. He hung there for a while until the boat driver's conscience made him come back to look for him.

He was lucky to be alive and he knew it. He is in tears at our feet but getting no sympathy. From time to time he stops the crying and threatens the driver and his mates. Eventually it is arranged that for the price of the cell-phone he had lost, he will not charge them with attempted murder. Apparently this happens a lot with the Dinka. The excitement soon settles back into sleep, interrupted briefly by sobbing and praying.

Was this little exercise in expedition therapy a success? On returning to Norway, Gangster realises that life is a world of possibilities and starts taking responsibility. Simultaneously, the Great White Explorer, fresh from another excellent adventure, realises that true happiness does not lie out in the world but inside himself. He decides to make the most of life where he is, instead of chasing another dream.

The problem with this fairy-tale ending is... we already know I am sitting in an airport waiting room about to go deeper into the rabbit hole than ever before. Gangster was doing fine, but sank back into the comfort of his welfare check. I failed him, the system failed him, he failed himself. Whatever the case, as you read this he is sitting on a stained couch, surrounded by beer bottles and cigarette butts, fighting the urge to wonder how he ended up at the beginning again.

Before I left for Uganda with Gangster I received a book called *Blood River*. The author did a six-week trip through the Congo and said it was hell. I know if I don't go, some loud-mouth American will do a Congo expedition with a support crew and a million dollars and claim it as the hardest thing ever. Frankly, I'm not going to allow that on my watch.

Besides, I have nothing better to do. My life in Norway is surrounded by pretty things but not overflowing with happiness. My experiment in the pace of mediocrity has failed, leaving me no choice but to try something outrageous. I don't know where this longing will take me, but I must see this to its end or endure it again later.

A pet project of mine for the last few years has been trying to walk from Mombasa, Kenya to South Africa along the coastline. I have a bit of time and need some 'harden the fuck up' training before departing for the Congo. Perhaps I'll pick up a bit of Swahili along the way. Now seems like a perfectly reasonable time to go for a walk down the Tanzanian coastline.

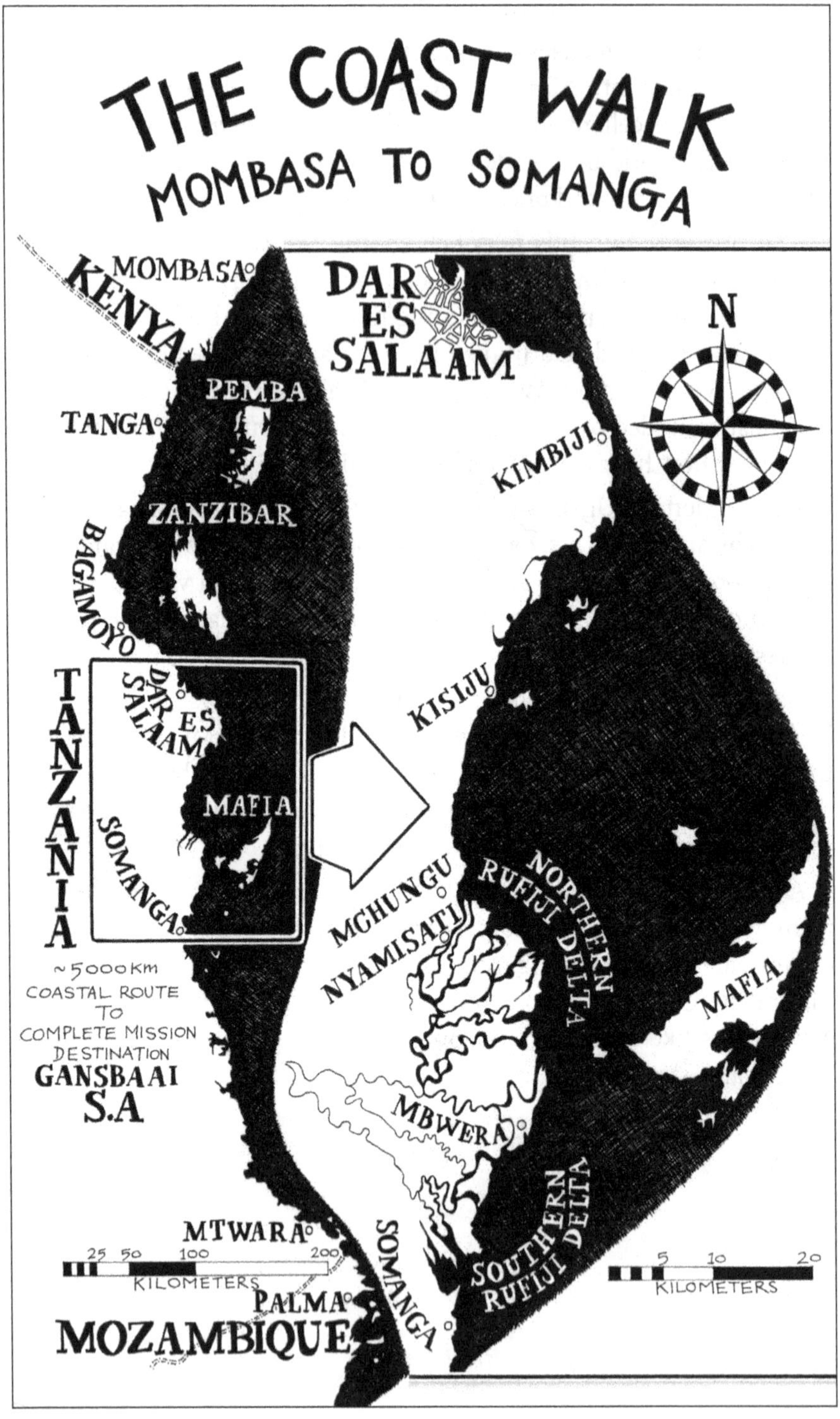

THE COAST WALK
MOMBASA TO SOMANGA
MOMBASA
KENYA
TANGA
PEMBA
ZANZIBAR
BAGAMOYO
DAR ES SALAAM
TANZANIA
MAFIA
SOMANGA
~5000KM
COASTAL ROUTE
TO
COMPLETE MISSION
DESTINATION
GANSBAAI
S.A
MTWARA
25 50 100 200
KILOMETERS
PALMA
MOZAMBIQUE
DAR ES SALAAM
N
KIMBIJI
KISIJU
MCHUNGU
NYAMISATI
NORTHERN RUFIJI DELTA
MAFIA
MBWERA
SOMANGA
SOUTHERN RUFIJI DELTA
5 10 20
KILOMETERS

A WALK

Song Of The Road

I lift my cap to Beauty,
I lift my cap to Love;
I bow before my Duty,
And know that God's above!

My heart through shining arches
Of leaf and blossom goes;
My soul, triumphant marches
Through life to life's repose.

And I, through all this glory,
Nor know, nor fear my fate –
The great things are so simple,
The simple are so GREAT!

—Fred G. Bowles

Day 1: February 3, 2009

As my bare feet leave the smoothness of the polished wooden deck and sink into the accepting sand, I make the transition from luxury-lodge guest to beach bum. I slip into the darkness with only a moment's thought given to the buffet breakfast being prepared in the candle-lit kitchen behind me. In my wake is the grandeur of comfortable beds, gourmet food and ice-cold drinks. Instead, I long for an uncertain sweaty existence. It seems a small price to pay for the purest freedom attainable to man on a physical plain: solo expedition. The fix comes from the simplest mission, and none can be simpler than going for a walk. It requires little money or planning.

Only by slowing down can you keep pace with Africa; the less you pay, the more you receive in experience. The only things that are expensive in Africa are comfort, convenience and speed, and since they are not indigenous, you pay import tax. If you want to experience Africa, you need to unclench your fist around her as best you can. The rewards are well worth it.

The physical discomfort of walking for hours a day also has its function. Learning to continue when it is not fun anymore is something we are forced to practice. It's called *discipline*, a vehicle to better things. Without that simple override switch, anything of substance will forever be out of reach.

If you have long enough to work on the project, pain becomes just another experience, as valid as any other and one that can be sublimated into whatever you wish. The mere fact that you go through pain, deal with hunger, roast in the hot sun and sleep in ditches is what makes it noteworthy. Then loneliness becomes solitude, tired legs become the prerequisite for the best rest ever and a beautiful view becomes powerful enough to stop the earth from spinning. The soul feels the need to suffer, at least as strong as the need for happiness, and inevitably has to endure the suffering to feel at peace. I figure it's best to get it out of the way while I still have a body that can handle it.

I know that not everyone has the need to go hungry or to overcome tiredness or fear. The manifestation each chooses for his or her challenges differs. Some choose *drama* and *excess* instead. But the principles are the same: you need to overcome something to gain the confidence and believe that you can shape your life.

My walking missions started as one thing and turned into another. The first one was because I was lost and out of options. In 2001, I struggled down the beautiful and mostly deserted coastline of East Africa for two weeks, experiencing the whole array of human emotions. By the end of it I had reconnected with the planet and myself, and felt I had found a way worth pursuing again.

I am heading south, not sure to where and not sure until when. If I do have a goal, it's to simplify: cut out unnecessary parts of the world around me and hope my thoughts follow. With no need to monitor the intricate web that holds my position in society, and without the need for talk, it is hoped the limitations of the 'I' can disappear at least temporarily.

After an hour's walk, my internal dialogue's stupidity is already clearer, and its repetition more obvious. My mind is tied to the outside world as with a piece of string; I hope it unravels into true silence so I can have a peek at what's underneath.

Past walks have taught me to take only the basics. Even the small day backpack will shrink as my necessities become niceties, shortly before becoming only extra weight. With every item left behind en route, I will move closer to my goal.

Pre-dawn reveals the scurrying movements of crabs amongst the abrasive coral rocks. I am forced to climb as the sea drives me and itself against the cliffs. As I again descend to the sand pit below, the earth swings past the sun pulling light from beyond the water in the greatest magic trick of all. A house sits like a crown on the cliff. Lush green grass sprinkled with kids' toys spills right to the edge. Before me is a sandy enclave with more toys, dad's toys. A ten-meter fishing boat is fittingly tied to a phallic white rock column. It's a page from a magazine about the rich and famous. I salute the unknown owner of paradise – "Well done, sir, I like your style" – before I jump, slide and climb up and over the opposing cliff wall of his private domain.

A sandy beach, the mental brochure of my mission, greets me on the other side. My naked toes splash in the thin layer of cool water that gently licks the sand; I know I might be seeing the best sunrise ever.

Hours later, a few battered canoes indicate a village close by. Needing breakfast, I take the first footpath I see. A broken gate, at ease and off guard, relaxes against a crumbling fence line. A posted sign presumably reads, "No Trespassing!" Surely it doesn't count if you don't understand the language? Besides, what can possibly go wrong?

It is a farm, but not the type you would expect in rural Tanzania. There is a group of camels and a pen full of llamas amongst the chickens, turkeys and fruit trees. I tip my hat to the universe, "nice touch." A few men on horseback pass by dove cages and challenge my right to be here. I smile and speak the two words I know in Swahili and in the wrong order. Suspecting mental retardation, they point me in the direction of town.

Soon I have a new friend and tour guide. We sit down for warm milk-tea and a few *chapatis* outside a teashop surrounded by a cloud of bees. On the dusty dirt track a Chinese-made truck pulls over. Young men in suit-pants and singlets empty from the back, laughing, joking and flirting with the roadside women who are selling roasted corncobs. I am not sure if happiness is synonymous with wisdom or with ignorance, but they seem to be doing okay here.

I do some last minute shopping: a cooking pot, some rehydration salts and a few packets of glucose biscuits. I find a five-hundred shilling note (enough for two packets of biscuits), crumbled in the dirt. Surely it is a sign that the journey is blessed. I give the money to my new friend and follow my restless feet.

At midday I have my feet up, eating a mango in the shade of an empty lodge. The caretaker looks impressed but doubtful at my feet as I tell him in African English of my plan to walk down the coast. African English is when a white person speaks English badly in the hope that black Africans will understand them better. Almost everyone who has been on the continent for more than two weeks has his or her own brand. Europeans in particular excel at it, and the Danish are the world champions.

For the rest of the afternoon the sandy beach uncoils past varying forms of ocean decoration. I steadily move south. To end a perfect first day, I lie down naked with the sinking sun on a deserted beach, watching crabs watch me, feeling the water as it feels me back.

I cook a curry-rice while the Indian Ocean purrs, but I am not yet hungry enough to eat my own cooking. After a cup of tea I follow the path up the steep cliff that blocks the ocean on my right. Above are some weekend homes, comfortable and luxurious without being obscene, reflecting their owners' taste not their bank balances.

Armed with my Swahili phrase book, I try to secure sleeping rights on the patio closest to the cliff. The ancient *askari,* or guard, with a bow and arrow slung over his shoulders, seems to understand but can't believe that a white man wishes to sleep outside the house. He calls for reinforcements from the neighbouring *askari.*

Some more African English and suddenly I am on the phone to someone. How did this planet ever run without them? Standing on my toes in the right-hand corner of the balcony, the phone receives one bar of reception that comes and goes like a house cat. The line is too bad to explain what I had thought was a simple request. The situation keeps coming back to me wanting a room. It is becoming more hassle than it's worth so I walk down to the beach.

Shocked, they come and fetch me a few minutes later, unlock the house and invite me in as if it was their own. Once again being white has proven to be the only character reference needed. I decline; the mere thought that the Great White Explorer might sleep in a house on his first night is an affront to my honour. But I see no harm in borrowing a mattress.

Day 2: February 4, 2009

A cockerel from a nearby village hoarsely shouts its crude rhyme, assuming the sunrise depends on it. I swing my pack onto my shoulders and proceed inland. Scouting yesterday indicated a large mangrove swamp will drown any chance of walking on the beach. In the darkness I walk a few circles before I find a road leading in the direction I feel is right. Years of experience, and countless times of losing my way, temporarily, and I still have unwavering confidence in my obviously flawed directional instincts. If you have instincts like mine, it's very, very handy to be lucky.

The early-morning walking sessions are not the easiest. Even without the sun, the humidity is a blanket and the cooling breeze is at its weakest. My legs are still stiff, there is no distracting scenery, and my mind is prone to ask the one question that must be avoided at all cost when morale is low: why? I must refuse to discuss it; it can only lead to tears. Given enough discomfort and a long-enough timeframe, you can talk yourself out of anything. When the sun rises aggressively on my left I know I am heading in the right general direction; not that I doubted it much.

Two schoolgirls in bright purple uniforms fall in a half-step behind me. "Good morning class, you may sit down," she says confidently. The day is wrapped one-dimensionally in a sheath of light across her large dark eyes, the contrast enhancing both. It looks like confirmation of her English from a real life *muzungu* is the best gold star she has ever received. She is a little bubble of pure happiness. We continue chatting for a minute but quickly exhaust the few words we know of each other's languages. She then repeats Swahili names for all the objects we pass and I yell out the English name. Their enthusiasm for learning is infectious, even if the Swahili words fall through me without even touching the side. I optimistically believe they leave a smear for future recognition.

Just around breakfast time, the white dirt road sways through the thick tropical surroundings to reveal a postcard. Shaded under a roof of palm trees, a village lies cuddled up by the ocean. In its calm bay, wooden boats of various sizes rock beneath their sails. Footsore and hungry, I eye up the most hygienic-looking teahouse. Choice made, I sit my unhygienic, sweaty self down on a miniature chair by a rickety wooden bench covered in red plastic, food stains and flies. With my knees up around my ears, I sip greedily on the scorching hot, disgusting, yet fantastically sweet cup of tea that cost me less than a cent.

My linguistic confidence plummets as I cause the entire street to break out in laughter after greeting an old man. Self-conscious, I grin and bear it with difficulty. I consider for a moment that they have the answer wrong instead of me. The town is nice and the reaction to my whiteness has been minor. I want to be left alone and go about my business in anonymity. Not much chance of that in rural Africa.

Bag full of mangoes, stomach full of breakfast, I walk down the beach heading south. As I admire the *dhows* dry docked under the palm canopy, I fantasise about taking one on a mission. By midday I am forced to abandon the coast completely. The mangrove swamp barrier has steadily driven me inland for the last hour.

After finding a proper dirt road, I make good time until I come upon a small village nestled amidst two mango trees. The trees are massive, their roots melt artistically into the light soil. Village life is lived in the boundaries of their abundant shade. Circles of men sit and play board games or lounge against grass mats that cover the ground like a patchwork quilt. It is an oasis of respite from the midday heat that would be rude to ignore. I collapse in the folds of the dark knotted roots of a tree whose age is measured in the ancient system it creates beneath the sandy soil. Between slow blinks I observe village life. Decorated by newspaper cuttings of dated football teams and cheap goods, a few shacks all sell the same merchandise through dark holes. A faded advertisement states strawberry-scented condoms will enhance your romance.

Eventually, I venture back into the furnace. Inland, the cooling breeze has stopped teasing, claimed to have a headache and gone to bed. An hour later I walk into another beautiful village, a cosy bay snuggled by a blue ocean. It is oddly familiar. My enthusiasm drops when I realise it is the same village I left this morning. The not-so-Great White Explorer is perplexed. Keep the sea on your left and the sun on your right. How hard can it be? No one else to blame, I laugh softly at myself and turn around. To the astonishment of the old man watching from the shade of his house, the white man that appeared from nowhere on foot goes back to where he came from.

Walking back I have plenty of time to figure out where I went wrong. I pass the mango trees village; it is still in the same state of rest as it has been for the past century. Barely an eyebrow is raised as I re-enter even sweatier than before. I stop for a few litres of water and a packet of biscuits before retracing my steps to where I joined the road.

The sun is right above me and I still can't figure out how I walked in a circle. When asking for directions in Africa one has to follow certain basic rules: always get more than one opinion, and never supply an answer in your question, as in "Excuse me sir, but is the town this way?" Most Africans will rather say what you want to hear: yes.

Another great misunderstanding is our cultural difference in measures of time and distance. Never, ever, get your hopes up or bet your last sip of water. In a foreign language the process is proving to be above me. I can't find enough material for an educated guess. The only option seems to be the mangrove swamp. This should be interesting.

Hour after hour, dead end after dead end, I search for a way out of this peculiar world. Roots grow straight up from the flat mud like hairs on rough skin. Strange trees are topped by thick clusters of leaves, their roots growing from the hips of skinny trunks to anchor them into the mud like women dressed in ball gowns. Morale is following the sinking sun. It is looking like a night in the swamp until I reach a river that marks the edge of the maze. On the other side there is no sign of any cosy town snuggled by anything. I have escaped a nightmare resembling the Blair Witch Project and the day might just have a happy ending after all.

Stripping down, I venture into the shallow stream while scanning for crocodiles. It never gets deeper than knee-height and I walk onto the opposing sandy beach with a smile wider than the river. Ahead lies open beach as far as the eye can see. A few fishermen sit around repairing nets. Either they see naked white men appearing from the swamp often, or they are just too polite to stare.

Once comfortably past the fishermen I sit down to smoke a Sportsman, the brand of particularly strong and cheap cigarettes popular with the locals. It is a perfect place for tobacco companies to dump the hard stuff. When people in the Third World live long enough to die from cancer they still just call it death. I suck deep on the drug and relish every breath. There is nowhere else I would rather be and nothing else I would rather be doing. Once finished with this mission it is not the long hours of sweat and the sore feet I will remember, but the small moments of immaculate bliss that follow them.

There is nothing to lose by leaving comforts behind every now and then. At worst I will come back appreciating them more; at best I will realise they were not that important. It may be that suffering is not needed to appreciate life. Some people seem never to need a reminder of how good they have it. When you do start taking things for granted, a quick refresher course is recommended. To discover what you need rather than what you want is surely worth a bit of time. Comfort is the chair you fall asleep in. The first thing that total comfort kills is curiosity, then true excitement. These are replaced with fear and boredom. I am almost sure that as you sit confined to your wheelchair in the old-age home, waiting for the nurse to change your colostomy bag, the comfortable days will not be the things you remember. That is, unless real suffering made them exceptional.

Later, still naked and now completely alone on the beach, I watch the stars. My thoughts are free to drift in whatever direction they choose. Dinner is a packet of biscuits, honey flavour, my favourite. The language of the wind and ocean is restlessness. Loneliness in nature is a joke. Feeling alone when surrounded by people is what makes life seem empty. How can you be lonely when all you are is being? Companionship has its time and place, but it would stand in the way of solitude during times like this. What would I say to another person if one were here? "It is beautiful, I am happy, I am tired." Useless words cheapen the experience by their everyday thoughtless repetition. They spoil the silence that gives rise to their perception. Language is one of the main structures used to define past and present. It is not possible to find the perfect moment, the timeless moment; even if it was, it would not be fast enough to describe it. In cities I feel lonely, bombarded by people scurrying about without seeing each other. There, I feel invisible and inconsequential; here, I feel small but connected.

Day 3: February 5, 2009

I suck on the sticky sweetness of a mango to make up for the water I have all but run out of. Again, the morning session is tough. Sand is everywhere; my pants are rubbing the skin from the insides of my legs and no amount of Vaseline can prevent it. No choice but to go naked now. Yes please!

Later when the sun has already been up for some hours, I am stopped by a three-hundred-meter-wide bay. I do what I always do when out of ideas, sit down and smoke a cigarette. I am halfway through when a canoe leaves the opposite bank.

Shuttling me across the bay is a man old enough to be timeless; a face like melted plastic and teeth long since fallen out. His bony body is moulded to his canoe seat as he chats non-stop, undeterred by the fact that I can't understand a word.

Long sandy beaches broken by large sea inlets become the theme of the day. Sometimes there are canoes, sometimes not. At the first major crossing I give the crocodile situation some thought. Before I swim I watch the bay for any sign of them. Since there is no other way forward, I convince myself there aren't any here.

Naked, backpack on, knife in my teeth and slightly sceptical I wade deeper into the cool salty water, losing confidence as the sand bank gives way to unknown depths. My backpack allows only a slow crawl, from which it is hard to look for approaching things with teeth. It is going painfully slow. As I move across eternity, the strap of my pack swings up to hit me on the bum. The unknown *bump* and resulting silent scream causes me to swallow salty water through the knife in my teeth. "You ffuugging irrgiiott, mmm," I mutter through the knife, clenched teeth and coughs of saltwater. Loosely translated is: "You idiot, you are here, now swim." I need to calm myself down and stop turning imaginary dangers into real ones. Eventually I walk out the other side, exhausted. I hang out the pack to dry and find some shade to collapse in. Mid-morning naps have become a part of my routine. Time for reading and writing, snacking and enjoying the view.

With nowhere to be and nothing to do, it's only boredom that makes me move again. Soon another bay lies in front of me, twice the size of the last and not a canoe in sight. Some nets mid-stream suggest people walk in during low tide, which means no crocodiles. With such irrefutable logic, I even leave the knife in the bag. Now that I am a trained professional, what can possibly go wrong?

Thirty minutes later, after every few strokes, I am frantically testing the water depths. I want this swim to be over now; I wanted it to be over some time ago. The pack is heavy and filled with water and the current is trying to carry me out to sea. Suddenly, I tap the sandy bottom and stumble onto the bank.

No rest yet, the sun is merciless in the open. With nothing but my grass hat on, the sun is acid on my soft white bits. My feet sink into the blistering sand as my tired legs struggle to reach the shade. Once there I collapse on my bivy and sip rehydration salts to wash the sea out of my mouth.

I lay there with no intention of moving when some fishermen walk past. Pitying the Great White Explorer, who is obviously falling apart, they invite me to their home. I am fed burnt sardines the size of goldfish and day-old porridge from a black dented pot. I wash it down with dirty water from a plastic cup that looks like it was chewed by a dog. No sympathy necessary, I left fussy on the river's other bank.

I reach the first milestone on the journey, Kisiju. It is a typical dirty fishing town with lots of men standing around trying to look like gangsters. I re-supply on biscuits and a new pair of shorts. It's already dusk when I take a canoe across the muddy bay south of the town. Dropped off in a lake of mud, I walk knee-deep in the black goo for a while. Some women catching mud-prawns smile at me and continue to chatter away, covered in earthy sludge from head to toe. Once out and above ground level, I remove the shorts before they can do any more damage to my raw thighs. Leaving them unceremoniously next to my squishy leg marks, I slip into the nice clean purple number.

Tired, but wanting to get some distance from the town, I walk into the night. It is a fantastic section. Basic fishing villages are scattered all along a narrow beach, decorated with fallen trees and small ocean canoes. As I pass two figures, one falls in beside me. He is a tall, gangly young man called Adam. I am unable to understand him but confident that no one who smiles so openly can pose any danger. We walk together silently for hours until he invites me into his village.

Normally I try to avoid people on a walk, but I figure why not give it a try, it being an authentic fishing village and all.

I am welcomed and join the men sipping hot tea and eating dried fish. Some are smoking marijuana but no one seems to be drunk. After tea I set my net up on someone's porch and fall asleep midway through a conversation with my host. Despite the friendly hospitality, my conversations all seem to follow the same short-lived script. "Where are you from? What are you doing? Why are you walking?" and then more often than not, "Give me some money."

After midnight I awake, tired of being surrounded by people, and pack up my stuff. My host follows me down the beach for a few minutes before asking for money. I refuse out of principle.

Day 4: February 6, 2009

The dark hours go by more quickly after pushing through a slightly painful first one. Every now and again I pass people, presumably fishing. Nothing is said; we share the distrust of darkness. Once light starts returning to Tanzania, I stop for biscuits and a Sportsman, while I pop a few blisters. It is pure paradise watching the world return to three dimensions.

I am a walking machine. I find a rhythm by which my body moves without the need for communication with my mind. The mind untangles itself from the various pains, becoming no more than an amused bystander. Another pair of socks is left behind; they, too, were a luxury.

I stop for tea at a skewed village beside a mangrove swamp. The English-speaking Abdullah Kharim, self-proclaimed drunkard and fine fellow, approaches me. We do the usual chitchat. I buy him a cup of tea and a few *chapatis*. He tells me about his life while giving me directions. When asked where I can find water, he looks at me very seriously, shaking his head in denial. "I am a drunkard," he repeats as though I had not heard him the first time. Eventually he does confess to know where the hated substance is.

The coastal character has changed. Sandy beach has been replaced by massive mud plains on which wooden fences poke out in erratically dotted lines to hang fishing nets when the tide is right. A short sandy step is held back from the mud by thick squat trees: old warriors the colour of ivory, scarred and damaged, stand bent and proud between their fallen comrades, their lives lived facing the tide.

Eventually the trail is lost in mud too deep to continue. I have to go inland. Already I have done more distance than any other day. I know I have to rest soon or take the chance of doing serious damage. Not just any place will do; if I sit down now it will be for a while. Getting back to this level of detachment will mean going through it all again.

Hours later I have not found a suitable place to rest. There are no humans in sight. With the sun behind thick clouds I am hoping the effort is in the right direction. I climb a tree and think I see an opening in the forest that could mean coast. It turns out to be a false hope that finally forces me to sit down. My right knee has been unimpressed for some time now and refuses to play anymore. In a little patch of shade on unruly grass, I roll out my bivy and the first-aid kit. I grab a few biscuits and lick my wounds for a while. My left leg is twitching like an amputated lizard's tail. Lacking eyes and ears, ignored by the brain since midnight, no one seemed to have bothered telling him it's time for a break.

My thirst makes me move again an hour later. I am hoping the overgrown path leads to people or to the coast. It has been many hours since I have seen any people to ask for directions. Through thick woods and *bushveld*, the path eventually brings my bleeding feet to Mchungu.

My elation at reaching this milestone is short-lived. Instead of a boat to take me through the Rufugi Delta, all I find is a drunken run-down village on a muddy river outlet. Even the ocean has left this derelict den. There are no boats here and no one is able to tell me where to find one. All I am sure of is that this is not a place where I want to spend the night.

I walk away planning to fall asleep roadside and reassess in the morning. A man on a bike stops to tell me where to find a boat and offers me a lift. I decline. Soon other entrepreneurs offer to take me to the town of the boat. Again, I refuse; I would rather sleep in the bush. On impulse I ask if there are any *wazungu* or foreigners in Nyamisati. "They are there."

My greedy brain considers a permutation: a chance to clean my wounds in a hygienic environment and have a proper meal. Surely the Great White Explorer will be greeted with open arms and animals slaughtered in his honour. Say no more, I am on the back of the bike. All thoughts of simplification are forgotten.

On the ten-kilometre ride we are blasted by a storm. We arrive wet and cold, but it is not enough to dampen morale. By now the *wazungu* are a clan of beautiful missionaries just waiting to be impressed by the real man that is going to show up at her door in time for the roast lamb dinner. I ask around in town for them; the first reply, "they are lost," puts an end to the little daydream. I do find a room with a shower and an omelette for dinner. Four walls of irregular size were painted by someone no doubt on their first assignment, and done with whatever colours were available.

The hunting tactics of the transparent geckos stuck to the walls and ceiling provide entertainment under the single light bulb, hanging a few feet between heaven and earth and wavering between light and dark. Hobbling to the communal kitchen I run into some rats the size of house cats. I find them disturbing at first, but after we establish our boundaries it works out just fine.

Day 5: February 7, 2009

Early morning: I awake groggy from painkiller-constructed nightmares. The commotion outside makes me think I am back in the army. I look out the window to see black men in orange life jackets running around, while yellow men in grey golf shirts and track suit pants blow on whistles and wave their arms. Reality sets in; I am renting a room on a Chinese fuel prospecting lot.

I limp down to the boatyard in search of a boat and breakfast. I am told with confidence, "The boat will come." So I wait and watch. Thanks, no doubt, to the Chinese, this town is by far the best developed I have come across. The Chinese may finally be the ones to tame Africa with their silent participation, but it is hard to imagine two cultures further apart. As the day drifts past I people-watch while reading and writing, my back against the pockmarked waterfront steps. Some kids fishing in the dirty water pull out a mutant-looking catfish. A man urinates five feet away before bending down to wash his face where he stands.

Small canoes hardly above the waterline are loaded with cargoes of fruit, people and basic necessities, coming and going like the tide.

Most of the men at the dock are sitting or lying in the shade; at their most active they might start a conversation. The women all have small businesses, selling a few pieces of dried fish or a handful of cashew nuts. Only the Chinese boats speeding past every now and again show any haste.

It is afternoon before the boat arrives. Its light pink coat of paint has long since worn down to one of my favourite textures: wood smoothed by use and water. I am not sure if it will take me clear of the delta – its destination is not marked on my map – but it's my only option, so I take it.

Piles of soda, blocks of ice, suitcases, pots, fishing traps, sacks filled with unknown substances, and plastic bags printed with pictures of Rambo form a bottom layer in the wooden shell. Kids and livestock are then inserted into the cracks. On top of this cluster more than thirty people are perched. I sense a bit of tension; it is clear to all that we are barely floating. The majority of people are ordered to sit in the back to keep the bow from digging into the water. They might have told me to move also but my Swahili has suddenly gotten even worse. It is a comfortable place to inhale one of the great river deltas in Africa. Half an hour later, a man starts to bail water from the boat. I know he is a bad boy, the multiple scars on his head tell me he needs regular beatings. It's worrying that he is only using a teacup; anything bigger wouldn't fit through the piles of gear.

We turn off from a main channel into a tight green alley flowing between islands thick with mangrove trees. A Chinese man chases us to inform us the channel has been closed for scientific purposes. Team spirit builds as we collectively shout expletives at the Chinese for making waves that nearly flood us.

I like traveling by boat. It's slow and overcrowded with no shade; conversely, there's no dust or potholes, you can smoke and the view is great. During the midday heat people are wrapping shirts over their heads and attempting to hide amongst their luggage. Conversation dries up as we hibernate in the heat.

Humanity returns to the boat by late afternoon. Old men are talking politics in the back row. I know because *Obama* sounds the same in any language. Halfway up, a woman shrouded in colourful cloth is flirting with the boat drivers. Some kids who could belong to any one of the women on board stare at me with blank eyes and snotty noses. The crew skips confidently along the boat, making jokes and showing off their balance, obviously trying to impress the women. I know because I have driven a few boats myself.

Our boat is filled with tourist guides. If we pass anything of interest, like an even more overloaded boat or a beautiful bird, my fellow travellers yell out excitedly for me to take pictures. I disappoint them tremendously when I don't rate a hippo worthy of a photo. Feeling I let the team down, I start a film shoot of the boat and its occupants. All is forgiven as they pose at my request. While I am at it, I snap a few of the best sunset ever.

The Chinese prospecting boat still zips past occasionally, but it slows down well before they reach us in fear of more abuse. Rows of workers in orange overalls sit back to back. The sample collector who is sent onto the swampy islands is easy to spot because he is covered in mud from head to toe.

After seven hours on the boat we have arrived at Kibanjo, nothing more than a few huts built on stilts in the mud. The one-hundred meters of waist-deep mud that has to be walked through to reach the first of the elevated houses seems less than inviting. The woman in the colourful *kanga* looks at me smiling and simply says "Kibanjo" pointing at the welcome mat of mud that completes her sentence.

I am led, mostly by myself, to believe that the boat will continue in the dark to another village further south to drop off some ice blocks. I stay on board to make the point that I wish to continue. The crew is obviously used to not understanding white people; they shrug at my insistence to stay on the boat before they enter the mud fields of Kibanjo in search of supper. Personally, it seems easier to go hungry.

The river mouth of the delta spills into the ocean against a strong wind. It's good to see the ocean again, and the space it represents. It's a full moon and it promises to be a good night for a mission. I curl up in the foetal position on the tip of the boat. It is the only flat surface available on this skeleton now that all gear has been unloaded. It takes a while, but I amalgamate myself within the tiny triangle.

I sleep peacefully until the crew returns. We slowly edge from the protection of the mini-harbour to face the brunt of the wind and the choppy sea. This boat is not made for the ocean, and as the swell grows it threatens to climb on board. The bright moonlight gives contrast to the few figures hunkering in the wooden hull, but allows no facial expression to gauge how serious our situation is. The engines roar after every wave. They are lifted out of the water to spin angrily in the air. A fish dives into the side of the boat, creating a moment of comedy amidst an otherwise sombre mood. We smoke and look into the distance, gliding over the uneven swell as gracefully as a South African on cross-country skis.

Shortly before dawn, we venture back into the tree-line and down a river outlet. I walk ashore for the first time since yesterday. It is only a twenty-canoe town, but it seems a vast improvement over the mud village. Dilapidated huts line the waterfront and a few figures sleep mummified in their blankets under a shanty roof. A fierce attack of mosquitoes forces me to set up my net at the first available spot, a hut identical in the dark to any other. Hopefully any bad guys will already be asleep.

Day 6: February 8, 2009

If people understand what silence reveals to them they would have been as close to God as the flowers of the Valley.

–Khalil Gibran

I awake from a few raindrops while Tracy Chapman sings "Cold Feet" in my head. Just as I bend to roll up my bivy, I am nearly hit by the wooden shutter of the house that is being pushed open. The rest of the huts soon wake up to the day, letting life into the street. I stand around, a bit unsure of myself, trying to look tough, feeling anything but. I am in the middle of nowhere. It is isolated and it is poor. The law would be many days from here and in this immense delta there would be many places to hide from it, even if it had the gas money or inclination to come by.

The Great White Explorer is on full alert as he sits on someone else's porch, watching his surroundings from a defensible position. Some men are looking at me with expressionless faces. It is 06:30 in the morning, what do I expect, song and dance? The lady cooking tea appears harmless, as do the kids staring with eyes still full of sleep. The young men returning from night fishing seem tired, and the only person who does more than say hello warns me to shift a few feet to the side. Apparently falling coconuts can be terminal.

A kid is playing in the dirt. I kick a makeshift football, composed of plastic bags tied together with bits of string, for him to chase on stiff little bowed legs. I tire of the game before he does. He starts crying when I sit down. I comfort him until he begins hugging me and calling me dad. No one comes to my rescue. I panic and look for a bucket of sand to stick my head in. Mum has been watching the whole time and finally comes over laughing like someone who knows all about being terrorised by a three-year-old.

A cup of warm brown sugar flavoured with some tea and a ride are organised for me by one of my boat drivers from yesterday. I walk into the waist-deep, muddy water and climb aboard a time-worn *dhow*. The sides of the wooden hull have been modified for ocean-going conditions; plastic bags are sewn with string to form a barrier intended to keep the sea out. Juma, the young man who escorted me, introduces the rest of the four-man crew. Ali is the Captain. Bearing slightly Arabic facial features and in his forties, he looks like a hard man. Mohamed, another teenager, greets me with no more than a nod. This is his world and he wants me to know it. The last member of the crew is an old sailor that seems to have come with the boat. His body is the same colour and texture as the wooden deck. Both have had all softness worn away so that only the hard knobby bits remain.

On impulse I wave back at the people going about their business. It is the signal for them to stop pretending that there is not a white man in their village. Suddenly it's a rhapsody of waving arms, smiles and shouts of encouragement. The only thing threatening back there was paranoia.

On this *dhow* no one speaks English and they express uncertainty toward me. My eagerness makes up for their lack thereof. I love old wood and things that float and did not feel like spending more time in that mud patch. A mission on a classic *dhow* in the Indian Ocean sounds like the *best day ever* to me. My excitement is contagious and soon we have some friendly banter going.

Juma is nice enough to allow me to get in the hull with bucket and scoop out water. "Thanks bro! But I don't think so. How about you get knee deep and bend over below the deck boards, and I will chuck the water over the side." He thinks it's hilarious that his cunning plan did not work. As we motor past the sandbanks of the murky delta and enter the enormity of the ocean, he passes water up in a modified plastic jerry can and I chuck it back to its source.

The Mafia Islands can be seen as hazy black dots on the horizon. We don't speak about camaraderie, but I sense it among us boat people. Boats represent freedom. A certain kind of man has been drawn toward adventure at sea for centuries, in boats not much different from this one. They preserve an uncomplicated design comprising a body of thick wood propelled by a mast and some tattered sails. A small deck allows three of us to stand with our backs against the ocean and our eyes on the horizon. In a sea of blue the only artificial colour apart from the plastic yellow rail is the dirty white sail and the rigging, which consists of colour-coded nylon ropes tangled and tied together.

As we near the beach at Mbwera the old sailor drops the anchor at a safe distance from some men standing shoulder deep in the ocean, erecting fishing nets in the gentle swell. Backpack on my head, I jump overboard, a little sad at leaving this crew behind so quickly, but happy to see sand again.

In the village hiding behind bushy scruff, blown in from the ocean wind, I am invited to join a feeding frenzy of young men at a plate of sardines. Afterwards I have the customary sugar and tea. Juma pays. It is a gesture far more appreciated than the cost of the transaction. Maybe there really was an understanding between the people of the boat?

A young man who can speak English latches onto me; annoying as it is, this is not unusual. I guess I am in an environment where there are so few opportunities, and here it comes in the colour white. The unidentified man and Juma follow me down the beach. I try to explain that I will be fine by myself, but the thought of a white man being able to survive without local help is so absurd it cannot be expressed or grasped with our limited language skills. This conversation is irritating me. I want to be walking and the fact that they think a white man is physically inferior to a black man, true or not, grinds on the Great White Explorer's ego.

Eventually Juma smiles, shakes my hand and walks back to do whatever he came to this beach to do. I try to persuade my new 'assistant' to do the same. He says that he is heading home which is that direction anyway, or at least I think that is what he says. He struggles to keep up with my deliberately fast pace. I can't go fast enough to shut him up. He keeps up his conversation from two steps behind me.

Worriedly, he says: "But you cannot pass this way."

"Thanks, but I think I will try anyway."

"Where are you going?"

"My destination, Mozambique."

Even more worried: "Do you know the way?"

"Not really."

His face twists in thought as he chews on this hard nugget of information, until eventually he blurts out, mortified, "BUT IT IS FAR!"

I get rid of him by accentuating, "I don't need you." I regret my loss of form immediately, but I am craving alone time. His spirit looks mortally wounded. After a good handshake and a few compliments on his English, he watches me approach the river outlet that has appeared a few hundred meters ahead. I can almost feel his disappointment as I call over a canoe as easily as hailing a cab in London and cross without delay.

It's bliss to be back on the beach and alone. Barefoot, totally content and fighting the urge to skip, I explore some lesser known rooms in my brain. When I do tire, I sit under a straw hut. Some kids show up and are paid to go buy me some biscuits from the nearest supplier.

While they are away an old man shows up. Dignified to his last grey hair, he sits down and we struggle through some topics. The hut is where he and some other musicians come to jam. He points proudly to his garden around it, young trees protected by man-made thorn fences. I think back to the guy who washed his face with his own urine a few days ago in Nyamisati. Only a fool would try to classify a nation by the actions of one man; I do it all too often. I ask him eventually if he would mind if I take a nap. He is insulted; I am too tired to care. When I open my eyes the kids have returned with the shopping, watching me, politely waiting for me to wake up. We have a few biscuits before I slip back into the sand.

It becomes clear that my map, carefully drawn in pencil on the back page of my diary, has some surprising shortcomings. Mbwera is not the end of the delta, as it would have me believe. The end of the swampy bay is nowhere in sight and no amount of positive thinking can trick me into an easy way round this obstacle. The finely-trained Great White Explorer immediately goes to Plan B: sitting down to smoke a cigarette while waiting for the universe to sort itself out. By the time I stub it out, I am still on the beach with nowhere to go but back.

Backtracking is always uphill. I arrive at the old man's house; he is still upset but gives me directions anyway. It's all in Swahili but I get the following: "You go straight, then you turn left, something about a boat, something about a bicycle, then you go straight some more until you reach Italy where you can go fuck yourself."

I am tired and annoyed, but it is somehow funny. Smiling grimly, I head inland. Eventually I find a boat to take me somewhere other than here and if possible in a southerly direction. The price is negotiated before we push off in the cracked, twisted and hollowed-out log. I squat on palm leaves to keep my butt dry, and my two rowers sit a step higher on planks. I am not sure where we are going and when you aren't going anywhere in particular, that's not the worst place to go. This is one of the biggest deltas on the continent – it would have been terrible if it was easy.

It's obvious we are going to be here for a while, so I decide to continue my Swahili lessons. Once I get fed up with bringing my drivers to the edge of hysterical laughter, I sing. They shake their heads and keep paddling me through the seemingly endless waterways. When we are deep enough in the labyrinth they stop and demand that I pay them. I tell them not to worry about it. The six dollars is tucked in my backpack, I even promise them a bonus. I am happy to have found a way through this latest obstacle at such a low cost, and what's more, my own singing has loosened a silence inside me. I carry on laughing at my own jokes despite the lack of appreciation from the uncomprehending paddlers.

Almost two hours later we pull the canoe onto a sandy beach below some huts under a mango tree. I hand over twice as much money as the boatmen had asked for. The Great White Explorer is a gracious man. These guys deserve six dollars for their work. My new best friends look at the money and hand it back. We have bonded so well that they refuse money for their labour. This must be the brotherhood of the boat again. "No, please sir, I insist you take the money, you have earned it." I eagerly stab the notes at him. As he repeats the amount I realise they are not asking for six dollars, but sixty. "Well, in that case, you can go fuck yourself." I give them ten dollars while still laughing, but now at my own stupidity. They seem to accept that they are not going to extract the exorbitant fee and offer me a joint. I don't want to be rude, so I accept. When in Rome! Today seems like a perfect time to bend the brain a bit.

A paddler explains that he can hire a bicycle and drive me to the next town. From there, it is only fifteen kilometres to the coast. It seems like another interesting adventure so I go for it. Stoned, carefree and happy, I jump on the back of the bike into the unknown. All goes well for five minutes but the bumpy, sandy road and hard metal frame soon make it uncomfortable. A group of kids playing soccer laugh at the Great White Explorer being driven through the countryside. I pay the bike man for his trouble and send him back. I feel better immediately. I follow the crooked road framed by tropical surroundings; I would rather be nowhere else.

Occasionally people walk beside me, but mostly they let me be. A particularly friendly guy invites me to his house for the night, but I am eager to get some momentum so I decline. He mumbles something about "lions and elephants" and "not safe." The Great White Explorer smiles his "do you know who I am smile" and continues with bravado. I walk on. The lush vegetation is regularly cleared by small villages and there are many people on the road. On cue, as darkness falls, all signs of civilisation disappear. The last toxins of the joint spark a wisp of unease: *did he say lions and elephants?* I walk for what feels like a very long time in a moonless night, without a single sign of human life. The slight unease grows to measurable paranoia.

The open blisters on my feet are aching to be separated from my shoes, but in the dark, on the uneven road, with tired legs, it would invite more cuts and bruises. Suddenly I am not having fun anymore. I am tired and a little scared, with no idea where I am.

Eventually a weak splatter of fire signals humans. I follow the overgrown path to its source and find a woman with three kids cooking under a tatty palm-leaf shelter. Too tired to bother with Swahili, I throw my bag down and slowly bend my stiff legs. While I am still trying to sit, she collects her kids and runs, leaving me alone around her cooking fire. I add up the possible outcomes of scaring her away and hurry in the opposite direction as fast as my uncomprehending legs will allow.

The incident does nothing to ease my mind. If she is that twitchy, chances are she has something to be twitchy about. Thirty minutes later I see another sign of life, a standard mud hut with smoke billowing out of its cracked walls. I knock on the flimsy door, which is tightly shut, trying not to sound like the big bad wolf. The voices inside stop abruptly, before starting up again in frantic whispers. No one rushes out to my assistance. The door stays firmly shut.

For a long time I stand outside, unsure what to do. Huffing and puffing would be no use, and my legs have locked. The shack opens and a man emerges. Serious damage is done to the Swahili language as I attempt to explain my situation. To his credit he seems to grasp most of it and allows me to hang a net outside his hut before retreating inside and closing the door behind him.

Later he brings out a grass mat, a radio, and some supper: five fish and a green plate, piled high with *ugali*. The fish are the size of my pinkie finger and half of it consists of head. Surely we don't eat that. But then there would be nothing left. In the dark it is hard to get any clues from my host on proper etiquette, and The Great White Explorer does not want to show his ignorance. I destroy the head with one bite. Instead of ignorance, I show stupidity. I pick minuscule fish bones from my mouth without drawing attention to myself.

We sit, listening to static, occasionally interrupted by a brief signal on his cheap radio. Only now and then do the airwaves converge well enough to reveal a few words. Something about Obama being an inspiration to the continent, then a brief refrain from a dance track.

Just like any man with a remote, it seems the process of searching for the channel he never finds is more important than the channel itself. We smoke cigarettes and stare contentedly into the dark. He stops tuning when he finds English football. Thousands of kilometres from my mozzie net under this banana tree, giddy commentators try to outdo each other whilst overpaid icons kick a ball around. Since he speaks no English I assume he is leaving it on the football for me. I would rather have silence, but I don't want to be rude.

It does occur to me that the radio is a great metaphor to my walk. All day long my thoughts change channels searching for something worthy of listening to. Primarily it's static, the crossing and overlapping of different thoughts. At times, it's a clear program of useless content, like an agricultural show in Swahili, or an exciting sporting match. Sometimes it's even a news flash. Mostly, I wish I could just switch it off and listen to my surroundings.

We fall asleep. The radio, still sprouting gibberish, is under his head. I presume he does not want to leave me alone outside. A few hours before dawn I fold my net, brush my teeth and offer the silent man a few cigarettes for his unquestioning hospitality.

Chewing on a glucose biscuit I walk down the dark road to whatever lies next. My body is asking, accusingly, why we could not have slept for a few more hours.

Day 7: February 9, 2009

A man's richness is in what he can live without.

—Henry David Thoreau

It is barely light by the time I reach a small town. A few goats and an aged *askari* stand around in the quiet streets. I find a cool concrete shopfront to sit on, and a wall to lean my back against. A few traders are on their way somewhere, bikes loaded with cheap merchandise pass by. They are the first of a thousand micro-businesses that will soon be flowering in the hot, crowded street.

One merchant stops to stare at me, occasionally pointing and laughing at the white man sitting against the wall. I am tired and hurting, I do not feel like being stared at. I think it is particularly rude and tell him so. He thinks this is even more hilarious. I slink off, defeated, feeling humiliated and very out of place. The Great White Explorer does not like to be ridiculed.

On the outskirts of town I get some directions to the nearest coastline. My blistered feet are hoping to go unencumbered in salt water and soft sand. With this promise, I coax my feet back into my shoes after a nice cup of sugar with tea. I start off down the mud-caked road. These are the hard miles, no beautiful or exotic coastline, without solitude or deep thoughts; only buses, mud huts, people on bicycles and continual reminders from my body that it doesn't think this is funny anymore.

After an hour the traffic subsides and the tropical vegetation creeps onto the road. Occasionally I jump on a truck to get through some particularly deep mud patches. Indian men stop to ask me what I am doing.

"I am going to the beach."

"But the beach is fifty kilometres away!" He looks concerned, and ashamed to give me the bad news.

I pretend not to be worried. "Fantastic."

I adjust my straw hat as they drive off, leaving me in a cloud of dust, alone on the road to digest this bit of unwelcome information. It takes me a while to build a logical construction of events that might prove that they have no idea what they are talking about. I don't mind the process. I have time, and anything that distracts my mind form my body is welcome.

Four hours later I walk into a shaded tea stand where the proprietor is having her hair fiddled with. I am happy to be here, wherever here is, and perhaps going slightly mad. I order some tea before wringing out my soaked shirt. I clean my blisters by pouring peroxide over them; enjoying the sting, a novel change from the dull pain of the last few hours.

I am told the beach is not far now; a short footpath diverging from the back of one of the mud and stick houses will lead me there. I follow its winding inclinations but give up, as it blatantly goes west and north. *Nobody panic.* I will just bushwhack in a straight line to the east. Finding the ocean is now an obsession. An hour later I sadly abandon that plan due to endless savannah and palm trees ahead. I don't even feel like going back to the teashop. I turn left at the village and keep walking.

I get more directions on my way out; Somanga is another twenty kilometres away. "The coast she is there." My eyes and head dip toward my worn shoes and the track they are on. It's midday and this is no time for anyone to be walking anywhere. Once out of town, I try to find a bit of shade, desperate not to be the centre of attention.

My search brings me to a set of carpentry tools lying around a half-finished door under a tree. The adjoining shack seems deserted. It is all too good to be true. I stretch out on the workbench that is made from logs the size of my wrist. Away from ants, in the shade and unmolested, I find quiet for the first time today. The flies are enjoying the buffet on my feet, but I have given up on petty concerns.

Two young men show up, and seeing the state I'm in, they give me space. Thoughtfully they hang a radio by my ear that emits that classic African blend of static and music that soothes the local's ears; to me it resembles nails on a blackboard. Sticking a few honey-flavoured biscuits in my mouth I slip into one of those afternoon naps where reality and dreams mix into a confusing and exhausting experience.

When I have rested enough to feel the flies again, the young men come over and invite me to have lunch – the standard pot of maize without seasoning. Food has lost its appeal. I have to keep moving, that is all I can think of now: walk, walk, walk.

After some careful directions, which I do not understand, I am back on the road. At times I dream happily for long periods before reluctantly ending up back in reality. Thoughts of quitting are now never far away. Every train of thought eventually stops at that station, only the duration varies. The pros and cons of stopping are endlessly reviewed. Sometimes, to my surprise, I haven't thought of quitting for almost thirty minutes, which reminds me that maybe I should quit.

A white man passes me in an air-conditioned 4x4, his driver doing a passable job of avoiding the potholes. Wearing a crisp white shirt and tie, he looks disbelievingly at me, trying to make sense of the sweaty figure under the grass hat, as if I was the one out of place. It is not good for morale. He is the first white person I have seen since starting. I feel like an American Indian looking at the end of my lifestyle as I know it. White people, especially ones in fancy clothes, mean civilisation. If they are around, you can be sure people here have realised true poverty. It is a social atom bomb.

The winding, buckling road that has forced cars to crawl for the past forty kilometres stops abruptly, replaced by a tarmac line, calm and obedient, waiting to enhance driving pleasure. To ruin a perfectly good neighbourhood, build a tarmac road past it, plant a cell-phone tower and claim it in the name of civilisation. This allows the world to move past fast enough for locals to see what they are missing, without a chance of ever catching up. It creates another dumping ground for the worst of our culture.

When the first outcast left Africa to become all that they could be, they started a process that has come back to threaten the survival of their descendants, including the ones who stayed behind minding their own bananas. Want, want, want will be the death of us all. But at the same time, need is the fastest growing product in Africa. It is an unnatural acceleration from the most basic of starting points to the most unrealistic, unnecessary and artificial of standards. Moving from one category on the need hierarchy to another is meant to be a gradual process in order to protect us from ourselves.

It's not all doom and gloom. Africa endures better than any place I have ever seen and maybe, just maybe, the meek will inherit the earth. It's hard to imagine that things can get any worse, and for all I know the boat that is Africa will float for a long time. Simplicity is good like that. I am not saying don't build tar roads. I am just saying roll up your window – transition is never pretty. Young men with no work or purpose drift around looking for a way to become the idols promoted by the West: gangster rapping, wife-beating, drug-dealing convicts, and the pinnacles of success. In these places, at every beer hall women sell their bodies and souls for the price of a warm beer and pay for it with their lives. Mid-sized towns look the same from Botswana to the edge of the Sahara. They represent AIDS-infested, desperate places where Africa meets civilisation halfway.

The vultures close in immediately. One cool cat after another tries an angle on me. I sit through two presentations by guys who picked up their 'How to take advantage of a white man' certification papers at the local whorehouse. No points are awarded for originality or cunning. I am too fatigued to pretend to care about their feelings. I tell them to leave me alone. The third opportunist is marginally better, perhaps only by comparison, so I play along. Maybe he knows where the beach is, or failing that, the fastest way out of this dump. After a week of walking I have arrived where I do not want to be and I need to escape before this pollutes the amazing time I have had.

I reach the beach. It's another swamp. My guide promises to start a holiday resort and name it after me because we will be best friends forever. I turn and walk away without feeling the need to say goodbye. I move slowly south through the ankle-deep pools under the yellow mangrove trees. I figure it can't go any place worse than this.

Eventually the swamp leads me back onto the mainland. Some kids are running after me yelling at my whiteness, making faces and being a nuisance. I pause to look over the scene, and my options. I realise it is over. This is not how I imagined it. Fortunately my body is at the last phase before damage is done which will take months to repair.

Mozambique will be there for another time. In my immediate future are things that need to be addressed in the real world – a world I am ready for again. I have had my simple journey. I have gotten what I came for. I lean on my backpack and tap a Sportsman from the crinkled pocket. I am tired, beaten, broken, and ready to get the hell out of here.

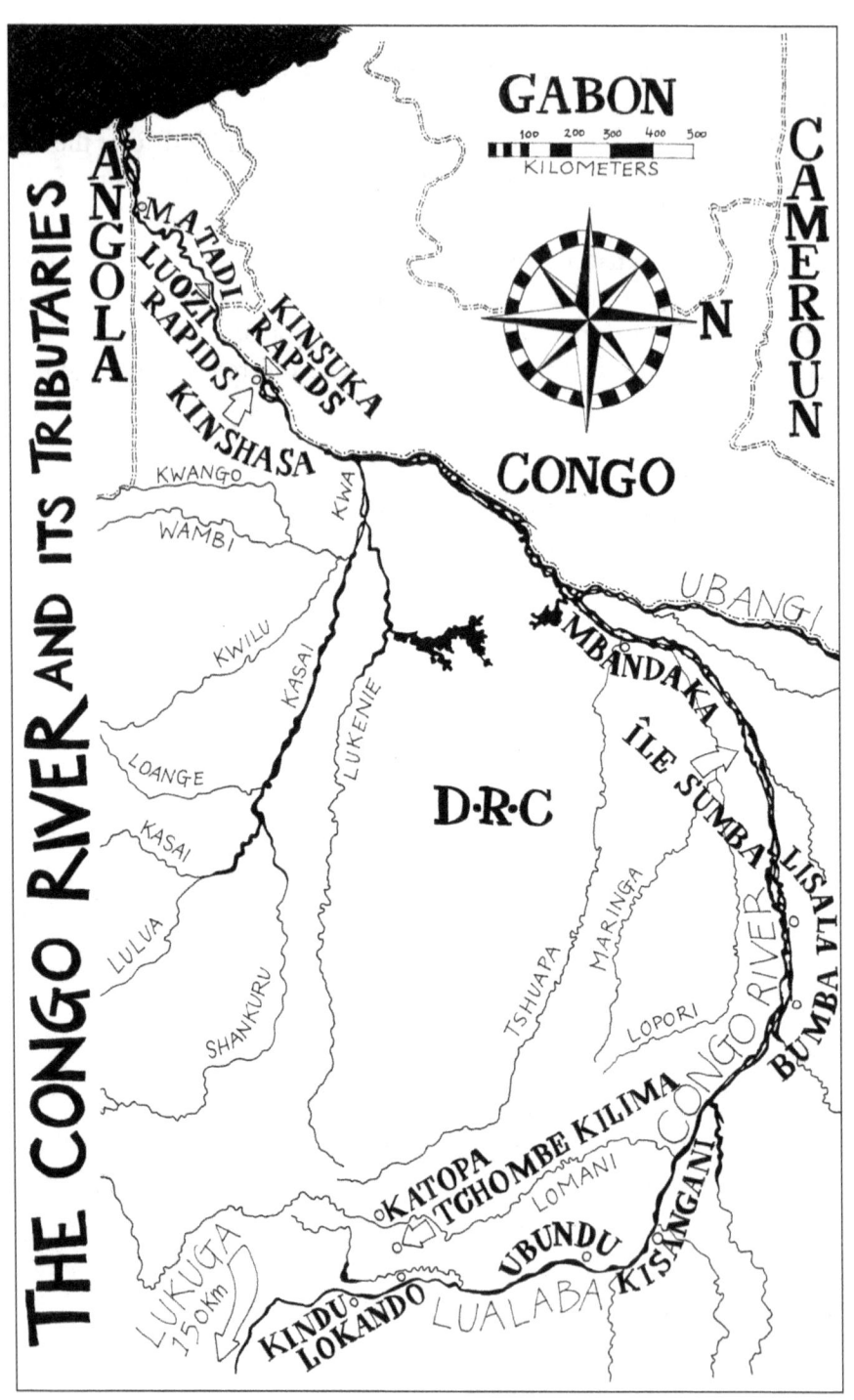

CONGO SOLO

He who has a strong enough why can bear almost any how.
—FRIEDRICH NIETZSCHE

THE ENDGAME

Black and white pieces sit in ones and twos like the endgame on a chessboard. We occupy our squares on rows of empty seats while the room holds its breath expectantly. There are no happy couples, no excited youths, no mothers, no children, no light reading, no idle chat, only serious men with serious thoughts. Airports are the lost and found of our dreams and I am in another waiting room to find out which one it's going to be.

The UN flight departed an hour ago, leaving us to fend for ourselves. I am guessing the old guy pacing up and down is too nervous to be a businessman and dressed too smartly for a missionary. This probably makes him both types of do-gooder, ready to hand out money and God to the less fortunate from his neat leather case that is too small to contain a laptop.

The remaining players' respective roles are easy to guess from the material they are intently reading or absentmindedly stroking. They are ready to tell their truths from a Bible or prospectus. It is not their occupations that interest me; it is their motivation I wish to know. There are easier places to do business, more accessible souls to save. Unless you were unlucky enough to be born in the Democratic Republic of the Congo, this is no one's first stop. Are they flying out of desperation, for passion, or for dreams of fame or fortune? Or perhaps like me, all of the above.

I close the book that brought me here. The words that made the challenge impossible to ignore. It makes for grim reading. It seems they eat people where I am going. I hope to avoid that but I am scared of something else. Fresh from another failed attempt at a normal life and low on confidence, it is giving up that I fear. If I fail in this mission, something is going to die inside me.

With every step in this direction my chances of a normal life decrease and with them the happiness I am told normality contains. What I find may overload the system. It could leave me unable to function in the world at all, or worse, bitter for having to live in it. I know from experience that completing an expedition is no guarantee of satisfaction, but I have nowhere left to look.

There was a time when I thought that a single expedition could colour all the grey spots. On the brink of another mission, all I seem to know is that, just out of my reach, there is a level of consciousness that makes everyday functioning seem like the slow death it is. There's not much to show for the last decade of searching, and my glimpses of pure conscious awakening have made the thought of life without expeditions unbearable. It has been too long since I have experienced the full flow of life. I know these moments offer only a brief respite, so I am returning to the *source* without expectation. I will take what She gives me, and if that is as good as life gets, that will do.

Ready Steady Go

Failure can be divided into those who thought and never did and those who did and never thought.
—Rev. W. A. Nance

When the time comes, we walk through drab, official-looking glass doors. Their blandness suggests nothing of the mysterious destination they lead to. The walk is short and directly onto the tarmac where a fifteen-seater twin-engine is waiting. A black registration is stencilled across its shiny metallic surface, the total of the airline's personality and the airplane's pretensions. Competition is non-existent. The only requirement is not to crash, and they know it.

The pilot's black pants and white shirt suggest respectability, and the stripes on his lapel identify him as someone with rank and responsibility. His dark wolf sunglasses tell another story. I know enough bush pilots to believe the latter. Formalities are kept delightfully simple. He leans over his shoulder, briefly putting us in the picture. Speaking French, his tone indicates that everyone should already know this, but it is stipulated in his contract so he does so anyway: seat belts, cell phones and ETA. He spins the silver flying machine around, revving the engine hard, giving it a last chance to brake before take-off.

A minute later we are rising in jerks and sputters, climbing a staircase over Lake Victoria, Africa's largest body of water. I flatten my face to get a glimpse of the Russian plane that landed in the lake last week. A tombstone made from its tail section, standing like a giant cross at the point of impact would be nice, but any sign of its carcass cut to shreds over the serrated wave blades of the lake will do. Instead I see picturesque fishing communities, white sandy beaches and scattered tropical islands that zoom out from the viewfinder.

We have a few stops on the way. In Butembo we skid to a halt on a dusty road across a hilltop into the middle of a shantytown lined by eucalyptus trees. We do not disturb the women walking straight-backed under bundles of firewood nor the bent-over figures working the soil; and plant growth as sparse as teenager's facial hair. I assume planes land in their gardens all the time.

Relieved, scattered applause ripples from the back of the plane as it rolls to a stop by a rundown two-room house. A few people stand outside ready to board. A do-gooder is replaced by a heavy sweaty Congolese man in an obscene suit with blobs of gold dripping from his fingers and neck.

The pilot finishes his cigarette, steps on the butt and walks back to the plane. The spiel is even shorter this time. My French is non-existent, but in retrospect it could have been, "Get down, hold on." The engines are revved, ominously, this time with even more urgency. Missionaries, diamond dealers and non-believers join in prayer as the plane attempts to clear the unnecessarily high tree-line at the end of the runway.

Next stop, Bunia. On my way to the airport building I stroll past a plane that someone seemingly forgot there years ago. A spare part never arrived, causing an infection to kill a machine that once defied gravity. In a dirty but official-looking building I wait my turn. A woman takes my money and passport. Soon I have a stamp that says Visa and République du Congo. I hope this is not going to be too easy – I'll be devastated.

It's a short flight to Goma. As we eke a slow turn over the mountains, my face is again squished against the porthole in macabre curiosity. This place makes the Gaza Strip look like a holiday resort and Al-Qaeda like disobedient schoolboys.

A few clusters of banana trees are unnaturally green, bright as algae between the grey rock fingers reaching out from the active volcano into the heart of town, squeezed between thousands of tin shacks that so inadequately shelter its population. In January of 2002, Nyirangongo erupted, releasing a stream of lava a kilometre wide and up to two meters deep, destroying twenty per cent of the town in the process.

Goma's problems do not start or stop with an active volcano. There is also the beautiful Lake Kivu, one of three lakes in Africa that holds huge quantities of dissolved gas at high pressure in its depths. In 1986, Lake Nyos in Cameroon erupted and released suffocating carbon dioxide, which killed nearly two thousand people in the surrounding area. Lake Kivu is nearly two thousand times bigger than Lake Nyos and has approximately two million people living along its shores. Occasionally, it burps and kills a few fishermen, but it is fair to assume a volcanic eruption in Goma could trigger a catastrophe.

It says a lot about Goma that no one worries too much about either of the natural catastrophes occupying their landscape. Eastern Congo, with Goma as its figurehead, has played a major role in Africa during the past fifteen years. No work of fiction could spin a deeper yarn.

A quick lesson in the Eastern Congo conflict begins with the Rwandan genocide of 1994. Hutu versus Tutsi. An invading force of Tutsi refugees living an exiled military existence in Uganda eventually stopped the slaughter of 800,000 people. The *interhamwe* or *genocidares*, mostly Hutus, ran for the border.

With the aid of 'safe zones' under Operation Turquoise, nearly two million refugees fled Rwanda; the Goma region alone absorbed almost half of those people. Thousands were greeted by a deadly cholera outbreak in the new Hutu-dominated refugee camps. The bad times kept coming. Hutu militias, of which there were nearly 30,000 living amongst the refugees, attacked ethnic Tutsis in their new homes. By 1995 North and South Kivu provinces were infected with instability and all international aid operations pointed to Goma.

Joseph Mobutu, Zaire's then-ailing dictator, seemed to ignore the east, as if it were a bastard child he dared not to claim. Meanwhile, Uganda and Rwanda sent troops to restore order, avenge the attacks and arm local supporters. The Hutu militia fled to regroup.

To further their cause, Uganda and Rwanda primed Laurent Kabila to overthrow Mobutu's crippled regime. At this point the conflict was no longer a residue of genocide: instead it turned into a regional war. In 1997 Zaire became the Democratic Republic of the Congo.

While Kabila nestled into his new position in Kinshasa, the Rwandan government became annoyed with his lack of response to the festering conflict in the East. Rwanda and Uganda were not the only players who vied for a stake in the mineral-rich and highly unstable Congo. At the time of the Lusaka Peace Accord in 1999, Zimbabwe, Burundi, Angola and Namibia were all involved: Africa's World War. Rather than stability these countries gained wealth through 'security' and mineral extraction.

The conflict is dressed up in ethnic colours, but it is all about business. The Kivu soil is some of the most mineral-rich in the world. As the third-largest producer of diamonds in the world and the womb of vast amounts of cobalt, copper, tin, gold, zinc and coltan, the DRC is a hotbed for unobstructed rape and pillage. No one knows who the good guys are. Even the current president, Joseph Kabila, came into power in 2001 when his father was assassinated. Apparently his allies didn't like him anymore.

The regional conflict officially ended in 2003. Countless journalists and war analysts maintain that it was the most costly war since World War II, killing nearly 5.5 million people (mostly from disease and starvation). While fat-cat generals and politicians stole billions, the local population was raped, enslaved, killed and occasionally eaten.

The airport in Goma is basic but it is an airport. The part of the runway not engulfed by lava is immaculate. Military gun posts built on fragments of lava rock from torn sandbags protect UN aircraft. Once out of the plane the pilot climbs into a 4x4 standing next to large piles of lava scraped away from the last natural invasion. He motions for us to jump in.

During a short drive we pass the planes of *Bora Air* (Swahili for better), *Safe Airline, Mango* and *Bravo Air Congo*. What these titles fail to mention is that the Congo is used to monitor the functional limits of Russian planes. Apparently it's a great place to see how overloaded they can fly with minimum maintenance before crashing. A few months ago one did not clear the lava pile at the end of the runway. It turns out the load master had a little import business of his own on the side. Unfortunately he did not inform the pilot that he had overloaded the already overloaded plane.

Inside the airport building the roof is missing in a few places. Scattered chairs take up residence in an otherwise empty arrival hall. A man is leaning against the wall smoking, while we are herded into a row of cattle gates to have our passports branded. I am confident since I have already cleared immigration in Bunia. With a visa in my dog-eared passport I stroll on over with my new best friend, the sweaty suit dripping with gold. As I had hoped, he knows Mr. Immigration by name. Unfortunately there seems to be a problem with my visa. "Oh really?" In a friendly manner I am instructed to stay until everyone has left so we can sort it out. This is more like it.

When I return to the office two days later everyone is happy to see me again. I feel better about the bribe knowing that I am a valued customer. I sit and chat to my new friends, smoking a cigarette in the departure lounge and waiting for my plane to Kindu.

I have been on red alert and at full battle stations since I arrived. The Congo is a war zone, and one of the most dangerous places in the world. I spent most of yesterday walking alone in the crumbling city of Goma. I watched my surroundings closely waiting for the apocalypse. Apart from the bribe that was so gently extracted at the airport, I have received less harassment than on an East African beach resort. Apparently since the governor sanctioned mob justice, things have calmed down. Soldiers are everywhere, and it is obviously a place ruled by the gun, even though the tropical green bursting out of the seams of the black rock gives it a vitality that even the gloomy volcanic air cannot dull.

When walking past women beggars, I have to shut my mind to what they might have been through. Even those who appear to be functioning have probably been gang-raped. The prevalence of rape and other sexual violence in Eastern Congo is described as the worst in the world. Research by the Harvard Humanitarian Initiative on sexual violence in Congo's eastern South Kivu province showed that sixty per cent of rape victims in South Kivu were gang-raped by armed men, with more than half of the assaults taking place in the victims' homes and an increasing number of attacks being carried out by civilians.

It might be the rape capital of the world, but I have my own problems. Erupting volcanoes, exploding lakes, a civil war and my biggest concern is my budget. Typical. A major problem with being 'poor' is that it takes up so much of your time. Despite my initial $80 visa and the additional

$100 bribe to get into the country, I am charged another $350 for the privilege of visiting the Congo. If I include air tickets to Kindu, I have now spent a third of my budget in one day, leaving me with $2000 to explore the Congo. The ease with which they relieved me of my cash in the first round is worrying. It could be worse, I could have been robbed at gunpoint or shot at.

There is no visible sign yet of the monster that is hiding in the shadows, ready to pounce. I distrust my instincts telling me that everything is perfectly small-town-calm. Around every corner I still expect to see a world falling apart. Where are the threatening immigration officers and intimidating soldiers? To make up for the lack of danger I have so far experienced and show you how brave I am for being in the Congo, I might have to mention that the country is still considered to be one of the most hostile places on earth. Maybe it is because of Goma's strategic importance, it is in some very powerful people's best interests that it is protected. Once I get to Kindu it's going to get worse, no doubt.

The Forest

Kindu, March 22, 2009

It's my birthday. The party is held over cold Cokes at the Vera Beach Resort. A few electric lights haphazardly poke out of the ground, lazily sharing their fluctuating glow with the pathway of crumbled rock, but regard our huddle of plastic chairs and table as the waiter's responsibility. Barbed wire curls in a spiral of metal thorns on the ground, separating us from the brown mass of water that flows past our feet. With no light to mark the other bank of its kilometre-wide track, the Lualaba could be mistaken for any old river at night. Strong bodies thrust a *pirogue* upstream, long tear-drop paddles are speared into the soft sandy bottom of the river and used as leverage against the current. We exchange passing greetings with the paddlers gyrating their hips to the Lingala music blasting out from the bar.

The topic of conversation is the imminent destruction of the planet. My companions are John and Terese Hart, an elderly couple here to make a last stand for bonobo apes on behalf of the six billion people that don't even know they exist. Until a few months ago I did not know of, nor care about, another variation of monkey. I am learning, however, that the bonobo is not an ordinary ape and that its evolutionary distance from the chimpanzee is a lot greater than I would have thought.

We share 98.4 per cent of our genetic make-up with bonobos. Some have even learned to use human language in captivity. As possibly the most loving creatures imaginable, it seems they also have a few things to teach humans. Sexual activity, grooming, or sharing food eases conflict between bonobos. Bonobos prefer to make love, not war; a lot of it, in every conceivable fashion. Sex in bonobo society is not about making little bonobos. Scientists claim that intercourse amongst the bonobo serves as a way of bonding, exchanging energy and sharing pleasure.

Sex is important in keeping the society together by maintaining peaceful, cooperative relationships and keeping everyone entertained. Besides heterosexual contact, both male and female bonobos engage in same-sex encounters. Orgies are not uncommon, and are used as an ice-breaking technique between groups. Female-female contact is a particular favourite. Unlike other apes, bonobos frequently copulate face-to-face, looking into each other's eyes. When groups meet in the forest, instead of beating their chests and starting a fight, they have a shag and share food. The more I learn about bonobos, the more I ask myself where humans went wrong.

Like all hippies, they don't stand a chance. Bonobos only occur in the Congo and only on one side of the river. Saving the last of the bonobos is John and Terese Hart's current priority. Terese first arrived here as a Peace Corps volunteer in 1974 while John was already in the forest working to document the lives of pygmy bush hunters. For thirty-five years they have been trying, in some form or another, to slow the Congo's environmental destruction. It has not been a total success. Not much in the Congo ever is.

Despite this, they bubble with excitement. It is hard to get in a word as they out-talk and constantly correct each other. A heated argument is easily defused by a warm gesture or a loving touch. Mama Terese often raises her voice to tell Papa John off, not because she is angry but because it is the only way to make him listen, and then only until he hears something he can run with. All do-gooding is done for selfish reasons. Or is it? If it is then it is more likely to continue in the absence of appreciation or inevitable setbacks. Their world is their own, and their work is their life. Their accents and body language are American, but they know this land and speak its languages as easily as their own. They raised their children here while they walked its forests and documented and protected its mysteries. They are that rare breed of truly integrated white people.

Later, walking home along the overgrown path, hopping over puddles and dodging potholes by flashlight, we talk about Africa and its future. It makes me think of Doug Erwin's quote from *The World Without Us*:

> Humans are going extinct eventually. Everything has, so far. It's like death: there's no reason to think we're any different. But life will continue. It may be microbial life at first or centipedes running around, then life will get better and go on, whether we are here or not. I figure it's pretty interesting to be here now, so I am not going to get all upset about it.

It seems to fit nicely in an environment that appears to be heading only one way. I think John and Terese might understand this. They are locking down what they can, for the future, but seem well aware that overwhelming odds favour it all coming to nothing.

With all the excitement of our own convictions, we hardly listen to each other. Occasionally the shiny face of a kid blooms in the weak perimeter of our flashlight that spreads ahead of us like a shadow. A few ask for money, most simply say hello. We do not stop, leaving them to giggle at their courage for speaking to the white people.

John is pessimistic about the future of Africa. This comes from someone who is as excited about life as a kid at Christmas, ready to whistle in any given moment. I don't think it bothers him too much. "We live from miracle to miracle out here, for that one small chance that comes by every now and again, against all odds." I smile. This is exactly why I have returned to Africa. I need to know that miracles exist. Since he is still here after thirty-five years, I assume he has seen a few. We agree that the chances of a happy ending for the continent are slim, but we also agree that if Africa is good for one thing, it is surprises.

As he points enthusiastically at the map duct-taped to the wall, I can't help but feel that I might finally have found what I have been looking for: the deepest, darkest, wildest corner on the planet. Mankind's ancestors left the continent millions of years ago in search of the unknown.

By the same genetic drive that pushed migrations across the globe I have been stumbling my way through the world to bring my life back to the beginning: the source, the heartland.

I know it is only the search that matters, but surely this, the last unexplored forest in the Democratic Republic of the Congo, may be just that – the last. Humans have been filling in the gaps on the planet since they figured out that if you go in one direction for long enough you end up where you started. TL2, as it is called on the map, is not the last unknown place on earth, but chances are by the time it is charted and turned into a national park, the others will be all but gone.

So it is there below that slightly crooked finger, a blob of green ink the size of a coffee spill, representing a forest of 36,000 square kilometres, that I will be getting my chance at the untouched and unknown. I have read enough about the Congo and its rainforest to know it will not be easy. Still, I feel incredibly fortunate to be here now. There are thousands of people with the same drive for the unknown, but I will be one of the few who gets a chance at the real thing. All the dragons have been slain apart from this wounded beast. I am not going to die wondering. I will help kill the last dragon, and good riddance. It's time to get a real job anyway.

Going In

It's not often I would admit to having a black man clenched between my thighs and enjoying it, but I have and I do. He is a nervous driver and I dislike being on the back of anyone's bike. The fact that proper medical help is two airplane flights away is something I try not to think about. "There are many ways to die in the Congo," John said last night and I refuse to list them right now. This is one of those times when you have to surrender. I know the young man can drive, he has had plenty of ruts, dips, and rickety log bridges to prove it. I came for the Congo – no use freaking out about it now.

It took three hours in a *pirogue*, carrying nine people, four bikes and scientific gear, to get from Kindu to Lokando. There we slept in a building that once had electrical power, glass windows and architectural intentions.

In the shy grey of early morning I watch Prosi, his cigarette, rolled from what was previously a part of my diary, dangling from his lips as he loads the dapper little red 100cc Yamaha. I study him strapping ever more to an already impressive load onto what resembles a child's toy more than a motorbike. In the jungle, unless your transport can fly, it needs to be easy to lift, small enough to fit into a dugout canoe and light enough on fuel to cover the lengthy distances between sips.

On the way out of camp we do a brief sightseeing tour of what must have been a functioning modern town in a civilisation long gone. Churches, schools and concrete are all turned to impressive ruins. Things from a time only old people speak of. We are speeding through a jungle track on 'the little red machine that could.' The trail started the width of a sidewalk. The knife that had hacked it open slowly grew blunt the deeper it cut, and we are now on little more than a dull brown superficial scrape through the surrounding green, in continual danger from the ever-encroaching undergrowth.

Every so often dead stems and bamboo beams spread over the road. I am a foot taller than my driver and my chances of being decapitated are increased by about the same amount. Wedged between the load, tied to the back and the driver, there is nothing to do but blink as they threaten to strike my head.

Prosi seems to have graduated from the Jim 'The Stuntman' Cummings' driving school. When in doubt, lean forward and go full speed. He loves it, with his toe sticking out of a split gumboot and cigarette at the edge of his smile. Every time I take my camera out he teases me with his only English, "Photo, photo, photo, photo." My standard reply never fails to crack him up, "smoky, smoky, always smoky, smoky."

I slap branches away from his eyes and remove ants from both of us. The bike in front of us flashes in and out of view in the thick jungle, trailing golden leaves in its slipstream, much like the kids in the few villages we do dissect, before they give up the chase and settle back on the jungle floor. We have already crossed one substantial river, the Kasuku, where we loaded the bikes onto a piece of wood resembling a plank more than a canoe. All our earthly possessions balanced an inch above the water in the hands of an old man in a ragged, collared shirt decorated with printed dollar signs.

A hundred small bridges punctuate our journey. Sometimes a single log as wide as a white line is the only link that connects the ends of a path constantly in danger of being smudged out; tightrope acts that would take me months before I could attempt them with any sort of confidence. Swirls of butterfly flakes – yellows, blues and whites – rise momentarily as we push and pull our load over streams, disturbing their beauty pageants held on the rotten logs below our feet.

The only other traffic are couriers who spend their lives moving up and down jungle tracks, pushing bicycles heavily loaded with baskets stuffed with jungle bounty. Occasionally a motorbike is briefly taken apart for CPR, life breathed back into dirty carburettors or spark plugs cleaned. The drivers have done it all before; no-fuss operations accomplished without panic.

By late afternoon we stop in a village, a copy of all the others we have passed. Fifteen surprisingly well-built huts stand on white sand, removed of all vegetation. Massive trees with outstretched branches, hold up the sky that seems to begin just above our heads. This is the end of the main road. We will leave the bikes here and continue on foot tomorrow.

Apparently there have been some problems with the locals. One of our field teams was threatened with shotguns. Oh really? I distinctly recall John saying to me he has never felt in danger anywhere in the Congo. Unfortunately that doesn't seem to apply to his employees. The story gets better. When the shotguns did not deter the Harts from exploring the forest, some spoilsports in the village reported them with false charges aided by backhanded payments to the secret police. Secret police. Can there be any term more synonymous with oppression? Only one adjective can make the words 'secret police' sound any worse, and that would be Congolese. The concept of state-sponsored psychopaths springs to mind. It took an official human rights complaint to get the Harts out of that situation.

Next, the village ordered its witch doctors to conjure up evil spirits, with their jungle voodoo, to swallow the intruders. Luckily the intruders had some strong magic of their own called Global Satellite Positioning. We are all interested to see what the next chapter in village relations will be.

Our little village in the heart of Africa wakes up like a million others. A cockerel yells "me me me", a baby cries, a woman moves in the dark, a fire is stoked to lick a blackened pot, a courtyard is combed with a broom of twigs. Children spill from warped doorways in cracked mud huts, half-dressed or completely naked, coughing and wiping their eyes.

I know we have a long way to walk, so I stand around impatiently for hours. The Congo doesn't notice. My mind wanders to the nighttime moments when the heat from the day finally left the earth; Prosi and I were cuddled close. In those moments I looked at him rolled up next to me under the mosquito net using his arm as a pillow. I should have offered to share with him when I realised that he had no net or blanket. However, where I come from, you don't share your bed with strange black men. I still get a fright when a black man tries to hold my hand, even if I know it is as natural for them as shaking hands. My first instinct was, if he ain't got it, he probably doesn't need it. If it was the other way around, I would have been offered the whole net, but I am still too white to share my breadcrumbs that easily.

We finally get underway. The first few kilometres wind past ugly overgrown fields, hacked from the jungles then surrendered back to its insatiable appetite. Suddenly, as if a door has closed behind us, we are in the real thing. Before, we had passed through the jungle. Now, we are in it. It grabs at my feet, catches my arms and slips down my neck. Falling could be painful and is a serious concern on a path littered with spikes. We cut branches to unravel the folds of the blanket thrown over us. We avoid hidden steps below dark brown puddles, and move down and up muddy riverbanks.

I would have believed I was the toughest man in the world if it wasn't for the fact that in front of me, keeping pace with the porters and myself, is a fifty-eight year old woman. Unwavering in her stride, Mama Terese makes it all seem ridiculously easy. When I comment on this to a porter he nods solemnly as if another has experienced the holy ghost, 'Mama Terese'; eyes widening, shaking his head in disbelief and wonder, "Ahh! Now you see."

The rest of the day is much the same, one foot in front of another, twisting and turning, fending off the jungle. Occasionally the challenge changes from jungle to savannah swamp. There is no gradual transition. One second you are dressed in jungle, and then, not a tree. With a single step you are in a wasteland of golden grass and clean blue air. The first reaction is awe and excitement. The view of the sky shakes off the claustrophobia you have been experiencing subconsciously for hours.

Your legs snap with vigour as they look forward to being unencumbered by roots and vines. Enthusiasm is dampened as your feet sink into the mud. After five minutes all you remember from the jungle is the shade. Your lower half disappears in the blond grass. Your feet search blindly for stable surfaces in the unpredictable sponge. Shoes are sucked off feet and ankles roll on hidden polls. When you do get the chance to take your eyes off the concealed path, the view is exquisite. Even the two biologists have no answer to why these bald patches exist.

Our line of slumped walkers draws longer and longer, spreading out more and more. After the third savannah of the day I am way up ahead with the lead porters. Thirsty and tired, endorphins have persuaded my brain to let them drive. The pace steadily increases until it is as close to running as you can get in this terrain. The sun is dipping fast and the porters have no desire to be caught in the dark.

Once back under the canopy the path becomes nearly invisible to my untrained eyes. Porters are flashing in and out of my view from as close as two meters away; swinging left and right around blind corners, jumping over obstacles. My feet and eyes have no time for deliberation, only reaction. I will not be able to keep this up much longer. No worries, though; when we reach water we will stop.

Before I even know it we have arrived at a stream, the porters have finished drinking from cups improvised using folded leaves. I realise with dismay that they never had any intention of stopping. I can't let them go now; soon it will be dark. If something happens to the group behind me I will spend my first night in the jungle as-is. As much as the ladies would dig the story, I would like to avoid it. I defy their almost-panicked demands, coming to a complete standstill, scooping the cold water over my head. For a second I think that I am fainting. The world zooms out on me. My eyes shut, I ride the feeling until I am back in focus.

By now the porters are frantically dragging me out of the little stream. For them the night holds more terror than discomfort. For the first time today, the journey is no longer enjoyable. My legs, which wanted to wait by the water, don't know how much more they can take.

An hour later the Lomami River blocks the path. It looks like a river in the jungle should: perfect. Massive trees, dressed in deep green, lean over one another to reach the open space the river provides. Their shadows are heavy in the last amber light as the sun makes a spectacular retreat.

My thoughts sputter in the dark, erratic like the fire we stare into. Despite the damp leaves below me being more comfortable than any bed, I am not really sure why I feel so content. To think I will be doing this for the next few weeks conjures a tug-of-war between the desire to push myself and questions of purpose. I decide that the problem with science is that no matter what anyone says, unless you're the monkey being shot into space, it's boring. I appreciate curiosity but resent rigid protocols; rebelling against them is in my DNA.

Back On The Trail

Just as I was starting to contemplate lying down in a column of soldier ants to make the misery stop, someone makes a suggestion. An 'explorer' is needed, someone to cover large distances into a previously uncharted part of the jungle, have a look around and document any signs of bonobo, hunting intensity or anything else of interest. They need a monkey, and I need space.

I do not stop to think it through. For me, adventure is normally the end of any good dream and has been known to lead to depression and insanity. I suspect a two month trek might be uncomfortable. I can pick my team. John, the old rascal, is my first choice. He is a terrible employee, we only hired him because he is such a good poacher, and we had to stop him somehow. The boss would spare him gladly; the longer he stays near base the more trouble he causes. He is taller than a Pygmy, looks old and smiles far too much to be a tough guy. I wouldn't leave home without him.

My second choice is more difficult to get. He is only twenty-three, but is smart, motivated and already doing the work of his supervisors. Because he was born in a village and is too young to order men around, he will be on a porter's salary of $65 a month for many years to come. Yet his future is bright for a Congolese because he has a job.

Heavy rain keeps us in camp until after lunch. Once the threat of falling trees diminishes, we force-march through the freshly washed jungle. It is green and winking silver from a million drops. Kissed by every leaf we passed, we are drenched before completing the first kilometre. No one minds. Whether it's rainwater or sweat, the outcome is the same.

As darkness approaches, we (and by we, I mean they) hack out an area barely large enough for a tent and a fire. My bivy is wedged between the two, next to a stream of fresh brown water. I have a suspicion that tomorrow is going to be a big one. As the fire loses enthusiasm, so do I. We both drift to sleep.

> *Hakuna muingine kama wewe*
> *Hakuna muingine kama wewe*
> *Hakuna kama wewe*
> *Hakuna kama wewe*
> *Ni wewe tulifuraha*
> *Ni wewe tulifuraha*
> *Bwana wa bwana ni wewe tu kuwa na ni wewe tu*
> *Kuwa na ni wewe tu*

It's a song, a poem, a whisper and a prayer. It's a way to let snakes know he is around. Like a hymn in church it hangs in the pre-dawn, mixed with the mystery of the fine mist from which it drifts. It is the sound of a man, happy and at home.

I grin as Papa John floats through the darkness, doing whatever it is that he does. I smile because everything is as it should be. As he whistles into camp, the light of the fire fades with the coming day. He flashes me a smile, "Uliamka Papa Hedriko." So genuine and perky, it is impossible to doubt that we are partners in some excellent adventure. At first I was embarrassed to be called Papa, but around here everyone is. The respectful yet familiar tone has grown on me.

Having dipped the coffee packet into his cup to make sure nothing is wasted, John uses a spoon to slurp up every last ounce of pleasure. It is as good as the day will get. When he is done, we will get into our wet clothes from yesterday, brush off the flies from our packs and walk until dark.

His smile has not faltered since we left the path yesterday morning for the unknown. I am not sure why he is so happy. I've been unhappy working cushy jobs in beautiful places where a month's wages for John could be spent at the bar in a frivolous night. Soon he will pull himself and his load up with the help of a tree. His load will stay on his back for the best part of eight hours. Once that is done, he will make more coffee and cook us some food, wash the dishes, then sleep for a few hours. Tomorrow he will do it all again.

Weeks ago I watched the same incurable zest from the porters doing the transect lines when we measured bonobo nest deterioration. They wake up cracking jokes and singing to themselves, even though they know that they will be doing backbreaking work for the rest of the day, for the rest of their lives. They will be away from their families for weeks at a time, constantly facing, what is to me anyway, a modest state of hunger. They work long hours in an environment where even the air seems to bite, while being slowly eaten alive for nothing more than a fish dinner and a few bucks.

There are few true jungle men like John. Walking and living in this claustrophobic, dark, humid environment is a constant battle for most people, black or white. They have no more interest in bonobo nest deterioration, and far fewer options, than I do.

I am starting to see the heart of darkness and I don't like its location one bit. These are not the Congolese I have read about. Instead of being scared of them, I admire them. Perhaps I am just lucky; surely they won't be so amicable outside the forest.

As Lengos sticks his head out of the tent, Papa John giggles. "You are up," he teases the man half his age. Little fuss is made about mornings. A cup of coffee is breakfast. We pick ants from our clothes, arrange our loads, switch on the GPS, and go.

When we sit down again it is four hours later and we are next to an unhealthy looking whitish puddle of water. Blocks of cold rice are shared out. The top is peeled from a tin of Anne sardines made in Portugal, its oil carefully dripped over the rice for gravy. Colourful butterflies, the size of small birds, flutter around seductively. They use their beauty as camouflage and are forgiven for behaving like common houseflies.

For barely five kilometres, we have walked, crawled, hacked and ripped through the inner fibre of the jungle. Apart from the odd observation we talk little. It's been a hard morning, mostly under *maranteceae*. Curtains of leaves hang from bad-tempered vines that have to be beaten regularly with a machete. The battle is occasionally broken by moments of bliss, like wading in a cold river or walking through enchanted jungle cathedrals, fairy-tale in size and devoid of undergrowth. It dwarfs us with arches tiled by gold and brown leaves settling together at the foot of massive pillars.

Lengos is clothed in a once-white, now-yellow outfit, torn and shredded like a shipwreck survivor. He swings the machete with the ease and precision of a boxer punching at shadows. Its wooden handle, polished by the sweat of rough men's hands, swivels as if his fist were attached. Cuts are delivered with surgical precision.

Behind him, mostly bent over or on my hands and knees, I force my way through. No gap he cuts seems big enough. Countless times Papa John has to untangle me patiently from his position in the rear. His khaki 1980s sports jacket is pulled up to his elbows. The white bowling hat I gave him is cheekily cocked forward in a Robin Hood style. All 5.5 feet of him stands straight in stripy black shorts mounted on skinny bowed legs.

He alone seems at ease in here, practically barefoot with a load I struggle to lift. I hardly ever see him move. Whenever I look back John seems to have been there the whole time; somehow appearing at the other side of obstacles, exempt from the normal restrictions of movement when in the burrows of his trees.

I am in awe of his powers because they surpass my understanding. He is living proof that spirituality exists; his perception is supernatural, his senses are sharpened by necessity of survival. In a world of near-uniform colour with shapes of every conceivable variation, he can see a snapped twig while walking amongst a thousand others like it. It might as well be magic when he stops his fast-floating walk, frozen in a stance with his face contorted in a frown, deciphering one variation on a million others. His nose and ears are ever-twitching, like a hard drive crunching data.

It is already getting dark when we drop our loads. I try to help set up camp, but feel like the little brother allowed to play with the big kids, only to be constantly under their feet. Everyone seems relieved when I sit down to write in my diary.

Put John anywhere in the jungle and he will build a home and have it fully furnished in less time than some people set up tents. Lengos is no slacker either. Soon we have a few square meters of civilisation on temporary loan. Where the wet logs meet, a little volcano of fire has formed. The smoke gently taps the first layer of the canopy just above our heads.

With coffee in hand and my aching back against a tree, I watch dinner being prepared. The salted and dried carcass of a fish, now resembling a piece of tree bark, is removed from a dirty mess bag. Judging by the frayed edges protruding from its grey oily coating, it might have been white originally and possibly part of a grain sack.

Over the nearest log the fish is hacked to bits with the machete. Blunt from chopping us along at one kilometre per hour all day long, it sends splinters of fish flying. A mineral water bottle, wrinkled and worn, is half filled with thick orange goo. Its top has long since been replaced by leaves stuffed down its neck, blackened with grime and grease. This palm nut oil is dripped into the most basic of pots. Fishing around in his dented coffee tin, John pulls out an onion the size of an eyeball and a tin of tomato paste only marginally bigger. Collecting the splinters of fish from the ground around him, he adds it all together to boil. Then John leans back to rip a few leaves from a nearby plant and uses them to touch the hot sides of the pot holding our priceless contents. It's the same plant he used earlier to make thread to sew his shoes back together.

Lengos has been inspecting the rice for an hour, removing impurities by hand, scratching away at the pile spread out on the plastic sheets in front of him. Satisfied, he washes the rice in the queer-looking water that is uncertainly making its way past camp. The quantity is reduced as more impurities are scraped off and discarded. I am not sure why we can't cook it all as is, but I am sure that if we could, we would. If available they will make enough for lunch tomorrow. Servings come in helpings as large as a plate can hold. Lengos gets the other plate and John uses the pot. No meal has ever tasted better.

At three in the morning I am woken by John cleaning the pot from last night to cook beans for today. My thoughts drift to what I would have been doing in previous years at the same time on a Friday night. I smile without regret.

Back on the trail, we soon return to the thick *maranteceae*. Cutting the curtain causes a confetti of dead leaves to sift down the back of my neck. If you're lucky they come without ants. The ants, like itching and flying things that bite, are constant. The only difference is the type. Some are a nuisance, others are a problem.

What makes the experienced junglier twitch in his sleep is when he inevitably ends up in a lake of ants while negotiating a natural bottleneck. When this happens, it is okay to panic, as long as you do so while you are running. If, as is all too frequently the case, there is nowhere to run from the red cables of exposed electricity, standard procedure requires that you stamp your feet and swear at the machete guy to hurry up. Only out of the danger zone do you stop and face the fiery streaks rushing up your legs toward any exposed skin.

If it is your first time, you might find it disconcerting how ferocious they appear with their oversized heads. You brush off what you can, knowing full well that the game of slap-and-tickle will continue for the next twenty minutes. Where the next bite comes from will be a surprise, but armpits, balls and ass are all especially memorable. The only consolation is that everyone gets to share in the fun.

After lunch I take over the machete from Lengos. He has been in hand-to-hand combat with the forest since yesterday, beating it back minute after minute. It's hard work, but rewarding to be fighting back and it makes the time go by faster. Looking at walls trying to find a crack to aim my sword at, I am glad I am not alone. Without these two standing confidently behind me, I would have felt we were attempting something impossible.

I realise it's game-on when I fall to my knees through a rotten log in the swampy ground beneath, filling the gumboots I have tried so hard to keep dry. Today the jungle will give me its best. The end of the day is still two hours away and between now and then it's going to hurt. I smile; it was getting too easy anyway.

It's not a test until *after* you are tired. The jungle continues to squeeze tighter with its claws. Exhausted, failing to cut clean, I forego technique for power, dragging meters of knotted green cable behind me. My idea of strength does not impress the jungle. I am a fly in its web. The blade is so dull that nothing but a precise angle-cut cleaves my shackles. I am well aware that swinging a blunt sword at my own body with a tired arm, desperately off-balance, while tied in knots and sweat burning in my eyes, blurring my vision, is a potentially unsafe situation.

The end, like the finale of any hard day, is a tease. Looking for clean water in a swampy patch of forest we find a hole that stinks less than the others. In sheer exhaustion we declare it fit for human consumption. A full day under the canopy and only nine kilometres to show for it. The path we cut with so much sweat will soon be washed away in the green tide, impossible to see for all but the keenest of eyes.

I bathe myself in the black pit, kept cool in the permanent shadows of its captivity. Restored, I return to camp and am handed a cup of coffee by John. He is dressed only in a towel, a multipurpose item that every self-respecting Congolese jungle man carries. His hard little body looks like polished wood in the last of the day's light.

Assisted by a candle melted to a stump, Lengos is studying his English notes. They are scribbled and squeezed onto a tiny piece of paper and copied from my "Learn Swahili" course. He is preparing for the next time he will drop a surprise English phrase out of nowhere. I bait him by asking if he knows he is named after the capital of Nigeria. He rattles off a list of global capitals greater than mine. He comes from a village down the road, for god's sake! Though the war ended in 2003, teachers and books are not only very new imports, but struggling ones at that.

Lengos is a good example of the hunger to learn that I have seen since my arrival. At night in Kindu, rows of students would sit outside the UN compound's barbed-wire fences using the powerful security lights to study. Even in the jungle, any morsel of knowledge is devoured. This is becoming a tradition after every exhausting day, when they have taken care of their needs and mine, my Swahili-English dictionary is passed round camp. By candlelight or the dim glow of a fire, someone is making notes, practicing a few words, or simply paging through it in wonder and want. I try not to reflect on all the opportunities I have to learn and still waste.

By 20:00 I am rolled up in my bivy. Sleep comes and goes between vivid dreams. The waking moments are used to stare at fireflies bragging with their lights. The forest waits till night to come alive. Everywhere insects transmit their piercing opinions: symphonies of unknown songs, sounds with calls of larger-life in the background. Reluctant to let the day go, I savour the moments awake knowing sleep is only a blink away. Later, rain joins the orchestra. Never hard enough to reach the jungle floor, it merely taps a thousand little drums far above my head. Awake and asleep, warm and comfortable, in my bivy with nothing to do but stare at the magic around me until day arrives.

John hands me my cup of coffee. We make the same jokes we make every day and laugh at them with an equal amount of pleasure. As I gently allow a sip of warm coffee to evaporate in my mouth, a leaf flutters from the canopy high above, swirling twice before coming to rest at my feet like a loving pet. John stops mid-whistle, a frown contorts his face, the lines knot into intense concentration. Two quick steps and he has the leaf in hand. He examines it intently until the frown reverses gear, replaced by a smile that makes you think he knows the punch line for creation. "It's good luck!" he declares, satisfied, as if the matter is settled once and for all, before returning to the log and his beloved coffee.

The day starts off with a delightful thirty-minute walk. I almost forgot how tight it became yesterday. It is the last we see of easy. Too soon we are buried alive, again. As the guys photograph and count a group of bonobo nests, I keep cutting forward, possessed by action. Coming through another seemingly solid wall into a relatively open space, I look up for a sign of sky. It is a reflex; I need to see it just to be sure it still exists.

For a brief moment I idly inspect the unusual insect that was sucking blood from me until I slapped it into a stunned state with the flat end of the machete. A green thing with a fly design, but produced in moth size. I am tempted to take a photo just in case it is a new species, but it freaks me out so I get rid of it. From my right I hear the slight rustling of leaves in a breeze. A harmless sound except that breezes don't come through here.

Parting a trail of leaves with the ease of an ocean wave, a snake is moving across my path. I watch fascinated and transfixed as the whip keeps uncoiling in a movement that seems to consist of no movement at all. I have seen my share of snakes. They are quite common. I do not love them, neither do I hate them. I leave them alone, they leave me alone. This relationship has worked well.

What causes my mental stutter is the sheer size of this one and the speed with which it moves. It is as thick as a man's arm, between two and three meters long with a green-bluish body and head as high as my waist and as big as my hand. Within seconds it has disappeared, leaving me staring numbly after it and already doubting if it really was as big as it seemed. Surely snakes that massive can't move that fast. My head shakes last as a full-body shudder vibrates from my feet up.

Eventually we reach the savannah that our satellite mapping system had predicted we would find yesterday. I feel like a prisoner who has tunnelled his way to freedom. The bars of the forest are replaced by a deep tannin-tinted lake spilling over the horizon. I am very possibly the first outsider to walk here. An endless sea of yellow, its brilliant serenity occasionally lapping at tiny forest patches in its midst. Defiantly, these dark islands hold their ground. Tall trees stand united and snobbish, forming cliffs rising above the golden tide. They are stranded by their enormity. As a treat a storm is closing in. The news is told by a thousand sounds, all whispering violence; the hushed warning slowly grows to a scream as the dark fist closes in.

The black clouds are set in brilliant sunshine. Wildlife twitches excitedly and resigned to the inevitability of what is going to happen. Thunder beats across the sky as the first of a billion raindrops can be heard racing toward us. Colliding with the world is a silent war cry. Soon all sounds become one, a universal static. There is no more I or us, we dissolve into the experience of true nature, where destruction is as valid and beautiful as creation. The tallest tree and the tiniest leaf attempt to bow, adding their voices to the mayhem. Rampant with electricity, the air riots and explodes.

It is too intense to last long. For a minute the calm after the storm is every bit as loud as the storm itself. Where the battle in the sky has cleared away the tension, a refreshed blue is left with small white clouds painting delicate patterns, enjoying themselves in the sunlight as if nothing has happened.

This, here, and now is a childhood dream coming true. Other kids dreamt of being rock stars, I dreamt of being Tarzan. It would not have been half as beautiful if it had not been for the effort to get here. There have been no half measures. This is as deep as it is possible to be in the Congo.

The machete dangles loosely in my hand; I absentmindedly wiggle it against the small blister. From my left hand on a red piece of string hangs the compass. To commemorate what will stand as one of the best moments in my life, I take some cheesy photos of my companions. They need no encouragement; Congolese are the world champions when it comes to posing. Pointing to the sky or pretending to read the GPS, they look like men who have fought their way here inch by inch.

We are all riding the high after being under the canopy for three days, even seeing the humour as we each have a chance at falling through the false bottom, waist deep into the swamp on which the grass is delicately balanced. The grass types, like the depth of the swamp below it, change constantly. From soft knee-high stems to shoulder length three-bladed paper knives. Blood, smudged by sweat, drips dramatically from the criss-cross of tiny scratches that cover my arms.

During the rain Lengos and John combined their load under the plastic cover that also serves as our lunch container. Luckily its contents had been gulped down earlier. Lengos, like me, has only been carrying his personal gear. Everything else had been on John's shoulders. He has not complained once, but now without it his step becomes a bounce. A wild horse should not do the work of a pack mule. Every so often he breaks into a run for no obvious reason, sniffing around inspecting grass polls with the intensity of a dog in the park.

Lengos and I stumble like drunks on a dance floor, crushing grass and splashing water, often falling through to our knees. The gumboots threaten to be sucked off my feet with every missed step. It's fun and games but a twisted ankle would replace *the best day ever* part of the schedule, with a week spent crawling back to base.

Just after 15:00, we reach the furthest point on our triangulation. Turning north and homewards, I am nearing my limit. I desperately want to see this day ending where I started: in front. A good point man needs to give and take, needs to know when to go round and when to go through. I have lost that edge, drifting round obstacles more often than fighting through them, taking us further off course with every side step.

I finally hand over the machete to Lengos when we hear a shotgun's muffled cough. It's close. This area is not a national park, but technically certain species are protected everywhere. It is normally these primates for whom the shotgun is used. Trying to forget how much I need to rest, we set off in the direction of the shot. Even Lengos, machete in hand, can't keep up with John. By nature he is a hunter and now he has the scent of prey.

Soon Lengos and I are alone on a narrow path trying to catch up and record trap locations at the same time. The situation is running away from me. I don't particularly like chasing people with shotguns. We are far from our own territory, and interfering with another man's empty stomach in a place where the law, as I know it, does not exist. John is already so far ahead I dare not shout after him for fear of revealing our position.

We follow the splintered remains of snares, fiercely hacked to pieces, as if they were satanic paraphernalia. One would never guess we lifted two hundred traps only last week. As we pursue the trail of carnage, I start to wonder if I have stumbled into a personal vendetta between John and an old foe, with John believing the white man will protect him. I have less faith in the power of my skin. An all-weather notebook is the total sum of my authority. The pen might be more powerful than the sword, but I still prefer to be the one holding the shotgun.

My boots are buckets filled with water sloshing around. My tired feet follow the trail long after I want to stop. We are trying to catch up with someone I don't want to meet. The sun wins the race.

We find John at a small stream; relaxed, whistling a tune after a good day at the office. He is forever picking things up in the forest: fruit, bark, leaves. Once he carried a small tree with him for ten kilometres. Earlier he tapped some sap from a tree. He now applies it, like old chewing gum, to a pile of wet wood before lighting it up. He doesn't make a fire, he starts it up with the ease of a housewife switching on an appliance. An intricate system woven together with three logs as its base; over this a pot is balanced on tiny edges and sometimes merely ash.

A fire made by someone who has made one every day of his life is a piece of art. Apart from filling our bellies with warm food, its light carves out a primal association with safety. Holding back a darkness as thick as death, it paints our little world in soft orange. Like a copy from a Marvel cartoon strip, small characters loom large with deeply drawn shadows framed in solid black. It is a picture magic could live in.

Beans for dinner, and they take hours. I spend the time staring into the fire, fascinated by the silent, peaceful, seemingly erratic display that fire portrays so perfectly. I play through the many highlights of the day, which in the moment were disguised behind sweat and fatigue. I smile as I remember Lengos patiently asking me to go round instead of through another thorny patch I had cut to shreds in my stubborn fight. I was trying to win their respect with my endurance, except they must have been thinking, "I hope the white guy gets tired soon and gives the machete back to one of us."

John sits quietly smoking his evening joint, then gives a little yelp, kicking away instinctively. Muttering to himself to hide his fright as he realises it's only a worm the size of a small snake that slithered over his foot.

After dinner, as I am about to climb into my bivy, I meet a spider the size of my palm. For a brief moment I play the scientist, trying my best to think of it as just another of God's little wonders. As it makes a move for my diary, it signs its death warrant. As big as it is, I have surprise on my side. I fall asleep with the contentment of a day well-lived.

Jungle Men

Life is not about how many breaths we take but about how many wonders we experience.

—Claudio

Trying to scrape some beans and rice from last night's pot, I neglect the sock that I am drying with a stick over the fire. Its nylon melts into a marshmallow of black plastic. Nothing but a leg warmer now, still, John is happy to have it.

For my next trick, I commit the schoolboy error of brushing my teeth in a puddle of ants. By the time I look down it's far too late. Apart from the physical discomfort there is also some mental anguish, as they take a particular liking to my penis. The guys pretend not to notice as I jump around the camp, naked apart from my two mismatching socks, picking ants from my pubic hair.

No sooner is this spectacle over when six men spill out from the heavy fog. It can only be the men whose traps we destroyed yesterday. This could be bad. At seeing a whiteface they stop, unsure. That is all John needs. Greeting them like long-lost brothers, he is handing out cigarettes before he is even halfway to them. They stand undecided on the path.

The hunters range in age from sixteen to fifty, short and muscular, hard-looking men. Dressed in the usual rag-tag of Western castoffs, all carrying machetes, but no shotgun. While John is shaking hands, Lengos takes out the GPS and proceeds to start a conversation into its deaf ears, informing a make-believe base camp of our position and situation. I position myself near the machete sticking out of the wet soil like a poor man's Excalibur.

John is not allowing them time to think. Laughing and joking like a court jester, he has them posing for the camera. The poachers stand no chance against the combined efforts of charm and superior technology.

If they had come for payback, all is now apparently forgiven. Just to be sure, I keep my shirt off and wear my best Jean-Claude van Damme scowl whilst I nonchalantly sharpen our machete with the metal file. My effort to look tough fails, but they jump at the chance to sharpen their machetes. Eventually they leave, stocked up on cigarettes, machetes sharpened, and carrying our last sugar.

We quickly head in the opposite direction. Our food finished and the furthest point of our journey reached, I make a tactical decision to leave the jungle-bashing and follow a faint human trail home. It is twice the distance but should be three times quicker. The little line flutters and stutters as erratically as a mosquito's flight path. In and out of the savannah for most of the morning, its sole reason for existence is to drip feed bush meat to the closest village, a day's walk away. Along its course we find two huts that function as base camps for deeper expeditions to protein. They have all the charm of hard migrant men's workplaces worldwide, only without the pornography. Tattered roofs made from a patchwork of leaves stand without walls. Dilapidated stretchers crafted from sticks and a few pots are scattered on the ground around a fire that is never left to die.

Over this fire primates are smoked and prepared for the journey to the markets in Kindu, their bodies shrivelled by hours on the rack. On their sunken faces fleshless lips draw back in final screams of agony, and childlike fingers clutch, in vain, to life. I have flashbacks of the genocide victims laid out in the Mirambi memorial in Rwanda. There is something satanic about burnt corpses, human or monkey, as if the soul has somehow melted to the bone. Only my privileged whiteness can afford the sentiment. Hunger does not have sentiments. For everyone here they are simply food; perhaps slightly more valuable than chickens. I have no doubt that, born in these woods, faced with a choice between farming or hunting, which I would choose.

We talk briefly with a slightly retarded young man who is left alone in the camp. We ask for directions, take photos and document the site, but are careful not to alienate anyone. If any of this is to be saved it will only be done with the help of the hunters.

Walking on a trail under a slightly overcast sky makes for a nice change. John's retelling of the fright we got when the poachers arrived in camp keeps us entertained. Every time one of us remembers something else about our reaction to the hunters we are in hysterics again.

I walk behind John for a change, watching the whites of his feet through the holes in his shoes. I am daydreaming when he curses and jumps back a few feet. I know what it means but it still takes me good few seconds to see it. Even Lengos struggles to make out the puff adder baking on the ground, daring the world to either go around it or die. Apart from slightly the wrong shape and a drop too much shadow, its camouflage is near-perfect in the tall yellow grass.

I would have stepped on it, no doubt. It would have taken a few days to die out here, slowly and painfully with plenty of time to regret not becoming a lawyer. The snake yesterday was three times its size, yet it had life somehow. This little slab of death-incarnate fills me with entirely different emotions: that age-old loathing and fear we feel towards something that has no emotion and carries death on the tip of its tongue.

I try to forget all the trails I have already walked and will still walk, so deep that I can't even see my feet. I know there are snakes but had hoped if I made enough noise they would move away. That little illusion is gone. That poisoned splinter sticks in my mind. A quote from Joseph Conrad's *Heart of Darkness* pops into my head: "No man here lives a charmed life." Again, I think of how few old people there are in the forest.

For the time being, I am too happy to dwell on the reminder of hidden dangers. My team has done well. We fulfilled a tough mission with humour. If I travel for another lifetime I will never have experiences more remarkable. The last few days are reason enough to venture to the edge of civilisation. Following this train of self-congratulation, I make the false assumption for the hundredth time in my travels that our experiences are over just because we are close to home.

As if rubbed out, the trail disappears. Neither of my two top jungle men can pick it up where it ends in a fallen tree. It's a blow to John's ego as he is forced to concede that the GPS knows better. I add my two cents in a plan to dissect a trail cut previously by the transect teams monitoring bonobos. The guys respectfully agree, but it turns out at least one of those two cents is bad credit. It means we have to go off-piste again. It is only five kilometres but it could well be another night out, this time with no food. Mentally we were already at the base, and for a few minutes, our heads drop. Hours later we break through onto a transect line, from which it is a mere hour's walk to base.

Privately I wondered if they would rather have worked with the cushy transect teams. For me this was an adventure, but for them it was only work. I know they would never admit to not liking it. Judging by their behaviour and the humour we have had, I think we have all received what we had put in. I also realise, as we all have a stumble during the last few kilometres on a relatively easy path, that it's time for a rest.

The locals think I'm crazy for running in the forest. Apart from unnecessary exercise, few like to be alone out here. Through the encroaching undergrowth and under fallen trees I push my body to calm my mind. I run for many reasons. Without the exercise I cannot sleep, and there is nothing to do at night apart from sleep or think and sometimes that becomes just too hard. Today I run because I do not want to hear the screams.

Someone had left a baby bonobo in camp. The mother ended up as bush meat. We cannot pay for orphans at the risk of creating a market, but somehow they persuaded the hunter to leave her. She stinks and is terribly shy. I hope we will become good friends, if she lives, which is doubtful.

The rope she had been tied up with has cut deep into her waist. Yesterday I got John to hold her down while I showed Alfonse how to apply the antibiotic cream. Scraping the maggots out of the wound she screams like the tortured child she is. During the process she bit my fingernail. The skin was broken but there was no blood.

I feel like a coward for getting Alfonse to clean the wound today, but I can't be anywhere nearby. Bonobos need love more than medicine; she will die if she doesn't get both. If she is going to trust me enough to give her the affection she so badly needs, I can't be associated with the pain that might save her.

When I return she is curled up on a few leaves in the middle of camp, tied to a hut and utterly miserable. The world has ripped her from the most loving environment possible. I have never seen anything so sad as that little ball of fluff, her head on the ground, wishing this new world would just go away.

I take my cassava dinner and go sit by the Lomami River. While I was running, I came upon Maurice sitting in a jungle clearing, looking small and alone. It wasn't just the fever. Malaria, typhoid, whatever it was, it makes no difference; it will be the death of him someday soon.

There is something far sadder than imminent death about him.

He was my tracker before John, and was another member of the small group of men who spend their lives alone in the jungle. I enjoy working with Maurice; he hardly ever speaks and he knows the landscape well. Unlike John, Maurice is a broken man, spiritually and physically. In his youth he was a Mai Mai rebel.

The Mai Mai are a group of rural rebels who have, like many other African resistance movements, tapped into a sense of spiritual protection. Mai Mai comes from the Congolese Swahili word for water. Their water is blessed and smeared on bodies to provide supreme warrior status for those who follow the doctrine. They protect their own, and change sides according to spiritual whims. Their fight is against the collection of fighters and governments who care little for the villages that feed their conflict.

Conflict is not a new phenomenon to this massive country. The first power to rape the Congo were the Portuguese, who landed here in 1482 to find a well-established King and stable Kingdom. The ManiKnogo greeted the Portuguese with open arms, who proceeded to export five-thousand slaves per year from 1530-1535.

On the crest of the nineteenth century, King Leopold II of Belgium took exploitation to a scale likely never seen before or since. As one of the architects of the great carving of the African continent, he created a personal bank account and called it the Congo Free State. He owned the entire country, the size of western Europe, as a private holding between 1885 and 1908. Forced labour was extorted from the natives who suffered outrageous abuses for European greed. Roughly half the population, nearly ten million people, perished during the Free State period before the Belgian government stepped in to take the 'property' from King Leopold.

As the entire continent teethed their way into independence, the Belgian Free State became the Republic of the Congo in 1960. Patrice Lumumba served as the new nation's charismatic prime minister, but not for long. Lumumba refused to play by Western rules based on Communist paranoia. The constant thought that your fragile nation could break into many pieces was enough to drive Lumumba into fits of confused rage. He is mostly remembered as an icon of liberation, but also for his execution: the CIA-authorised, Belgian-led murder and deposition of his body parts into acid.

Following five years of instability and civil unrest, Joseph Mobutu took over with backing from the USA, and proceeded to do with the country as he wished, as long as he never spoke of going Communist. He was ruthless, often executing political rivals in public, but to his credit, he also had style. He built palaces to mimic European wonders, changed the name of the nation to Zaire in a process of *authenticité* or *africanisation*, and hosted the famous boxing match 'The Rumble in the Jungle'. In his thirty-plus years of dictatorship he became the world heavyweight champion of kleptocracy, a system that degraded all the nation's infrastructure. Mobutu's glory days ended in 1997 when he was exiled to Morocco. He took with him millions of dollars in state funds, and enjoyed the wealth until he died later that year, after living a full, and by all indications, happy life.

The same cannot be said for my tracker, Maurice. He, like the other ninety-nine per cent of the population, were at the wrong end of the stick. His life consisted of survival and he chose to be a fighter and not a victim. He is alive possibly because of that, but the burden of that choice is too heavy for his old shoulders. Unfit for society, he stays out there in the forest, just him and his demons.

I shelve the issue of choice and history politics as I hear the bonobo screaming in the dark. Everyone is ignoring her; she is only a wild animal. To escape my thoughts, I go over to look at her as a distraction. She has strung herself up with her leash and is covered in ants. All she can do is yelp as they eat her. When I have removed the worst, she slides into my lap, arms around my hips. The little bundle of hair and grey skin, limbs shrunken like an old person, she looks up at me with eyes that beg not to be left alone. Bonobo mothers hold their young twenty-four hours a day. I have just been adopted.

A BIKE RIDE

The first hour was pure bliss, the second was okay, and by the sixth I was over it. It had seemed like such a good idea this morning as I saw the bike leaning against a bunch of bananas. It had all the potential for *the best day ever*: adventure on the horizon, a physical challenge, the unknown, and a good friend to explore it with. We even ate breakfast for a change.

It seems the whole village had come to send us off. Standing around, making small talk, fiddling with the bike, tightening bolts that held nothing, adjusting cables that led to imaginary brakes, while checking the lumpy and cracked tires for adequate pressure. Confirming and reconfirming where I am going and when I will be back.

John had arrived in his best outfit, a baby blue Fat Albert shirt and sharp blue jeans, white hat cocked forward with a red ribbon looped through. I could tell it was a big day for him. Lapping up the excitement, borrowing this, promising to deliver that, he is full of importance from the task assigned. He displays that human need to feel important, to dress up in your best and to have a purpose. Chances for a person to take responsibility are rare here, and grabbed as eagerly as, or even more so, than a day's wage.

An old woman, with a face that gave up smiling years ago, makes some snide remarks to John. I suspect the old rascal either broke her heart, or never did. The rest of the crowd treated us like the first people to go to the moon. Back then, I thought this torture machine looked like a bicycle and a nice change from two months of walking. Back then, I didn't have a world atlas of bruises on my inner thighs. Back then, I still sat on the seat, its awkward angle long since having forced me onto the carry-rack above the rear wheel. Back then, the nails used for pedals did not feel like spikes. Back then, I complained a lot less.

To be fair, there were some highlights. There was the young man with his homemade guitar who played us a few tunes where we found him alone, practicing only for an audience of trees. There was the joy of a road that leads to somewhere I had never been, with a good friend as a companion; and of course the stunning scenery.

The first stop was at Lengos' village to meet his two wives. I used to tease him about who he sleeps with on his first night back from the forest, but now I see the practical value of polygamy. Marriage here is foremost a matter of convenience. The first girl is his age, probably a childhood sweetheart, but already at twenty-three she is showing signs of wear and tear from the hard work that is required by African women. The second wife is a strong, younger number, ideal for helping out in the house and fields. This eases the duties of his first wife, keeping both wives younger in the process. Everyone is a winner.

White people are rare around here, so I am given the VIP tour.

Nothing fancy, because they have nothing fancy to give, only respect far above that which I deserve. Before we can leave I am offered a bowl of rice and some cooked bananas. In return John gives them a one-serving coffee packet.

It was only a gesture, but I think I might be starting to understand. Nowhere have I come across a culture that asks for so much as the Congolese; not begging, just asking. It begins to occur to me that there might be equally as much giving as asking, but that I haven't noticed because I am not the one doing it. In all my travels in Africa I have been out-given by Africans, particularly if the equation of personal income, physical exertion and thoughtfulness is taken into account. I have infinitely more and yet they give so much, so easily. When I give, it is usually things that I do not need. The same cannot be said for the things that I am given.

The so-called "Third World" uses things long after the West has discarded them. It is where objects end up for their last tour of duty. If an African gives you something you can be sure they would have used it – excess is rare.

In *Shadow of the Sun*, Kapuscinski writes of a Nigerian man to whom he had given money because he could not tolerate the coldness between them. He jokes about how much closer the friendship becomes the more he gives. I had thought this was sad, having to give money to make friends. How fake the friendship must be. But perhaps it is not so unusual an arrangement. Someone has to start the giving and this might even be a good way to go about it. When we give expecting something, we are not really giving at all, we are trading. This concept is hard to grasp coming from my nothing-for-nothing culture. Here, in the depths of the Congo, giving is not even based on need; it is based simply on giving.

In a country with so little it appears that the only way to get by is by giving. Life survives on credit. In a country this disorganised, that produces so little, family and friends are a universal safety net. The slightest misfortune can be devastating. Often the only way to get by is to receive or take; which might explain all the terrible wars.

I am not an idealist. I know different rules apply for white people. Being white in the Congo, you can prepare yourself for constant demands to give, often it doesn't even matter what you give as long as you give something. A typical conversation can go like this:

"Give me your watch."

"No."

"Okay, give me money."

"No."

"Okay, give me a sip of water."

Dealing with this constant demand is challenging, and something at which I don't excel.

Because we have so much more to give, the scales can never be equal. If we give without question, we will be exploited eventually, if not initially. Even if we deserve to be exploited, we will upset the culture and create beggars along the way. We simply cannot give to everyone we meet; there are just too many who are just too needy. Giving too much will ruin the balance as surely as giving too little will make you selfish.

Somewhere in this complicated tangle of cultural misunderstandings about giving lies another important part of the puzzle to why aid has been so unsuccessful in Africa. Giving is the core of the aid equation. We need to realise that we are dealing with different expectations over the value of X. It seems that aid given by an anonymous face does more harm than good – we need to find an alternative. With John guiding me in the process of giving, it allows me to experience the joy of the process without the complicated calculation of how to save the Congo.

The Congo, surprisingly, has a better version of poor rural village life than any other place in Africa I have visited. The jungle provides most things needed to live. The huts are nicer, the roofs are higher, the walls better-made, the chairs more comfortable, the people better-fed and more prone to dance. Those I have met, at least here deep in the forest, seem a lot more aware of their surroundings. They are able to collect from their world what would have been sufficient in years past. As in all of Africa, everything constructed is temporary.

The reason for our little bicycle mission is power – our lack of it. The generator in camp has broken down and we have a pile of dead electronics. Our first attempt is at the village outside our camp, a long shot but worth a try. The chief has gone, leaving his battery and a plain solar panel on the ground between some pecking chickens.

Five men surround it, each eager to add his expertise. In a familiar scene, a group of boys watch the men carefully, informal training for when they too can take part in the ritual of fixing things they don't understand. It takes a few minutes to reach agreement on negative and positive poles. Now we tie this to that, bypass the other, remove the first, force this in here and there you go. No one seems surprised when the light does not come on. The next contestant steps up for a turn, as the 'expert' slumps back, disgraced. Biding time until he can return to the inner circle, he recognises a clue over the shoulder of the current participant.

The circle grows smaller as it becomes clear that this is not a five-minute job. The sun takes its toll and soon the few remaining men move into the shade to completely dismantle the appliance. One hour later everyone agrees that the reason it is not working is because it is broken.

From there the journey brings us to the church. Like everything else around here, it has seen better days. The ends are frayed and it is structurally unsound, colourful and still standing with the help of some cleverly placed bamboo scaffolding. It provides running water straight from the roof and the toilet flushes with buckets. This is considered modern, even if everything is covered in a red dust from the dissolving bricks. Buildings here cannot hide behind appearances; rather, Nature has removed their pretensions by scrubbing them with a steel brush. Their true essence is revealed through the personality of the people who inhabit them.

A short man with the swagger of a street fighter and the pinched look of an accountant greets us at the door. The cross around his neck marks him as a priest. His black suit pants and ridiculous pointy shoes seem oddly enough to go well with the red t-shirt that states, 'Snack Bar Is La Difference.'

I would not know fashion if it fell on top of me. The Congolese however, love their clothes. In the cities one can see street kids with self-made bling buckles, loosely tied without belts to pants too large for their malnourished bodies. Even out here, days away from anything that can be considered a town, everyone has at least one outfit that beats anything that I have crumpled in my tent back at camp.

It's curious that such an impoverished society should be so vain. The women are forever playing with each other's hair. In the towns they have taken to large nylon wigs, so unnatural that they are best described as hats. Here they mould their hair in any direction you could imagine and a few you couldn't. Even the little boys have fancy patterns cut into their scalps. John wore a pair of North Face shoes this morning that are much nicer than I could afford. So much for feeling sorry about him walking barefoot in the jungle; he just didn't want to get his shoes dirty.

The fact that I am sitting here now, with a sweet cup of tea in my hand, suggests that it wasn't all that hard; perhaps just tougher than a bike ride should be. Armed with the right equipment it would have been easy. I am not referring to clothing that breathes, shock absorbers or gears; just a simple seat would have sufficed.

After tea I have my first shower in months. I thought I would have enjoyed it more, but it turns out to be only water falling from the sky. Washing with a bucket is not much different and it's still no match for a fresh jungle stream.

I talk to Theophilus, the street-fighting accountant/priest. He knows English, which is refreshing after two months without it. He turns out to be indescribably boring and predictable. He parrots ideas from a two-thousand year-old manual written on another continent, and then he seems surprised that the locals resist it. I have heard his whole story before and am happy when the two porters, Boniface and Alfonse show up. They disappeared for a month, preferring to spend their money before returning to make any more. I slip them a packet of cigarettes with the enthusiasm of someone who has learned a neat new trick. It works a charm. I am happy they are happy, even John is happy; perhaps because he can now smoke his in peace, perhaps because he can't help himself.

In the Congo I never know what the day is going to bring. I try to enjoy the feeling without growing attached to it; it will inevitably leave me to fluctuate between Africa's balance of extremes. It might seem strange to think of life as an illusion at first, but if you think about it long enough, it becomes clear it is too strange not to be.

The day is spent trying to charge some batteries with the church's marginally more sophisticated solar system. We need a new plan. John apparently knows of a generator in a village not far from here. Tomorrow we will track it down. After a sombre lunch around a plastic table, with colourful plastic posters of Jesus and Mary on a dull grey wall watching over us, I ask for the bill. It comes as a shock. They have slapped *mondele* tax on me: thirty dollars for a night. I am close to losing my temper. Actually, I do. It's hard to argue a point that is so ridiculous. Eventually I go to my room, pack up my stuff and leave what money I have on the table without bothering to say goodbye.

When John hears the price he is furious. It takes ten minutes to calm him down enough not to make a scene. I don't want bad vibes and feel guilty for having just walked away, so I return later to talk calmly to the priest. Theophilus is almost in tears at my sudden departure and blames it all on the bishop, a Bill Cosby look-alike, whom I disliked almost as soon we met. He is a man given superiority by his position and demanding respect for the same reason. I make him feel guilty to such an extent that he says I should come back and stay free of charge. We all just want to get rid of the bad taste of the sudden ending, so I agree and move back to the dismay of John who has already found us another accommodation.

After breakfast with three priests who do not speak to one another, in a building that God does not live in, I meet John outside. His plans have changed. Now he wants someone else to get the 'grrrrrrr', as generators are called here. I calculate the chance of it showing up the next day if I don't go myself, and decide they are not good.

Next, John tries to buy fuel from the priest. They don't want to sell, sending John over the edge. He throws his toys out and creates a scene in the middle of the village. I get on my bike and leave them all still shouting at each other in the road.

In Manala town, twenty-five kilometres farther, we try again. Yes they have a 'grrrrr', but it has gone and should be back tomorrow. I have nothing better to do so I pretend to believe it. There is another generator in town, which is broken. Because I am white they think I might be able to fix it. I know better, but I humour them. The owner has no tools. We stare at it for a while. I hit it a few times, then I leave. The rest of the day is spent in the shade reading and writing while John gossips, waiting for a 'grrrrr' that more than likely will not show up. Bored, I eventually go for a walk. John is pretending to be asleep, just in case I ask him to join me. Only mad dogs and Englishmen leave perfectly good shade for no reason.

The sky is so blue and clear that the day seems like a canvas that can be painted with anything you want. I walk for a few hours. The only people working in the heat are the women, who are chopping wood, washing cassava roots and carrying loads in finely woven baskets on their heads. The groups are usually talking happily together, chewing fruit, and making fun of the white man, but there are some loners who seem less happy. They are burdened under heavy loads, too tired to look up. The only noise they make is the gentle hiccup of their flip-flops on the sandy path.

On my return I am introduced to Gilbert. I don't recognise him, but apparently I gave him a can of sardines a month ago when we met on a walk in the jungle. He insists I stay at his house, and repays me many times over by providing full board for two days.

Late afternoon, the near-empty street starts filling with people spilling out with the afternoon shadows. A group of women sit and sing at an informal church gathering in someone's yard. Dads are playing with their children and clusters of kids hang around everywhere. Everyone stops and stares as two men push a bicycle past. The basket on the back reveals two feet, the colour of old teeth, sticking out. Following a few hundred meters behind are two women stumbling, screaming and wailing. The village draws back from the sight of death. Twenty minutes later another woman runs by hysterically. I have never seen sorrow expressed so forcefully. In my culture we are taught to handle it mostly internally, as if to stop it from infecting the world. Here they vomit it out, to expend it as quickly as possible. They might as well mourn hard, because if they mourned long they would never stop; people die here all the time.

Gilbert calls me over to show me his new baby, lovingly being breast-fed. I come close, ready to make the appropriate cute baby noises, he pulls the blanket from the baby to reveal a tiny girl. Her legs are little grey bones without meat, with hand-like claws attached to the ends. I am horrified and feel physically ill. Unable to watch this loss, I mumble an apology and excuse myself.

It's the final straw. The natural environment has unique challenges, but being amongst people again destabilises my psyche. In every village we have passed through, I have been a spectacle that has drawn crowds, an important actor that has an unfamiliar role to play. I can't help them with their misery; I can hardly witness it.

Watching the streets drain of people as rain begins to fall, I take a chair away from the family's episode and sit alone until well after dark. John and then Gilbert approach to tell me to come in; in case I had not noticed it's raining, but I can't bear to leave the solitude of the empty street, the wonderful quiet. Eventually I walk back to the house. Soft voices float from inside along with the faint light from a paraffin lamp. I can't cross the threshold of the peaceful family scene. I turn around before the light reveals me. I walk to a shelter on the other side of the village. The rain steadily increases along with the darkness of my mood.

From the huts around me I can hear kids crying. Kids, everywhere, kids. Out here kids are having kids as often as they can. Overpopulation is a time bomb ticking all over Africa; more so than anyone realises. It makes me wonder why billions of dollars are spent on prolonging life when the only possible chance we have is if there are fewer of us? I am not suggesting we stop trying to cure people, but why isn't stabilising or reducing population every poor country's first concern? Anything else is a vaccination for a patient bleeding to death.

Eventually I bring my bivy outside. Tonight I am going to have to risk offending my host; walls will not suffice.

John wakes me at 05:00 to ask for medicine, and I say a prayer to Ibuprofen myself. At 05:30 he is back wanting to leave for base camp. He is worse than I am when it comes to planning.

He is far from being the coltish boy running and whooping in the savannah a few days ago. His shoulders have dropped as if he has the responsibility of the world upon them, floundering in an environment he was never made for. He has three kids here, and his need to seem important is as clear as his failure to do so. The overplay of his own importance and his shiny new clothes are a burden he can't carry. Just like John cannot play a game of averages, the average person could never play at his life's game. I like him more for that.

Maybe John's mistake is wanting to fit in. Perhaps he should rather just be a freak and be judged by the end product, rather than trying to please everyone and falling short. We all have that need to fit in and to be accepted, measuring ourselves by the norm. We spend so much of our lives in an attempt to be understood by people we don't understand, pleasing people we don't like, and gaining the respect of people who aren't respectable.

As John finishes up his business in town, I watch a family load their life onto a bicycle. The father is a self-educated nurse/pharmacist playing doctor for lack of better options for him and the communities he cares for. With him comes Mum, a three year-old girl, a ten year-old boy and a box of medicines. They walk from town to town selling hope and sometimes cures. I am impressed that they can fit a shop and all their possessions on an ancient push bike, but what really intrigues me is how close they seem as a family.

The boy, with eyes still full of sleep, holds the bike while Dad ties on the precious box of cures. Mum gathers her few possessions up in a shawl, while the baby girl hums happily around her feet. Our paths would cross again, and every time we met, on a jungle track hours away from any villages or setting up shop in someone's living room, they were together and seemingly content.

I give them, and the millions of other little scenarios playing out under me, a thought every time I fly over the continent at thirty-thousand feet. How seemingly small, fragile and inconsequential their existence could seem but amazing how much value they generate in it. Their entire family takes up no more space than a bicycle and the circumference of their feet. How hard they have to fight for even that little space, and how it highlights the obese materialism of the world I come from.

Getting To The River

Living in the Congo shakes open the prison house of my dispositions and lets all the wicked hoodoo Adah's run forth.

—Barbara Kingsolver

Kisangani could have been one of the great jungle cities of the world, except that there is absolutely nothing great about this place. The Congo and the Tshuapa rivers hold nature ineffectively at arm's length as the city lives in purgatory, a drawn result between jungle and civilisation. Neither side is going anywhere, and I don't see any possibility of development or a natural takeover.

On the street some kids are kicking a deflated football between open sewers. Women in little groups weave each other's hair. Men sit around radios playing checkers with bottle tops. Some women look dejectedly at the corncobs they have burnt over charcoal stoves. A young man is selling mobile phone airtime from a shoebox. Beside him sits an older man behind a stack of cigarettes carefully arranged on top of each other. The next shop belongs to a little girl who watches the street from behind a pile of mangoes laid out on an old plastic sheet.

The same products at the same time, at the same place, at the same price. There is no obvious difference between any of the thousand similar square meters of personal industry patched onto the city's streets. A city where three languages – Lingala, Swahili and French – are spoken in equal measure, sometimes so mixed the speakers do not even know which is which. Yet it is a culture that has no space for individuality as the Western world understands it. Perhaps this why it has been so susceptible to exploitation from individual leaders.

The city seems to reject the thought of anything new apart from the fancy diamond-dealer offices. Buildings are constructed from old materials; the process of breaking them down has already started well before they are finished, intending to fix the electrical faults or to get to the bad plumbing. Anything freshly painted desperately tries to blend into the dust. Even the vegetation refuses to draw attention to itself; tall trees have been cut to half their height, their legs painted with simple Congolese flags for some presidential visit a long time gone. The only things that flourish are plastic bags; the faded, flower-like rubbish sprouts everywhere, floating on green and blue scum-filled puddles and wedged in between every cracked piece of pavement still clinging to the soil.

Tonight is a no-power night. As the sun disappears blandly behind the smoke of charcoal fires, only a few paraffin oil lamps light the communal borderlands beyond the main road. It serves as a living room and business opportunity to anyone and everyone. Pieces of tar stick on the road like scabs. Few cars pass. Lights are mostly from cheap motorbikes snaking around pedestrians and bicycle taxis. Non-reflective moving parts are interwoven like raindrops coursing down a window, all picking different paths on the same potholed road. The scars of wars can be seen on buildings and felt as the gathering dark turns Kisangani into an eerie ghost town.

Kisangani is a city that can't bring itself to perform at the pace required for such a label, so it moves about like a collection of small towns. The streets are full but never packed, the shops sell the basic and advertise the luxurious; it's a promise they are rarely expected to deliver.

The only surprise in this grey scene is how safe I feel. I hardly ever get hassled and have never been threatened. There is something about the streets and the noise that I can't put my finger on; a subdued exuberance, people are laughing and living but almost as if they are in school and someone is monitoring. It's a theatre I cannot lose myself in. I dislike being on the street because I feel I do not belong here.

The 'Heart of Darkness' is a label that will hang over the Congo for a long time. The cliché is turned on its head when you find out it is your own heart that leans in that direction all too often. In the jungle the demanding environment brings it out. It makes you snap at a porter at the end of the day when he fumbles while trying to help you. In the city it's harder to recognise, the crowds absorb it better, there are more rules to follow, more guidelines, but as soon as you are frustrated, it starts beating in your chest again.

Congo has not been as bad as I was lead to believe. Expect the worst and you might be pleasantly surprised. Things are probably as bad as it gets. There is still a line of decency even if it is among crooks. They rarely rip you off for the same thing twice, and they are open to negotiation.

To navigate through the web of con men a good interpreter is a must, and it's okay to be paranoid; they are out to get you, but don't start feeling sorry for yourself. You signed up for it when you crossed the border. Feel sympathy for the honest interpreter who, for all his charm and education, will never have a proper job. Feel bad when he sinks into his chair at the sight of a visitor to his country being blatantly robbed by his Government. I came here daring the Congo to break me. It has come close, and might in the end. Still, this is all a game, a choice; for him, it's the reason life will never get better. Africa does not seek out an opportunity to make things harder; here people have already experienced things as hard as they can get.

Adjusting to the Congo's system is demanding. Anyone with a position even slightly resembling authority will use it to get money from you, and once you learn to say "no" to all but the gravest of requests, you realise it was just a request framed as a demand. In the Congo this behaviour is called entrepreneurship.

I don't have a problem with greasing a few palms; the world needs to turn. If you can tip a waitress for bringing you a cup of coffee, surely a few dollars to an official who hasn't been paid for a while is acceptable. The depth of this 'shadow' economy is staggering. I have been to four customs offices for routine check-ins, and have as many visas. Added to my portfolio, I have letters from various state departments all guaranteed to grant me access to God himself, as long as he doesn't work in another office. None of these passes are given without palms dripping with grease.

I wouldn't have it any other way. Coming to the Congo and complaining about bureaucracy would be silly. The warnings could not be clearer. Rated as the worst place in the world to do business, is a good indicator that things might not work perfectly. Government officials remind me of automotive mechanics; everything is always twice as bad and three times as expensive as you expected. The last guy always did the job wrong, with sub-standard parts, and it's impossible to tell exactly where your money went. The lesson is, never ever take it in if it ain't broken.

I merely observe as another official shows up at my hotel, staring as gravely as an undertaker at the documents in front of him. For ten minutes he does not blink or speak, looking at the same page, as if reading the mind of my passport with some official power beyond this physical plane.

I simply shake my head at the Director of the Ministry of Tourism as he demands $500 and offer him $10 instead. I sit back in the Chief of Immigration's office without looking surprised when he tells me the papers I got from the Ministry of Interior are completely useless. I even hand over a dollar for gas money as he goes to consult with yet another chief.

I sit in their offices for hours to find out how they can help me to make it all better. I look them in the eye as they sell me their lies. All I ask is that they look down. In that second when they break eye contact to look at the floor, they own the lie. Only then I hand over the cash. You learn to appreciate the little things out here.

No, I am not complaining, I swallow it as best I can, but if some damn bicycle courier tries to overcharge me by ten cents, I'll bite his head off. Which is exactly why power corrupts; we will all eventually do whatever we can get away with.

I was close to giving it all up yesterday. I've been waiting for my kayak to arrive and no one knows when the strike at customs will be over. The final straw, after a month of lethargy and endless red tape, was being summoned from my meeting with the Chief of Immigration and the Ministry of the Interior where I was accused of being a diamond dealer. Turns out I could make it all disappear, I just had to pay the administration fee. I told them to fuck off.

If I lose my temper less than twice a day, that is a good day. I was born with a good one, but even for me this is a bit excessive. In the jungle it seemed it was only me, but in the city there is a lot more aggression. I have seen the same thing in Sudan, but there I was largely unaffected. It's not the fault of the Congolese, they are, contrary to what I was lead to believe, quite friendly; a bit demanding and prone to arguments, it's true, but no one is perfect.

Suddenly Africa is out to get me: everything is late, everything is broken. I have lost my mental buffer, I need to get it back or I will fail, or worse, make a mistake that I can't undo.

How much is this dream worth in time and money? What is the value of my pride? It is the only thing still keeping me here. Anything apart from serious injury or death would be quitting, and then where would I be? Once you accept a challenge, if you quit you not only lose your goal, you accept the burden of failure. Committing to an adventure is like money owed to the Mafia.

I could not bring myself to do it. Every thought eventually lead to leaving and ended with an exclamation mark. Snippets of conversations stuck in my mind. My own words written three months ago in my diary – "I fear just giving up" – refused to be washed down the drain of self-pity. Still, if it had continued for another day I would probably have been on a three-day bus ride to arrive at wherever I was going, filled with self-loathing at letting the Congo win.

Today starts badly. After standing in a square for two hours waiting to receive a money transfer, I see Hassan forcing his way upstream through the crowd, oblivious to everything but the door. I get a hand on him. He looks at me. I don't know him well, we briefly met in Kindu. Amidst the chaos he gives me his number and tells me to call. He seems genuinely glad to see me.

He expresses more kindness than I have experienced from the few other whites I have met out here. Even my own countrymen could not been bothered to move an inch out of their way.

Hassan, and later Claudine, could just have invited me for a beer but they made me feel welcome. All it took was a relaxed night with some good people, speaking English and laughing for the first time in weeks. Suddenly there was hope again; suddenly I felt I could do another three months, that things are changing, that luck has turned. This is hope. Hope buys time. Hope releases energy.

I mention to Hassan that his hospitality is far above what I have received from other foreigners in the Congo. He justifies his generosity with a profound anecdote:

> *I was a student in high school when the trouble broke out in Lebanon. A boy from my class came to me one night; he was a Christian living in the Muslim part of the city. The fundamentalists had started to round them up and his family was in danger. He begged me to get him out. I did not know him that well, but did what I could for him. I could not ignore him; I had known him and his family my whole life.*
>
> *It was impossible not to be involved in the war, and eventually I was forced to take sides with my people. I did what a young man does in war and became a soldier. As the years went on, my role in the situation grew.*
>
> *On returning from an overseas trip, I was ubducted at the airport and taken to a house in the Christian part of the city. Inside the guarded compound, I was given a number and thrown into a room with five other men. One by one they called out the number, followed shortly by a gunshot.*
>
> *There were two of us left when they called my number. I knew that death was waiting for me outside the door. The fear made me forget my number. When they called it out the third time without me standing up, they read my full name from a list and ordered me up.*
>
> *In the room next door some soldiers were resting. One of them heard my name being called and thought he recognised it. When they took off my blindfold, instead of seeing my killer, it was the boy I had helped ten years ago.*
>
> *Since then, I use every chance I get to help other people; you never know when it will be your turn.*

My driver has just driven through a police roadblock without stopping. I am not sure what his intentions are, or where he thinks he is going with my kayak strapped to the back of his bike, but it's clear the situation is beyond my control. I am left to watch as the police commandeer a pushbike and eventually a motorbike in hot pursuit.

The fact that I had to get off my hired motorbike so that it could make it up the first hill, should have been a sign. I should have expected trouble when I climbed on and the seat fell off, but by then I was riding on optimism.

The getaway driver and his dysfunctional motorbike stalls not long after the chase begins. By the time I arrive, the driver is in tears sitting on the ground, regretting his panicked decision. If he thought I was going to help him, he is mistaken. I make it clear I think he is an idiot and fire him on the spot. I feel sorry for the guy, but not enough to pay his way out of this.

As usual, within minutes we have the road blocked by spectators. Occasionally the knot unties for a rubbernecking bicyclist. Eventually I find a new driver, and we siphon the gas from the previous driver's tank.

The police ask me for a commission for obtaining a new driver. It's standard procedure to ask, but they make the mistake of justifying it. I point out that it is the new driver who should pay the commission, since he is the one receiving the money. They think it over for a moment and turn on the young man. A teenager called Blaze is on an unbranded bike. It is so small that my kayak strapped sideways on the tiny carrier rack leaves him to sit on my lap as we drive off.

It is tricky driving with a wide heavy load on a bad road. He takes it on with the confidence of someone who is too young to have crashed much. Not bothering to ease himself into the limits of his situation, he soon learns that if you are the width of the road you need to slow down or you will hit a few things on the way. Unfortunately, the first thing he hits is a military officer riding on the back of a pushbike.

I hear the *thunk* of the kayak hull as it strikes, and then the wobble as Blaze tries to gain control of the seesaw. Next is the skidding of the rear tire as it loses its grip and then the tunnel vision as impact with the road becomes unavoidable. We skid a little but the kayak strapped to the back helps to minimise the cuts and scrapes on both of us.

The crowd forms instantaneously, and turns on me for being white

– therefore suggesting the chance of a cash payback. Since I wasn't driving, and a little angry myself at the sudden deceleration, I nod to subtly convey my displeasure with their attitude. Stunned by my subsequent outburst and probably having long carried grudges with speeding bike riders for covering them in dust and forcing them off the road, they shift their focus. Blaze is looking dejectedly at his bike lying in a pile of dust and misery at his feet, my kayak tied to it like a crucifix.

The lieutenant is livid, but not as much as his soldiers who have just arrived. They start slapping Blaze around. Someone is peeling a piece of bamboo for what I assume is an imminent and proper hiding. An old woman carrying firewood is yelling abuse and two bike couriers seem eager to get involved in the slapping. The roadside scene is becoming dangerous.

The soldiers are slapping ineffectually at Blaze. As he pulls away, they spin around one another. Reluctantly, I get myself in the middle of the hurricane. I create a bit of a pause in which I point out that we are the only ones hurt. Luckily both of us have some blood on display. Five minutes later, after some intense apologising and a promise to never, ever, drive that fast again, we are bending pieces of the bike back into place. Blaze hands over a fist of dirty brown notes. We drive away very slowly.

I am squeezed between the kayak and Blaze on an uncomfortable seat, but I can still appreciate the amazing trees we are driving under. If the Congo has taught me anything, it's to never wish for the next moment; it's definitely not going to be perfect and most probably even more uncomfortable. Optimism is foolish in the Congo. Expect the worst and be happy when it's not as bad, and always remind yourself you did not come here for 'anything easy.'

We are on a single-lane track eroded by heavy trucks. Only one is moving. They are all heavily loaded with a last layer of plastic containers tied to their outsides in large ribbons. One truck has its engine laid out on the ground. The metallic smoothness of its cylinder block looks out of place on the dusty track. Black men covered in yellow mud are digging stuck machines out of holes; their contrast reminds me of chocolate dipped in caramel.

Scattered villages with single streets stand on white patches in the overwhelming green. Every front door faces onto the road that all life must pass through. The huts are identical; every village has a church made from bamboo poles and a market with a rusty piece of metal serving as a bell. Apart from the trucks, the only traffic is people walking and piles of gear wheeled around like stage props.

Most of the people we pass look at me with an expression I don't like. The ones who do speak ask for money or cigarettes. I pass a white man on a bike and stop. He is a bald-headed German cycling down the west coast of Africa and thinking about coming up again on the east side. I could not think of anything worse; every day on that bike must just be a copy of the last. Your head is down counting the kilometres while everyone on the roadside asks you for money.

One of the first things he says is, "I am always alone." On my mission I can escape the crowds, sleep on an island, and paddle in silence for long hours, while he is continually surrounded by people who do not care for him. He has been stuck in an unchecked internal dialogue for the past eleven months. Still, I admire his commitment and endurance, an achievement I would not wish to duplicate.

I can't help but wonder how my little Congo trip has affected me? What new lines or scars will my own reintegration to society reveal? It is no secret that insanity occurs way more often in isolated individuals. We don't realise it but even the smallest interaction with others is an exercise in reality maintenance, something we have both been without for a while. He is the first tourist I have come across in four months and I am the first Great White Explorer he has met since he cycled into central Africa six months ago.

We stand there in the shade, talking. It is soon clear we have little to say to each other. We have both spent too much time in our own worlds to walk over onto the other's so quickly. It's ironic that we start traveling as young men thinking we will have stories to tell, but end up with less to say.

July 11, 2009

Keeping my gaze at waist level I avoid eye contact. I have no wish to speak. I am too nervous to allow my thoughts to wander. Slowly and deliberately I double-check every strap on my life jacket before carefully closing the latch on the back of my boat. The kayak is too heavy to lift so I drag it like a sled through the old dockyard, over railway lines and through knee-high grass. I sidestep the piles of guns stacked in intricate and clever structures on crumbling cement slabs beside rusty railway cars.

The soldiers are everywhere. Half-dressed young punks and sombre-looking old men yell comments at me. I pretend not to hear. If I get drawn into a conversation, it will turn to money. Asking is one thing, but when they have guns it's another. For now it's friendly banter, but I am aware the choice of tone lies with them. I nod at some officers staring sceptically. Then I slide my kayak through the human faeces into the water.

I had hoped it would be like getting back on a bike, but after four months the kayak feels strange and heavy. It's a good thing I bought that extra bottle of Ibuprofen; at best this is only going to hurt a little. My arms stutter as I draw the first stokes. The paddle, still covered in airport fragile stickers, drags slowly through the brown water. It is a distinct kind of scared, the one you get when you begin a journey you might not come out of alive.

I do not bother to look back at the soldiers; we mean nothing to each other. I am happy to be alone, if only I could stay that way. I have no idea how the people downstream are going to treat me. It occurs to me that I don't know the Swahili word for crocodile.

I can hear the roar of the whitewater, but it takes me ten minutes just to paddle to the middle of the river. Before entering the rapids splitting off into the left channel, I drift past a rusty old ferry that was cut loose in the battle of Congo's deterioration.

Every book I have ever read about the Congo River described it as being sinister, even evil. For a few seconds I feel it, the repulsion and horror, feelings I have never felt on a river. It occurs to me that it is only my fear, and indeed it disappears as I grow accustomed to my surroundings.

Getting to the left side is harder work than it should be. I am weaker, and the water is stronger than I expected. Some fisherman scream frantically at me, pointing to the river ahead. Their panic threatens to infect me. I make it to the bank with little space to spare. The rapid doesn't look like much but the whirlpools at the bottom make me uneasy. I slip down a smaller side channel; today is a good day to make it easier.

It is ironic that the older I get, the more afraid I become. By all rights I should fear less. Experience has made me a better judge of risk and has helped me to keep a calm under pressure. I am more equipped now than ever to deal with tight situations. Contrary to popular belief, bravery is not a young man's game. Being a young man and fearless is not the same as being brave. Without fear there can be no courage.

Thirty-four years of risk taking with a one-hundred per cent survival rate, and I have yet to break a bone in my body (I don't count fractures). There have been more than a handful of close calls and one or two escapes could be categorised as miraculous, but I have yet to spend a day in hospital due to injury.

So why do I get more nervous as I get older? I have less time left to live so by definition less to lose. Perhaps the problem is that I know that it is not due to my tiger-like reflexes that I am still alive. Somewhere along the line I started to think that my *luck* might run out. There is less motivation to take big risks and nothing left to prove.

If I had to be honest about the reasons that I used to run big lines in my kayak, a very large part is because of the respect I got with it. I was good at it, and I liked being good at something. The exhilaration felt better than anything else I knew. Those reasons are almost irrelevant now. I am old enough to know that respect gained from unnecessary risk-taking is not a basis for any kind of relationship. It never was. *Courage* defines the persona of myself that I liked, but the real 'I' knows how scared I can be.

I wonder if every man remembers the day that he realised he is not young anymore. For me that day came in Kisangani. When I looked in that mirror, after six weeks of inactivity and drinking myself to sleep at night, it looked back unforgivingly with sagging man-tits and a beer belly. Once I looked closely the rest fell into place: a receding hairline and fluff growing out of my ears and nose.

My body is my existence. Everything has been built around it, mentally and physically, and yet I have hardly ever stopped to contemplate a life without it. The times when it has performed at its peak have given me more bliss and taken me closer to God than any prayer in church ever will. I know there is still plenty left in the tank; as I write Lance Armstrong is going for his twelfth Tour de France. From now on my body will make demands, and I will listen if I still want to play.

I always said that when the time came, I would say thanks for the memories and move on from this lifestyle. I have been playing for longer than most and feel enormously privileged for that. However, the transition has proved harder than expected. It seems as you get older, learning becomes harder than unlearning. Soon, I might have give up outrageous adventures.

Call Of The Wild

Have you suffered, starved and triumphed, groveled down, yet grasped at glory.
Grown bigger in the bigness of the whole?
"Done things" just for the doing, letting babblers tell the story,
Seeing through the nice veneer the naked soul?

Have you seen God in His splendors, heard the text that nature renders?
(You'll never hear it in the family pew).
The simple things, the true things. The silent men who do things –
Then listen to the Wild – it's calling you.

They have cradled you in custom, they have primed you with their preaching,
They have soaked you in convention through and through;
They have put you in a showcase; you are a credit to their teaching –
But can't you hear the Wild? – It's calling you.

Let us probe the silent places, let us seek what luck betide us;
Let us journey to a lonely land I know.
There is a whisper on the night-wind, there's a star agleam to guide us,
And the Wild is calling, calling... let us go.

—Robert William Service

July 24, 2009

I arrive in Bumba and there is a boat leaving. After a week of chasing something similar in my little red Solo kayak, I find the M/B Nyawera in the collapsed and overcrowded dockyard. It is stopped for a Congo-reason that no outsider will ever understand. It is the last in a row of barges, which seemingly had no inclination to move.

By the time I get to the M/B Nyawera, I am starting to feel a too familiar feeling of frustration and helplessness. Congo is becoming a lesson in not giving up. I can only hope it has some benefits.

I put my case to the Captain. I know I am at his mercy as he looks down at me from the upper deck. His face arranged deep in thought, he ponders taking a *mondele* on board. Being white can swing both ways in the Congo, like just about anything else. I am not above begging, should it be necessary. If he does not allowed me on, I will spend a few more unpleasant weeks' wait in a nowhere town.

By myself I can go no further: it's too dangerous. The next town after Bumba is Lasala, and after Lasala is "The slaughterhouse." Where the locals have an unfriendly reputation.

Who said cannibal? No one said cannibal, *calm down tiger*, you are alone out here. It's too late, *someone definitely did say cannibal*. Reluctantly I give in to the voice. Sensing it might have a point, I order a check of my mental files. I don't have to look far, my research has left an impression. The headlines go a bit like this:

> The Congolese have grown wary of outsiders – they have plenty of reasons to distrust Western intruders, or the *mondele*. At least one region along the Congo River – 'Ile Sumba' – has been dubbed the abattoir, or slaughterhouse. Cannibals from the Engombe tribe live nearby and have been known to abduct and kill explorers.

"What about crocodiles?" The thought is not enough to stop me, but it certainly slows me down. Suddenly what has been pure bliss has a nagging undertone of fear. *There are no crocs here, even if there were they would swim a mile away from humans.* It does not silence the nagging voice.

I know it's not completely safe, but my excuse for leaving the barge at night is a valid one. In three weeks I will paddle the largest volume rapids in the world. Somehow I have to keep at least some of the fragile fitness I have worked so hard over the past three weeks to build up. That, and it's really nice to be alone for a few hours. I have been on this noisy and crowded floating slum for over a week now.

Someone definitely said *cannibal*. My need for solitude diminishes. Maybe tonight I will just do a short run, there's still time before I get into the rapids below Kinshasa, no use overtraining.

Back on the barge the evening's evangelical session is just ending. The barge comes standard with no less than three priests. Hopefully this has more to do with the Congolese need for religion and the accompanying singing, than as an added safety feature.

To get to bed, I have to climb a mountain of charcoal and corn sacks. It's a challenging venture, never dull and ever-changing, made harder at night by the family asleep at the base. I step on only a few of them curled up on the cool metal sheeting of the barge. Finally, I get a toehold on the mountain of goods of which the highest peak is my bed.

You would think the difficulty of the route is enough to keep the riff-raff away, but a moat filled with crocodiles could not keep the numbers down. On top of my boulder, a six-by-four-meter crumbling square, we are fourteen people along with personal belongings, piles of merchandise to trade and sell, one live monkey, two parrots (one grey and the other green) and more than three hundred dried fish neatly stacked in folders made from jungle vines.

The floating village looks like a cross between Noah's ark and a garden shed. I thought the barge was full days ago. I was mistaken; there is space here for everything except hygiene. Everyday our capacity swells with more people and goods.

It would not be possible to fit everyone on the barge without the terracing effect created by mounds of merchandise. Overloading should be an Olympic sport; it is an art and medals are guaranteed for the poor. Necessity beats science every time. It is possibly the strongest of human motivations and the last thing to break.

People sleep over the edge of the barge like the aftermath of a domino world record attempt. Everyone is touching in some way or another. The unlucky ones are sitting with knees drawn to their chest. Behind me, on a substantial slope and an insubstantial space, some guy has crawled up unseen, sleeping one slip away from a three-meter drop onto the metal below. It's true the family will break his fall, but from there it's one bounce into the water.

You would think I would feel sorry for him having to sleep in such an uncomfortable position, and I do, but I like personal space more. I am relieved when Rambo chases him away. I know his name is Rambo because it says so on his arm, tattooed in faded black ink next to the misshapen scorpion. The man scampers away to a spot even more uncomfortable. At least one of us is better off.

The radio that has been broadcasting static for the last ten minutes suddenly allows Madonna to sing "Material Girl". I assume I am the only one who speaks English; the irony of the song is all mine.

Soon a few more stragglers sneak up looking for a space to sleep. Unsure of the correct etiquette, I put in a few elbows for the team. My subdued efforts are not needed. Rambo and Sarge take a more direct approach with crowd control. Sarge plants his feet shoulder-width apart – "We are full." I don't understand the dialogue, but the ultimatum is clear.

When faced with men who are more familiar with violence than yourself, you will be the one backing down no matter how good your argument is. Besides being dressed in battle fatigues of the DRC military, the two are naturally intimidating figures. Judging by the way the invaders scrambled, it's not just white paranoia.

I attempt to express my allegiance by slipping them a packet of cigarettes. This gesture earns me new friends and security at the same time. I don't think I need it, but when you are alone in the Congo you can never have too many friends.

When I walked on board, security was not first on my needs list – food was. My father gave me three pieces of advice when I left home after high school. The first piece was perhaps the wisest, most practical words ever spoken. "Always make friends with the chef." With this wisdom I found Mama Grace and her troop. I heard her speak Swahili and within three minutes I had been adopted into the clan. I am not too old to play the poor-little-lost-boy role.

I am now property of the barge. Everyone wants to chat, everyone wants to be my friend. I feel like a politician, holding babies, waving at people I don't know and pretending to listen. God knows why anyone would want to be famous – it's exhausting.

In the morning the three stooges are again trying to out-Amen and Hallelujah each other as they wave their arms in the air. The one fool has a megaphone used in the hopes of making his sermon sound more official and thereby getting an edge over the other two. They are all demonstrating what they would do with the devil if he should dare make an appearance. The rough edges of their egos are soothed by the hymns rising in whispers from voices still asleep in the dark of the pre-dawn.

By the fourth song and fifteenth hallelujah, men are gyrating their hips obscenely while praising the Lord. It's not something you would want to watch with your mother and definitely not associated with divine worship as I know it. It is however not physically possible for a

Congolese person to hear music without gyrating any more than it is for a dog not to move his leg when tickled on the belly.

We start the day's journey with that annoying *beep* that seems to come standard with the reverse gear for anything big enough to run something over without noticing. The frayed steel cable is untied from the bank and the hundred-meter long metal suitcase is spun on its axes by the tin can pusher, which consists of nothing more than two rooms built over a very large engine.

Soon a message is relayed from Mama Grace that coffee is ready. I slide toward the edge of the blue canvas that covers the mound. Once committed to the steep slope, there is a tricky step over a stack of smoked fish. From there I traverse over someone's house onto a tiny ledge. There I can check for any changes that have occurred on the route during the night. It is important to keep a controlled descent to the deck. The difficulty rating of the last few feet depends entirely on what type of life-form is tied up or asleep at the base. Yesterday it was a goat, which is easier than chickens; mostly because they rebound better after being stepped on. Even though the height is manageable, the short jump over the fleshy step is performed onto a landing strip twenty centimetres wide, covered in cooking oil and sliding into the Congo River.

To keep this exercise from getting easy I recommend using one-dollar sandals that come standard in rainbow colours and are guaranteed not to have any grip. Climbing back is equally tricky with coffee in one hand and daypack in the other. My supplies are held in a red plastic shopping bag containing a diary, book, sunglasses and an empty sunblock container. Once on top of the mountain I settle in for the first shift of the day.

There are three types of days on a river barge: sunny ones, cloudy ones and ones where something happens. Sometimes they overlap. Today reveals itself early with an innocent sound. The slightly frictional *thud* as the barge slides onto a sandbank is followed shortly by the frantic whine of the diesel engine trying to undo the momentum it has worked so hard to achieve.

The deep breathing of the engines suddenly roars into a rebellious growl as they protest against the impossible demand for movement in the opposite direction. After a few minutes of fruitless revving, the engines shut down, leaving the boat silent and motionless mid-river. I try to find my Zen but all I can think is: This is what happens when you have a half-million dollar piece of equipment and do your depth-checking with bamboo poles.

I have seen barges in this position along the way, their crews and passengers ensnared on a sandbank where they will stay until the wet season floats them down river. I suppose you have to be Congolese to be able to endure sitting in a squatters' camp for two months under a hot sun waiting for the river to rise. Because air transport is unaffordable, this is the only means of travel between Kisangani and Kinshasa. On this barge are people from all walks of life with families and jobs to go to. Unlike me, they do not fret any delay; the Congo has taught them acceptance. Personally, I don't even care in what direction we move as long as we move. Cannibals or not, if we are stuck I am off this boat by tomorrow morning.

Pirogues are dispatched to search for deeper water before any more efforts are made to clear the boat from the sandbank. In the Congo, performing simultaneous tasks to save time simply increases your chances of something going wrong. By the erratic lines the *pirogues* are paddling and from the frantic hand signs between them, I am guessing they aren't finding any answers. The shallow sandbanks surround us.

To get off the sand we will have to attempt a feat equivalent of reversing a container truck out of a traffic jam. Rambo, only half joking, books a space on my kayak. I make a mental note to bring him along as protection if I do abandon ship. Logic says that they must get stuck often and that they would have a system for fixing the situation, but logic gets confiscated at the border. You even have to pay $50 to get it back when you leave again. If you try to sneak any in, it will only make you miserable. Instead pack a sense of humour and a hunger for adventure.

The pusher detaches, either in search of an alternative route or to abandon us. Not once in the last week has any information been passed down to the masses. On none of our frequent stops at dockyards or dodgy villages has there been any warning of departure. When we are at anchor, at any moment the air horn could blow giving you five minutes to be on board or leave you in the middle of nowhere with only the clothes you have on.

The captain's coping mechanism with the obese overloading is to deny that there are people on the boat. The unspoken message is that you should feel privileged to be here. Maybe the captain knows exactly what will happen next, and he prefers not to be a liar?

It's not immediately clear what the plan is, but it looks complicated, a word that does not go well with 'plan' around here. Tying the pusher to the front might be the last option before going back to brute force. The engine is placed at an angle presumably trying to blow the top layer of sand away to dig us out.

It huffs and it puffs but it cannot blow the sand bank away. After all that commotion we are still exactly where we were. Next, they move people away from the affected corner in the hope that it will help us slide off. Most of us have realised that chances for a speedy solution are lost. People are starting to abandon the barge, taken to the side by *pirogues* appearing from nowhere.

Soon the whole barge population is forcibly offloaded, apart from the VIPs like the pastors and Kabila's nephew. A few big mamas stirring their cooking pots refuse to leave. The crew yells at them for a bit, but it's more for effect. When a one-hundred kilogram woman says she will not move, there is very little that can be done.

Once most of the passengers are on the closest island, the barge rises about ten centimetres. It's still more than one and a half meters underwater, but the progress is encouraging. I can see we are getting serious when the crew is issued with safety equipment; one of the fifteen guys gets a pair of gloves, and another a lifejacket.

Steel cables are dragged to the front. To help, a few stowaways are rounded up to wrestle the frayed cables through bedrooms and kitchens, past boiling cooking pots, under the golden arc of a little boy pissing and over piles of fish looking on with that peculiar, "I can't believe I am dead," look in their glassy eyes.

I decide to get a bit of training in while the operation is underway. It's all so exciting I lose interest in training and do my part by entertaining the crowd from my kayak. I warm them up with some paddle twirls before going into the Eskimo-roll, which is guaranteed to bring the house down. "I would like to thank the academy, my parents and the fans, without you this would not be possible. Thank you, I love you all." Talking to myself and laughing at my own jokes have long since stopped being weird.

When the barge finally shifts I finish the show off with a 'Mezza' happy dance. I would have liked to get the Mexican wave going, but I lack the hand signs to demonstrate it from my kayak. I do manage to get a fair amount of hooting and hollering out of them. It seems no one was really looking forward to spending the next few months out here anyway.

I have the feeling it's a bit soon to start celebrating as I see the barge spinning ever so slowly out of control downstream. The pusher is frantically trying to reattach itself. Five hundred tons of steel with its own agenda is an accident waiting to happen. Eventually it all crashes into the bank with the sound of thunder. People are reloaded and we continue our journey.

From eleven till four in the afternoon, as the sun sits heavy over the Congo, everyone slips into a state of reduced consciousness. The crowds have shrunk with the shadows. All are hiding under and inside anything that resembles protection. People crouch under sleeping mats and cover themselves in blankets. Some even wear woollen beanies. I have never been able to understand how being wrapped up in a blanket in thirty degree heat can be of help, but it's a system used all over the continent.

Sarge looks comfortable under his yellow umbrella decorated with pink flowers. His daughter gets passed up from time to time by a wife, who I never see, and plays on his lap. A few of the men in our group have wives on the boat but do not feel the need to hang out with them. It is possible they are afraid that they will hinder the women in the task of preparing food, so they sit and talk the day away.

The flow of *pirogues* is never broken. Without barges these people would have no contact with the outside world. The barge is a floating marketplace. *Pirogues* peel on and off, selling their wares of fruit, meat, beer and fish that come in all sizes, shapes, and conditions such as live, smoked or dried. The whole family is involved. For the duration of their brief business hours, nimble boys or big fat mamas jump from *pirogue* to *pirogue* tying their little stall onto the barge. Men and women of all ages are bartering against the clock as the barge takes them ever further downstream from their homes.

For most of the passengers, buying and selling is a means to pay for their tickets, investing what limited capital they have in packages made from vines that they fill with protein of any kind to resell when they arrive in Kinshasa. The professional merchants, like Mama Grace, live permanently on the barges, trading clothes for fish.

Instead of the naked savages one might expect from people so isolated, they are often dressed in colourful Western clothes. Some paddlers even have matching outfits and judging by the down jacket and beanies, practicality is not as important as style.

If a *pirogue's* cargo is exotic enough, like a crocodile tied up, or a giant catfish, it captures the imagination of the whole barge. Fresh fruit and veggies are another show stopper. The barge might even slow down as people force their way to the edge, waiting for the pineapple, coconut and mango stall to float down to them.

Villages scraped from the surrounding forest are never far apart, and their entertainment seems to consist of yelling at barges that never stop. Our passing existence is the only sign of a world outside the trees under which they sit and drink *pombe*, the local brew. At hardly faster than a walking pace we move through this timeless world. The sides of the river have been lost for some time now, replaced by islands the size of suburbs and channels larger than all the rest of Africa's rivers combined. Over us hang clouds compressed into shape, sometimes carpeting us with its humid haze. The isolation completes the feeling of detachment from the rest of the world.

From side to side we follow pointing wooden arrows hung in trees, expecting that they will still indicate the best way through the endless sandbanks below. The captain has a GPS but he has yet to find the willingness to use it; instead he opts to lock it up safely in his room.

Late afternoon is the time everyone awakes from the midday coma, knowing we are another day closer to our destination. The only thing that dampens my awe at the water around me is the knowledge that it is all going to compress into a gorge. The idea that I am going to paddle through it seems absurd.

A village of three hundred-plus people and there is not a washing basin in sight, but luckily we are on the second largest washbasin in the world. Bent milk powder tins or modified plastic containers tied to string are cast to collect water. Few Congolese drink the water from the river; most have the foresight to fill a few containers at a borehole when the chance presents itself at an overnight or loading stop.

The Best Day Ever

The sunset speaks a sonnet of colours just as I am called down for dinner. Mama Grace likes a good meal herself, and as a professional merchant she normally comes up with a feast. Fish of some type, a few cooked bananas, rice or my favourite, cassava bread. We sit in our little huddle, her on her bed, and me on the ventilation pipe protruding from the hull. We are wished countless *bon appetites* as the human traffic flows ever past.

As the night church service starts, I slide my kayak from the light of the barge to the amazement of the crowd. I am desperate for a few hours of solitude, some exercise and that feeling of floating in space brought by paddling at night. My days are filled with ups and downs, but these hours in the Congo's darkness carry only bliss. It is near midnight when I leave the cool water again to climb back onto the barge. It remains illuminated and silent under a great spotlight aimed at the bank. The once-bustling crowds are now peacefully asleep.

I wake up at 05:00 with stomach cramps. I suspect it has come from 'cheating' on Mama Grace and accepting some of the many other dinner invites I get daily. I find it really hard to say no to food. My mouth might very well be the death of me one day. When you share a toilet with three hundred people, diarrhoea can be an inconvenience. A stroke of genius is the fact that the toilet is also the only shower.

Congolese are more aware of how many days pass between washing than myself and this means that the toilet gets about three hundred washes a day. It's probably still not kosher but if, like me, you have been in the Congo for four months, you start to do math differently. I suspect that when news of this unhygienic squatters' camp leaks to the outside world, an NGO will be formed to tackle the problem. It's not all bad. Lining up for the toilet is a great way to spend time. I make a few new friends amongst the regular customers like myself.

News of my problem is soon a topic for discussion amongst every household on the barge and presumably the villages are spreading the news by drums. Support is provided uniformly through verbal encouragement. Many people who only speak Lingala or French still want me to know they are thinking of me and demonstrate that they know what the problem is. By 09:00, on my third visit to the toilet, some pills appear from somewhere. I try to pay for them but am told to shut up and swallow the nameless little red and yellow capsules. Under the careful observation of the entire barge and to their delight, I am declared fit again by afternoon. Just in time for dinner.

Between Light And Dark

Before I slide into the darkness, Mama Grace touches my arm and looks me in the eye to be sure I am listening. "Be careful and don't go far, this is Engombe's place." Neither the gesture nor the warning is needed. She is far too large a lady to ignore, and she tells me the same thing every night. I have seen the same resigned look in my mother's eyes, both no doubt thinking I should be on a leash. I am not oblivious to the situation, so I stay close and careful. Only for a while.

I paddle the length of the barge as it lies tied to the side for the night, leaving myself a downstream escape, if it should be needed. Every lap I go just a bit further upstream. It's unnecessary but happens by reflex. I am not too worried. I have a clear picture of how it will go wrong. A fishing canoe will come up and check me out. The mood will grow hostile as they realise I am helpless. All I have to do is make sure no canoe comes near. If I even see one silhouetted in the darkness I am straight back to the safety of the barge.

After almost two hours, it's time to go. But first, just one more lap. Reluctant to leave the peaceful night, I go further than I should. I just want to see what's behind that island and then I am coming straight back. Under a big moon, the world is reflected in silver, fresh, clear and exquisitely quiet. There is no one out here but me.

I have already turned back when it becomes clear: they have timed their ambush to perfection. Hiding in the shadows of the trees and breaking the cover at precisely the right moment, five or six *pirogues*, four men to each, scream angrily and charge at an angle that will cut me off from the barge and from hope.

Their cries are punctuated by softer sounds: the sound of air being sucked into a vacuum, the sound of paddles digging into water, and more importantly, the sound of speed far greater than I possess. In perfect unison the men bend double, throwing their body weight onto long thick paddles. The distance between us is closing fast. A creek boat versus a war canoe. It is a race that will only have one winner.

There is no chance I will outrun them so I go straight at them. I hope the show of confidence will calm them somewhat. It has the opposite effect. They go ballistic as I switch my angle at the last moment, aiming straight for the middle of their small fleet. The unexpectedness allows me to break the line, a tiny victory soured by the speed of their recovery. Instead of turning the seven-meter *pirogues*, they simply spin on their heels and are racing after me again.

I can see the barge in the distance. A single, silent point of light, impossibly far from the darkness I find myself in. I will not make it, but every meter closer increases the chance they might hear me. I have been screaming for a while, roaring at my attackers. I'm hoping that the barge has finished singing at the evening church service.

In seconds they have me surrounded again. Another quick turn buys me a few more meters but less than I hoped. The situation is worsening. The men in the canoes are using their paddles as clubs and swinging wildly at me. One blow strikes the back of the kayak. The plastic muffles a blow that would have cracked bone.

Pirogues are closing in around me. They have worked out my technique, and with superior speed and manoeuvrability it will not be long now. The spotlight of the barge and the light at the end of the tunnel is still impossibly far. I am moving in a dream, the one where I can't run fast enough. The frenzy on the *pirogues* grows with every missed attempt to grab me. They are in a murderous rage and I am out of luck.

Somehow I keep them off for a precious two hundred meters but it's becoming clear one of the swinging clubs is going to connect soon. I break through the surrounding circle one more time. The closest canoe, now only two meters away, throws a rope over me. The second it takes to get my paddle from under it is all they need. My hands go up, my running is done.

Tulia, Tulia. Calm, calm, everybody be calm. By pure chance *Tulia* is one of the words that translate into Lingala from Swahili. The fact that I speak an African language causes hesitation in the swinging of wooden clubs at my head. A toehold in a rockslide perhaps, but I take what I can get.

There might be more overlapping words, I just have to find them. Until then it is of the utmost importance I project *calm*. Like aggression, it is airborne. The guy behind me is still swinging his paddle. It seems impossible that he would miss me at this distance. Perhaps they are only trying to scare me. I try to ignore the sound of the heavy blows falling around me. I maintain eye contact with the guy holding me, I have to make a connection with him and I need to do so quickly.

A heavy staff churns the air before splitting the water next to me. Another crashes into my kayak. The cluster of boats are all coming together, jockeying for a better position from which to swing their paddles. The guy holding me seems to have started thinking. I keep repeating it, "Calm, calm." Steady voice, bringing my hands down slowly, saying the word even slower, trying to express it with every cell in my body.

After every third calm, I try other happy words in Swahili. *Rafiki!* "Friend!" They seem to recognise the word. The guy holding me raises his hand for the happy slugger behind me to stop swinging. It's a welcome intervention and a relief that lasts for about a second. He starts roping my kayak onto his boat. I have never been tied up before, and I don't like the feeling one bit. As I watch his hands and hear the grating of the nylon rope against the metal of the grab-loop on my kayak, I want him to stop, badly. With the hollow sound of paddles banging against canoes and people screaming victoriously, they start to drag my kayak and me upstream. I would rather not go.

Any resistance now can set the whole freak show off again, but if I do nothing I end up in the village and that's a trip I don't think I will be coming back from. It is the worst moment of the whole incident so far.

Up to now my mind has been moving fast, in short sentences. It flashes up possible answers like a quiz show: true, false or pass. For the first time I have a chance to grasp the severity of my situation. My kayak is parallel to the *pirogue*. I try a light push on its edge to see if there is a chance I can flip it over and make another run for it. It's bound to buy me a hundred meters or so, but if they catch me again the most likely outcome will be blunt trauma to my head. Once you opt for aggression you better be ready for a fight; it's a door that doesn't close well.

I am trying to slow them down while being as cooperative as possible. Most of them have stopped screaming, and at least accidental death is out of the equation for now. The next plan that flashes through my head is to flip the kayak over and make a swim for it. It's not much of a plan and it would mean I lose the kayak, a sacrifice I am willing to make, but a last option.

"Sir, I have friends on the boat, I want to go back to them." Trying to imply that they will also come looking for me. I know they hate the military down here so I make no threats. They yell something back at me that is not positive; more importantly they stop paddling to do so. I must simply keep them talking. "*Pesa!*" "Money!"

I can see I have hit another correct note. My hands try to convey the message that I have some and that they are very welcome to it, just as soon as we are back at the barge. By the way they are looking at each other I can tell a whole new possibility has opened up. For the first time I allow myself some hope. Greed is stronger than hunger.

As I sit in my kayak below a man's knees, he bends over and screams into my face. A dribble of spit hangs from the corner of his lip and he looks mentally unbalanced. The only word I understand is *Jina,* "Name." Between negotiations I try to calm him down before he reignites the whole scene again. I try a few different answers. He grows more frantic with every incorrect answer I give.

Another two canoes have joined us; one has a pregnant woman cheering the men on. It's all in danger of getting away from me, again, when I hear a sound from a world outside this dark place. Shouts! This time from further away. Looking, I realise the current has moved in my favour. The shouts are coming from the barge. Glowing like the light at the end of the tunnel, it is no further than three hundred meters away.

They have heard me and guessed what is happening. The added stimuli overloads the scene. Everyone knows that witnesses have suddenly changed the stakes. I know it is over, all I have to do now is tread lightly and I will walk out of this. The river wraps itself around the base of the metal box on which floats my village. We gently slide our cluster of boats along its rusty sides.

Aggression cracks back and forth between the two groups. The barge wants their *mondele* back, and they want him now. The Engombe are not used to taking orders and are hissing with venom far more potent than their small group could ever deliver. In a slow movement I reach up to let my hand glide over the smooth man-made surface, in search of a grip that will stop the whole situation. Midway along the barge, my fingers close around a ventilation pipe.

I am mostly forgotten as the two groups broadside each other with abuse. A boy bends down on the deck to reach my ropes but his hand is slapped away. It is a temporary setback. With every passing moment their fury is seeping away. Shortly thereafter another arm slices from the spotlight beam covering the boat and unties me. The firmness of the cool metal under my wet feet affirms life.

There has never been a clearer distinction between light and dark than the one drawn by the spotlight of the barge. I am safe inside it, even if I can still touch the darkness outside. My friends have formed a group around me. Robert leans his lips to my ear and whispers, "Did they hit you?" I know a positive response from me will force this proud man, who has been trying his best to show me a good Congo, to act and that it is something neither of us wants. "No, No, Robert, everything is OK." To illustrate the point I reach my arm down to the figure standing below me in the dark. He takes my outstretched hand and shakes it. I am not angry. I am happy to be alive. The only fault here is stupidity, and that's all mine.

The Engombe do not wait around to see what happens next. They let themselves be taken by the current, disappearing within seconds into the night.

Behind my back in the insect-filled beam of light, my entire village is buzzing with excitement. I feel sheepish, and turn to look up at Rambo and Sarge. "Security, security, where is security?" The boat explodes into laughter. I am followed by a thousand "I told you so's." And just in case I haven't noticed, more warnings that it is not safe to paddle at night.

For the next two weeks any wise-ass in need of a laugh, parrots, "security, security," as I approach, and sets the entire barge into hysterics. The Congo as it turns out, is full of wise-asses.

Kinsuka

This morning as I watched the sunrise, I have the calm of a man set firmly on the rails of destiny. Resigned to my fate, I am happy that the moment is finally close after months of anticipation. That calm grows into a sensation that words cannot describe. A very personal experience of knowing and being. I try briefly to capture it in my diary but something makes me stop. Even if I did have the talent to describe it I am too selfish to do so. What I feel sitting alone while watching the sun seep out of the Kinshasa skyline will remain *mine* for the time being.

"You are about to do something very special," Jack says across the breakfast table. Jack is right. Today is the final revelation of a mission that started five months ago. Soon the Congo will be finished. A fork in the road, perhaps like every other moment of my life, except I recognise this one for its importance and therefore I have been able to suck every last meaningful drop from it – a rare occurrence in a life cluttered with meaningless days and actions.

When I asked to join her team of fish researchers, Melanie expressed concern about me paddling alone. I explained to her that paddling solo is only psychological. On water this big there are few paddlers good enough to get to you if you are in trouble, and even fewer capable of manoeuvring to the side if they did. It's not a place for mistakes, alone or otherwise. My rationale does not remove the fact that sometimes it's just nice to be scared with someone else.

The depth sonar in my boat makes it the heaviest kayak I have ever paddled and I sense that I'm not adequately prepared. It has been a long time since I have paddled anywhere near the skill and confidence level required for this operation. Flat water and a few basic rapids, requiring no more than a forward gear, might mean I can tighten my belt again, but there is still far more rust on me than I would like to admit.

Now, gazing at the river, fear wraps around me like steel cables. I know I want to do this, I am just not sure I can. In the back of my mind is a voice that says *this might be a good time to leave the planet*. After a great mission, my book is almost finished, everything is in order with the ones I love. To not come back from the largest rapid in the world would be as good as I could hope for. *Nobody panic*, it's just a voice. My only regret would be the pain I'd cause my mother.

The one hundred and forty-kilometre section starts with fourteen waves coiled almost evenly over a distance of a kilometre before they disappear around a corner into who knows what. None are smaller than thirty tons, some are just more aggressive than others. The river is behaving like water should, but on a scale far superior to anything I have ever come across. Water is going in opposite directions and fluctuating up and down with meters of variance. Open like massive jaws, it is capable of swallowing anything that had previously thought itself superior. It is an unpleasantness where no plan in the world will do any good.

The speed dial is cranked up as I enter the first wave. My dismay rises exponentially as I sink further into the trough. The waves are bigger once you are in them; from the side you only see halfway above the waterline. Sucked into its lowest point, it looks a very long way to the top. Climbing the mountain of water, my momentum slows as I reach what feels near vertical. A prayer forms on my lips: "Please don't break on me." It is an irrational hope, sooner or later it will. I need to accept that fact now or risk panic when it does.

I am feeling every bit the plastic toy that I am inside the careless grip of a river whose banks are littered with pieces of metal barges chewed to the bone and spat out. I throw my body at the crest, fighting its momentum with my own, and break through. The second wave is even easier, granting me a clean line on a smooth surge.

By the third wave my luck runs out. This time my lunge into the chest of the beast is rejected. In a frozen moment, my precious momentum is arrested and then reversed. I am flipped end over end in a boat over two meters long. I cartwheel back down the pile I just came up, straight into the cogs of a hydro-machine with enough potential to supply power to all of sub-Saharan Africa. Like a train entering a tunnel, vision is lost and sound intensifies.

Normal thought becomes impossible. Upside-down in a kayak with adrenalin pumping, you have perhaps forty-five seconds of fight before you lose the strength to live. It is not a statistic one should think about while it is happening. Unfortunately it's the only thing I am thinking. Moving inverted and blind at forty kilometres per hour, unable to breathe and with pressure equivalent to 1.3 million basketballs per second being applied to every part of my body, I panic. Frantically my brain searches for a way out, for alternatives that don't exist.

My body detaches, setting up automatically for the roll it has done ten thousand times before. It runs into an unexpected snag as my head hits the GPS unit mounted on the back deck. A fact registered with the utmost disappointment in the very blurred emotional state of mind that is serving in the absence of full consciousness.

The body luckily is not concerned. Its job is simple. As mechanical as a combination lock, it goes through the process of stopping the clock that the mind is so worried about. It knows that rolling in this carnage of converging currents while in the crest of the wave is impossible, even without the complication of the GPS transmitter. Unlike my mind, it knows fighting the water is not an option. Instead of fearing the next wave it is planning on using it. Still upside down, slipping over the back of the wave, cultivated reflexes use the force of the current to get into position. Everything is happening in increments. Single steps in a timeline of fluid motion.

The next sliding white wall falling from above forces me back down the wave. I am bouncing like a rock in a tumble drier. On the third bounce, easy as you like, my head flicks my body over landing me upright surfing backwards down the face of the giant. I am going too fast, in the wrong direction, but at least the oxygen clock has been reset. I have just enough time to turn the kayak around before the next wave. I brace into it with more confidence. A good bitch-slap was needed as a reminder that I know what I am doing.

After the sequence of waves, the river flattens in a peculiar way, shifting constantly as if trapped in a shaking container. Swelling and shrinking, it breathes unevenly inside the confines of the stumpy black cliffs, long since crumbled to little more than pebbles.

The river is unlike anything I have seen before. Rapids are little more than flat-water configurations in unheard-of sizes. Waves emerge where currents meet. Exploding bursts carry little threat, but enough power to send me skipping like a flat stone in any direction. At times currents form under me and simply toss me aside with little fuss and not a single look back.

It's beginner kayaking on a life-threatening course. A glance at my GPS says I am moving nearly twenty kilometres an hour. The effect is doubled by clearly-defined currents moving at the same speed in the opposite direction. Again I am reminded of trains, except their momentum seems inadequate.

Most of the time I am lost below the waterline in the river's indentations. I make decisions on the occasional clear glimpses in the distance. Two or three hundred meters is the extent of my visibility. Reaching the bank will be extremely hard, and only if I am not picky about where. I know that the river has been kayaked once before. Without that knowledge I would never have committed to running it blind.

This must be what it feels like to walk in an earthquake, jumping from one moving mass to another as the surface crumbles below. Once I have adjusted to the surreal environment I start enjoying the absurdity of it. Except for the whirlpools: they still scare me. I use the outer rings of smaller whirlpools to slingshot away from the big ones. Pits of doom are carved out in the muddy water, some fifty meters long with Cyclops eyes five meters across.

When paddling big water, momentum is everything and straight lines are impossible. Success consists of being knocked around like a pinball, rolling up one mountain and down another, charging into solid currents and using that recoil to ascend the ones behind. When I do lose momentum, there is nothing to do but wait, completely out of control, for a surge to throw me in a particular direction. Sometimes I look straight down at my kayak pointing vertically below, other times I see only sky. It's the first three-dimensional kayaking I have ever done.

Every now and again the whole river crashes like an ocean wave; stopping me abruptly or helping me on my way. Immeasurable opposing forces push against each other forming big boiling walls, often higher than my head. The overpowering roar of the water and the howling of the wind allow no other sounds in the murky grey morning. I might as well be the only person in the world. The walls of the canyon grow. The rapids stretch further apart. The water becomes more manageable. The day speeds on.

I stop once to check that the depth sonar is working. I stop again to take photos of a barge sitting above me, its back broken over the rubble of basalt boulders.

I know I am going fast; part of me is turning this into a race. Ego is its only motivation. Part of me says slow down, take in as much as you can, there is nothing in that other world that can compare. Small and large streams are increasingly gushing in from banks. Waterfalls sixty meters high, drift serenely alongside frenzied rapids that burst through patches of green vegetation.

Eventually, tired and complacent, I make a mistake. The penalty is a few moments of dread as I paddle uphill from a section that might just kill me. It is a nice reminder. I should focus. I should know better than to give in to an inclination to rush.

Before I get to the next rapid I see a small cove, a white sandy beach backed up and guarded by a sheer cliff. I have seen few people, and I would like to keep it that way. After a stressful day, all I want is to be left alone. Climbing the cliff, I throw some firewood down. Soon I have a pile big enough for my needs with enough to spare for luxuries.

There is no satisfaction greater than a sweet cup of coffee over a campfire after a day of adventure. I sip it slowly, watching the yellow hills of the Bakongo region. Few trees stand above the scraggy dry grass. It is a landscape that seems more harsh than hostile. The cliffs are sporadic; anywhere else they would be spectacular. Here the river takes all the glory.

Once coffee and food have been consumed, I have time to think. All day long I have felt swept away, part of a hydropower that has no earthly equivalent. The flow of water here is stronger than all the rivers of the USA combined. It should be impossible to kayak, but somehow it is not. I imagine if you could ride a lava flow it would feel like this.

In some ways the day has been an anti-climax. Not that I would have wanted to or could have handled much harder. It's just that it never reached the Zen of some other solo missions. I suspect it is because I had not trained properly. The fear was too great; it stopped me from surrendering to the moment, it kept us separate. Nothing I have done this morning can be classed as technically difficult. If I had been down it before and my boat was light, it would have held few demons. But there is something about being in the Congo and alone that has made me feel more exposed.

Extreme kayaking is not a sport where you can have a quickie. In skydiving you can have a jump every month or so and still enjoy it. Kayaking is a ladder, and once you get to the top, you fight to stay there. Fear is as natural, constant and persistent as gravity. Without strong wings you fall. My inability to train for this mission was forced on me, and that realisation softens the disappointment. Instead of bliss I merely feel happy to be alive. But if alive is all I wanted, I could have stayed home.

It seems that after nearly six months I might survive the Congo after all. Ahead of me is a future I have not been able to see or even attempted to imagine. During this mission, the size of the present tense has not allowed it. I am now only a week away from finishing. Soon I will go back to a world I have hardly even thought about since this started

I sit on the smooth black boulder in a night without sky. No stars are visible through the haze that has hung over the entire day. An orange wind blows in from the distance. Like lava, the fire crawls through the night. How can something so beautiful be so destructive? The fire soothes my mood. I fall asleep to the roar of the rapids.

I wake up at midnight with these words on my lips that want to be written:

"Thank You for the flat rock I sleep on.

Thank You for the peace I feel.

Thank You for the chance to live my dreams."

The Horror, The Horror

Most literature that comes out of the Congo is negative. Sooner or later Joseph Conrad's label, "the heart of darkness" is mentioned. It's a catchy phrase, I am fond of it myself. I came here to see what the scariest place in Africa is all about, to have a peek at where evil lives so rampantly. My experience turned out to be better described in the word *humbling*. The majority of people I got to know were far better human beings than myself and doing what they can with the unfair hand that life dealt them.

It's a place with few rules, and things can get out of hand. It is a place where bad things happen often, but it is also a place where people dance in the street. The Congo has been a revelation. If this is as bad as it gets, everyone can stop panicking.

It is the heart of Africa, but it is not the heart of darkness. The place and the people are far from evil. The times when I got into trouble were without exception under the influence of 'I know better.' It will not be a tourist destination for many years to come and if you don't like getting dirty, you have no business there. If you are, however, willing to pay the price, it holds adventure of epic proportions.

I will not pretend to know the Congo. I have only been here six months. All I can do is analyse my experiences. By design and by luck, I have had many diverse adventures. I cycled the footpaths and back roads, walked through the jungle, lived in the city, paddled some remote sections of river and lived shoulder-to-shoulder with Congolese on a barge for six weeks.

In Goma, I expected chaos and anarchy. I spent the day alone, walking and getting lost in town without a single threatening moment. Flying into Kindu, I was ready for the aggressiveness that I had been lead to believe was synonymous with Congolese. A friend of mine's mother described them as dogs, a breed between Dobermans and Rottweilers.

What I did see in Kindu was a guy running seven hundred meters after me in the market to give me a bar of soap I had forgotten. I saw guys go through three telephone SIM cards to find me one that worked after I returned a broken one. I saw a moneychanger so trusted that the money does not have to be counted. Again, I walked for hours alone at night with not a single threatening word or gesture directed at me.

When my time came to leave Kindu, I thought it would get dangerous in the jungle. Once there I lived closely with the locals and found them to be honest, hard-working, decent people. For the vast majority it was an honour to work with them. In the remote villages, where we occasionally spent time amongst the most primitive and sheltered people imaginable, they were mostly downright friendly.

When I left the jungle to travel west, I was petrified. All my preparation had been in the east. Surely that was where it would get out of control. I knew little of the language and my contacts were almost non-existent, but the greatest obstacle I faced in six weeks in Kisangani was boredom.

On the barge I lived with three hundred people in what was little more than a slum. On top of each other with no personal space and with nowhere to go, we watched each other for over a month, day in, day out. Not once was I disrespected, threatened or taken advantage of. I can assure you it is not because I am nice a guy. I am a moody number that can go days ignoring everyone around me. I can be downright rude, and the fact that they didn't kill me after six weeks together says a lot about them.

Brymer's thesis on extreme sports refers to Abrahams' 1986 warning to, "Be careful when reporting experiences to avoid, as far as possible, the danger of reducing the experience to a merely typical or representative experience, for to do so would lose the spirit that resides within the actions."

In a way all explorers are journalists. We report from places others can't go. We speak from experience and not fiction. We are blessed with no special powers or skills, often simply able to make the sacrifices needed to live and experience things others cannot or will not. We can fuel our passion only by allowing others to live vicariously through us; our aim is to experience, not explore. Our alternative lifestyle acts as a balance for the system as a whole; for all the men and women who feel the call of adventure but for whom it is too far removed. People are fascinated by the things they cannot do themselves. Our accounts of those experiences are a window for them.

Some of expeditioning's basic lessons like overcoming fear and discomfort, facing the unknown, and living with less, are valuable lessons for our time, perhaps even more so now than ever. We have a responsibility to tell the truth or become at best storytellers, or worse, liars. The best explorers and seekers will always find themselves apart from society and alone. Only a fool will pay the price for a life lived on lies. Unfortunately the truth is a very poor seller, no one knows what it looks like. Truth really is stranger than fiction.

Because all experience is subjective, it is not easy to report honestly. Film is cumbersome and complicated. Just by considering writing about an experience, you compromise it. We become conscious of how the experience will reflect on ourselves. You think about what colours can enhance or blog, and what they will say about you. Me, Me, Me.

For the longest time I could not understand how books about the Congo could make this place sound so terrible. It has only been five years since Tim Butcher's journey that formed *Blood River* and nothing of major political significance has happened in that time. I have spoken to many people who have been in Congo since 2004 and before; they all agree that his book is a self-serving fabrication. I would like to give Mr. Butcher and other authors the benefit of the doubt and assume that they came here scared from their research and never let go of that mindset; continuing to look at everything through fear, seeing things that just aren't here.

I am grateful to John and Terese Hart for a lot of things, but mostly for adjusting my focus. Their relaxed tone allowed me to see the Congo without prejudices. John might be a bit oblivious in his eccentric professor way, but I believe his interpretation after living, walking and paddling through the Congo for thirty-four years. Terese might be one of the most remarkable and tough women I have ever met, but she is not Laura Croft. She is still just a woman and a mother who raised her three daughters there. Perhaps as scientists they have chosen to understand, not judge. Whatever the reason, they both have lived and loved without the fear that so obsessed and blinded others.

Thankfully, it is possible to find something of real value in a trip even if you are trying to sell yourself and the experience. Amazing and inspiring feats done to impress people, or to gain their respect, are not worth much. If I need to tell the world how tough I am, it only shows how fake I am. It shows that I need others to justify my existence, and by doing so, I have failed myself.

I was once called, "The greatest explorer you have never heard of," in a magazine. It's sensationalising, but I like the idea of being great and of being 'underground'. I wear my non-commercialism as a badge of honour. Every time I see the other guys get the big funding (or any funding for that matter) I get jealous and reconsider my stance. It's tempting, but by making our most intimate moments public, we prostitute them.

There is nothing wrong with film. It is entertaining and educational and it certainly seems like a nice job, but the fact that we attribute to it a quality that it cannot possess, reality, makes it almost a lie. I have no problem with HD camera-wielding teams spending millions on producing films that educate and entertain. They are needed to show people who would otherwise never be able to see. These films are mostly made to recipes that they know the public likes: a little bit of inter-group drama, a lot of suspense on either side of the ad break, a spoonful of controversy and some do-gooding, all brought together with a healthy dose of identification with the excited, eccentric host.

The people I admire most are those who have escaped this Ego gravitational pull, at least to some extent. People like Pete Meredith, Justin Venable, Dale Jardine, Dan Yates and Fleming Smich. People who you have never heard of but should have. Guys who go on missions and forget experiences they hear others sell for money. I don't know what their motivations are, but I would like to think that they push themselves to have experiences so pure that they will not need justification from anyone else.

The older I grow, the more ridiculous this human need to draw attention to ourselves looks, and ironically, the more important my need to be acknowledged is. It is a delicate balancing act. Without recognition, your world shrinks until you are all alone. By surrendering to this need completely, you may lose that fragile inner grip on something authentic, something real.

There is a more meaningful type of expedition: self-exploration. Rather than chase extreme experiences that attract attention, people on a path of self-exploration quietly embark on inward journeys. This is true art with real value, done by real people under ordinary circumstances. People who suffer without asking for anything more than the experience. People doing everyday jobs, living everyday lives, with no need to draw attention, no desire to drag a film crew around or to write a book. They are going deeper into their own heads and hearts, fulfilling their need for adventure by entering territory open to no one else. The bigger the obstacles, the better the mission. I am daring to glimpse into that option, one that requires the ultimate strength but that provides the purest freedom.

Diary Quest

Must I still continue the quest
On this strange and wandering stream
A prey to this gloomy land's pest
And banished from sunlight or gleam.

The natives declare it flows North
The Savants describe its course West
Livingston all his powers put forth
To win the strange secret, and rest.

Livingston was old but loyal
Of a courageous heart and well tried
He roused up his soul for the trial
He made a supreme effort & died.

Then Cameron came to the field
Young, stout-hearted, eater & brave
But the river refused to yield
The knowledge of the flow of its wave.

Westward from Tanganyika's shore
We flew to the trial of might
Determined to die or explore
The wild lands which stood on its right.

–H. M. Stanley

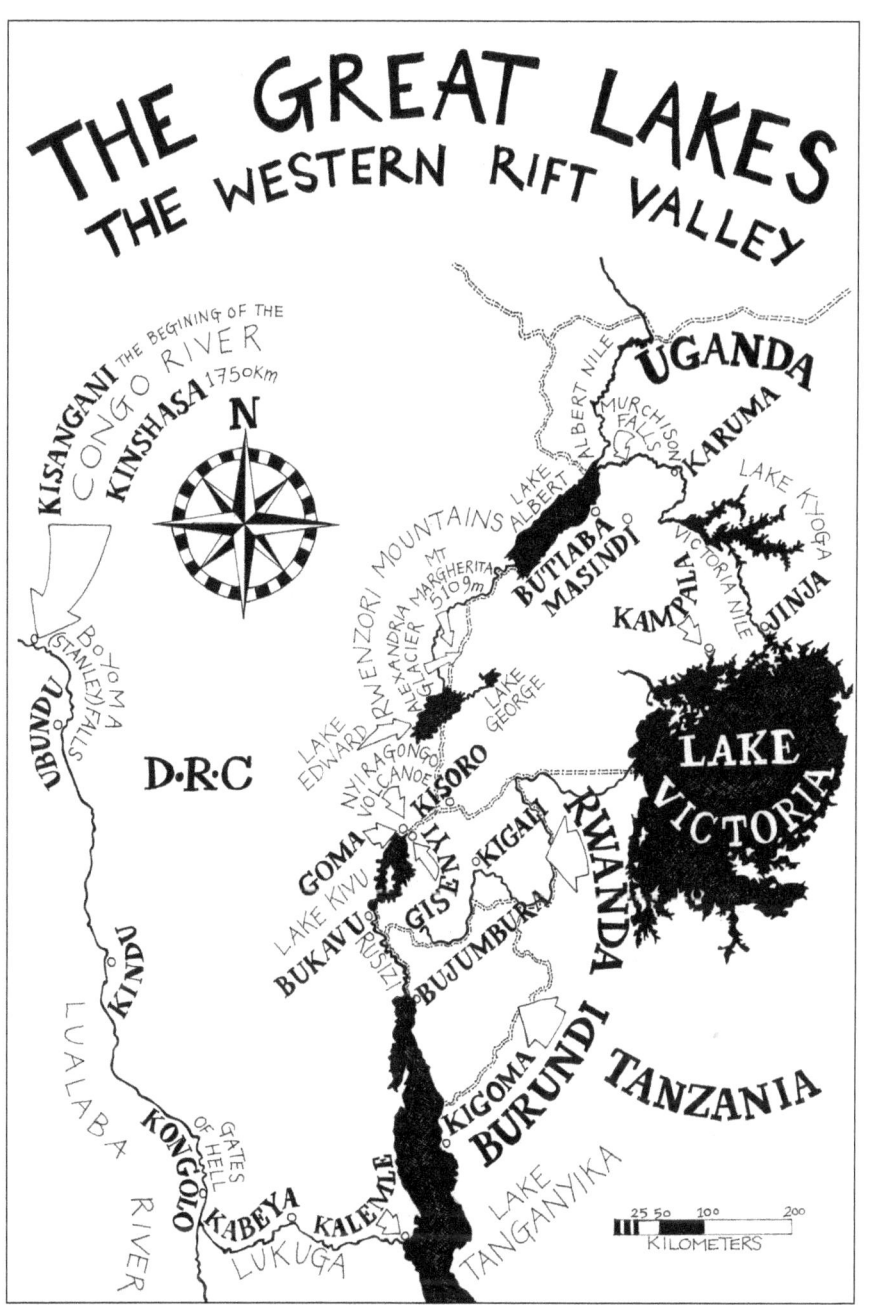

THE GREAT WHITE EXPLORER
http://greatwhiteexplorer.blogspot.co.uk/

SO MUCH FOR SQUASH

Monday, October 4, 2010

It is not the first time I have felt that everything I have done before has merely been training for what lies ahead. But that does not make it any less true. If you can see past the challenges, they are not big enough. This is also the reason I have retired from Great White Exploring about five times. I always repeat, "That's the last one, surely. From now on I am getting serious about my future. Perhaps start a relationship with a pot plant? Adventure education has taken me as far as it will."

Then, I spend four months in one place and next thing you know, minding my own business, an idea arrives. This time I had just come back from Thailand and settled into Jinja, Uganda, started my own business and began playing squash when I got an email from Ben Stookesberry.

The last and only time I had heard the name was in 2009; I was neck-deep in the Congo and he just wanted to touch base. In other words, he had an itch for the Congo that needed scratching. I pretended I did not understand: it would be ludicrous to take an American whom you don't know and who has never been to Africa into its very *heart*.

In his next contact, Ben was more direct. He and a few kayakers wanted a proper African expedition. For the few professional kayakers who come to the continent for an expedition instead of just a surfing safari, this normally means a week on the Zambezi, a week on the Nile and a few creeks along the way, finishing with a run down the Murchison Falls section.

Since I am retired, I distractedly encouraged him and said I would paddle with them on the Nile for a bit – it would be a nice way to get my yearly Murchison run in and keep my sponsors happy. It was only when he said he wanted to kayak the Rwenzories (Mountains of the Moon) that I started to really listen. Then he mentioned Rwanda, and soon thereafter, the C-word.

After hearing Congo, I do a Google search: it turns out Ben is a National Geographic action hero. I have no idea what this means, but if I were one, I would have it on my business card. Further checking indicates that he and the other members of the team, Jesse Coombs, Christopher Korbulic and Darin McQuoid can all kayak in a straight line; amongst other things they have the record for the steepest mile in kayaking. This is a worrying fact since they might expect me to do some proper kayaking, instead of just standing around speaking bad Swahili. Any which way, I resignedly move my retirement plans to next year and check the outfitting in my Expedition Solo. The universe has spoken.

Our trip will be a circular route around the Great Lakes area of Central Africa. We will start in Jinja, Uganda, with a few days of big-water kayaking in paradise, then down to Murchison Falls National Park for a week in Africa's version of Grade V whitewater. Still in Uganda, we will proceed to the Rwenzories: Africa's highest mountain range. There we will spend ten days in the African alpine zone in the hope of finding some kayaking gems. After one full day's rest, we will continue to Rwanda and Lake Kivu to put onto the Rusizi River that forms the border between Congo, Rwanda and Burundi. Take-out is in Lake Tanganyika at Bujumbura.

From there we'll go by boat to Kalamie in the DRC, paddle the Lukuga until it joins the Lualaba, later to become the Congo River at Kongolo. We will have another day of rest, hopefully avoid any local shenanigans and drop into *La Porte de l'Enfer* or Gates of Hell section (love the name), for a big-water ride through one of the world's most mysterious gorges. We finish in Kindu, go by road, if it exists, to Bukavu, cross Lake Kivu by boat to Goma, hike up an active volcano, take a picture and come home conquering heroes. Let's just hope we survive the Nile River Explorer's bar on our first night back. To quote the great Jo Henry, "What could possibly go wrong?"

This is not just the most comprehensive African river exploration of our generation, but it is so by far. No team has traversed across as many landscapes, attempted such dynamic paddling or risked what we intend to accomplish. I want to thank Ben, Jessie, Chris, and Darin for making their first trip to Africa a proper one, and for trusting me enough to dive into the deep end. When most people speak about the fear of the unknown, I bet they have no idea what you four must be going through right now. Eddie Bauer, you surprise me. After watching 'Summit on the Summit', I thought you might just have no idea of what you are sponsoring us to try. After checking up some more, it seems you like it hard. Respect. If nothing else, at least we can add the word "expedition" to this trip with a clean conscience.

BECAUSE IT IS THERE

Friday, October 22, 2010

'Why?' is the most-asked question in the business. It's a tough question, without a definite answer, but one that has to be asked. The classic answers are: 'Because it's there' and 'If you have to ask me, you will never know' – both great one-liners that mean little. On most long expeditions, there will be days where you are lonely, hungry, bored, sick or all the above. If you don't know why you are out there, the option to quit becomes a lot more appealing.

Pre-trip jitters are in their own way one of the most challenging and special times of the mission. By definition, fear and doubt are uncomfortable. On the most basic level, dealing with them establishes commitment to overcome obstacles on the journey. On a deeper level, it makes you reassess your life. We live in a world of opposites, filled with irony, and our actions arise from the same flavoured mix.

Perhaps all achievement is born out of insecurity: I have done many a stunt to impress others. By doing something that no one else has ever done, that no one else is likely to want to do, I reinforce that I am different. For a compulsive individualist, this is oxygen. We all have our roles to play. I wish I was the guy who sings beautifully, but this will have to do. Unfortunately for my 'brave' man illusion, it has become clear to me that the brave people are not the ones risking their lives playing boyish games.

Psychoanalysts may diagnose a death wish, but missions like these enhance the appreciation of life. It is no coincidence that death and rebirth are related in all forms of religion and spirituality. When you accept that you are going to die, and that it will be sooner than you think, it becomes impossible to merely go through the motions. Life without passion holds no appeal.

Deeper yet is the need to escape the mundane aspects of everyday existence. Escape from a world that incessantly tells me how to live, what to do and how to behave. Escape from my own shortcomings, escape from the duality of mind and body. Escape from the goals I set and continuously fail to achieve. A pointless act of defiance, shouting "fuck you" at no one, "I will live my way even if it kills me." Simultaneously there is a need to move toward something, of needing something more, of completing oneself through effort. To be tested to the core is as good a reason as any; it is in that place that we learn most about ourselves. On an expedition, I can be perfect for a day. It is the thing I do best, and being your best is being complete.

In a world filled with interpretations, truth exists only in nature. There you cannot even lie to yourself. She does not tolerate bullshit. You come before her with respect, fully present and ready to give one-hundred per cent; anything less and she will have your head. Ultimately going on a journey that puts your life at risk is not a decision made by the mind. Reason does not support it. Everyone knows that Africa is not a reasonable place, but if we can express that neither are we, rather we strengthen the bond with the continent. People are not conscious beings, just ask any marketer. Irrationality is part of a collective unconscious found in the early explorers, in the new ones, and in the places we will be venturing into. When George Mallory was asked why he climbed mountains, he said: "Because it's there." I wonder if he knew he was talking about the *need*, not the mountain.

The issue of motivation is indeed beyond words, or even petty needs. When we surrender to the unknown, faced with the magnitude of the powers, it compels us to realise how insignificant this body is compared to the forces of nature. We are all walking on eggshells – nature will have the final say – the solid ground we take for granted is just another illusion. Someone recently pointed out to me that our greatest moments are the ones where we lose ourselves; moments when we become not only more, but become everything. I have breathed in life in its purest form a few seconds here and there, and all I want is more of it.

These moments by themselves are inadequate, offering only brief respite. Grabbing onto them can be as destructive as any addiction. Their value is found in the glimpses they provide of what is possible. I have come to hope that perhaps the intensity and clarity of these experiences can be used for more than cheap thrills. There is more to this world than what we perceive and perhaps one day, I can slip through the gap these experiences briefly provide, to live permanently in that place of *boundlessness*, also known as *happiness*. Not the superficial 'satisfaction of needs' type happiness, but the real thing. The happiness of *being one with the moment*, no matter how it presents itself. Ultimate freedom.

STAGE ONE

Monday, October 25, 2010

I am late to the arrivals hall and a few dollars poorer, thanks to the military checkpoint outside the airport. A few taxi drivers stand around trying to scrounge business from the last tired foreigners arriving through the glass doors. I look around, worried, for any sign of my new best friends. It's never easy going into the unknown, especially with a team you have never met. They are going to have to trust me as I will have to trust them; losing them at the airport is not an ideal start.

One by one they emerge from the harsh neon lights into the garden outside where I have been waiting. Strong handshakes and straight looks are exchanged; we weigh each other up as fast as possible. The ride back is filled with small talk and petty details that tell me nothing. It is only when I see them sitting in their kayaks that I relax. If nothing else these guys can kayak. I could tell that even before we got to the rapids.

The first week is done, and it has been a good one. Showing people who share my passion around my backyard is a joy. Learning from them as they look at it with new eyes, a pleasure. As can be expected when getting stuck into the big stuff, it has not all been plain sailing. Jesse took a swim from a monster hole on the first day. He came out okay, but it's not what you want at the start of a mission in a strange continent. In this game, like most others, it's all about confidence. He, like all of us, knows that things will only get harder. Tomorrow we start the infamous Karuma to Murchison Falls section, and all indications are that it will be the highest level in years. Yes please.

WITHOUT THE SEX SCENES

Tuesday, October 26, 2010

The days of the great explorers who walked onto blank continents and sailed into unending oceans are gone for good. Eventually, the explorer of whom I am already a cheap clone will fall from the gene pool through lack of use. People like me are wannabes, lucky that there are some places that have not had their mysteries trampled by previous generations. The Murchison Falls section of the Nile is one such place, a place that epitomises 'Wild Africa'. Few have heard of it and fewer still have actually done it. If my calculations are correct, if completed, this will be the seventh descent ever, my fith. It is a terrifying place to love, but fear is the price you pay to be allowed into nature's VIP lounge.

In an attempt to sound brave, some great white explorers might write extensively about the size of the rapids. They might even conclude that they are the biggest rapids on the continent, second only to the Black Gorge (I made up that name) on the Congo River. Or they might point out the lack of access in remote wilderness. Some might even be so direct as to mention the densest concentration of hippos in the world (statistically the most dangerous animal in Africa) and the healthy Nile crocodile population. Personally I would not dream of using such childish tactics. Basically the place is larger than life and what happens down there is straight from a Wilbur Smith novel, but without the sex scenes. The reason I keep going back is because it makes me feel like Tarzan.

Murchison

Thursday, October 28, 2010

And so another page in my relationship with an extraordinary place is written. Every journey has had its own cast of characters and individual flavour. Some have had closer encounters than others, some more humour; but in the end they have all been overshadowed by the place itself.

Perhaps it is coincidental that I should have my first flawless run now that I do not look at it as a challenge that needs to be overcome, rather like a place where I love being. A more likely explanation is that I have found a route through the eighty kilometres to minimise the risk, and that I have begun to know the location of the territorial hippos and the best way to react to crocodile encounters. It is tempting to believe that it is the Great White Explorer's skills that brought me through another run; the next time before I put in, I will realise again that it is not.

There are many moments that stand out from the past two days, but perhaps the most striking is looking back upstream at a stairway of whitewater stretching over a kilometre long, descending in giant steps seemingly from the sky. For the first time in six years, I think maybe one day we will come down the middle.

Doubt surfaces as I lay safely in my sleeping bag. Is it possible to ferry above Murchison Falls? Yes, easily. I put it down to too much coffee and ignore the doubt. The next morning, my mind occupied with logistical issues, I hardy give the matter any more thought. Just before put-in Ben calls me over to look at the line again. Either it has changed or we all misread it the day before. From a different angle it seems impossible. It is doubtful I would have made it and the consequences would have been fatal. Murchison Falls is a place where my generation's skills and mindset are not up for the challenge. If this section survives for another fifteen years, it could become the place where the next generation of kayaker comes to test superior skills.

Perhaps there will be someone who will also fall in love with this place, someone who will consider tying his paddle to his hands, strapping himself to his boat, sewing in his spray deck and fitting an aqua lung. His Jet Ski rescue team will foul up the natural serenity, and I will grumble about the chopper filming him. It will be worth every tsetse fly bite and more to watch someone ride one of the giants from top to bottom.

Much more likely, Murchison Falls and its sisters Karuma and Uhuru, will merely fade away under the pressures of a Third World economy and its need for power and oil. It will become a legend and the legacy of the few petty humans who were willing to risk a bit more to experience one of the world's great natural cathedrals. Oil has been found in the national park and new lodges are being built. Murchison is far from spoilt but the tide is turning for one of the last bastions of truly wild Africa. I will not complain about it much, I would rather focus on the positive. I have a Class V local run, with more channels than I can run in a lifetime, where you can stop in the eddy and watch a herd of elephants washing as a pod of hippos play-fight. What could there possibly be to complain about?

OUT OF THIS WORLD

Thursday, November 11, 2010

The Mountains of the Moon is exactly that: out of this world. Seven years ago I was part of the first team to snowboard these equatorial glaciers, or more accurately, the first man to roll down the mountain with a board strapped to his feet. Surprisingly, five thousand meters was not the best place for my first lesson. This time I am part of the first team to kayak Africa's highest mountain range.

Ascending its slopes, hardly an hour goes by without a 'wow' view and not a day without a complete change of scenery. Starting down in the lush jungle, we climb through bamboo forest, walk over plateaus with more variations of green, yellow and rusty red than I knew existed. We skirt past high-altitude lakes until eventually the fairy-tale Afro-alpine zone with its giant mutant plant life is stripped to the bone by ice and snow; only the wind and rocks remain.

It takes me a few days to settle into the slow pace of the mountains, but when I finally do, I realise I have been missing a key component of the activity. Walking has always been equated with physical exertion. In my life there have been some amazing walks, of which the highlight must include a thousand or so kilometres down the east coast of Africa and two months in a virgin Congolese forest. The physical stuff is nice, but perhaps for the first time in my life I walk without anything to prove to myself because I am already where I want to be.

We have all kinds of weather and usually over a two-hour period. The heavy rains stay away until our descent starts. Within an hour of the last hut, the path turns into a stream, at times waist-deep, giving us a final little challenge and preparing optimal water levels for us on the Bujuku River. The only question is whether we should put in before or after the ridiculously steep section. My vote is for lower down, with thick jungle and a steep gorge I suspect long, hard portages that will eat up days we could spend on the more promising propositions during our great African kayak extravaganza.

Ben bites his lip and tries not to look devastated when Chris also votes for lower down. As I am learning rapidly, he is not one for half measures. This attitude is equally as challenging for me as expedition leader, tasked with everyone's safety, as it is inspiring on a personal and professional level. Where we put in is still plenty steep. It has been three years since I kayaked on a creek, and I am aware that I will be the weak link, a turnaround from the 'Murch' section where the guys must have had similar doubts.

After a quick reminder that this is the life I have chosen, I adjust my elbow guards, say a quick prayer and get ready to take my medicine.

Watching Chris glide ahead like he is walking though the mall, makes me feel even more agricultural. It is hard to tell if there are many medium-sized rapids or just one really, really long one. It is soon clear: we had discovered a classic. This is no gimmick run, this is the real deal and made for kayaking.

Before I know it, I am slapping high-fives like I was born in the USA. I might even have slipped in a playful rail-grab or given an air punch. I maintain that no matter what Ben and Chris might suggest, I did not say "awesome" even if it was that kind of day.

The Death Of Logic

Friday, November 12, 2010

After three weeks of experience bombardment we stop for a break in Kisoro, Uganda. Apart from being thirty minutes from the border with Rwanda, it is also a chance to catch up with an old friend. A few things have changed since our last meeting nearly ten years ago: Kidd recently got married and added a PhD after his name. I have less hair.

I know we will be welcome at his house, but am reluctant to call for help when our dirt track through the jungle becomes a dead end behind a truck jack-knifed across the road. The offending driver looks glumly at the edge of the cliff; the twisted truck expresses the same thought as me: "This doesn't look good." The Great White Explorer's contribution to the situation is to point out that he should have known better than to try this road with something that size. Our driver, Tabu, takes a more helpful approach. Lucky for us, he has the rare kind of physical and mental presence to walk up to hundreds of unknown people and take charge. I met him a few hours earlier when I flagged him down by the side of the road. Since then I learned he has twenty-one children, is a former warrior of the Acholi tribe, served in Idi Amin's army as an intelligence officer, loves Uganda and most importantly, he used to drive trucks in Mobutu's Congo. In other words, he has played in the Super Bowl for digging out trucks.

Within thirty minutes Kidd arrives at the other end of the jam. He has brought with him the only safety equipment that makes any sense in a situation like this: five litres of red wine. If we are going to be here for the night, we might as well enjoy it. We have hardly shaken hands when the truck moves. Before anyone else even knew it was big enough, Tabu slips through the gap between cliff and truck, firing up the hill with his chequered minibus, five kayaks on top, as if he has just entered the Central African rally championships. Kidd and I delay conversation as we try unsuccessfully to catch up in the slippery, potholed darkness.

Eventually, after the first shower in over a week, I sit down with my old friend in front of the fire place. It seems a perfect time to have my first drink in ten months. It is a hilarious evening of inappropriate tales, exaggerated adventures and good-natured abuse of each others' countries. Chris takes story of the night with 'The Indian Scarf', blowing my 'Cannibals in Congo' and Ben's 'Paramilitary in Colombia' out of the water. The youngest and quietest member of the expedition is turning out to be a dark horse. On my first impression, from all the people who climbed off the plane that night in Entebbe, I felt most comfortable with Chris. His eyes project a stillness, which makes it all the funnier when his dark side surfaces.

Our rest day turns out to be just as amazing as any day of adventure we have had so far. We all know that there are few things as precious as an old friend and the forgotten art of hospitality. For two days, the boys and I are showered with an abundance of it. In the north of Sudan people don't say *thank you*, they say *you are welcome*, as if giving is the pleasure and not receiving. The Kidd family believes in the same mindset. For them it is never a case of counting how much they have already done, but instead how much they can do.

I am indebted to them and all the other Samaritans who have taken me in during my travels; givers that might never write a blog, people you will likely never hear of even if they have stories that surpass my own. If it was not for the selflessness of people like them, not only would my life not have been possible, but it would not have been nearly as pleasurable.

Expeditioning is, in the end, a humbling affair. We come in with the cameras and the death-defying stunts but what do any of these things really count for in daily life? It is the people who can turn every day into a chance to give, to laugh or to experience that are the ones we should strive to be like. They are the ones who have "made it."

Optimistic

Sunday, November 14, 2010

Is it possible to start a day visiting a genocide museum and have hope for mankind by sunset?

Rwanda in 1994 marks a low point in human history. Over a million people killed by their neighbours, families, and friends in a three-month orgy of horror. Twenty people per minute slaughtered, up close and personal. Here every adult has a story, either as a hunter or as the hunted. The museum states that five per cent chose not to take part and five per cent chose to act heroically. For some reason this statistic stands out more than any others. Perhaps because of what it tells us about our species and its obedience to the statuesque and authoritative. If you think your society will behave differently, I suggest you read the Milgram experiment and then ask yourself if you can still be sure.

I try my best to absorb every story, every quote, and every picture inside the museum's dark building, not because I want to but because I feel I have to at least see what we are capable of, even if I cannot understand it.

We are all capable of evil just as we are of love; let us not fool ourselves that we are bigger than our culture. Evil hides in our make-believe, sterile world. It is not absent, it is not tamed, it is merely 'civilised'. I would like to think that such horrific examples of our capacity to look the other way and blindly follow our leaders are diminishing.

In the afternoon we have interviews scheduled that I would rather cancel. One of the reasons we came to Rwanda is because it is one of the success stories of the continent. Miraculously as the turnaround appears, it seems to matter little in the face of where they came. However, with every interview, my admiration for the people and the country grows, not in spite of the genocide but because of their reaction to it. Rwanda is a society in a hurry. They have experienced rock-bottom and have vowed *never again*. Rwanda has risen from the ashes to become a regional leader, but more importantly it has done so by being realistic. Government strategies are built on the best of African culture and not Western ideology. Politicians are held responsible to their voters by contracts, and corruption is almost unheard of.

This is no utopia, nor is it even a free society. There are soldiers on every corner, and party politics, inevitably based on tribal allegiances, are suppressed. It was hate propaganda that sparked the 1994 genocide; as a result, free speech is not allowed. The first stage in oppression is a division of 'us and them'. Once we believe that they are not like us, we can look down on others; next we can believe that they don't feel like us; once we cross this bridge we can start to hurt others. Here the party line is: There is no more Tutsi and no more Hutu, only Rwandans. The hope is that the very real divide can be suppressed long enough that the new generation might forget about it or realise its true insignificance.

The measures can be classed as oppressive. It would be easy to find faults in the new government: there are many. At our core we are all the victims of like and dislikes based on propaganda. If more governments stand up for the right thing instead of playing on emotions, Africa could be a better place. I don't know if this could work anywhere else or under any other leader.

President Paul Kagame is no Nelson Mandela. As world leaders go, he probably has more blood on his hands than most. My opinion is a murky reflection in a mess I will never understand. It seems to me that no one else could have resurrected the corpse of a society he freed from the greatest horror of our time and rebuilt it in such a short period.

How you judge improvement is a matter of opinion. I use a simple measure: Is it a better place to live under the current regime than it was before? In Africa this can normally be measured on the most basic of human needs. Security, when you don't have it, is all that matters. It is impressive that Rwanda is now one of the safest countries in Africa – but to measure Rwanda by this is inadequate – anything apart from total annihilation of the population would be an improvement. In a country with just about every challenge that could face a nation, perhaps the best measure that can be used is that it is a place where everyday people can be optimistic.

Nobody Panic

Wednesday, November 17, 2010

On every mission there are moments that have the potential to stop it in its tracks, moments with consequences so monumental that even a spoonful of Nutella won't cheer you up. Sometimes they are associated with danger, more often they are logistical. When the immigration officer in Goma hands us back our passports with our visas annulled and our entry denied, we are looking at such a moment.

Expeditions should not have many rules. Since there is nothing common about sense, however, some have. Our only rule is jokingly quoted but of the utmost importance: *Nobody panic!* Our visas from the embassy in Kampala are worthless to anyone apart from the Congolese embassy who made $550 from the ink squares. The new regulation, unbeknownst to all but the border post, is that you have to get your visas issued in your country of origin. When the official tells us to return to Rwanda, we stand around in the rain. What she does not know is that we are going to get into the Congo, I am just not sure how.

We throw ideas around to minimise the damage and are ready to cut our losses in the Kivu Province, with the hope of trying another border post further south. Fifteen minutes later the door to the Congo opens slightly wider as we push $850 through the crack. Apparently we can get 'Special Passes' that grant us the pleasure of seven days in the not-so-Democratic Republic of the Congo. When we ask about the chance for an extension once inside, we are told "There is always a chance." We thank them for the opportunity, but a verbal thanks is not what they are looking for: another $100 and we have our 'Special Passes'.

In an effort to help us get our budget back on track, Bryce offers us accommodation at the International Rescue Committee. We make it there just in time to watch the second half of the Springboks vs. Wales rugby match. The finale to our day is spent in the unexpected surrounding of a beautiful house overlooking Lake Kivu.

Goma, alongside having possibly the worst political mess in the world and being surrounded by some of the most unpleasant armed groups you could imagine, sits on the banks of a lake filled with poisonous gas, capable of killing every living thing in the vicinity if triggered to bubble to the surface. Goma is built on the slopes of an active volcano, Nyirangongo.

I have been wanting to see its volatile insides since I first visited in 2001, but security in the outskirts of this town changes like the weather. This time round, the line to the top seems open and under armed escort, we make for the three-thousand metre cone. Getting to the top, we hear the lava churning down below but the cloud of carbon dioxide obscures the pool. After eating our two-hundredth can of tuna on the trip with some crumpled bread, it finally opens up; at first just a slash of red, but once night settles, visibility grows. Feet dangling over the very edge of a crater three kilometres wide and two thousand meters deep, we looked into a pool of molten lava (love the world molten) perhaps seven hundred meters in circumference. Some people can watch a camp fire for hours and others find equal pleasure in watching water run. In this moment we watch a combination of the two, imploding and exploding on itself. The venue is breath-taking, the view unbelievable, we are watching the earth's core bubbling up.

We set our bivys on the only flat spot available, meters from the rim and possibly the windiest place in Africa. It is also possibly the coldest I have been for quite some time. More realistically, not that long, since I was on a glacier last week. The fact that it is freezing matters little, somehow it might even add to the experience. The guards' tents flatten repeatedly until they eventually give up and roll themselves in them. Apart from the moments when I feel I might be blown off the mountain, I love being wind-blasted on the side of a crater boiling with a power I can't comprehend.

Another Statistic

Saturday, November 20, 2010

Instead of leaving Goma on a big old ferry, we pack into a bathtub toy with sixteen other people, all substantially bigger than any of us and dressed a whole lot louder in Congolese fashion. Once wedged in, we skip across the lake, bouncing from wave to wave and bombarded with Lingala music for two hours until we reach Bukavu, the capital of South Kivu. From our first impressions it seems more of a functional city than Goma; vehicles with a purpose other than NGO or UN zig-zag on the crumbling roads and muddy strips.

It is unbelievable but entirely possible that Bukavu has seen even more misery than Goma. In 2006 it was overrun by rebel forces, who proceed to try to rape every woman in the city, giving it the dubious distinction of 'rape capital of the world'. Security has improved but remains fragile. Rumours suggest that three weeks ago, the same rebel group, now incorporated into the Congolese army, took the airport from DRC and UN soldiers in an effective show of power.

Our indispensable partner in this ambitious project is the International Rescue Committee. They are the most prominent NGO in Congo and this is their biggest base. They run four programs from here, the largest of which is a community-driven reconstruction project: helping communities to help themselves. It has a budget of $160 million and is estimated to benefit 1.8 million people. In most communities, villagers have chosen accessible drinking water as their second-highest need after education. Clean water is a real crisis, only fifteen per cent in rural areas and forty-two per cent in urban centres have access; the fact that they still choose education as their top priority says a lot about the Congolese desire to improve their situation.

Before you, like me, ignore these statistics, you should realise the following: water-borne diseases are the biggest killer of children under five, with half of the world's hospital beds at any given time occupied with its victims. In the countries on our route, clean drinking water sounds harmless compared to say, civil war, but as I am quickly learning, the struggle to obtain clean drinking water is one of the major obstacles that prevents the development that could lead to more stable societies.

To see first-hand what the crisis is about, we drive for hours through rolling green hills with many little streams trickling into the valley below. Water seems the least of anyone's problems. The area outside Bukavu remains in danger from the many rebel armies hiding here. Superficially everything is idyllic, apart from women my mother's age carrying loads I would struggle under. Notably, we see hardly any men carrying anything at all.

Our destination is a few neat huts built on the side of yet another hill. Once we step out of the car we are cheered until we sit down in the town hall/church, a dark building with holes for windows and well-worn wooden benches. We are bearing witness to the opening of a simple water system. The project has cost only $50,000 and being gravity-fed means it has little maintenance. It should supply water to three thousand people for the foreseeable future. This is a useless statistic, if you, like me, don't know what life is like without water at your every convenience.

At first I am puzzled by the passion with which the village sings the national anthem. Their allegiance is to a government that has not changed a water pipe since the Belgians left fifty years ago, but Congolese are proud to be Congolese. I assume that the passion is for humanity's belief in ideas and a need to belong to something larger, instead of to their non-existent leaders.

The speeches are above my struggling Swahili, but touching because of the people who stand up and speak. There is pride expressed from those who, perhaps poor for most of their lives and victim to uncontrollable forces, are participating in accomplishing something concrete.

What draws my attention most is the women. It is disturbing how vulnerable I know or believe them to be. My thoughts keep going back to the security briefing we had earlier in the day. Fresh social unrest has broken out just south from here, full military operations that will no doubt lead to the scattering of militia and the pillaging of every local community in their path. Our own trip down the border river, the Rusizi, is in jeopardy because of the new development. The important point is, we get to choose whether we would like to be brave, they just have to pray another storm will pass.

There can be few places worse to be female. The fact that illustrates this best is that in Bukavu there is a hospital that is the world leader in vaginal reconstruction for rape victims. Try to forget that statistic. By all rights, women here should be quivering in the corner and not be organising committees to improve their daily lives. Clean water is fundamentally a woman's crisis, because it is women who have to carry forty litres, spending a minimum of an hour a day fetching water from often-unclean sources, or even more draining, caring for their sick children due to waterborne diseases.

By allowing them to choose water as a priority, it gives them the opportunity to participate in the realisation of the project. Not only does it free up hours in every day to spend on income-generating activities, but it empowers a very important part of society. It might even start to address the very reasons this place is in such a mess.

FEELINGS, DO THEY MAKE YOU SOFT?

Friday, November 26, 2010

As I lick my dry lips and carefully check that my spray deck is on properly, I have the feeling I might be doing something I shouldn't. I push through the doubt and when I finally shoot out of the bottom of the rapid, I am happy I have. It is just paranoia after all.

It is hard to know the difference between irrational fear and instinct, but fortunate is he who can. Often there is no clear right or wrong option, only the safest one. And if safe was all I wanted, I would have stayed home in Jinja. Too often when trying something no one has ever done, there are only three likely outcomes: success, quitting, or serious injury and beyond. The difference in the three are often forces outside of your control. But this is the nature of the beast: risk.

Anyone who is good at what they do – be it marketing, sports or hairdressing – will tell you they trust their instincts. There are rational explanations for people making the right choices based on information they could not have known beforehand, but only because we live in a rational world. If you choose this option and believe that all there is to know is already known, then that is your boring truth. Keep me out of it. Whatever the real reason, I think we all agree that people who can go successfully beyond facts are the ones who excel in any and all fields.

There are ways to sharpen these skills, such as practicing to trust your feelings. Personally I have found meditation extremely helpful, but I am yet to find a definite answer for when to choose fact over instinct. Due to necessity I am often forced to choose nonetheless. Never has this been more so.

Our current goal is a first descent of the Rusizi, the river that forms the border between the Congo, Rwanda and Burundi. Due to recent rebel activity, we cut plans for the last eighty kilometres between Burundi and Congo; it is flat water anyway. We focus on the prize: fifteen kilometres of what we believe could be some of the steepest, big-volume creeking in Africa. This (creeking) means more water going over more rocks at a faster speed. About the only positive thing going for us is that the left side of the river belongs to Rwanda. African politics 101: Rwanda is the size of Wales, has the densest population in Africa, is a relative fortress of stability in Central Africa, and possesses an army lacking a sense of humour that kicks serious ass.

After a frustrating morning trying to find the exact put-in at the second of two hydro stations, we are halted by a soldier who refuses to let us proceed without permission. Given where we are, it is a reasonable request. We would have loved to have permission, but no one wants to take responsibility for something they cannot grasp. Rwanda being possibly the only country in Africa where a dollar bill can't negotiate and will offend by trying, we go back to the car.

We try several avenues, and after being delayed two days are no closer to knowing who is actually qualified to give us permission. This is enough reason to walk away from the project, you would think. Unfortunately, as the goal of advancing river exploration in central Africa was always going to involve some bending of protocol, the line is looking as blurry as ever. With a new dam proposed to be built and the area likely to remain on a political knife-edge, we realise that this might be the last chance anyone gets. That, and we really, really want to.

I know as expedition leader that 'want to' is not enough. I start to make alternative plans after being blown off by the mayor and wait for the boys to return from a scouting mission with some hired motorbikes. They report that the locals are calm and show me photos taken from the rim. I see a truly spectacular canyon and monstrous rapids; desire takes over common sense once again. Ben is keen and Chris is undecided. As leader I will have the final say, but for once it is a decision I do not want to make. We still have preciously little info on what we will find down there. Our greatest enemy, the all-mighty Rwandan army, has become an obstacle to be avoided. Their reaction to us, if found in a delicate area with bags full of cameras and no official papers, is expected to be less than accommodating. If caught we will be on our own, unable to drag our 'friends' into our mess. With all this on the table, and my mind made up, I am surprised that I still want to have a crack at it.

The river and the area are enough of a challenge under any circumstances, but with the added element of doing it without permission, we all know that we are on the line, possibly past it, and we haven't even started yet. We promise ourselves that if any more complications arrive, we will back down, pack up and go on our way. The plan is simple: we go down nice and slow, and as far from the soldier who stopped us as possible. Unfortunately, the only put-in we find is within sight of the dam. As soon as we are on the water, we can see people watching us from there. This really should be the end of the trip, yet again I am surprised at how easily we decide to run the first drop and then see what happens. The river is beautiful, but I have walked away from beauty for a lot less and rationally should have done so again. My mind is spinning with the decisions, the repercussions and the consequences. Strangely, inside, it feels right. We continue.

The first rapid lasts five minutes, we stick around for a few minutes waiting for hell to break loose. When it doesn't, we run another rapid and then another and another. The whitewater is everything we had hoped for and more. The rapids flow into one another uninterrupted. Our suspicion of the locals lessens as an ever-growing mob cheers and encourages us down the river. Once they realise what our plastic boats are capable of, they even start making suggestions on how to approach future obstacles.

I thought I had been to most of the big gorges in Africa but it turns out only to have been the known ones. To find myself in something of that scale, almost unknown, is worth every drop of sweat, every public bus ride, every fly-infested nowhere border town I have invested time in, ever. Dwarfed by lush green mountains rising up to a thousand meters above us, we are drawn in ever deeper, with a constant eye on the banks for trouble, by the river with every foot of its relentless gradient. Only one portage is required on day one, and the three of us quickly fall into our roles: leapfrogging, filming and scouting without instruction. All the while we keep an eye on each other, hardly ever talking. The hush of the river's static, thick and comfortable over us in the narrow valley, is only occasionally broken by short sentences of appreciation.

We spend the night under an overhanging cliff, waking sporadically to stare at the full moon and the silhouette of the mountains overlapping in the cut behind us. We rise with the sun's signal to start off another big day.

Below our camp, I change my line to accommodate the camera, making the schoolboy error of not scouting around the corner for the variation, and pay the price. Being ahead of the boys and knowing that swimming is not an option, makes the beating easier to handle, but being rag-dolled in a fully-loaded creek boat is an experience I find unpleasant. More portages appear on day two and I am struggling to come to grips with the unusual reactions of a heavy boat, being a bit too fast or to slow for the majority of the day. At times I am annoyed, at times I am scared, but most of the time I would rather be nowhere else.

To avoid detection from possible soldiers downstream, we take out at the last big rapid. An army of impromptu porters are eager to carry our boats out of what seems to me a challenging affair. Three-quarters of the way up, a storm unleashes, dragging a curtain of water toward us through the warped valley. As hard, warm drops trash our little selves and a pair of goats, we stand precariously on an unknown slope deep in the heart of Africa, for once my mind and heart agreed.

I would never live a better day.

EPILOGUE

Be it life or death, we seek only reality.

—Henry David Thoreau

Looking back on it all, I could not have spent the time better. My 'hardships' do not even deserve to be called sacrifice. It has not all been happy, but it has been good. It would be impossible for it not to have changed me. I can only hope it is for the better. This is by no means guaranteed. There will be scars, but overall I feel stronger than before. In time I will forget what it was really like and my memories will resemble photographs. This search for peak experiences has been the driving force in my life for as long as I can remember. The closest to an answer I have found was in nature. With Her help I have felt like a god. For a few seconds here and there I have inhaled pure life. Fleeting and built on air, but it's a lot better than nothing at all.

After all the craziness and blessed adventures I have had, I wonder if perhaps a sunrise anywhere over water is not the purest moment of them all. Seeing the sun rise as you lie, no tent or roof barrier, surrounded by sky and the morning noises that sound like silence, allows your soul to take freedom sips through your blinking eyes. No story to tell but the reality of Earth's rotation. I know now that I had my special time and my special mission; that I need not repeat it.

I will never have a greater mission than the Congo. I have loved adventure and nature and they have been good to me, but Nature cannot love me back in the same way. Perhaps that is why I could love Her so unconditionally?

I have tried giving it up many times but could not. The large dull hole it left in my life throbbed until it became unbearable.

Physical risk was too important. A simple and effective form of achievement, it fills the self with the confidence to take down larger prey. The more you achieve, the more confidence and the more achievement. Maybe those achievements can in some way answer a larger question for me? I have developed a path, by accident or subconscious design, that allows me a view of life from a different vantage point. As a tool, solo expeditions have been no more or less valid than religion: A vehicle from which to find meaning in life.

Perhaps I missed the turn off to normality – wife, kids and a steady job – or perhaps my road was never going there. The thing about life is we already know the ending is death. Personally I have tried to at least give the bits in the middle every chance of surprising me. We all start and end the same, but what happens in between might be up to us.

Nature taught me to surrender completely in her presence. I repaid my trust in direct communion with the supreme Consciousness that I am now convinced exists. She has shown me that experiencing God requires nothing more than being completely present in any second.

These glimpses of what life can be like has made me thirsty for more. As I realised looking at the stars after not being eaten by cannibals: this is not a balanced life. Peak experiences, as much as I have valued them, are nothing but sips of pure life passing me by in a raging current, out of my reach, no matter how hard I try. It is not enough anymore.

My world of adventure might have provided me with glimpses, but they are only available at the risk of the ultimate prize. Being in nature confronts you with eternity, forces you into the now, and if you spend enough time alone in it, you find metaphysical speculation. When we lose belief in what we are doing, we lose the value of what we are doing. Whatever our passions are, we must feed them, we must invest in them, and we must build them, even if they are castles in the sky. By being hard it becomes beautiful, by being irrational it becomes necessary.

Walking and paddling through endless scenery I have come to know myself as well as I could ever hope to and found a surprising thing: I am not me. With enough self-knowledge and understanding came my first real thought, ever. I have watched my thoughts run around aimlessly. I have watched them identify with courage and fear, seen them enjoy happiness and depression through preconceived ideals of attraction or revulsion. Among these clouds, nothing has ever been clearer to me than the knowledge that 'I' am not that which floats around in my head. If you are not the separated 'I' any more, then you become part of everything and then you are God. Could it be that simple?

I want this Oneness to be the norm, not the exception. For this to happen the ego must die, not just in the seconds where Nature puts me in my proper place. Every accomplishment I have ever achieved has lost its shine after climax. Soon the ego realises that it is only as good as its last trick. Only in the seconds that I forgot myself have I felt pure bliss. Unfortunately I have spent a lifetime building the ego, chasing the bliss. To destroy it might very well take the rest of my life.

The time has come to go to the next level and expeditions by themselves will not take me there. For the first time, I know with absolute certainty where I have to go next. Spirituality offers options that do not require the stimulus to continuously be increased. The more your practice deepens you, the less stimuli you need to get-off on. I might not have been searching for adventure in the first place. A wise yogi once told me that God lives in the eternity between the in and the out breath. I think I am starting to understand.

Life slips by us second after second as we live in the past or future, with so many wonders to pursue, so much life to drink in, there is no more time or need to hide from the present. I used to play that game because I believed the present did not have enough to offer. Now I look at the Present and I feel myself dissolving into its endlessness. I do not regret those times; all is as it should be. Expeditions have taught me that perception is the only difference between adventure and hardship, that if you can't carry it you don't need it, that failure is a better lesson than success, and that there are a million people worse off than I could ever be and happier for it.

There is something different to learn this time. I have nowhere left to go in search of my peak moments. I might be able to replicate them by going to the same levels of risk and commitment but this mission has taught me that expeditions and adventure by themselves can't bring me much further. There might be more levels above where I have been but not many; even a cat runs out of lives sooner or later.

I do not know exactly where this path will lead, only that I am tired of trying to force it. Life has lived me from the start, I know that now. He let me play, but I have played enough. No more wandering, I want to go Home and for the first time I know where Home is.

I worry if I will like the answers that I find inside myself. We are right to fear this process. The guardian of the threshold is powerful, immensely powerful, with an enormous capacity to terrorise the psyche. All great mysteries are grand: the bigger the dragon, the bigger the treasure. This discovery unveils a thought: I will go into darkness and learn to live with it. Never did I imagine that I would find the opposite, nothing but hope, nothing but light. I have figured out why those perfect moments, previously confined to expeditions, have been so hard to duplicate. I realised the missing ingredient: the absence of ego. He who loses that gains everything. I truly believe that must surely be the ultimate prize.

I have stepped onto paths that lead into places so dark that I had no way of knowing what they held, no way of knowing that I would come out alive. Loved that feeling of complete surrender, surrender to the future and whatever it holds and surrender of the self as you embark on something bigger than 'I'. Never before have I stood and stared at such a precipice as I do now. I have looked at this challenge before and walked away. Today I fear no longer. The quest has lead me here by leading me to everywhere but here. Without knowing it, my journey has taught me skills to enter into the void with a fighting chance.

It is ironic that after a life of adventure, my greatest challenge holds no danger apart from relinquishing the ego. It is ironic that after fifteen years of traveling it will happen with my eyes closed. It is ironic that people would understand it more if I told them I was about to wrestle a crocodile.

The Ultimate Realisation is close enough for me to grasp in this lifetime. I don't suspect it is going to be easy though. It comes at a point when I had hoped that I may rest. Rest? Rest for what? Indeed, what would I do if I rested for the remainder of my life, just to continue in the next one. I would live with daily dissatisfaction, with mediocrity.

Beyond this frontier is not achievement; there will be no status updates or photos. The underlying search for truth cannot be done in front of the camera because it is a personal journey. The path that lies ahead of me is Spiritual, that is all I know. Uncool words like God, energy and karma. I don't even know what to tell people about what I am doing, I just know its bigger than anything I have ever done.

I am starting to believe, really believe, the world is nothing but possibility. There will be steps backward, forward, sideways, jumps, leaps and bounds. I can see this was always my task. I have been training for nothing but This. There is no indication that I will succeed, but the fight cannot be in vain. Whatever happens, I surrender. Wherever the path goes it is beautiful. This is exciting times my friend – a grand adventure – surely there can be no greater.

A MOTHER'S PRAYER

Dear God Almighty Father, You are Love and You are Faithful. You are the Creator of all earth and of every man and beast on it.

Thank you for the awesome person, Hendri, whom you created for all of us to cherish, enjoy, admire and love. Thank you for allowing him the freedom to take his time to seek the Truth. Then, after he did find You – as he confessed to me and close friends that there was no doubt in his mind that God really exists – You took him one morning by the hand to live with You in heaven.

You create and bestow on each of us special gifts, with the will to use them to bring Joy and Glory to You. Hendri showed us what a life looks like when you use each of those gifts to the fullest. He did not leave one of them semi-developed or unfulfilled.

You allowed and protected him through all these years to live out the dreams You had planned for him. As a human being he was truly beautiful, inside as well as outside. He brought light and happiness to many and was blessed with a brilliant mind for all to enjoy.

He was not merely another good human being. He was a ball of fire, passion and drive, and had a zest for life that is uncommon to, but appreciated and admired by, most. His whole life was a voyage to understand himself, other people and the world around him!

Forever exploring, forever seeking and forever enquiring!

Gracious God thank you for blessing me with this very special son! I will always cherish the exceptional relationship we shared. He always made an effort to make me feel special and keep the bond between us strong regardless of a personal journey across the world. I am so grateful to have such fond and precious memories of my Hendri. I saw him grow from lively boyhood, through rough teens, and restless twenties, into an incredible person with an amazingly mature mind and soul.

He was at total peace with himself and the world around him when he left this earth. He told me this a few weeks before his death. It was as if he had successfully completed his search for the meaning of life, and had shared his wisdom and love with each person who needed to cross his way.

God you gave, and You took away. Praise the Lord because He is Good. Please bless and comfort each of us here. May we find the Peace that surpasses all comprehension as we know and accept that Hendri is with You, and that he is undoubtedly now LIVING HIS BEST DAY EVER!

Amen

LIFE CHRONOLOGY

1975-1977 Hendri is born on 22 March 1975 in Ottosdal, North West Province of South Africa. He is the only son of Henk and Marie (neé Faul) Coetzee. He inherited the family name of Johannes Hendrik.

1978 (age 3) His parents return to Pretoria, after farming for a couple of years, where his father takes a job in the SADF (South African Defence Force).

1979-1981 (age 4-6) The family is transferred to Durban, Kwazulu-Natal Province, where Hendri attends an all English nursery school. It was his very first exposure to English, being born and bred in an Afrikaans family.

1982-1986 (age 7-11) These years he spends in Oshakati, Ovamboland in Namibia where the family stayed during the time his father served in the Border War (Angolan Bush War). He had his first experience of malaria in Oshakati followed by many more attacks in years to come. The worst was when he got cerebral malaria in 1985, but had a miraculous recovery.

1987 (age 12) His family moves back to Pretoria, and Hendri finds fitting into a big city school a big challenge. He was physically a late developer and on average a year younger than his peers. He started playing more serious chess, participated in drama, continued with karate and played school rugby.

1991 (age 16) He leaves formal high school, Hoërskool Zwartkop, to attend Technical College. He hoped to complete his Grade 12 early, rather than having to go the formal way, because he wanted to finish school as soon as possible. At this stage he was still considering a career in Law.

1994 (age 19) He decides to take a job at a Kibbutz in Israel. For the first time he tours outside his native country and Namibia. He made some good memories there, not the least working on an ostrich farm. Later, three school friends join him and together they toured Egypt, Turkey and Jordan before returning home.

1995 (age 20) Still unsure of a career path, Hendri gets work as an assistant to the manager of the Kaokohimba Safaris in Namibia. This was his first exposure to working in the tourist industry. After returning he decides to become a commercial pilot. His training went well, but just before he qualified he pulled out.

1996 (age 21) His father, who had by now retired from the SADF, encouraged him to do a one-year training programme to qualify as a Medic at the SA Medial Services Academy in Pretoria. He also qualifies as a Parabat. He starts keeping a diary from about September this year until his death.

1997 (age 22) He gets a job as assistant to a helicopter business, doing tourist trips over the Victoria Waterfalls in Livingstone, Zambia. Later that year he is employed as a river guide for Safari Par Excellence. For the first time he feels like he found the career that suited his passion and skills perfectly.

1998-1999 (age 23-24) He works seasons as a whitewater guide and video kayaker for different companies in Morgan Town and Fayetteville, West Virginia on the New, Gually, Green and Cheat Rivers.

1999 He spends time as a safety kayaker in the Blyde River Canyon, Mpumalanga Province, South Africa.

2000 (age 25) He works for Adrift in Uganda and becomes a kayaking pioneer on the Nile. Also, he decides to take up studying and enrols at the University of South Africa, distance learning, to do a Bachelor's degree in Psychology. He completed the degree in a record time of three years, where it normally takes a minimum of four.

2001 (age 26) Hendri now starts to meditate more frequently. He rafts a trip on the Tana River in Kenya. Towards the end of the year he does a solo unsupported 800km walk from Mombassa, Kenya to Bagamoyo, Tanzania. For the entire journey he carried equipment weighing no more than fifteen kilograms.

2002 (age 27) He does the first snowboarding descent of the Rwenzori Mountain range (Mountains of the Moon) in Uganda as a camera man for a Swedish lead expedition. He learnt to snowboard within a few hours.

2004 (age 29) He leads his first big expedition to raft the Nile River, the longest river on earth, from source to sea, starting at Victoria Lake in Uganda and finishing in Egypt. The trip was made into a documentary film by National Geographic. The last part of 2004 he works as canyon and mountain guide for the Swiss Outdoor Association in Interlaken, Switzerland.

2005 (age 30) He completes the Nile Source to Sea on the Akagera expedition. Fluid Kayaks starts a sponsorship which lasts until his death.

2006 (age 31) On the Blue Nile he leads the K-Factor Team departing from Ethiopia to where the Blue and White Niles meet.

2007 (age 32) His curiosity about solo expeditions takes him alone down an eighty-kilometre stretch of whitewater in Murchison Falls National Park, Uganda.

2008 (age 33) UNISA grants him an Honours degree in Psychology. He got his first job in the psychology field as juvenile delinquent therapist in Voss, Norway. He takes one young man on nearly a month long expedition (The Mandari) on the Nile, as part of the therapeutic and rehabilitation process. His diaries now turn into documents intended to be part of this memoirs.

2009 (age 34) In preparation for his Congo Solo expedition, he continues his walk (1000km) down the East African coast. He also embarks on a transformational six-month solo trip to the Democratic Republic of the Congo. He is on the Congo River for 2300km on a river barge before kayaking solo on the Congo River from Kinshasa, alone and with hand paddles. For this expedition Hendri was nominated as Adventurer of the Year and was awarded a close second place.

Early 2010 (age 35) He attends in-depth meditation courses in Thailand and returns to Jinja in Uganda. He prepares his manuscript for publication.

October 2010 The Great Lakes Kayaking Expedition begins. It was intended to go from the source of the Nile in Uganda, to the Rusizi River in Rwanda, to the Lukuga River in DRC, and eventually into the main Congo River confluence. Wins the Expedition of the Year Award awarded by Ryder of the Year. After his death this specific award was renamed the Hendri Coetzee Award

December 7, 2010 While paddling on flat water with two companions, a crocodile emerges from the Lukuga River and grabs him by the shoulder. He is taken under and never seen again.

LIBRARY & REFERENCES

Abrahams, R.D, Eds. V. Turner & E. M. Bruner. 1986. *Ordinary and Extraordinary Experience in the Anthropology of Experience*. University of Illinois Press.

Asher, Michael. 2006. *Khartoum: The Ultimate Imperial Adventure*. Penguin Books.

Assal, Munzoul A.M. 2004. "Displaced persons in Khartoum: current realities and post-war scenarios." PhD diss., University of Khartoum.

Bayart, Jean Francois. 2009. *The State in Africa: The Politics of the Belly*. Polity.

Beker, Gavin De. 1997. *The Gift of Fear: Survival Signals That Protect Us From Violence*. Little, Brown and Company.

Bowles, Fred G. 1962. "Song of the Road" in *Granger's Index to Poetry*, 1215. Columbia University Press.

Breytenbach, Deon J. Pers Comm.

Briggs, Phillip. 1995. *Guide to Ethiopia*. Bradt Travel Guides.

Briggs, Phillip. 1998. *Uganda: The Bradt Travel Guide*. Bradt Travel Guides.

Brymer, George Eric. 2005. "Extreme dude! A phenomenological perspective on the extreme sport experience." PhD Diss., University of Wollongong Thesis Collections.

Butcher, Tim. 2008. *Blood River: A Journey to Africa's Broken Heart*. Vintage.

Castaneda, Carlos. 1968. *The Teachings of Don Juan: A Yaqui Way of Knowledge*. University of California Press.

Churchill, Winston Spencer. 1972. *My African Journey*. Hamlyn Publishing Group.

Coleridge, Samuel Taylor. 1996. *Everyman's Poetry*. Orion Publishing Group.

Colson, Charles. 2005. *The Good Life: Seeking Purpose, Meaning, and Truth in Your Life*. Tyndae House Publishers.

Collins, Robert. 2002. *The Nile.* Yale University Press.

Conrad, Joseph. 2008 reprint. *Heart of Darkness.* UBS Publishers.

Cotter. 2003. The Vision Quest.

Diamond, Jared. 1997. *Guns, Germs, and Steel: The Fates of Humans and Societies.* W. W. Norton & Company Inc.

Dostoevsky, Fyodor. 2000. in Viktor Frankl's *A Man's Search for Meaning.* Beacon Press.

Dowden, Richard. 2009. *Africa: Altered States, Ordinary Miracles,* Portobello Books.

Erwin, Doug, William James. 1907. "The Energies of Men." *Science* 635:321-332.

Feuerstein, Georg. 1998. *Tantra: The Path of Ecstasy.* Shambhala Publications.

Flanagan, Richard. 1994. *Death of a River Guide.* McPhee Gribble.

Forbath, Peter. 1997. *The River Congo.* HarperCollins.

Forsyth, Frederick. 1974. *The Dogs of War.* Hutchinson and Co Ltd.

Frankl, Viktor. 2000. *A Man's Search for Meaning.* Beacon Press.

Fries, Annerika. "Soul Growth." www.archive.org/stream/quotablepoemsana007889mbp/quotablepoemsana007889mbp_djvu.txt

Gettleman, Jeffery. 2008. "Mai Mai Fighters Third Piece in Congo's Violent Puzzle." *New York Times,* November 21.

Gibran, Kahlil. 1923. *The Prophet.* Knopf Doubleday Publishing Group.

Goddard, John. 1979. *Kayaks Down the Nile.* Brigham Young University Press.

Guest, Robert. 2004. *The Shackled Continent: Power Corruption and African Lives.* Macmillan.

H.M Stanley. 1961. In Richard Stanley, Alan: *The Exploration Diaries of H.M. Stanley.* Vanguard Press Inc.

Hesse, Hermann, 1943 (reprint 2008). *The Glass Bead Game*. Picador.

Hesse, Hermann. 1951. *Siddhartha*. Penguin Books.

Jung, Carl. 1938. "Psychology and Religion: The Terry Lectures." Yale University Press.

Kapuściński, Ryszard. 2002. *The Shadow of the Sun: My African Life*. Vintage Books.

Karnazes, Dean. 2005. *Ultra Marathon Man: Confessions of an All-Night Runner*. Penguin Books.

Kingsolver, Barbara. 1998. *The Poisonwood Bible*. HarperCollins.

Kruger, Celliers. 2008. *African Veins*. House of Orange.

Malan, Rian. 1990. *My Traitor's Heart: Blood and Bad Dreams A South African Explores the Madness in His Country, His Tribe and Himself*. Grove Press.

Meredith, Martin. 2006. *The State of Africa: A History of the Continent Since Independence*. Free Press.

Moorhead, Alan. 1954. *The White Nile*. HarperCollins.

Mutwa, Credo. 1998. *Indaba, My Children: African Tribal History, Legends, Customs and Religious Beliefs*. Payback Press.

Nietzsche, Friedrich. 1886. *Beyond Good and Evil*.

Nietzsche, Friedrich. 1888. *The Twilight of the Idols*. Maxims and Arrows.

Osborne, Authur. 2000. "Be Still, It Is The Wind That Sings." V.S. Ramanan.

Petraitis, Richard. 2003. «From Simbas to Ninjas: Congo's Magic Warriors.» www.infidels.org

Reader, John. 1997. *Africa: A Biography of the Continent*. Vintage Books.

Renton, David and David Sedon Leo Zeling. 2007. *The Congo: Plunder & Resistance*. Zed Books.

Russell, Joan and D.V. Perott. 2003. *Teach Yourself Swahili*. McGraw-Hill.

Schultheis, R. 1996. *Bone Games: Extreme Sports, Shamanism, Zen and the Search for Transcendence*. Breakaway Books.

Service, Robert William. 1916. "Call of the Wild." In Garvin, John William, Eds. *Canadian Poetry*. McClelland, Goodchild & Stewart.

Shakespeare, William. circa 1599. "Henry the V."

Shipman, Pat. 2009. *To the Heart of the Nile*. HarperCollins.

Snailham, Richard. 1977. *A Giant Among Rivers*. The Scientific Exploration Society.

Stanley, Henry Morton. 1988(reprint). *Through the Dark Continent Vol 1&2*. Dover.

Stevenson, William. 1976. *90 Minuets At Entebbe*. Bantam Books.

Tagore, Rabindranath. 1916. *Fruit Gathering*. The Macmillan Company.

Tayler, Jefery. 2000. *Facing The Congo*. Three Rivers Press.

Thesiger, Wilfred. 1996. *The Danakil Diary: Journeys through Abyssinia 1930-34*. HarperCollins.

Thoreau, Henry David. 2007(reprint). *Walking*. Arc Manor.

Thoreau, Henry David. 1995. *Walden; Or, Life in the Woods*. Dover Publications.

Trefon, Theodore. 2004. *Reinventing Order in the Congo*. Fountain Publishers.

Weisman, Alan. 2007. *The World Without Us*. Picador.

Wolpe, Joseph. 1958. *Psychotherapy by Reciprocal Inhibition*. California: Stanford University Press.

Yogananda, Paramahansa. 1946. *Autobiography of a Yogi*. Yogada Satsanga Society of India.

Zu, Lao. 2008. *Tao te Ching*. Jeremy P. Tarcher/Penguin.

Websites

monusco.unmissions.org

http://www.un.org/en/peacekeeping/missions/past/unamirFT.htm

rescue.org

www.bonoboincongo.com

www.johngoddard.info

Photograph Credits

All Photgraphs © The Hendri Coetzee Trust, unless indicated below.

Page II Bottom © Waldo Krahenbuhl

Page III © Shearwater Rafting, Victoria Falls

Page IV Top © Natalie McComb
Bottom left © Marcus Wilson Smith
Bottom right © Leyla Ahmet

Page V Top and bottom left © Marcus Wilson Smith
Bottom right © Dr Ian Clarke

Page VI © Marcus Wilson Smith

Page VII Top and bottom © Marcus Wilson Smith
Middle © Chris Prior

Page VIII Top and bottom left © Ailsa Guest Smith
Bottom right © Chris Lee

Page IX & X © Chris Lee

Page XV & XVI © Chris Korbulic

www.ingramcontent.com/pod-product-compliance
Lightning Source LLC
Chambersburg PA
CBHW062042080426
42734CB00012B/2530